M000119635

Quantitative Research Methods in the Social Sciences

Paul S. Maxim
The University of Western Ontario

New York   Oxford
OXFORD UNIVERSITY PRESS
1999

Oxford University Press

Oxford   New York
Athens   Auckland   Bangkok   Bogotá   Buenos Aires   Calcutta
Cape Town   Chennai   Dar es Salaam   Delhi   Florence   Hong Kong   Istanbul
Karachi   Kuala Lumpur   Madrid   Melbourne   Mexico City   Mumbai
Nairobi   Paris   São Paulo   Singapore   Taipei   Tokyo   Toronto   Warsaw

and associated companies in
Berlin   Ibadan

Copyright © 1999 by Oxford University Press, Inc.

Published by Oxford University Press, Inc.
198 Madison Avenue, New York, New York 10016
http://www.oup-usa.org

Oxford is a registered trademark of Oxford University Press

All rights reserved. No part of this publication may be reproduced,
stored in a retrieval system, or transmitted, in any form or by any means,
electronic, mechanical, photocopying, recording, or otherwise,
without the prior permission of Oxford University Press.

Library of Congress Cataloging-in-Publication Data
Maxim, Paul S., 1950–
Quantitative research methods in the social sciences / Paul Maxim.
     p.   cm.
   Includes bibliographical references and index.
   ISBN 978-0-19-511465-2
   1. Social sciences—Statistical methods.   I. Title.
HA29.M2968   1998
300'.7'27—dc21   98-18953
                                                         CIP

Printed in the United States of America
on acid-free paper

To Justin and Louise—may they never lose the joy of discovery

Contents

Preface

Science consists of a body of substantive knowledge and a way of assessing the validity of that knowledge. Many other intellectual endeavors claim to produce knowledge and understanding. What uniquely sets science apart from those enterprises is method. The method of modern science, however, is based on a curious logic. As Popper told us, science cannot "prove" the validity of assertions—even those limited to the empirical realm. At best, the logic of science can show us where we err. Thus, the method of science is the method of elimination. By marshaling our insights and our resources, we attempt to strike competing explanations off our list of possibilities. At its heart, then, science is a cynic. It accepts anyone's explanation but believes none. It is perhaps for this reason that Benjamin Disraeli wrote, "The pursuit of science leads only to the insoluble."

Still, like intrepid travelers, most of us who do science come to appreciate the journey as much as the destination. Just as we are thankful for the knowledge and wisdom we gain through getting where we are going, so many of us come to appreciate what science teaches us as we search for an elusive "truth." The vehicle of the scientific journey is the substance of this book—methods.

For several years I have taught an introductory graduate course on quantitative research methods and have struggled to find an adequate text. Little exists between what we use in our undergraduate courses and the highly advanced and specialized monographs directed toward research professionals. It is the objective of this book to fill this niche—to provide a reasonably sophisticated discussion of methods that builds upon the student's undergraduate background while still providing an overview of how the various issues and techniques employed in the social sciences interrelate. Hopefully, with this material and an intermediate level statistics course, the graduate student will be prepared for the more specialized literature traditionally addressed in doctoral seminars. On the other hand, the material covered in this text should stand students who do not plan to go beyond the master's level in good stead.

This text is designed to form the basis of a one-semester graduate course, either on its own or in combination with instructor-selected readings from the literature. While I have attempted to provide a broad range of examples in the book, I find that the value of any text is enhanced when combined with selections from contemporary research. I have also attempted to produce a text that will serve as an ongoing reference for those entering their professional careers. Thus a variety of classical and up-to-date citations are offered that point to more detailed or advanced discussions of particular problems and topics.

Clearly, a review text cannot hope to cover all the issues faced in contemporary social science research; however, an attempt has been made to address the more significant and generic ones. It is also the case that the topics selected in any survey book will reflect the biases and experiences of the author, and this text is no exception.

Chapter 1 presents an overview of the philosophical basis upon which contemporary neopositivistic, quantitative social science is based. Positivism has become a "dirty word" in some sectors of the social science community. This is unfortunate, since this approach to research has managed to generate a cumulative body of knowledge that has done much to push us beyond the realm of mere description and speculation. It should also be noted that while positivism as a philosophy of science took many body blows over the last two to three decades, it has overcome several serious philosophical weaknesses and still provides the umbrella under which a sizable portion of the productive social science community works.

Chapter 2 moves from the broad philosophical basis of scientific methodology to a discussion of the basic building blocks of social theory. Attention is paid to how concepts are formulated and designed, and to how their linkages generate the raw material of social science research—propositions and hypotheses. The problem of functional form is explored in some detail, since this is one of the biggest hurdles researchers need to overcome as they move from general theory to the nuts and bolts of quantitative analysis. In Chapter 3 we broach that ultimate quagmire, causation. Or, more specifically, with the issues involved in deciphering the logic underlying the beasties known as *causal models*. The first part of the chapter deals with many of the theoretical and philosophical aspects of causation. The second part illustrates the implications of those aspects for the statistical analysis of causal models.

Chapter 4 addresses topics more often dealt within statistics texts, namely, the logic of statistical inference and the problems of Type I and Type II errors. Complementing this is a discussion of the concept of statistical power. Statistical power is an issue that has been given lip service for many years, though rarely addressed in practical research. Recently, the problem of statistical power (or more properly, the lack of it) has started to receive greater attention in the general research community. Simultaneously, it is becoming a more active area of research in the statistical literature.

Chapters 5, 6, and 7 examine the process of sampling. Sampling is crucial in all the sciences, but it is of particular importance in the nonexperimental sciences. More than most of the activities in which we engage, good sampling requires an extraordinary combination of statistical acumen and "in the trenches" methodological savvy. These three chapters attempt to summarize the core of an extensive volume of literature. While Chapters 5 and 6 touch upon the basics of sampling methodology, Chapter 7 explores a few common problems not normally covered in introductory expositions. Some of the more salient issues relating to measurement error and applied sampling are revisited in Chapter 12, after the discussion of measurement.

In Chapter 8 we examine the logic behind the classical experiment and observe how the basic paradigm has been modified to encompass quasi-experimental designs. The research into quasi-experimental methods, particularly by Campbell, has done much to vitalize the applied side of our discipline. The logic of quasi-experimental designs is the basis for much of our evaluative research. This chapter also addresses what many "experimentalists" consider the illegitimate child of research methods—the survey design.

If theory is the right leg supporting the scientific edifice, then surely measurement must be the left leg. Chapter 9 examines the broad issue of measurement and its included concepts of reliability and validity. The chapter also deals with a number of related issues, and with questionnaire construction, in terms of problems in measurement.

Chapter 10 follows upon the problems of measurement as introduced in Chapter 9 and proceeds with a discussion of classical test theory. Although classical test theory has largely been superseded, it is still important as a basis for understanding the procedures that have come to replace it, and much of the existing literature, as well. Chapter 10 concludes by demonstrating how even moderate amounts of measurement error can lead to erroneous inferences in standard statistical procedures.

A more recent procedure that has come to replace classical test theory is confirmatory factor analysis. Chapter 11 provides a brief introduction to structural equation models, particularly as these can be used to address problems of reliability and validity. The basic confirmatory factor analysis model is then extended to illustrate how measurement problems can be addressed effectively in causal research.

As already mentioned, Chapter 12 deals with the problem of data collection methods and measurement errors. This chapter addresses a number of issues that typically fall in the cracks between sampling and measurement. Unlike texts that deal solely with the theory and statistics of sampling, this book reflects the recognition that social sampling is primarily a vehicle for delivering a measurement instrument. The performance of that instrument is very much influenced, not only by the construction of the instrument itself, but also by the manner in which the instrument is delivered.

Chapter 13 addresses that chronic bugaboo of research: missing data. All researchers talk about missing data, but few successfully address the problem. This chapter examines why some traditional approaches to handling missing data are often unsatisfactory. It also explores some more recent and more successful attempts to deal with missing cases and missing items.

Chapter 14 deals with interpolation and smoothing. These procedures can be seen as an extension of the discussion of missing data for aggregated distributions. While often useful in their own right, the techniques also provide a sound basis for understanding micro simulation.

Finally, Chapter 15 discusses the growing field of computer-intensive procedures. The discussions of randomization tests, jackknifing, and bootstrapping provide an introduction to one direction that some of the research in statistical inference is taking. Jackknife and bootstrap techniques, in particular, have opened a new vista for both theoretical and applied methods.

A work of this type is never accomplished in isolation. I owe a debt of gratitude to many colleagues and students who have offered freely their ideas and criticisms and support. For having taken the time to read and comment on significant portions of this manuscript, I am grateful to T.R. Balakrishnan, Louis Culumovic, Paul C. Whitehead, and the late Dick Henshel. Those of us who have the occasional privilege of reviewing articles for the professional journals appreciate the effort involved in that task. What is true of reviewing a single article is multiplied manyfold when it comes to reviewing a book manuscript. The unnamed reviewers who found the time to read this text and offer their guidance and comments deserve special recognition.

Significant portions of this manuscript were written during my 1994–95 sabbatical year spent at the Statistics Institute at the University of Copenhagen. A particular note of thanks is extended to Hans Oluf Hansen, whose hospitality, collegiality, and singular intellect enlivened many a difficult day at the word processor. I am also indebted to Danmarks National Bank for their scholar's residential program, which turned a good sabbatical year into one of exceptional enjoyment and productivity.

Department of Sociology   P. S. M.
The University of Western Ontario
May 8, 1998

1

The Scientific Method

Empirical science has two major objectives: to describe particular
phenomena in the world of our experience and to establish general
principles by means of which they can be explained and predicted.
—Carl Hempel

Science is a social enterprise that attempts to provide answers to our questions about the state of the world. Thus, it shares a common goal with many other humanistic endeavors aimed at knowledge accumulation and truth assessment. Judged on this basis, science is no different from philosophy, religion, or even some forms of magic. What sets science apart from these other activities, however, is the singular method it employs. That is, science attempts to avoid the arbitrary or received wisdom inherent in most religious forms of understanding; it shuns the mysticism of magic, and attempts to evade the tautological basis of knowledge upon which many fields of philosophy are based.

The scientific method is unique in that it is a procedure almost anyone can learn; it bases its assessment of the truth value of propositions on observations of nature; it is open to public scrutiny; and, most importantly, when properly employed it allows for the potential disproof of even our most cherished personal beliefs.

While the basic procedures of science are relatively straightforward, the tools developed by practicing scientists to carry out those procedures have become very complex. This is particularly so in the social sciences, where elaborate designs and intricate statistical procedures are often used to "tease out" subtle relationships that are generally masked by a variety of competing processes and by data of questionable quality. It is for these reasons that many procedures discussed in later chapters will appear to bear little resemblance to those presented in introductory undergraduate methods texts. In day-to-day research, nature rarely gives up its secrets willingly. Thus, it is not surprising that even the most successful researchers often have a desk drawer full of failed projects.

Ironically, a common complaint levied against quantitative social science is that our data are often too poor in quality to meet the assumptions underlying our "high powered" methods and statistics. In fact, just the opposite is true. High quality data with little error often "speak for themselves." That is, where the relationship we seek is strong and clearly defined by the data, we do not need powerful statistical procedures to tell us whether the relationship might exist or not. On the other hand, the more error prone the data, the more difficult it is to separate a true relationship from the background noise within which it resides. A good analogy is that of a radio receiver. Strong local stations can be picked up very well by an inexpensive pocket radio. Weak signals from distant stations, however, require intricate and expensive receivers. Often, the most interesting questions we address in the social sciences are based on subtle and shifting relationships embedded in a loud matrix of noise.

Since the late 1960s, developments in social statistics and methods have appeared at a prodigious rate. This is partly because of a demand to address ever more complex problems, and partly a result of the realization that answers to some traditional problems are wanting.[1] For many, the inability of the social sciences to generate definitive answers has been unsettling. This unsettledness has often manifested itself in an arbitrary rejection of state-of-the-art tools. Thus, we see calls for a return to a more pristine, qualitative method based on "common sense" and everyday experience. Sadly, this longing for certainty and simplicity reflects an archaic notion of science. As an undergraduate, I was exposed a popular methods text by Selltiz et al. first published in 1951. In it, a short quotation appears from a paper by Jaspers that bears repeating. According to Jaspers, "Whereas ancient science had the appearance of something completed, to which the notion of progress was not essential, modern science progresses into the infinite" (Selltiz et al., 1959: 4). Science then, is an ever evolving activity that rarely provides absolute truths but, when successful, increasingly enhances our understanding of our world.

PHILOSOPHICAL PERSPECTIVE

The study of methods in the social sciences consists of two foci. The first is what might be termed *methodology*: that is, a study of the underlying approach or philosophy of how one goes about studying social phenomena. The second focus is on the application of specific procedures or *techniques*. These are the specific tools and procedures used to carry out the study. The social sciences are not monolithic in their acceptance of what is the most appropriate method for studying social phenomena—debates rage in the discipline about whether we ought to follow the "scientific method," the "historical method," or another fundamental approach. Within each of these methods, specific techniques (which may or may not be common to more than one approach) are used to collect and manipulate social facts.

The utility of specific techniques, like the meaning of data produced by the application of those techniques, is secondary to questions relating to the validity of the underlying methodological approach. Consequently, we will begin with an examination of the basic principles underlying the *scientific* method in relation to the social sciences. Of necessity, the overview will be short. The reader is advised, however, that the literature on any of the issues covered is extensive, and time spent on the references in the notes and in the Further Readings section at the end of the chapter will pay significant dividends. Once the basic philosophical framework has

---

1. Yet a third factor, sociologically speaking, is probably the professionalization of methodology, which tends to create its own demand. That is, as the social sciences become more specialized, members of the subgroup of self-defined methodologists often engage in the study of methods for its own sake, independent of the need to address substantive problems. The study of methods begets journals of methods which, in turn, demand articles to fill blank pages.

been laid out, our attention will shift in later chapters to specific techniques and their applicability and application to social issues.

The primary orientation of this text is to follow what is currently termed the scientific method as the principal approach for studying society. As indicated previously, opinions differ in the social sciences, particularly in sociology, about what is the most appropriate methodological framework for the study of social phenomena.[2] Crudely stated, the debate appears to be polarized between those who advocate the application of universal scientific method—the approach that evolved in the natural sciences—to the study of social phenomena, and those who often follow more empathic or metaphysical approaches appearing under such rubrics as historicism, hermeneutics (e.g., Hirsch, 1967; Habermas, 1971), and phenomenology (e.g., Schutz, 1967/1932).

A typical depiction of this dichotomy is expounded by Barbara Frankel, who suggests in an article entitled "Two extremes on the social science commitment continuum" that there are two polar positions or commitments in the social sciences. One commitment assumes one basic method (but perhaps many different techniques) underlying "science." The other commitment assumes a multiplicity of methods (again with many different techniques associated with them) under the rubric of science. Briefly, Frankel categorizes the positions as follows. Under the first, or unified science model:

> This understanding of science prescribes a hypothetico-deductive logic of investigation, quantifies results, states its conclusions in propositional form, and demands that these propositions be falsifiable in principle. Its project is the discovery of causes, and its unit of study is ideally typified by the atom. Although there is a marked problem as to the way in which such atoms (i.e., minimal units) ought to be conceptualized at the levels of organization that social scientists investigate, the general strategy is to reduce sociocultural phenomena in order to study them, with the aim of attaining that well-known trio of traditional scientific goals: prediction, explanation, and (where possible) control of the behavior of discrete variables. (Frankel, 1986: 354)

Under the second, or pluralistic model:

> any systematic effort to learn about nature may qualify as science, and a plurality of methods for unlocking her secrets is acceptable. Pluralists assume that research methods appropriate to the study of nonliving, living, and specifically human aspects of the natural world may well be fundamentally unlike one another. In particular, they assume that because humans are self-conscious beings whose behavior is not independent of their notions of the way humans are supposed to behave, the social sciences may normally require different methods than any of the natural sciences. At this end of the continuum, the logic of investigation is as likely to be inductive as deductive . . . , and results may not be quantifiable, nor even fully replicable. Conclusions are not always stated as propositions—and if they are, these may not be strictly falsifiable. . . . (Frankel, 1986: 356)

---

2. An excellent compendium outlining the range of approaches to research in the field of education can be found in Section 1 of Keeves (1988).

Many commentators (Frankel included) have the mistaken belief that truth evolves from compromise, that by triangulating the methods of science with those of a supposed antipode, knowledge is created. Indeed, knowledge of some kind may arise from such an activity, but it is unlikely to be scientific knowledge. Compromise may be a worthy objective in the political arena, but it has little standing in the world of logic. The intellectual inadequacy of the so-called dialectic as a form of logic—with it notions of thesis, antithesis, and synthesis—is a prime example. As a colleague once noted, if science were truly dialectic, then it would be possible for a congress to pass legislation repealing the law of gravity! This is not meant to imply that knowledge is not generated in the arts and humanities—far from it. It is just that this knowledge and understanding, as valuable as it may be, is not science.

The fundamental approach of this text might best be described as *neopositivist*. To understand this term's referent, it is necessary to look at a historical movement we might call classical logical positivism. While the methodology associated with conventional science has a long and illustrious history, the most prominent attempt to develop a systematic philosophy of science in recent times is a movement known as logical positivism. Logical positivism as originally proposed has few contemporary adherents, but its ghost refuses to rest. The movement had its origins in the rise of the Vienna Circle in the 1920s (Ayer, 1959). Several illustrious philosophers and scientists are associated with this school, including Carnap, Neurath, Gödel, Frank, Hempel, and Ayer. The school as a formal entity met its demise with the rise of Hitler in Germany and the takeover of Austria by the Nazis.

The rise of logical positivism added a vitality and vibrancy to the way people thought about the scientific enterprise in the early part of the century. This movement and its philosophical thrust are well summarized by R. W. Miller (1987: 3):

> In the first half of this century, when Russell, Schick, Hempel, Carnap and many others made positivism a source of major innovation, the general, a priori rules of method were supposed to be concerned with logical form. Thus, one great question of methodology—"When does a set of hypotheses, if true, explain why something happened?"—was supposed to be resolved by analyzing the hypotheses and the event statement to see whether the former consisted of empirical general laws and statements of initial conditions, together entailing the latter. The other dominant question in the philosophy of science—"When does a body of data confirm a given hypothesis?"—was to be answered by providing general rules, valid in every field, describing appropriate patterns of entailment connecting hypothesis with data.

How successful were the Vienna Circle's solutions to these fundamental questions? The answer is equivocal, depending upon what elements are considered and whose analysis is accepted. The Vienna Circle was never as homogeneous as either its apologists or its detractors would have one believe. Although important disagreements arose among members of the circle, there were core elements around which those members had basic agreement. Reviewing the core issues is worthwhile, since reactions against some issues and elaborations of others have molded contemporary views of the scientific enterprise. Among the core elements of logical positivism that deserve particular attention are the rejection of metaphysics, the centrality of empiricism, the concept of verifiability, the rise of nonrealism, and the role of covering laws.

The Rejection of Metaphysics

The logical positivists reacted against the overwhelming adherence to metaphysics that dominated European philosophy of the time. To many in the Vienna Circle, European philosophy had more in common with the mysticism of Bishop Berkeley or Herman Hesse than with pragmatic science. Phillips highlights a wonderful passage in which Michael Scriven states:

> The Vienna Circle or *Wiener Kreis* was a band of cutthroats that went after the fat burghers of Continental metaphysics who had become intolerably inbred and pompously verbose. The *kris* is a Malaysian knife, and the *Wiener Kreis* employed a kind of Occam's Razor called the Verifiability Principle. It performed a tracheotomy that made it possible for philosophy to breathe again. (Cited in Phillips, 1987: 39)

While the history of philosophy is replete with attacks on metaphysics, the critique raised by the Vienna Circle was quite specific. The Vienna Circle attacked metaphysical statements with supposed knowledge content that did not contain either logically verifiable or empirically testable components. It is from these twin issues of logical and empirical adequacy that the term *logical positivism* is derived. The logical positivist position held that existential questions relating to issues of existence, the Divine, or transcendent values, were not legitimate issues for scientific scrutiny. Metaphysical utterances might have emotive meaning, but as logical or empirically laden statements they are substantively nonmeaningful, or "meaningless," as Carnap (1931/32) maintained.

The early social sciences were particularly vulnerable to charges of wallowing in metaphysics. In a paper written in 1931, Otto Neurath (1931/32) decried the adherence of much contemporary sociology to empathic and metaphysical modes of explanation such as those espoused by Dilthey and Schutz. Neurath addresses the particular problems in such sociological classics as Sombart's *Geisteswissenschaft* and Max Weber's study, *The Protestant Ethic and the Spirit of Capitalism*. As he says of Weber, "Max Weber's prodigious attempt to demonstrate the emergence of capitalism from Calvinism clearly shows to how great an extent concrete investigation is obstructed by metaphysical formulations" (Neurath, 1931/32: 310). In contrast, Neurath praises the form of Marx's theorizing:

> Marxism is, to a higher degree than any other present-day sociological theory, a system of empirical sociology. The most important Marxist theses employed for prediction are already formulated in either a fairly physicalistic fashion (as far as traditional language made this possible), or they can be so formulated, without the loss of anything essential. (Neurath, 1931/32: 309).

Undoubtedly, Neurath took this view because of the materialist underpinnings of orthodox Marxist theory.

It is extremely tempting, when considering the logical positivist's strident distinction between metaphysics and science, to wonder why so much was made of this issue. For most people, the separation of science from metaphysics is probably a reasonable distinction that merely places two different types of intellectual endeavor into their appropriate domains. After all, we are familiar with many such distinctions such as the separation of church from state. For the logical positivists, the distinction was paramount for two related reasons. The first reason is clearly a political one, since it allows science to exist as an autonomous entity of status and integrity similar to or higher than other intellectual pursuits. As Ayer (1959: 16) states:

> Its merit is that it removes the temptation to look upon the metaphysician as a sort of scientific overlord. Neither is this a trivial matter. It has far too often been assumed that the metaphysician was doing the same work as the scientist, only doing it more profoundly; that he was uncovering a deeper layer of facts. It is therefore important to emphasize that he is not in this sense describing facts at all.

The second reason for the radical distinction is a variant on the slippery slope argument. If one admits that some of the rationale behind science is metaphysically based, then by extension the whole scientific edifice is only as strong as its weakest metaphysical underpinning. Hence, science again loses its political if not its intellectual independence.

The Centrality of Empiricism

The principle of empiricism assumes that there are basic perceptions upon which scientific theories and constructions are based. As Carnap (1969: 108–109) states, "The elementary experiences are to be the basic elements of our constructional system. From this basis we wish to construct all other objects of prescientific and scientific knowledge."

This assertion by Carnap rests on the fundamental Kantian notion that there is indeed a reality external to human perception. For Kant, external reality would exist regardless of whether it is correctly perceived by humans, or even whether humans were around to make the perception. Thus, for science, the ultimate assessment of truth-value is based upon some form of experiential test. This position may be contrasted with, for example, that of Berkeley, who intimated that all external reality was merely a construction within the mind of God. In essence, Berkeley believed that thing we call reality is indistinguishable from a dream.

It should also be noted that the term "positivism" is often used as a synonym for "empiricism"; however, it must be recognized that positivism is but one version of empiricism. Furthermore, not all forms of empiricism are positivistic. Skinner's questioning the value of theory in psychology (Skinner, 1950) and Paul Samuelson's (1963, 1964, 1965) "operationalist" agenda in economics illustrate adherence to empirical procedures while rejecting the theory basis of logical positivism. Similarly, the contemporary adherents of hermeneutics and phenomenology also claim to be empiricists while rejecting the very core of logical positivism.[3]

The Concept of Verifiability

The logical positivists also developed what they termed the verifiability principle of meaning. This idea was adopted as the crucial element that supposedly separated the realm of metaphysics from that of science. *Verifiable statements or concepts were those upon which one could draw empirical confirmation.* Thus, excepting legitimate tautologies (as in mathematics or logic), any statement or concept not backed by an empirical referent was considered gibberish or nonsense. Verifiability assumes that *proving* the existence of certain relationships given the right experimental design and the availability of appropriate data is possible.

Ultimately, the verifiability principle was the Achilles' heel of logical positivism as originally proposed. Verifiability assumes that it is possible to prove that a scientific law, theory, or proposition is "true." This is an extremely difficult endeavor for several reasons. First, if we propose a general statement to the effect that all As are Bs, then no specific subset of observed As can support this proposition. It is essential to observe the entire population of As. For example, it is widely known that all mature squirrels are either red or black. Thus, a reasonable proposition is "If A is a mature squirrel then A is either red or black." Indeed, one can travel far and wide and collect innumerable samples of squirrels and this thesis will appear to be supported. At what point does one declare the proposition confirmed? Unfortunately, never, since it requires a complete enumeration of squirrels to confirm this truth. In fact, there is a small town in central Canada called Exeter, where a group of white squirrels resides. These squirrels are not albinos, but a legitimate white variant, as indicated by their nonpink eyes.

A second problem for verification arises when the available evidence appears to support two different hypotheses. Classical notions of "proof" or confirmation, it was determined, could not readily distinguish among competing models with more or less empirical support, but more on that later.

The Rise of Nonrealism

Because of the apparent contradiction between the verifiability principle and the empirical difficulties in observing such concepts as atoms (electrons, neutrons, etc.), many logical positivists became *nonrealists* or, as they are currently termed, *instrumentalists.* The realist position essentially asserts that when a theory is well supported,

---

3. An excellent exposition of the limitations of hermeneutics and phenomenology is to be found in Phillips (1992). In a strange attempt to democratize science, Robin Dunbar (1994) asserts that science is a "genuine universal, characteristic of all advanced life forms" and that as such, all societies—and even animals—engage in science. While Dunbar acknowledges that science is primarily a method for testing hypotheses and inferring conclusions, he draws his conclusion as to the universality of science from his implicit belief that science is primarily crude empiricism. Dunbar's view of science, while perhaps noble in intent, captures only part of the enterprise for science is much more than mere observation.

entities and relationships covered by the theory can be treated as "real" or "true." Instrumentalists, on the other hand, are far less likely to assume that theory claims, especially those concerning unobservables, are true. Thus, as Phillips (1987: 40) states: "Scientific theories could not be true or false, but as tools they could be economical, useful, or instrumentally helpful; theories were hypotheses designed to predict facts (facts being sense experiences, or rather, reports of sense experience as propositions), but they could not be conceived of as true descriptions of an underlying physical reality." For most social scientists, the realist approach is a form of reification. Reification, of course, being the mistaken belief that one's theoretical constructs are not merely proxies for empirical entities but are indistinguishable from those entities.

The realist/instrumentalist debate is of more or less concern depending upon the extent to which disciplines rely upon unobservables within their theory frameworks. At one pole in the social sciences are demography and economics, which seldom appear to use unobservables; at the other pole is psychology, which is replete with such concepts. Sociology lies somewhere between.

Although most practicing scientists are probably instrumentalists at this time, the realist/nonrealist debate is still a very active one among philosophers of science (see, e.g., Leplin, 1984; Harré, 1986). The issue is not close to being resolved, probably because, as R. W. Miller (1987: 10) notes, "anti-realism is unbelievable (for many of us) while realism is unsupported."

Covering Laws

Early positivists generally followed the belief that one could discover and define covering laws from which all subsequent propositions and hypotheses could be deduced. This tenet underlies the *logical* dimension of logical positivism. Often, this aspect of logical positivism is termed the nomological–deductive approach to theory construction. The covering law requirement, which has been most admirably defended by Carl Hempel (1965), remains one of the most debated and problematic aspects of the logical positivist approach for the social sciences. The concept appears to have been based on an ideal type of how physical scientists construct and exploit theories. Experience has clearly shown that this approach is difficult if not impossible to implement in the social sciences, and is rarely, if ever, employed in the physical sciences. As Roy D'Andrade (1986: 26–27) notes:

> What seems to have happened is that Hempel and others took an ideal form, general law, as the prototype of a "generalization." The social sciences and psychology then measured themselves, and were measured by others, according to how closely they fit this ideal. Once the ideal was in place, the useful and slowly improving generalizations of psychology and the social sciences looked so far from it as to raise the question whether they were science at all.

What the social sciences have done and continue to do is to develop limited generalizations. Clearly, limited generalizations are not fundamental laws, but is it necessary for a discipline to have covering laws to be called a science? The growing consensus among philosophers and methodologists is that the covering law criterion (if can be met) is more likely in the realm of sufficiency rather than necessity. For, as D'Andrade (1986: 27) queries, "Is not a good science one in which the scope of the generalizations fits the extent of regularity found in the phenomena?" Thus, rather than forming a hierarchical system in which covering laws are hegemonies, current views of scientific theories tend to the position that they are systems of interrelated generalizations. The goal of normal social scientific activity, then, is to try to increase the specificity of the domain and the boundary conditions associated with those generalizations in a way that increases their precision without sacrificing their programmatic utility or explanatory power.

THE DEMISE OF LOGICAL POSITIVISM

Logical positivism contributed a great deal to the philosophy of science, but ultimately, was not without its failings. Many crucial elements came under scathing critiques and were found sorely wanting. The verifiability principle is a prime example. As Phillips (1987: 42) concedes,

> the verifiability principle suffered the same fate as the "Elephant Man"—it became a contorted monstrosity that choked to death under its own weight . . . it led to problems about the meaningfulness of scientific laws and theories. Furthermore, logical positivists were never clear about the status of the principle, for if it was to be regarded as a meaningful principle about what was meaningful, then by its own test it was not (for it was not testable or verifiable)!

Other aspects of logical positivism also fell to the surgical knife of the logician. The notions of covering laws, and of primal observations as the basis for scientific theories, did not withstand sustained scrutiny. Furthermore, empirically oriented philosophers and sociologists gradually came to the conclusion that most scientists (and most sciences) rarely meet the tenets laid out by the Vienna Circle. Even physics, which was held up as the scientific ideal, failed most tests. Yet, many sciences from chemistry to biology to geophysics to psychology have clearly made substantive progress. As happens with many intellectual movements, the prime thinkers behind the positivistic movement started to run out of steam. The major contributions appeared old-hat, the diversity within the movement became underestimated, and the failings were overestimated. Logical positivism had lost its radical vigor and was increasingly seen as the intellectual establishment against which any young Turk could score easy debating points.

NEOPOSITIVISM

With the end of the logical positivist school in the late 1960s, there arose a "new philosophy of science" that tended to be nihilistic (or anarchistic, according to Paul Feyerabend). Ironically, many tenets of this new philosophy of science were based on the metaphysical principles the Vienna Circle itself had found so problematic at the turn of the century. Thus, we saw parallels being drawn between physics and Zen Buddhism within the natural sciences (see, e.g., Capra, 1979, and discussions in Talbot, 1981), and a return to phenomenological and hermeneutical approaches in the social sciences. This new philosophy was based not so much on an alternate programmatic methodology, with its own constructive agenda, but instead, upon the simple goal of destroying the positivist edifice. Thus, in one assault on classical positivism, Feyerabend (1975) argues for an acceptance of methodological anarchism—a type of "anything goes" philosophy.

In many circles it has become fashionable to identify oneself as "antipositivistic" to be politically correct. The label, however, does not tell us much about where one stands. As Collins and Waller (1994: 17) note:

> There are a wide range of positions which might be called "antipositivist." From the mildest to the most extreme these include: (1) Rejection of a particular philosophical program, especially the Vienna Circle's logical positivism in its most extreme formulations such as those of Carnap and Ayer; one might also reject milder versions such as Popper's falsification doctrine. (2) Rejection of formal or quantitative methods. (3) Rejection of the possibility of any generalized knowledge—the alternatives are to endorse localized, historically or culturally particularistic knowledge—or skepticism about any knowledge whatsoever. (4) Rejection of science as a political or moral evil.

This abandonment of the core of the classical scientific method is not new. Often, in particular disciplines, practicing scientists become demoralized by a seeming lack of progress due to the limitations of existing methods and technique. As Phillips (1987: 50) states:

> From time-to-time in any of the sciences, researchers are likely to face problems that seem insuperable given the methods that are available in their current armamentarium. This situation naturally leads to a certain loss of heart, and to flirtation with methods and ideas that in more certain times would not be touched with a barge-pole. A clear example is provided by the history of the biological sciences over the past two hundred years; at times the complexity of living organisms seemed unmanageable, so that researchers abandoned the "mechanistic" orientation and swung over to rampant romanticism and vitalism. But when a breakthrough occurred in "hardnosed" methodology, the pendulum swung back.

A contemporary example of an attempt to orient the social sciences to a form of idiosyncratic thinking is presented in Box 1.1.

What was not noticed by many adherents of this new philosophy of science was that most of the flagrant limitations of classical positivism have been recognized by the more thoughtful supporters of that position, and that major efforts have long been taken to ameliorate those aspects found wanting. Rather than throwing out the intellectual baby with the bath water, traditional positivists were busy revising their understanding of the scientific method.

The outcome of that reconceptualization is what might be termed the neopositivist movement. This school retains the crucial strengths of the traditional scientific method while rejecting what we now consider to be several naïve and simplistic assumptions

---

■ **Box 1.1**

A *NATURALIST'S* VIEW OF SCIENCE

As proponents of an alternative to traditional scientific methodology, Guba and Lincoln (1988: 81–82) espouse the following:

> Naturalists assume that there exist multiple realities which are, in the main, constructions existing in the minds of people; they are therefore intangible and can be studied only in wholistic, and idiosyncratic, fashion. Enquiry into these multiple realities will inevitably diverge (the scope of the enquiry will enlarge) as more and more realities must be considered. Naturalists argue that while the rationalist assumptions undoubtedly have validity in the hard and life sciences naturalist assumptions are more meaningful in studying human behaviour. Naturalists do not deny the reality of the objects, events, or processes with which people interact, but suggest that it is the meanings given to or interpretations made of these objects, events or processes that constitute the arena of interest to investigators of social/behavioral phenomena. Note that these constructions are not perceptions of the objects, events, or processes but of meaning and interpretation. The situation is very much approximated, the naturalist would say, by the ancient tale of the blind men and the elephant—provided it is conceded that there is no elephant."

How does this approach address the basic elements of the scientific method?

---

followed by many classical positivists. This is not to say that current positivist conceptions of science are without criticism—this is far from the case. Still, progress has been made.

It is possible to identify the significant aspects that we currently use to distinguish the "scientific" method from other forms of knowledge acquisition such as magic or religion.[4] Among these elements are the following:

- a reliance on the senses (resorting to empiricism)
- the a priori statement of methodological principles
- the replicability principle
- the communicability of results
- an institutionalized skepticism (conservativism)
- the potential to falsify any hypothesis

By saying that we rely on the senses, we are essentially reaffirming empiricism as a core element of scientific practice. The ultimate arbiter of theoretical validity

---

4. See Nettler (1970) for a thoughtful discussion of various approaches to systems of under-standing and explanation.

is sensory truth or the truth of experience, as distinguished from revealed or logical truth. As Nancy Cartwright (1989: 4) notes, "Questions about nature should be settled by nature—not by faith, nor metaphysics, nor mathematics and not by convention nor convenience either."

The a priori statement of methodological principles essentially means that the rules of the game are established before the onset of any investigation. By stating the principles of procedure "up front," the researcher creates a situation in which the working hypothesis can fail—that is, it can be potentially refuted if certain procedures are followed. After-the-fact approaches suffer the limitation that anything can be explained within one's theoretical framework after the outcome is known. Thus, with ex post facto reasoning, a hypothesis cannot be refuted.[5]

Further, clearly stating one's methodological principles implies that the rules of inquiry can be transmitted from one individual to another, from one generation to another. Science, or more precisely, the scientific method, can be taught. It is not an innate cognition or *awareness* that some people have and others do not through some quirk of birth. This requirement moves the practice of science at least one step away from simple metaphysical existentialism.

Closely associated with the ability to state and communicate the rules of the scientific method is the notion that if similar procedures are followed elsewhere, other researchers ought to obtain similar results. This is known as the replicability or the reproducibility principle. The advantage of replicability is that a system is put in place that can minimize scientific fraud and ferret out honest procedural mistakes. Implicit in the replicability assumption is the notion that social events are not unique, but are manifestations of a more limited set of events that can be either established or observed on successive occasions.[6] Without replication, there can be no prediction of events or processes that cannot be foreseen. If replication is not possible, then logically all events and processes are unique. Unique entities, in turn, are not subject to falsification or general explanation. Thus, without replication, science is not possible, nor are generalizable theory and explanation.

The issue of communicability entails two facets. The first is the prescription that results ought to be disseminated to the public (i.e., published). In practical terms, the public consists of other scientists interested in the phenomenon under study. The crux of this requirement, however, is the notion that by publishing results, other scientists can examine, replicate, and criticize one's methods and findings. Ultimately, this should allow for an expansion and accumulation of knowledge while simultaneously resulting in the stillbirth of fallacious or poorly conceived ideas. A

---

5. This is one of the major criticisms levied against many so-called psychodynamic theories in psychology. Unlike the behaviorist models proposed by Skinner, those proposed by Freud are not open to refutation. The same problem arises with dogmatic Marxism. Adherents to this paradigm refuse to specify the conditions under which the theory might be rejected. As Lakatos has so forcefully stated the case: "This is the hallmark of their intellectual dishonesty."

6. An alternate view is what is known as "historicism," which holds that human events are essentially unique manifestations and that any similarities are largely coincidental. Thus, the role of the "social scientist" is to examine the specific circumstances that generated the event of interest. For a critique of this perspective, see Popper (1960).

second facet of communicability is that scientific knowledge is public knowledge in that it can be transmitted from one human being to another. This can be contrasted with some forms of religious knowledge, which are of a totally personal nature (e.g., Otto, 1957).

Finally, the notion of institutional conservativism or skepticism is intended as a mechanism for further checking the veracity of results. While it is allowed that individual scientists may be carried away by exuberance and enthusiasm for their pet projects, it is expected that the broader profession can take a more balanced, or even jaundiced view of the findings. Ultimately it is hoped that if sufficient institutional impediments are put in place, only ideas with a high degree of veracity will be placed on the stockpile of knowledge.[7] One way to conceive of this position has been referred to as the democratization of knowledge. In principle, anyone can overturn the theories of the most lordly, established giant of a field. Further this will (ideally) not be taken as disloyalty, but as loyalty to a higher ideal—an institutionalized loyal opposition in science—rather like that which arose in parliamentary politics.

Many other elements have crept into modern science in addition to the foregoing principles. For example, we have seen the replacement of the validation principle with the idea of refutability; the acceptance of stochasticism as an element of both theory and hypothesis testing, and the acknowledgment that practical science is a social activity that sometimes possesses what might be termed a *nonrational* or metaphysical component. This latter notion has led to distinctions between science as an enterprise of discovery and science as an enterprise of justification.

All too often, we would argue, the critics of positivism appear to have confused form with content, or more specifically, what Reichenbach termed the context of discovery with the context of justification (see Hoyningen-Huene, 1987). The context of discovery is that aspect of science that leads to the generation of ideas and insight. The context of justification, on the other hand, is that aspect of science responsible for assessing the truth value of one's claim. To advance as substantive disciplines, science requires both components, but it is its context of justification that makes science unique. Thus, for example, Feyerabend's call for methodological anarchism is based on the insight that scientists rarely (if ever) followed the nomological–deductive technique in developing theoretical insights. As Feyerabend notes, nearly all the great contributors to science "broke the rules." This was probably true. The greats did not, however, break the rules of assessment or validation; rather, they broke the supposed rules of discovery.

Science is a social activity, carried on by human beings who seem to generate insights from all sorts of directions.[8] The scientific method does not distinguish itself from other approaches to knowledge based on the acquisition of insight—it is

---

7. Individual scientists are also not beyond engaging in deliberate fraud and falsification of results. Excellent investigations of some of the more infamous cases are to be found in Broad and Wade (1982) and Kohn (1986).

8. This is not to say that paradigm or theory formation and hypothesis generation is completely irrational. Practicing scientists spend a great deal of time reviewing and criticising existing theory and attempting to draw inferences, both deductively and inductively, from existing bases of knowledge. For a fuller discussion of the logic of discovery, see Nickles (1980).

distinguished by how it purports to assess the truth claims of those insights. Thus, the members of the Vienna Circle were misguided in rejecting *any* role for metaphysics in science, for the context of discovery is probably the least logical and mechanical of all human enterprises. To reject the scientific method based on aspects of discovery, however, is to engage in a non sequitur.

Just as the context of discovery is sometimes confused with the context of justification, in the social sciences, questions of method are often confused with questions of substantive theory. As R. W. Miller (1987: 5) suggests:

> Even if many interesting social hypotheses deserve to be defended against positivist criticism, social science in the hermeneutic style often seems to be little more than the self-expression, interesting or dull, of the investigator. Whether certain feelings of empathy or enlightenment are real sources of insight seems a subject for scientific argument, not an unquestionable premise for inquiries utterly different from natural-scientific investigation. Similarly, the hermeneutic assumption that social processes are governed by the subjective factors that empathy and introspection might reveal seems an appropriate topic for scientific inquiry, not a defining principle of a special logic of inquiry.

The scientific method as applied to the social sciences is also rejected by many because of a misunderstanding of the nature of the natural sciences. Often it is heard that human affairs are not subject to *scientific* analysis because humans are not predictable in their behavior whereas natural objects are. At best, this view is based on an outdated notion of the natural sciences; at worst, on complete ignorance of the substance of the natural sciences. Contemporary physics, for example, argues that basic particles are inherently unpredictable in their individual behavior.[9] Common sense dictates that humans and human affairs do have some order and predictability to them. Social behavior, therefore, may be intrinsically more predictable than many "natural" events.

The second edge of the rejectionist's sword is that human affairs are not susceptible to scientific analysis because they are teleological (i.e., goal-oriented). Ironically, this view only serves to simplify the applicability of the scientific method since, if it is true, there ought to be more readily identifiable patterns in human behavior than in the behavior of natural objects.

LOGIC AND SCIENTIFIC THEORIES

At some point, any discussion of social science method ultimately involves references to theory, for it is the development of valid and useful theory that generates the enterprise of science in the first instance. The most sophisticated methods and techniques that one might devise cannot make up for fundamental inadequacies

---

9. Interestingly enough, chaos theory illustrates how inherently deterministic systems can behave in such a manner that they appear indeterministic or purely stochastic. See, for example, Bunde and Havlin (1991) and Crilly, Earnshaw, and Jones (1993).

in the manner in which questions are posed. Of course, considerable debate exists about whether any of the social sciences have actually generated a genuine, full-blown theory with all its attendant bells and whistles. Dumont and Wilson (1967), for example, suggest that at best we have spawned numerous *theory sketches*. No matter how highly developed one perceives social theories to be, a well-formulated proposition remains the crucial first step in any successful piece of research.

Elements of the Axiomatic Method

While the term "theory" is broadly defined in the social sciences, from our perspective it is best used to describe a set of interrelated propositions or hypotheses. It is partly due to the assumption that these propositions are logically related that logical positivism has been depicted as nomological–deductive. Sometimes this approach is also known as the axiomatic method, since ultimately some propositions within the theoretical nexus are assumed to be true independent of empirical evidence. The axiomatic approach to theory building has several identifiable elements. These include:

- a system of postulates based upon previous research, concepts, or studied guesses (conventional wisdom)
- definitions of key terms in the postulates plus a statement of undefined terms (i.e., terms with definitions that seem self-evident)
- logically derived conclusions from the postulates that are subject to test through empirical observation (i.e., to be distinguished from a tautology, a statement that is true by virtue of the rules of the language alone)

As with any approach, there are both advantages and disadvantages to the axiomatic method. Among the many advantages are the following.

- It can lead to parsimony and economy of expression.
- It makes for ease in exposing defects in one's reasoning process, and in forcing the researcher to explicate his or her assumptions so that they can readily be checked by other scholars.
- It encourages researchers to integrate otherwise segmented observations into a coherent whole.

Among the limitations, we note these two:

- At present, the nonstandard terminology of the axiomatic method is troublesome to the user of the system.
- As with all deductive approaches it yields no new information: that is, information that does not appear in the original postulates.

Several introductions to axiomatic theory construction have been written, with two of the more popular and accessible being those by Gibbs (1972) and Reynolds (1971).

Classical logical positivism often treated theory statements within a very narrow school of logic that we call the Cartesian framework. This is a deductivist, deterministic model based on the Aristotelian paradigm known as the syllogism. For example, consider the following statements:

All dogs bark.	
Fred is a dog.	Explanans sentences
————————	
∴ Fred barks.	Explanandum sentence

The syllogism consists of a major premise ("All dogs bark.") and a minor premise ("Fred is a dog."), which are known as the explanans sentences, and a conclusion or explanandum sentence ("Therefore Fred barks."). If the first two sentences are true, then by logical necessity the conclusion is true.

The syllogistic form is explored in detail in most introductory discussions of logic (e.g., Copi, 1967). For our purposes, considering two conditions is sufficient. Assume that a major premise of the form 'if p then q' and a minor premise of the form 'p' are both true. Then, the conclusion must be 'q', and 'q' must also be true. This formulation, known as "affirming the antecedent" (or in its Latin notation, the Modus Ponens), characterizes the example above concerning Fred. A second valid argument may be formulated by again asserting the major premise 'if p then q,' but then assuming as the minor premise 'not q.' If the explanans is true, then the explanandum (conclusion) must be the truthful assertion 'not p.' This latter formulation is known as "denying the consequent," or in Latin, the Modus Tollens. To clarify the matter slightly, both forms are reproduced below in a more conventional format, along with a parallel substantive example regarding the reliability and validity of scales.

Affirming the Antecedent (Modus Ponens)

If p then q.	All valid scales are reliable.
p.	The Srole scale is valid.
—————	—————————————
∴ q.	∴ The Srole scale is reliable.

Denying the Consequent (Modus Tollens)

If p then q.	All valid scales are reliable.
Not q.	The Srole scale is not reliable.
—————	—————————————
∴ not p.	∴ The Srole scale is not valid.

The Modus Ponens and the Modus Tollens, however, do not exhaust the logical possibilities for the minor premise. Again, assume that the major premise 'if p then q' is true. If the minor premise is 'not p,' and this is true, then we *cannot* formulate any conclusion regarding q. Typically, however, one might be tempted to conclude 'not q' for the explanandum, but this would constitute what is known as the "fallacy of denying the antecedent." The reason for this fallacy is that q may result from other factors besides p.

Similarly, if the minor premise is 'q,' a conclusion of 'p' would also be fallacious. In this instance, one would be committing the "fallacy of affirming the consequent." The reason for this fallacy is the same as that for the fallacy denying the antecedent. Again both forms are reproduced below in their conventional format along with the substantive example regarding the reliability and validity of scales.

Fallacy of Denying the Antecedent

If p then q.	All valid scales are reliable.
Not p.	The Srole scale is not valid.
$\therefore$ not q.	$\therefore$ The Srole scale is not reliable.

Fallacy of Affirming the Consequent

If p then q.	All valid scales are reliable.
q.	The Srole scale is reliable.
$\therefore p$.	$\therefore$ The Srole scale is valid.

As we will show, the value of the classical syllogism is limited to instances in which the explanans concerns binary phenomena (e.g., true/false, yes/no) in a deterministic relationship. One such instance, however, is central to science and that is the acceptance or rejection of the null hypothesis.

Disconfirmation and Science: The Role of the Null Hypothesis

The verifiability principle was the founding and faltering principle upon which classical logical positivism was based. Unfortunately, verifiability in science turned out to be something that could not be verified. Rather, as Karl Popper wrote in *The Logic of Scientific Discovery*, the strength of the scientific method was not its ability to verify, but instead, its ability to refute![10]

Ultimately, it is difficult, if not impossible, to test propositions directly in science. This is primarily because it is not inconsistent to assert that all observed As are Bs, but that there are some unobserved As that are clearly not Bs. The formal logic behind this can partially be understood by resorting to the classical syllogism (see Hempel, 1966: 6–8). Let us consider an arbitrary hypothesis H, and one or more implications, I. Thus, to follow Hempel,

---

10. Although Popper is credited in modern times with having introduced the concept of refutability within science, it is probably more proper to attribute its rediscovery to him, since the essential logic can be traced back at least as far as Hume (see Smart, 1968: ch. 6).

If H is true, then so is I.

But (as the evidence shows) I is not true.

$\therefore H$ is not true.

Again, as Modus Ponens, any argument of this form must necessarily be true; that is, if its premises (explanans) are true, then its conclusion (explanandum) is also true. Thus, if the premises are properly established, the hypothesis H that is being tested must be rejected.

Now let us consider a variation on this form.[11] Suppose the evidence, I, is concordant with or confirms H. Thus, we have:

If H is true, then so is I.

(As the evidence shows) I is true.

$\therefore H$ is true.

This form of reasoning (the fallacy of affirming the consequent) is deductively *invalid* because it is possible for the conclusion to be false, even if the premises are true. A further clue about why this may be so is to be found in the issue of necessary/substitutable relations, dealt with in more detail in a future chapter. Simply put, the evidence, I, could easily be the manifestation of more than one cause, or it could be due to some spurious factor totally unrelated to H. It is because of this limitation in logic that scientists work in the negative; that is, they attempt to disconfirm the null hypothesis to tentatively affirm the working hypothesis. Referring to our dog Fred, we should be aware that barking by a beast does not necessarily a dog make. Seals and some other animals also bark.

It is worthwhile examining the structure of the null hypothesis model in greater detail. As suggested, if one cannot directly affirm some hypothesis, H, then it may be possible to confirm it indirectly by disconfirming its complement, null-H. Thus, we may propose,

If null-H is true, then so is I.

But (as the evidence shows) I is not true.

$\therefore$ null-H is not true.

Since the situation is set up as a dichotomous outcome, showing that the null hypothesis is *not* true leads us to accept the validity of the working hypothesis. Ultimately, this formulation relies on two facts: H and its complements are (a) mutually exclusive

11. An excellent discussion of this logic from a Bayesian point of view can be found in Howson and Urbach (1989). Also see Johnstone and Lindley (1995).

and (b) finitely enumerable. If H and null-H can be expressed as mutually exclusive dichotomies, there are usually few logical problems associated with testing. More often, however, the working hypothesis, H_w, is only one possible alternative drawn from the set $\{H_i, i = 1, \ldots, n\}$. In this instance, all H_i, where $i \neq w$, are eligible null hypotheses. The various H_i may not be mutually exclusive, and it may be difficult to specify the complete set of i alternatives. Furthermore, several H_i may be adequate explanations in that they are congruent with the implications, I, to varying degrees. In this instance, the task is one of deleting the least adequate among the H_i.

Unfortunately, the classical syllogism has several other drawbacks. In an oft-quoted example, Salmon (1971: 34) considers the following:

Nobody who takes birth control pills as directed gets pregnant.

George takes birth control pills as directed.

∴ George does not get pregnant.

The structure of our syllogism is clearly correct; however, given that George is a man, few would regard this syllogism as an explanation of *why* George does not become pregnant. Clearly, taking or not taking birth control pills (even as directed) has nothing to do with George's not becoming pregnant. Depending upon how we wish to criticize this example, the fault lies along one of two dimensions. First, we might argue that the major premise ("Nobody who takes . . .") is a misspecification of the target population. That is to say, there are clearly unspecified ancillary assumptions here regarding birth control pill usage and pregnancy. The appropriate target population is obviously limited to presumed fertile women within childbearing age. George is outside this target population; hence the explanation is specious.

Second, we might argue that while the structure of the syllogism is correct as far as it goes, it is a misspecification of the overall causal model. As will be addressed in a later chapter, the model is inadequate because it does not include several intervening variables, the primary one being "sex."

Overall then, what is the salient point here? The point is that the formal structure of the syllogism may be a necessary condition for adequate theorizing but it is not a sufficient condition. Further analysis will also show that it need not be a necessary condition. Consider again our first example. Asserting that all dogs bark contradicts empirical reality because some dogs, such as basenjis, are assumed to be mute. For all intents and purposes, however, we are often willing to accept the major premise as correct, since the number of mute dogs is quite small. Still, a more precise statement would be "The overwhelming majority of dogs bark" or "Ninety-six percent of dogs bark." Thus, if Fred is a dog, we cannot say with certainty that Fred will bark—it is only highly likely that Fred will do so.

Clearly under these circumstances, the classical syllogism is limited as a useful form of logic. As previously noted, few if any of our assertions about the social world are universals of the form of the major premise stated above. At best, we couch our major premises in the ceteris paribus assumption of all else being equal. Unfortunately, "all else" is not always equal, or even equal most of the time. Thus, we have been forced to abandon the simple, but elegant form of the classical syllogism, with its strict deterministic form, and revert to other types of logic. The most common alternative (which we will explore in the next chapter) retains the form of the syllogism, but introduces an aspect of probability into the structure.

Although many other types of logic beside the classical syllogism exist, there has been an unwillingness or inability among social scientists to explore these in any great detail. Some attempts have been made, however, to explore the applicability of elementary stochasticism, and several sciences have toyed with fuzzy set theory.[12] Still, this is a greatly underdeveloped area within the social sciences in both theory and methods. Few practicing social scientists still espouse a strict determinist model, but as Paul Meehl (1986: 323) has stated: "Nobody has succeeded in presenting a useful meaning of scientific explanation that is totally unlike the Hempel model."

Despite the formal logic employed, then, positivist science uses the deductive approach to retain internal consistency in its models. This is achieved because deductivism is a closed system by definition. To avoid being tautological, however, the final propositions generated by the model are left open to empirical assessment. If the model's logic is sound, empirical disconfirmation undermines the basic principles or propositions upon which the system is based; therefore, the theory is rejected. Unfortunately, as we have suggested, the simple logic inherent in the syllogism is not always adequate for dealing with the problem at hand. Since most relationships in the social sciences appear to be at least minimally stochastic, it is difficult to know in any given study whether empirical disconfirmation (a) negates the basic premises, or is just one of those fluke results due to sampling variability, (b) constitutes support for a competing hypothesis, or (c) is due to an inadequate empirical test.

Making Theories Untestable

Some years ago, Clifford Shearing (1973) published a short but invaluable essay on how to make theories untestable. Shearing's comments have likely saved the fragile egos of many social scientists who cannot face the prospect of having their insightful discourses on the state of the world shot down in flames. After all, few of us really *like* to be proven wrong. Shearing's advice is quite simple: there are two primary lines of defense in one's quest for irrefutability.

1. "Make certain that no empirically refutable statements can be deduced from the theory."
2. "Ensure that the theory is internally inconsistent. That is, take steps to ensure that one's theory does not form a deductive system where all the propositions of the theory can be deduced from a set of axioms."

---

12. Three basic patterns of logic define most of our modes of analysis: deduction, induction, and inference. Although the study of logic has had a long and illustrious history, it still provides a great deal of scope for disagreement and debate. A good introduction to many of the issues and quandaries of formal logic can be found in Poundstone (1988).

Point 1 can best be carried out by doing one or more of the following:

1. "Provide no operational definitions for any of the terms in the theory."
2. "Provide no propositions in the theory."
3. "Ensure that the relationship between terms remains as unclear as possible."

While Shearing's sage advice (1973: 33–37) may be sound for maintaining the steadfastness of one's pronouncements, adherence to these rules does little to advance scientific knowledge. After all, assessing the truth value of propositions is the crux of the scientific endeavor. Shearing's tongue-in-cheek observations, however, go to the heart of how one might start to generate good theory, or at least, good propositions.

Other Approaches

Other basic approaches to theorizing do exist, even within the Cartesian framework. Hegel's dialectic with its notions of thesis, antithesis, and synthesis readily comes to mind. Generally, however, the dialectic is discussed outside the ambit of formal logic, since the notion of *implication* cannot effectively be applied to dialectic thought (see Copi, 1967: 14–17). This framework also contravenes Aristotle's law of noncontradiction—the assertion that a phenomenon may not have an attribute and its opposite simultaneously (i.e., a thesis and its antithesis).

On a personal note, I suspect that the dialectic is more applicable to a substantive model of social process rather than a model of formal logic. Society may function dialectically, but the dialectic is probably not a valid model for assessing the coherence of statements purporting that substantive model.

The Hypothetico-Deductive Method

How, one might ask, do all the foregoing elements fit together for testing theories or hypotheses? Traditionally, the formal model that ties the components together is termed the hypothetico-deductive (HD) method and consists of four primary steps:

1. Propose some theory, T.
2. From T draw a series of logical predictions or hypotheses, H, that propose empirical or observable consequences. The H should be stated along with any caveats or ceteris paribus assumptions.
3. Collect data for testing H using standard test procedures (e.g., experimentation).
4. Decide whether T is or is not disconfirmed depending upon whether the data collected in step 3 are or are not congruent with H.

As we have seen, each of these components can be elaborated in substantial detail. It should also be remembered that the HD model is not without its critics—ranging from those who reject the framework in toto to those, such as the Bayesians, who would keep most elements but with substantial revisions. For those who work within this general framework (that is likely, most scientists), the most significant methodological problems are those of specifying what forms relevant testing data in step 3, and how one ought to deal with step 4 when inconsistent results are obtained (i.e., some elements are disconfirmed and others are not).

There may be no definitive answer to either of these two problems beyond saying that the determination of what is accepted as relevant data and what is strong disconfirmation relies upon a consensus of the scientists who work within the specific paradigm. Still, formal attempts have been made to address these issues, the foremost being that of Imre Lakatos.

LAKATOS AND THE RESEARCH PROGRAM

Students of the history of science soon come to realize that the precepts of the philosophy of science are rarely followed completely by practicing scientists. Thus, while we might follow the Popperian theme of falsification as the primary vehicle for assessing the likely (non)truth value of propositions, not all disconfirmations lead to a rejection of particular propositions or the theories from which they are drawn. If this is the case, is there some way of reconciling a general adherence to the basic method we have discussed with the reality of how scientists decide the merits of individual theories? Imre Lakatos (1965, 1978) thinks so. Lakatos argues that we have to broaden our perspective and look at the entirety of what scientists do. From this perspective, scientists in particular fields are tied together by what Lakatos terms a *research program*. According to Lakatos, "The programme consists of methodological rules: some tell us what paths of research to avoid (*negative heuristic*), and others what paths to pursue (*positive heuristic*)" (Lakatos, 1970: 132).

Implicit in this analysis is the notion that most research programs (theories) are broad entities that have a certain level of a priori credibility. That is, they fit most of the known facts at some point in time, or at least most of the most crucial facts. Lakatos recognized that research programs do not appear through some form of divine revelation but evolve slowly through trial and error. A research program consists of two components. First is a *hard core* of givens based on known relationships, axiomatic assumptions, and key deductions that are essentially unchallenged. These relate to the negative heuristic and are generally considered off-bounds to direct assessment within the particular framework of a research program. Around this hard core is a protective belt of *auxiliary hypotheses* that are the substance of day-to-day scientific tests. These are an integral part of Lakatos's positive heuristic. The auxiliary hypotheses are accepted, rejected, modified, or even replaced according to the outcomes of various investigations. The important point is, the rejection or need to modify any one or several of these auxiliary hypotheses is not sufficient reason to reject the whole theory.

Ultimately, the value of a theory is based on how well these auxiliary hypotheses fare, and on whether competing research programs provide a better explanation and better fit to the data. As Lakatos (1965: 133) states in his uniquely jargonistic style: "A research program is successful if all this leads to a progressive problemshift; unsuccessful if it leads to a degenerating problemshift."

The real value of the Lakatos model is that it explains why we do not have the immediate abandonment of a valuable theory simply because several implied hypotheses are rejected. In many branches of science, hypotheses derived from successful theories have been rejected without undermining the credibility of the core theory in the short run. The reason for this is that often there are hidden lemmas or ceteris paribus assumptions that are not immediately evident. Furthermore, as technology and scientific ingenuity evolve, not all empirical findings turn out to be what they appear at first sight. Again to quote Lakatos (1965: 134):

> While "theoretical progress" . . . may be verified immediately, "empirical progress" cannot, and in a research programme we may be frustrated by a long series of "refutations" before ingenious and lucky content-increasing auxiliary hypotheses turn a chain of defeats—*with hindsight*—into a resounding success story, either by revising some false "facts" or by adding novel auxiliary hypotheses.

Another interesting observation by Lakatos is that research programs require continuous growth to survive. Successful research programs not only incorporate new facts as they arise, but can generate new relationships. This Lakatos calls the *heuristic power* of a research program. Two examples of contemporary research programs perceived to lack heuristic power are Marxism and Freudism. As Lakatos queries somewhat facetiously, "What *novel* fact has Marxism *predicted* since, say, 1917?" This view is echoed by Thomas Kuhn (1970: 8–10), who suggests that what distinguishes pseudosciences like astrology from *real* sciences like astronomy is that despite failed experience in both cases, pseudosciences generate no puzzles that can lead to a revision of the science's tradition.

A further consequence of Lakatos's conceptualization is that one classical notion put forward by the logical positivists—that of the *crucial experiment*—is not valid. Research programs do not experience instantaneous death upon the revelation of the results of a single experiment or finding. Instead, they wither away at a rate decided by the relative success of competing programs.

CONCLUSION

In this chapter we have attempted to provide a general framework for explaining how at least some forms of social science research are conducted. As with all models, this one is not complete; some dimensions are certainly more fully developed than others, and considerable debate continues over the status of most of the individual components of the model. It will likely be noticed that much of the discussion draws heavily on the literature in the philosophy of science. There are many reasons for this, not the least of which is that it is the intellectual domain of philosophers to consider such questions. Most applied methodologists and substantive researchers are usually too busy trying to conduct what Kuhn terms "normal science" to step back and systematically consider why they do what they do.

Often, the explanations espoused by those who think about why scientists do what they do are not much more advanced than any other social explanations. Just as this is true regarding the actual practice of science, so it is true of the normative statements of what scientists ought to be doing when they do science. Ultimately, the determination of how science is and should be done relies on considerations of what advances the discipline. Often in the past century when philosophers' analyses have been at odds with actual practice, it has been the analyses that have changed, not practice. This is not to say that day-to-day social science has been immune to philosophical and methodological insights. Popper's discourse on the issue of falsification and the fuller development of Bayesian logic have had profound impacts on how social scientists structure their research. Yet, the basic framework of the hypothetico-deductive model has remained largely unchanged since the last century, despite the rise and fall of logical positivism and the ministrations of many critics.

Having proposed this methodological framework, we must also acknowledge that some elements of the study of social phenomena do create substantial problems. For example, unlike most phenomena within the domain of the natural sciences, humans appear to be teleological in their orientation. Thus, it is legitimate to raise the question of whether our subjective explanations of why people do what they do should or should not be the subject matter of what we explore.

Having noted this, it is well to heed the warning issued by Pawson (1989: 8), who tell us:

> Whatever its merits, prescriptive methodology is not something one can apply in any straightforward sense. Set against the task of defining the ultimate character of the whole history and scope of science, philosophers are faced with a choice of (a) producing a favoured model which is exemplified by certain episodes in certain disciplines but whose very language is so conditioned by this context that one needs some inventive metaphorical extension to make it apply to other forms of inquiry, or (b) trying to give credence to the width of scientific endeavour, in which case they produce prescriptions so broad and bland that even the most *ersatz* of scientists can say "we'll drink to that."

Ultimately, the value of the scientific method is that it is the least fallible method we have yet devised for assessing truth in a world full of fallible truth seekers. Contrary to some opinion, adherence to the scientific method does not entail commitment to yet another ideological religion. Should a more useful method appear in the future, the scientific method will be relegated to the status of a transitory philosophy that served its practitioners well, but left the doors open to its own succession.

Further Reading

Fetzer, J.H. *Foundations of Philosophy in Science.* New York: Paragon House, 1993. An anthology of classic articles in the philosophy of science including those by Hempel, Popper, Quine, Kuhn, and Lakatos. Excellent coverage of philosophical thinking from the early logical positivists to more recent developments.

Giere, R.N. *Understanding Scientific Reasoning*, 2nd ed. New York: Holt, Rinehart & Winston, 1984. A solid introduction to the philosophy of science and the processes underlying scientific reasoning.

Hausman, D.M. *The Inexact and Separate Science of Economics.* Cambridge: Cambridge University Press, 1992. An analysis of how a social science with one of the strongest traditions of formal theorizing deals with the problem of assessment. While addressed primarily to economists, this text has much to offer all researchers conducting empirical research in the social sciences.

Howson, C., and Urbach, P. *Scientific Reasoning: The Bayesian Approach*. La Salle, IL: Open Court, 1989. This book provides an introduction to the problem of inference and the issue of dealing with theories as probabilistic as opposed to deterministic entities. The Bayesian approach to the issue is explicitly laid out. The authors also outline the logic underlying classical statistics as proposed by Fisher, and Pearson and Neyman, and provide a very insightful critique of that approach.

Phillips, D.C. *The Social Scientist's Beastiary*. Oxford: Pergamon Press, 1992. Phillips outlines a number of bugaboos that challenge standard scientific methodology for the hearts and minds of social scientists. Phillips provides an especially devastating critique of phenomenology, hermeneutics, and other such "beasts."

Popper, K.R. *The Logic of Scientific Discovery*. London: Hutchinson, 1959. While somewhat dated, this book by one of the century's great contributors to the philosophy of science is still worthwhile reading. Popper's work is a starting point for most contemporary literature—both critique and commentary.

2

Theory Formalization

*In a natural language the relational terms are so diverse and
ambiguous that their use when stating an empirical generalization
virtually precludes defensible tests of the generalization.*

—Jack Gibbs

What is known as theory in the social sciences varies considerably from one discipline
to the next. In much of sociology and anthropology, for example, theory connotes a
substantial literary discourse, rich in metaphor and highly emotive. Proponents claim
that explanatory power within this framework arises from the ability of discourse
to create an empathic or intuitive understanding of the phenomenon under study.
In other sections of these disciplines, and in much of psychology and economics,
the term "theory" most often connotes a highly specific entity, often presented as a
symbolic calculus. While less empathically appealing, this type of theory is valued
for its clarity, specificity, and parsimony of expression.

No matter how theory is perceived, all valid theoretical statements contain two
basic elements: concepts and expressions of functional relationship between the
concepts. Concepts and relationships are the basic building blocks of any scientific
theory, and the clearer and more precisely these are developed, the easier it is to
evaluate a given theory. In this chapter, we focus on some ways in which concepts
are developed and how they might be linked together to formulate testable theories.

WHAT IS A THEORY?

Intuitively, theories are sets of verbal statements that synthesize the behavior of
empirical systems. Depending upon one's point of view, theories either describe
the behavior of empirical systems or provide sufficient explanation to allow us to
understand "why" those systems behave as they do. Wherever one stands on this
matter, the adequacy of either description or explanation involves the ability to make
successful predictions.

The classical logical-positivist view on this matter assumed that, in principle, theories could be completely explicated by discovering a series of covering laws and then
pursuing all the logical entailments. This paradigm, which appears to have tenuous
links to the construction and exploitation of theories in the natural sciences, seems
completely foreign to the social sciences. Still, considerable intellectual energy was
expended in the two decades spanning the 1960s and 1970s to develop sociological
theories within an axiomatic framework. Despite those efforts, there is little legacy of

any substantive importance in the literature on social theory. Perhaps the lack of true axioms or social laws has been the greatest stumbling block; perhaps it is other factors. Regardless, the nomological–deductivist approach has not borne a great deal of fruit. Instead of covering laws and hegemonic propositional systems, most working theories are loose affairs that consist of a series of models of varying degrees of complexity and explication, with several auxiliary hypotheses called in when needed. Furthermore, most working scientists, who should have a natural affinity to the axiomatic approach, find the logical algebra of linear equations a far more adaptable research tool than the axiomatic approach borne in the textbooks of symbolic logic.

Based on this view, we are probably well served by Giere's (1988: 85) definition of a theory:

> My preferred suggestion, then, is that we understand a theory as comprising two elements: (1) a population of models, and (2) various hypotheses linking those models with systems in the real world.

The author elaborates his second point as follows (Giere, 1988: 86):

> The links between models and the real world below are nothing like correspondence rules linking terms with the things or terms with other terms. Rather, they are again relations of similarity between a whole model and some real system. A real system is *identified* as being similar to one of the models.

What, then, can we conclude regarding the status of theories in the social sciences? First, it is evident that the general concept encompasses a variety of explanatory forms—some of which are so divergent that they appear to have little in common at first glance. Second, the only apparent consensus on the ontological status of theories is that they should be internally consistent and potentially open to refutation. And sometimes, even those requirements are waived. Third, excruciating difficulties exist with the linkage between our theory language and attempts to operationalize it.

It is for these reasons that many social scientists, and especially quantitatively oriented researchers, have opted for a much narrower (some would say arbitrary) definition of theory, while others have abandoned the term entirely. Instead, these people have generally opted for the term *model* to describe their theory statements, and they speak of model construction or model formalization when referring to their attempts at theory construction. The switch in terminology may be more political than substantive, although commentators of all stripes do seem to acknowledge that "model" is a distinct and far less encompassing term than "theory."

Whether we speak of theories or models, however, several issues need to be addressed. A primary one is that some association needs to be made between the ideational world and the empirical world. The English philosopher Hume, for example, made a fundamental distinction between the world of ideas and the world of facts. This practice of viewing two realms—that of ideas and that of facts—remains with us today and is a fundamental issue within the philosophy of science. It is generally accepted that some form of "truth" can be determined within each realm. Thus, for example, statements of relations among ideas are assumed to be true if they follow certain rules of semantic logic. To repeat an example presented by Quine (1953), both the following statements are deemed to be true:

1. No unmarried man is married.
2. No bachelor is married.

The first statement is true by logical necessity, since one cannot be in some state A and not A simultaneously (i.e., married and not married). The second statement is analytically true if we assume that the term *bachelor* and the implied concept, *unmarried man,* are synonymous. The important point here is that both sentences are true independent of the state of the world. This class of truths is variously identified as "linguistic" or "analytic" truth.

On the other hand, the statement "The median age in Canada in 1985 was 31.1 years" is a statement of purported fact. Its truth value is not based on its logical or semantical veracity; rather, its truth value is based on its empirical veracity.

What is the nature of the relationship between semantic relationships (statements) and empirical facts? In other words, how closely linked do those ideas we call theories need to be to their empirical referents to be considered valid or invalid? This is a central issue for scientific theories.

One extreme view is that a perfect relationship between a concept and its empirical referent must exist. This position is termed *radical reductionism.* As Quine points out, however, this position is "unnecessary and intolerably restrictive." To follow the radical reductionist argument to its logical conclusion would require our theories to be as complex as the reality they purport to describe and explain. In essence, nothing is to be gained by generating theory, for it is only by allowing for a parsimony in our theory language that theory becomes worthwhile. Theories become useful to us when linguistic terms and relations cover classes of empirical events and relationships. To follow Quine, then, "more reasonably . . . we may take full statements as our significant units—thus demanding that our statements as wholes be translatable into sense-datum language, but not that they be translatable term by term" (1953:39). Within this framework, the problems facing scientists as they attempt to test theory become more complex. Not only is there still the issue of linking some semantic concepts to empirical phenomena, there is now the issue of deciding which are the essential semantic elements that need to be linked and which can be omitted.

Put in a more pragmatic framework, let us assume that we have a reasonably complex theory. Is the theory necessarily disconfirmed if a complete correspondence appears neither between the concepts of the theory and their empirical referents, nor between the semantic relations of the concepts and factual relations among the empirical referents? Since we do not require a direct correspondence between the semantical and the empirical worlds, some slippage is to be expected. These are critical questions for which no definitive answer currently exists, or probably ever will. How critically one views this problem is likely related to whether one supports a realist or nonrealist (instrumentalist) stance. One might expect realists to be those seeking a closer correspondence between their theory statements and the empirical world. From an extreme instrumentalist perspective, it might be argued that one should care only about the degree to which a theory makes successful predictions, no matter how well individual theory components correspond to their empirical counterparts.

We can develop a better appreciation for the role of theory in methods, however, by looking more closely at the constituent components of theories intended for empirical assessment.

THE LANGUAGE OF SCIENCE: NOUNS

Substantive science consists of statements of relationships among concepts and, as with all linguistic statements, statements in science are composed of nouns (things, concepts) and verbs (relations between things). The *things* we talk about are concepts, which may themselves be verblike gerunds (e.g., "coping"). As Kaplan (1955: 527) tells us, "The process by which a term is introduced into discourse or by which the meaning of a term already in use is more exactly specified, may be called *specification of meaning*. This process is ordinarily explicated by the concept of definition—a logical equivalence between the term defined as an expression whose meaning has already been specified."

A central question for understanding the research enterprise is: How are concepts formulated? Interestingly, researchers have conducted little formal empirical research on this issue although considerable anecdotal material exists. Further, much of the discussion surrounding this issue has been prescriptive (e.g., Hempel, 1952) rather than descriptive. Without formal evidence, therefore, Greer's (1989: 38) assertion that "the natural history of psychological meaning is from sense data to symbol to the individual's system of meaning to the resulting interpretation of the experience" seems reasonable.

If this is the situation, then it appears that concepts arise initially for labeling and identifying observables. Thus, the task is one of generating a symbolic (usually linguistic) referent for the sense datum and providing a definition for the symbol that denotes the essential and unique characteristics of the sense datum. Concepts so generated are often defined as first-order concepts. We can link those first-order concepts to other concepts to form second- or higher-order concepts.[1] When we join or linked those lower order concepts to form complex concepts (as in sentences), their meanings often change so that we formulate a different view or understanding of the symbols' original referents. Thus, our definitions may start as referents to sense data, but over time they are modified and infused with meanings that can affect how we view the sense data. Instead of simply reflecting the sense data, the symbols then become a mechanism for organizing the sense data. Ultimately, this iterative process can result in concepts changing how we draw boundaries around the sense data.

Experience also teaches us that when lower-order concepts are embedded in a metatheoretical framework, or linked to form a model or theory, higher-order concepts can be generated. Establishing whether those higher-order concepts are valid requires

---

1. See Steiner, 1989, for an interesting discussion of the application of mathematical symbols to the natural sciences.

us to conduct further empirical investigation. As Bierstedt (1959: 125) asserts: "It is necessary to rely upon the investigation itself in order to determine whether or not the properties the definition ascribes to the concept actually do belong to it, whether, to put it bluntly, the *definiens* does in fact define the *definiendum*, whether, in short, the definition is 'true.' "

Because of this process, some concepts will arise and be linked to their empirical referents in a "bottom up" format while others will be linked to their referents in a "top down" fashion. That is to say, sometimes we start with an observable or sense datum and then seek an adequate construct to act as its referent, while in other instances we will start with a concept or construct and attempt to find an adequate empirical referent.[2] In either instance, it is necessary ultimately to specify and link the concepts to their observational referents and vice versa.

Concepts must be clearly defined in order for us to understand them. The drafting of such definitions can be pedantic but useful exercise, since a great impediment to the generation and transmission of knowledge is a lack of common understanding of what basic concepts stand for. Thus, trying to determine what we mean by *anomie*, or *locus of control*, or *alienation* is not necessarily an exercise in navel gazing. Consider the latter term—alienation. If used outside a specific context, most social scientists will quickly raise the question about whether it is meant in a Marxist, Durkheimian, or psychiatric sense. The sophomoric exercise of defining one's terms is often overlooked in everyday science, but it is essential to the full development of any working theory. Comparisons of supposedly "like" studies in reviews of literature often show that contrary results are a consequence of different modes of conceptualization rather than truly contradictory empirical results.

As John Madge (1965: 28) notes in his discussion of the differences between American and British understandings of the term "billion"[3]:

> It is undeniable that any such discrepancy is a nuisance, a barrier to perfect communication. In this case there may not be any very compelling reason to choose one meaning rather than the other, but one doubts that in the long run, two peoples who want to share the instrument of language will have to agree between themselves which usage to adopt.

While the issue of *meaning* is the subject of substantial debate in the philosophical literature, some analytic distinctions provide a reasonable framework for generating workable definitions. It is common for scientists to speak of different levels of definition based on level of abstraction. A typical hierarchy of definition consists of three levels, referred to as *real definitions*, *nominal definitions*, and *operational definitions*. A real definition is usually considered to be the underlying or true meaning of a concept. For example, the real definition of a chair is assumed to be the quintessential or prototypical concept of the entity that exists in the mind

---

2. While the terms concept and construct are often used ambiguously and interchangeably, we will adopt the convention that a construct is a concept that is embedded in a specified theoretical framework.
3. That is, a thousand million (10^9) in the United States and a million million (10^{12}) in the United Kingdom.

of the observer. Nominal definitions are linguistic representations of real concepts. Practically speaking, nominal definitions are akin to dictionary definitions. Thus, for example, Webster's dictionary defines a chair as "a seat with four legs and a back rest, for one person." This may be distinguished from a stool (which has no back rest), or a bench (which has room for more than one person).

It is current vogue in some circles to deny real definitions and assume the semantic basis of nominal definitions as the starting point for defining concepts. That is, some people assume that whatever cannot be verbalized, cannot be conceived. Clearly, they do not share the frame of mind of former U.S. Supreme Court Justice Potter Stewart, who declared that while he might not be able to define pornography, he knew it when he saw it.

Finally, operational definitions are the empirical referents to which real and nominal definitions are applied. As Gwynne Nettler notes in his book *Explanations*: "For scientists, the experiential reference of operational definitions is an advantage. Such definitions tend to be clear and certain. The clarity and certainty gained by this mode of definition are a result of both its empirical base and its referential restriction: *The term shall be used to refer to what this test tests and nothing more.*" (Nettler, 1970: 14; italics in original)

A continuing weakness of the logical-positivist framework is the difficulty in identifying linkages between levels of definition—especially between nominal and operational definitions. Formally, definitions are supposed to be linked by rules of correspondence, but we have very little to say about them except that ultimately they rely on intuition. More than 30 years ago, Nagel noted in *The Structure of Science* that:

> It is pertinent to observe, however, that no one has yet successfully constructed such definitions. Moreover, there are good reasons for believing that the rules of correspondence in actual use do not constitute explicit definitions for theoretical notions in terms of experimental concepts. (Nagel, 1961: 98)

The difficulty inherent in specifying rules of correspondence undoubtedly contributed to the rise of behaviorism in psychology and radical operationalism in other fields (e.g., George Lundburg's work in sociology). We might note that radical empiricism is often seen as a safe refuge by many, especially after they have spent considerable time trying to decipher some obtuse, and illogical theory. Undoubtedly, there are few sociology graduate students who have not thrown their arms up in the air with the utterance of "Who cares what Durkheim or Marx 'really meant' anyway?"[4]

Box 2.1 provides some soruces of definitions in the social sciences. These provide an excellent starting point. Ultimately, one must refer to the professional literature for the most current developments.

Theory in Measurement: An Aside

It is often pointed out by critics of mainstream social science that the process of measurement (i.e., the relating of facts to concepts) is itself a theory-laden enterprise.

---

4. Or, to quote Bridgman (1928: 7), "the true meaning of a term is to be found by observing what man does with it, not by what he says about it."

■ **Box 2.1**

A SAMPLING OF DICTIONARIES IN THE SOCIAL SCIENCES

There are many sources for nominal definition of key terms within any discipline. Textbooks, review articles and original research studies provide fertile grounds. The easiest entrance however, is through one of the many social science dictionaries. The following list is by no means exhaustive, but provides a flavor for what is available in most major libraries.

Bannock, G., R.E. Baxter, and E. Davis, *Dictionary of Economics*, London: Hutchinson, 1989.

Gilpin, A., *Dictionary of Economic Terms*, (2nd ed.) New York: Philosophical Library, 1970.

Gould, J. and W.L. Kolb, *A Dictionary of the Social Sciences*. New York: Free Press, 1965.

Mitchell, G.D., *A New Dictionary of the Social Sciences*. New York: Aldine, 1979.

Pearce, D.W (Ed.), *Macmillan Dictionary of Modern Economics*. London: Macmillan, 1992.

Petersen, W. and R. Petersen, *Dictionary of Demography: Terms, Concepts and Institutions:* Westport, C: Greenwood Press, 1985.

Pressat, R., *The Dictionary of Demography*. Oxford: Blackwell, 1985.

Reading, H.F., *A Dictionary of the Social Sciences*. London: Routledge & Kegan Paul, 1976.

Seymour-Smith, C., *Macmillan Dictionary of Anthropology*. London: Macmillan, 1986.

Sutherland, N.S., *Macmillan Dictionary of Psychology*. London: Macmillan, 1989.

Walsh, D. and A. Poole, *A Dictionary of Criminology*. London: Routledge & Kegan Paul, 1983.

Essentially, we are told, science is not objective because the scientist observes only what she or he wishes to observe. Undoubtedly, this is true—one tends to "see" only what one looks for, and what one looks for is a theoretical imperative. That observation and measurement are theory guided, however, does not undermine the "objectivity" of the scientific method, which is to find ways of rejecting the null hypothesis.

A more important criticism revolves around the comment that theories cannot be tested with observations defined, or constructed, or conceived by that same theory. Inherently, this situation creates a tautology, since the validity of a theory is being tested by the observations the theory defines as valid. Again, we can avoid the problem by taking a step back and separating the substantive aspects of a theory from the theoretical aspects of measurement. As Ray Pawson notes,[5] "There is, however, no circularity involved in the use of theory-laden measurement provided that theories

---

5. See Pawson's Chapter 4 for a detailed discussion of this problem.

drawn upon in the construction of the instrument are not the same as those tested in the application of the instrument" (1989: 27).

Characteristics of Concepts

While it is no mean feat, developing an adequate definition of a concept is only the first step in using it within the scientific paradigm. Concepts have several characteristics that need to be recognized and explicated. Essentially concepts come in two varieties—constants and variables. For example, religion is a phenomenon, but it is not a variable. Whether one follows any religion or none, one's level of religiosity, or the specific creed to which one adheres are all variables. Things that do not vary are constants, and while constants have a use in science, they should not be confused with variables. Often, social scientists become sloppy and refer to constants when they really mean to refer to variables. For example, we sometimes see references to *crime* when the topic of interest is *variations in the crime rate* or *how much criminality*. Similarly, the term *education* is used when we really mean *level of education* (or more often *years of schooling* or *test scores*). The key distinction here is that variables vary—they have more than one level—whereas constants are just that: they do not change.

Although we will go into this in more detail in a later chapter, the issue of variables raises the issue of levels of measurement. Distinguishing between qualitative and quantitative phenomena is common in some circles, as if the two were categorically different. In essence, what most social scientists call qualitative data (or "qualitative research") are simply data measured at a low level of measurement. That is, using a common scaling typology, qualitative data are nominal or ordinal level measurements as opposed to interval or ratio level. We must recognize that nominal level measurement is really one type of "quantitative" measurement. Nominal level measurement can be as simple as presence/absence or existence/nonexistence. Multiple categories are simply polytomies. Basically, anything that can be observed can be quantified. The quantification may not be very sophisticated or offer very much information, but it is still there. Anything that cannot be potentially measured—that is, quantified—is metaphysical and is therefore outside the realm of scientific inquiry (try religion).

Levels of Analysis

Some sociologists spend a great deal of time considering whether "social reality" is a phenomenon sui generis (Durkheim's conundrum). Ultimately, this question reduces itself to the individualist/group debate. Durkheim and his intellectual predecessor, Comte, would argue that a group is more than the sum of its parts. Others, such as George Homans (*The Nature of Social Science*), would argue that a group is merely the aggregate of the individual egos—nothing more, nothing less. In the resulting ideological slugfest, the followers of Durkheim suggest that Homans is guilty of reductionism; Homans and his followers argue that the Durkheimians are guilty of reification (see also the very worthwhile article by Nagel, 1955).

We cannot propose to solve this debate here; however, as every economist and demographer knows, making certain predictions at the macro level but not at the micro level is possible, and vice versa. For example, we can make fairly accurate predictions about the rate of mortality for a given population in the coming year. Much more unpredictable, however, is the identification of individuals in that population who are likely to die in that year. Clearly, the population at risk consists of an aggregate of individuals. On the other hand, our understanding of behavior (as defined by our ability to explain and to predict) is obviously related to the unit of analysis.

THE LANGUAGE OF SCIENCE: VERBS

Once we have achieved some consensus on the meaning of concepts, the next step is to examine the manner in which concepts might be related. The assertion of a relationship between two or more concepts is called a proposition. Thus, to state that "poverty causes crime" is to present a proposition. A *hypothesis*, on the other hand, is a conjectural statement relating two or more variables. Our proposition that "poverty causes crime" can be phrased as a hypothesis by converting the terms "poverty" and "crime" into variables. The statement "The propensity to commit a criminal act is inversely related to level of income" is a hypothesis.

Scientific hypotheses also require the statement of facts and not values. Thus, the statement: "John is a good person" does not qualify as a hypothesis since the term "a good person" is a question of values, not fact. Some apparent value statements can be posed as statements of fact, however. To state "The more one gives to charity, the more likely one is to be perceived as a good person" is a hypothesis, since it involves a question of fact: to wit, Do people think others who donate to charity are good people?

Hypotheses must also be open to refutation. The statement that "poor people have less money than rich people" is true by definition. It is a tautology in that being poor necessarily implies the condition of having less money than "the rich." Tautological statements cannot be refuted because they are true by logical necessity.

To summarize then, the following factors distinguish hypotheses from propositions or more general assertions: a) the subjects and objects of hypothesis statements are variables, b) hypotheses are conjectures of fact and not values, and c) hypotheses must be subject to possible refutation; that is, they must be "vulnerable," to use Popper's term.

So far, we have discussed the noun parts of hypotheses and some general characteristics of hypotheses. Scientific hypotheses can also be characterized by several logical relationships, that is, different linking characteristics. While constructing many typologies of relational characteristics is possible, the following five dimensions are either those most often alluded to, or those explicitly identified in the research literature.

1. Reversible/irreversible
   - Reversibility implies: if x then y, and if y then x.
   - Irreversibility implies: if x then y, but if y then no conclusion about x.
     [Note that in statistics, these relationships are termed nonrecursive and recursive, respectively.]

2. Deterministic/stochastic
   - Deterministic implies: if x then always y.
   - Stochastic implies: if x then probably y.
3. Sequential/coextensive
   - Sequential implies: if x at t_0 then y at t_1.
   - Coextensive implies: if x at t_0 then y at t_0 also.
4. Sufficient/contingent
   - Sufficient implies: if x then y despite anything else.
   - Contingent implies: if x then y but only in presence of z.
5. Necessary/substitutable
   - Necessary implies: if and only if (iff) x then y.
   - Substitutable implies: if x then y but if z then also y.

Variations along these dimensions determine how one variable affects another. Later we will discuss the issue of causality. Traditional notions of causality required that the relationship between two variables be characterized as sequential, sufficient, and necessary. Not examining the nature of the relationships implied in many hypotheses has led to substantial confusion and wasted debate over the years.

If we return to our "poverty causes crime" example, abundant cross-sectional evidence shows that poverty and crime do indeed coincide. Since the nineteenth century, however, the debate has followed a pattern. First, it was proposed that "poverty caused crime" either through some mechanism of necessity or by reason of a more ephemeral concept such as relative deprivation. Labeling theorists later pointed out that "crime causes poverty," since being labeled a criminal limits one's life opportunities. The more sophisticated among us then quickly came to the conclusion that the relationship was reversible, so that "poverty can cause crime and crime can cause poverty." Thus, the relationship is perhaps best viewed as reversible as opposed to irreversible.

Few social scientists view relationships as deterministic, therefore, it is almost axiomatic these days that the poverty–crime relationship should be characterized as stochastic. Similarly, since we often think in "causal" terms where asymmetry is necessary, it is unlikely that the relationship would be identified simply as coextensive. Asymmetry within causal models often implies temporal precedence; therefore, we may wish to assert that this particular relationship requires sequentiality.[6]

Poverty is clearly only a contingent condition for crime, since the overwhelming majority of "the poor" never become official criminals. Clearly an intervening or contingent factor is required to produce the phenomenon. Similarly, crime has more causes than mere poverty. In fact, many factors might be reasonable substitutes.

Thus, the apparently simple proposition that "poverty causes crime" takes on greater substantive meaning when we define it as likely to be all of the following:

- reversible
- stochastic

---

6. The whole issue of causation and what it implies is exceedingly complex. A more detailed discussion of the issue is presented in the next chapter.

- sequential
- contingent
- substitutable

The process of generating good propositions and translating them into unambiguous, testable hypotheses is not easy, especially when several interrelated linkages are involved. Still, it is upon this base that the methodological edifice rests and, as suggested earlier, no amount of methodological wizardry can improve faulty theorizing.

FORMALIZING PROPOSITIONS

A great difficulty facing social scientists is the problem of converting verbal explanations of propositions to some type of symbolic or mathematical form that can adequately express the intended relationship. For many students of the social sciences, going from a verbal statement to a structural equation involves a level of magic that would put Houdini to shame. Even those who have a "handle" on the matter often become frustrated at their inability to express the "full intent" of the relationship in symbolic form. Some of these frustrations result because any attempt to define systematically a relationship in symbolic form, or metalanguage, generally involves a higher order of specificity than we are willing to provide. Other frustrations result from the inherent limitations of the symbolic system (calculus) we choose to use, while others result from personal lack of familiarity with thinking in such a fashion.

While we cannot provide a complete exploration of all possible approaches to this problem, some guidelines and examples can make the task less daunting. We will start with simple bivariate relationships and expand that discussion to include the multivariate situation.

Bivariate Relationships

Perhaps the best starting point is to generate a graphical representation of what it is that we mean to say. While classical path analysis has fallen out of favor in recent years (for valid statistical reasons), the graphic framework afforded by this approach does provide a useful start.

Let us assume that we start with a simple hypothetical proposition: "There is an inverse relationship between aggregate income levels and rates of crime." We may diagram this relationship as follows:

$$\uparrow \text{Propensity to crime} \longleftarrow \downarrow \text{Level of income}$$

Current practice in most of the social sciences is to transform discursive statements into the symbolic form of linear algebra. This need not be the case but it is convenient, since most assessments of the validity of theoretical propositions rest on the use of conventional statistical analysis (which uses either scalar or linear algebra as its symbolic language). Thus, a typical first step in formalizing this relationship is to construct a linear equation of the following form:

$$Y = \beta_0 - \beta_1 X + \varepsilon$$

Where Y is the dependent (left-hand side) variable "crime rate" and X is the independent (right-hand side) variable "level of income." Following most criminologists, I have substituted "crime rate" for "propensity to crime," since measuring outcomes is much easier than measuring tendencies. This small change, however, introduces some slippage at the outset. Whether we can live with it is the first of a series of important decisions that must be made. This model can be estimated using standard regression procedures, thereby providing an expected value of β_1. The intercept in this instance is usually of little value and is simply considered a scaling or "nuisance" parameter. Once β_1 has been estimated, its interpretation is that for every one unit increase in X, there is a corresponding β_1 increase in Y, and this increase is constant over the entire range of X.

Some students rail at the simple "linearity" assumption implicit in this model and suggest that few, if any, social relations follow a straight line. That is, few relations have a constant rate of increase in Y along all values of X. This is likely true for this relationship. Intuitively, it seems (at least to me) that crime rates ought to be more sensitive to changes in X as X tends toward extreme values. This change in meaning of the fundamental relationship can be had simply by changing what we call the "functional form" of the relationship.

Thus, for example, we might write:

$$Y = \beta_0 X^{\beta_1} \exp(\varepsilon)$$

or, to simplify estimation,

$$\ln Y = \ln \beta_0 + \beta_1 \ln X + \varepsilon$$

In this instance, we have produced a model commonly known as the log-linear model. This model really has two components of interest. First the relationship is a power function, where Y is related to X through the exponential β_1. When X is exponentiated, Y is related to X through a simple β_1 multiple of the power result of X. Ultimately, the function is one of geometric growth.

A model that straddles the traditional linear model and the log-linear model is the semilog model, often used to define exponential growth curves. This variant is very similar to the one just discussed but is defined as follows:

$$Y = \exp(\beta_0 + \beta_1 X + \varepsilon)$$

or

$$Y = \ln \beta_0 + \beta_1 X + \varepsilon$$

Commonly, X is some measure of time, in which case, the slope, β_1 can be interpreted as the average rate of growth in Y per unit time.

More complex "two-variable" models can be developed. For example, it is possible to specify a quadratic form such as:

$$Y = \beta_0 + \beta_1 X + \beta_2 X^2 + \varepsilon$$

Depending upon the signs associated with the β_is, the curve may be either concave or convex. Although this model is substantively a bivariate, or "two-variable" model, the change in specification leads to the realm of multivariate models, since more than one slope is being estimated. Further extensions of "two-variable" multivariate relationships lead us into the realm of time series or ARIMA (autoregressive integrated moving average) models. These models allow for estimating models involving autocorrelation.

Without entering a time dimension into our models, we are assuming that the process being investigated either is static or has achieved equilibrium. For example, if we collect data on crime rates and poverty rates across 100 randomly selected cities, it might be possible to detect a simple linear relationship of the form: $Y = \beta_0 + \beta_1 X + \varepsilon$. The inherent equilibrium assumption here is that the parameters in the model, β_0 and β_1, are time invariant. That is, within the range of sampling variation, those values will be consistent, say, from year to year.

Now, each of these different functional forms has a different substantive interpretation of the nature of the relationship between crime and labor force participation—a substantive meaning that is not captured by the simple graphic presentation defined by our original statement (Propensity to crime ⟵ Level of income). Even the incorporation of up and down arrows (↑ and ↓) into the schema does little to advance the cause.

Some commonly encountered functional forms are diagrammed in Figures 2.1 to 2.9. Often a simple plotting of the function provides a more intuitive understanding of the functional relationship. Again, we will attempt to keep matters simple by sticking to bivariate models. Figure 2.1 represents the simple straight-line model of the form $Y = X$. To simplify matters, the graph has assumed that the y-intercept is at the 0,0 point and that the slope is 1. The most salient characteristic of the line in Figure 2.1 is the monotonicity of the slope. That is, the slope is constant over the full range of X, and the change in Y is consistent for any unit change in X.

Figures 2.2 through 2.4, on the other hand, represent a family of exponential decay or growth functions. Another way of viewing this is to recognize that the slope is accelerating with X. Figures 2.2 and 2.4 are growth functions: Figure 2.2 shows

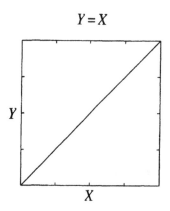

Figure 2.1. $Y = X$.

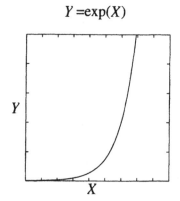

Figure 2.2. $Y = \exp(X)$.

positive growth starting slowly and then increasing exponentially as X increases. Figure 2.4, while still a growth curve, indicates that the greatest rate of growth is for low values of X. As X increases, the slope decreases, thus producing incrementally smaller increases in the value of Y. Figure 2.2 characterizes the spread of epidemics in early stages; Figure 2.4 represents a mature epidemic, where increasingly fewer uninfected individuals are left in the population.

Figures 2.3 and 2.5 are similar to the two preceding graphs, except that they are decay functions. That is, Y decreases as X increases. In Figure 2.3 we see slow decreases in Y at low values of X but increasingly faster rates of decrease in Y as X moves toward the more extreme values. Figure 2.5 presents the opposite type of exponential decay function, with greater rates of decrease in Y appearing at the lower as opposed to the higher values of X.

Figure 2.6 represents the classical U-shaped curve, where values of Y are highest at the extremes of X. Unlike the exponential family of curves, U-shaped curves are

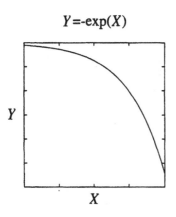

Figure 2.3. $Y = -\exp(X)$.

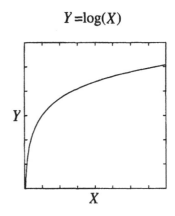

Figure 2.4. $Y = \log(X)$.

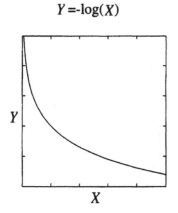

Figure 2.5. $Y = -\log(X)$.

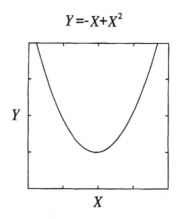

Figure 2.6. $Y = -X + X^2$.

characterized by a line slope that actually changes direction—in this instance from negative to positive. At the minimum value of Y, the slope is 0. ∪-shaped curves appear to characterize many social relationships. One example might be a child's propensity to commit deviant acts (Y) as a function of degree of parental control (X). The likelihood of being deviant is probably greatest among children whose parents impose no restrictions on their children and among children whose parents are extremely rigid. Parents who impose moderate levels of control, however, are least likely to produce deviant children.

By changing the sign of the implicit slope parameters in the model, it is possible to produce a convex or a ∩-shaped curve. In this instance, Y achieves its maxima at the midrange of X rather than at the extremes. Practically, quadratic or ∪-shaped functions are estimated with $Y = \beta_0 + \beta_1 X + \beta_2 X^2$ as the structural equation functions. These functions differ only according to the valence of the slope and the convexity of the curve.

Figure 2.7 illustrates a cubic function, where rates of change in Y are both positive and greatest at the extremes of X but relatively flat in the midrange. By raising X to the fourth power, we achieve the "bathtub" curve illustrated in Figure 2.8. A variant of this functional form is familiar to demographers in that it models the mortality function of many populations with age. Among most human populations, the likelihood of mortality is highest at infancy and at extreme old age. Throughout young adulthood and middle age, the mortality function is flat. Clearly, for any real population, the exact shape of the bathtub will be slightly different; most populations, as with bathtubs, have a steeper slope at the head of the tub and a gentler slope at the foot. This slight change in shape can be accomplished by changing the values for the parameters implicit in the model. The general shape of Figure 2.8 is also reflected in another commonly used function in demography—the Weibull distribution.

Finally, Figure 2.9 illustrates a logistic curve. The logistic function is used in logit analysis where Y is represented as a proportion in the range 0 to 1. In the midrange of Y (between .25 and .75, say), the slope of the curve is almost linear. At the extremes,

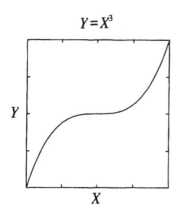

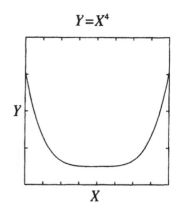

Figure 2.7. $Y = X^3$.   **Figure 2.8.** $Y = X^4$.

Figure 2.9. Logistic curve

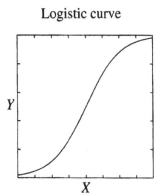

Logistic curve

the curve is similar to an exponential growth curve and an exponential decay curve. The logistic function is defined by:

$$\ln\left(\frac{Y}{1-Y}\right) = X$$

By isolating Y, we obtain:

$$Y = \frac{\exp(X)}{1 + \exp(X)}$$

In both instances, it must be remembered, the dependent variable is of the range $0 < Y < 1$.

These graphs show but a few of the many functional forms that can be generated within the framework of a two-variable model. Clearly, as one enters the multivariate realm, the possibilities become virtually endless. This exercise does have significant implications, however, for theory construction. Traditional approaches to sociological theorizing, in which variables are identified and simple linkages between them are specified, fulfill only half of the researcher's theoretical obligations. Functional form is an important consideration, for a misspecified function could easily lead to the acceptance of a false null hypothesis (i.e., a Type II or β-error). Even where the null hypothesis is rejected, it is likely that an incorrect specification of the functional form would lead to an underestimation of the model's goodness of fit.

Hasty and sloppy theorizing often leaves researchers with little idea as to the appropriate functional form to specify. In these instances, there is a strong incentive to seek the functional form within the data rather than in positing the relationship a priori. Simple data dredging by specifying kth-degree polynomials, for example, may help to identify the underlying form. On the other hand, at best it may also lead to overfitted models and at worse, to the specification of spurious relationships.

Summary

Decisions about functional form can be rationalized by asking ourselves a series of questions:

1. Is the function continuous or discrete? If it is discrete, does it consist of several discontinuities (steps) or just one?

2. Is the function monotonic or segmented?

3. Is the function linear or nonlinear?

4. Is the function intrinsically nonlinear or nonintrinsically nonlinear (i.e., transformable to linear)?

Table 2.1 presents some commonly used functional forms. Some are intrinsically linear in that they are additive in the parameters; others are nonlinear in that the parameters are not additive. While theoretically relevant, nonlinear models often pose practical problems for parameter estimation. Most modern statistical packages, however, include nonlinear estimation procedures. Often, those procedures are time-consuming and are sensitive to initial, or starting values, thus making them less popular than more direct estimation procedures such as ordinary least squares (OLS). In some situations, however, it is possible to "linearize" the equation through a suitable transformation, thereby allowing standard generalized least squares approaches to be used. For those nonintrinsically nonlinear (i.e., transformable-to-linear) functions in Table 2.1, a linearized form is presented. Procedures for estimating and transforming nonintrinsically nonlinear functions into ones that are additive in the parameters are presented in several sources (see, e.g., Mosteller and Tukey, 1977; Draper and Smith, 1981: ch.5).

We will now examine three pieces of research to explore the issues surrounding theory formalization in more detail.

Table 2.1. Some linear and transformable-to-linear models

MODEL	STRUCTURAL EQUATION	LINEARIZED MODEL
Line through origin	$Y = \beta X$	NA
Straight line	$Y = \beta_0 + \beta_1 X$	NA
Parabola	$Y = \beta_0 + \beta_1 X + \beta_2 X^2$	NA
Polynomial of kth order	$Y = \beta_0 + \beta_1 X + \beta_2 X^2 + \cdots + \beta_k X^k$	NA
Power function	$Y = \beta_0 X \beta_1$	$\log Y = \beta_0 + \beta_1 \log X$
Exponential decay or growth model asymptotic to zero	$Y = \beta_0 \exp(-\beta_1 X)$	$\log Y = \beta_0 + \beta_1 X$
General exponential decay or growth	$Y = \beta_0 \exp(-\beta_1 X) + \beta_2$	$\log(Y - \beta_2) = \beta_0 + \beta_1 X$

EXAMPLE: RETURNS TO EDUCATION

A fundamental assumption of most students is that one's lifetime earnings are related to the level of education acquired. The economic theory behind this is relatively straightforward. Classical human capital theory notes that education entails an opportunity cost to the individual due to forgone earnings and the direct costs involved in acquiring the education. To encourage workers to undertake further schooling, there must be a likelihood of higher lifetime earnings as compensation. Those higher lifetime earnings are justified, however, only if more schooled workers are more productive than less schooled workers. Ultimately, a long-term equilibrium will be achieved between lifetime earnings and schooling such that expected earnings will encourage enough people to pursue the amount of higher education required to fulfill market demand (see Polachek and Siebert, 1993, for a detailed theoretical treatment of this topic).

The basic income–education relationship put forward in the economics literature is that of Mincer. Mincer's model suggests that income $= f$ (schooling, experience). In other words, income is related to how much schooling one obtains, and how much experience one has in the labor market. Thus the three terms that need defining are *income*, *schooling*, and *experience*.

Definitions

Income. For income, Mincer uses the U.S. Bureau of the Census definition of earnings: that is, income obtained through wages and salaries.

Schooling. The operational definition for schooling used in most of the literature consists of "years of formal education." This is usually estimated by summing the highest number of years of elementary school achieved (grade level), the highest number of secondary school years achieved, and the number of years of postsecondary education acquired. The normal range is between 0 (for no formal education) to 18+ for those with postgraduate university degrees. While this operationalization clearly has the advantage of simplicity (both for conceptual and data analytic purposes), no element of *quality* is included regarding either the type of education (training) received, or how much is actually learned.

Experience. Usually this term is operationalized as the number of years in the labor force. Functionally, Mincer defined experience as current age minus years of schooling minus 6. Again this formulation has the advantage of simplicity. However, it does not consider periods outside the labor force (which may be especially important for women), nor again, the *quality* of the experience. For example, some workers receive substantial on-the-job training and others do not. For some workers, experience is enhanced by staying in the same industry as long as possible; for others, the quality of their experience is enhanced through an exposure to a variety of work environments.

Whatever its theoretical limitations, Mincer's model is explicit in its relationships and captures much of the empirical variation in earnings. Written as a regression equation, Mincer's model is defined as:

$$\log \text{(earnings)} = \beta_0 + \beta_1 \text{ schooling} + \beta_2 \text{ experience} + \beta_3 \text{ experience}^2$$

As is typical of most earnings models, the dependent variable log-income is regressed on the independent variables, since this transformation addresses a large portion of the heterosckedasticity problem often encountered with income data. Income also appears to have decreasing marginal utility, such that the perceived value of incremental units decreases as one's total income increases.[7] Mincer (1974, Table 5.1) estimated this equation based on the annual earnings of American, white, nonfarm males for the year 1959. Based on the available data, the following results were obtained:

$$\log \text{(income)} = 6.20 + .107 \text{ schooling} + .081 \text{ experience} - .0012 \text{ experience}^2$$

Since the model is represented in only three dimensions, graphing Mincer's results to obtain a visual representation of the model is easy.

From Figure 2.10, the implications underlying Mincer's functional form are quite evident. Each incremental year of education represents a constant log-dollar increase in income, while experience shows a decelerating rate of return as one heads toward one's retirement years. For those not practiced in thinking in terms

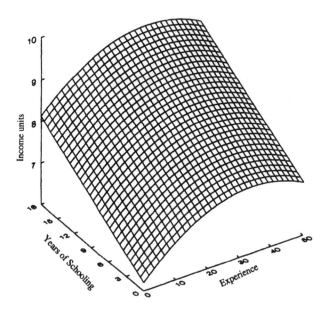

Figure 2.10. Graph of Mincer's income function.

---

7. Whether a simple logarithmic transformation captures the utility function of income is open to empirical debate; however, research going back to the time of Bernoulli seems to suggest that it is adequate for all intents and purposes.

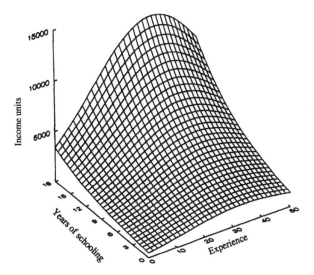

Figure 2.11. Exponentiated version of Mincer's equation.

of log-income, it is possible to convert the relationship back into original dollar units by exponentiating the entire right-hand side of the equation. This leads to the representation in Figure 2.11. Clearly, in raw dollar terms, the incremental impact of schooling and experience becomes much more exaggerated.

EXAMPLE: THE PROFESSIONALIZATION OF PSYCHOLOGY

As a second example, we will focus on a far more complex study than Mincer's. Frank, Meyer, and Miyahara (1995) put forward a thesis that the prevalence of "professionalized psychology" depends on the sociocultural configuration of a society. Specifically, they argue, societies that have strong sociocultural norms regarding individualism are more likely to give rise to and to support the development of professionalized psychology than do "other polities." They argue that this is so even when other key social and economic factors are considered.

Since the authors use a linear structural equation approach to testing the model, they outline the essential model using a type of path diagram. In the path diagram, the linkages between the structural factors are identified along with the relationships between the structural factors and their empirical referents (operational definitions). A modified form of the original path diagram is presented as Figure 2.12. As in the preceding example, we will start with a definition of key terms.

Definitions

Dependent variable—professionalized psychology. The term "professionalized psychology" appears to rest on conventional interpretations of the terms, since it

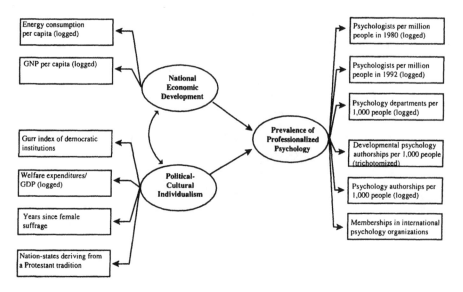

Figure 2.12. Path model of cross-national variations in economic development and individualism on prevalence of professionalized psychology. (Adapted from Frank, Mayer, and Miyahara, 1995.)

is not defined directly in the article. There are, however, a couple of sentences that help to clarify the meaning of the term as used in the study. Specifically, we are told that:

> our indicators describe only professionalized aspects of the field, rather than, for instance, its prominence in mass culture. (Frank, Meyer, and Miyahara, 1995: 362)

and

> Because we are concerned with the scientific and professional field of psychology *in general*, not with psychology as used in the treatment of individuals, we exclude specialized medical applications like psychiatry and counseling psychology. (Frank, Meyer, and Miyahara, 1995: 364)

Unfortunately, this article is inconsistent in its use of nomenclature or terminology regarding the dependent variable. That is, in the title the authors refer to the *prevalence* of professionalized psychology, while other places (including the path diagram) cite the *prominence* of professionalized psychology. Undoubtedly, this confusion is the result of sloppy editing; however, the difference is important. Prevalence refers to a measure of occurrence, of tallies or counts. Prominence refers to a quality of distinction or eminence. Since all the operational indicators used are reflections of quantity, we will assume that the titular nomenclature is correct and that references to prominence are mere editorial slips.

Independent variables—individualism. The concept of an individualist polity is clearly less intuitive to the professional audience than is the dependent variable. Thus, the authors provide a clearer description of the term. They write:

> Individualism refers only partly to sociocultural arrangements encouraging individuals to be completely autonomous and uncontrolled. More importantly, it encompasses the rise and legitimation of models of society in which the individual is seen as a central constitutive element: the sovereign source of public life. . . . (Frank, Meyer, and Miyahara, 1995: 360)

Further,

> We use indicators to determine the degree to which the status of individuals is especially central in national societies. (Frank, Meyer, and Miyahara, 1995: 365)

Economic development. The second independent variable, which is considered a key control variable, is economic development. This variable is not defined outside its operational indicators and is assumed to be self-evident.

Linkages. The model is clearly defined in a combination of narrative description and the path diagram outlined in Figure 2.12. Specifically, the working hypothesis stated the author's intention

> to test cross-nationally the relationship between levels of national political–cultural individualism and the centrality and prevalence of professionalized psychology. Our core problem is to show the simultaneous effects of overall development and of political–cultural individualism on the [prevalence] of psychology, and in doing this, we also test these relationships against the effects of other relevant variables. (Frank, Meyer, and Miyahara, 1995: 364)

and the null is stated as follows:

> We test this relationship against an obvious alternative—that *any* form of economic development or modernization generates a greater prominence [prevalence] of psychology.

Although the narrative does not so state, it is clear from the path diagram and various references that the model is strictly linear in its functional form. "National economic development" and "political–cultural individualism" are considered causally prior to the "prevalence of professionalized psychology." The two independent variables are assumed to be correlated but not in any causal sense.

Controls. A strength of this study is the emphasis placed on identifying causality and spuriousness. The authors controlled for several variables that might have a confounding impact upon the primary relationships, although these were not incorporated into Figure 2.12. Among the variables considered by the authors were:

- English-language bias
- national population size

- government revenue as a proportion of GDP
- social disorder and economic development
- expansion of tertiary education
- volume of general scientific activity

The model of Frank, Meyer, and Miyahara is fairly typical of much practical theorizing in quantitative sociology and psychology. The graphic imagery of the path model fits well with the mathematical formalization of structural equation models to produce both a succinct model and an intuitively appealing imagery.

EXAMPLE: LAND ON DURKHEIM (OPTIONAL)

As a third example of how theory might be formalized, we turn to an article by Kenneth Land (1970). Land's approach is to use the calculus as a notational vehicle for specifying the model. The notational system used is elementary, and no attempt is made to pursue derivations. Consequently, even those with no background in calculus should find the presentation relatively straightforward. The article deals with how one aspect of Durkheim's theory of the division of labor might be formalized. Land is not alone trying to formalize Durkheim's sociological classic, but his efforts seem to have gone beyond those of others (see also Zetterberg, 1965).

The task of specifying social theory in testable terms is not a trivial one. This is especially the case with classical theory. As Land (1970: 262) notes:

> A difficulty confronting any formalization of a classical social theory is that many specific models may often be formalized from a single classic because of its generality of application and diffuseness of structure. That is to say, classical social theorists were often satisfied with ill-defined concepts and indeterminate theoretical structures because these characteristics suited the expansiveness of their goals and their penchant for a rather loose fit to empirical data. The modern social theorist, therefore, can rarely claim to have captured the "complete" meaning of a classic in his more rigorous restatements of classical social theory.

We will focus upon two aspects of Land's work. The first is the issue of defining the key terms; the second is the nature of the relationships among the terms.

Definitions

Dependent variable—division of labor. Clearly, the key concept in this study is *division of labor*. It is also the concept that Land finds most problematic to his task. Land (1970: 265) points out that:

> Classically, there are two general ideas associated with this concept: occupational differentiation and functional interdependence, that is, the exchange of goods and

services among occupational groups. It can be argued, however, that the first phenomenon implies the second. That is to say, an increase in the degree of differences of individuals with regard to sustenance activities (that is, an increase in occupational differentiation) implies an increase in the degree of their functional interdependence. . . .

On the other hand, if the rate of exchange of goods and services increases (that is, if functional interdependence increases), then it follows that individuals *may* engage in different activities (that is, occupational differentiation may increase) although it is not necessary that they do so in order to maintain a given level of functional interdependence. Thus, an increase in functional interdependence is a necessary but not a sufficient condition for an increase in occupational differentiation. . . .

Based on this discussion, Land (1970: 266) provides the following definition:

The level of the *division of labor* in a society is the degree of differences among members of the society with regard to their sustenance activities.

Independent variables—dynamic density. The two primary independent variables from Durkheim that Land incorporates in his model are *dynamic density* and *competition*. Since dynamic density is the more central and more complicated of the two, we will deal with it first.

Land indicates that according to his reading of Durkheim, "this term refers to the actions and reaction of persons upon each other. A specific action–reaction sequence between two individuals can be called and *interact*. The number of interacts in a society per unit of time is called the *dynamic density*" (Land, 1970: 263; italics in original). Operationalizing dynamic density is difficult, so both Durkheim and Land use a proxy variable termed *material density*. Material density is assumed to be the product of a few readily operationable indicators, including population size, urbanization, and the efficiency of the technology of communication and transportation. Specifically, Land suggests that material density be operationalized as follows:

$$\text{population size} \times \frac{\text{population in urban areas}}{\text{population size}}$$

$$\times \text{ efficiency of communication and transportation}$$

$$= \text{population in urban areas}$$

$$\times \text{ efficiency of communication and transportation}$$

Since dynamic density is defined as (number of interacts)/time, it is possible to make the substitution of material density for dynamic density and operationalize dynamic density as follows:

$$\frac{\text{number of interacts}}{\text{time}} = K \times \text{population in urban areas} \times \text{efficiency}$$

$$\text{of communication and transportation}$$

where K is simply a normalizing constant.

This use of a proxy concept for another higher order concept raises an interesting issue. If material density is close enough in meaning to dynamic density to be considered a valid proxy, then is it possible to distinguish between the two? Perhaps the conceptual difference between the two is fallacious, in which case one ought to be deleted from the conceptual framework. If a valid difference exists between the two, we might also question the need for an abstract concept that is difficult to operationalize but is adequately represented by a proxy. Surely considerations of parsimony would suggest that the practically inessential concept be dropped from the model.

On the other hand, if the conceptual distinction between dynamic density and material density is sufficiently great that the two are deemed necessary within the theoretical model, any practical test of the model will be severely misspecified unless both variables are included.

Competition. According to Land, competition "represents no conceptual or measurement problems," so we are left to assume that the definition of the concept is adequately covered by conventional understandings of the term.

Linkages. Given the identification of the key concepts, the next step is to identify the relationships among the concepts. In general terms, Land states:

> The basic relations with which we begin are that the level of competition in a society is a monotonic increasing function of the level of dynamic density, that the level of the division of labor in a society is a monotonic increasing function of the level of competition, and that there is a feedback loop from the level of the division of labor to the level of dynamic density (1970: 266.)

The key phrase in this quotation is "monotonically increasing function," which identifies Land's perception of the implicit functional form in Durkheim's work. From this, Land specifies three functional relationships as follows.

- *The level of dynamic density in a society will tend to increase if its existing level is lower than that 'appropriate' to the level of the division of labor.* (1970: 266)
  Note: It is essential to recognize that there is an important caveat to this proposition, namely: the process is not instantaneous. Over time, however, the process will stabilize or become stationary.

- *The level of competition in a society depends upon, and increases with, the level of dynamic density in a society.* (1970: 267)
  Note: Unlike the preceding proposition, level of competition is assumed to adjust itself almost simultaneously. Thus, the time dimension is almost irrelevant.

- *The level of the division of labor in a society will increase if its existing level is lower than that "appropriate" to the level of competition in the society.* (1970: 267)
  Note: As with the first proposition, it is assumed that stability in the relationship (stationarity) is achieved over time.

The definitions of symbols and primitive terms used by Land in his attempt to formalize Durkheim are listed below.

Dependent variable

$L(t)$ the level of the division of labor in the society at time t

Independent variables

$C(t)$ the level of competition for scarce goods among the members of the society at time t

$D(t)$ the level of dynamic density in the society at time t

Dynamic density is, in turn, composed of three more primitive concepts:

$U(t)$ the level of urbanization in a society at time t

$T(t)$ the level of efficiency of the technology of communication and transportation in the society time t

$P(t)$ the size of the society (population) at time t

Model. The first step in Land's model is to recognize that dynamic density $D(t)$ is a function of three exogenous variables, $U(t)$, $T(t)$, and $P(t)$. This relationship may be formally stated as:

$$D_t = D_{t-1} + k(\Delta U)^a \, (\Delta T)^b \, (\Delta P)^c$$

that is, D is a function of D at $t-1$ and changes in the components U, T, and P from $t-1$ to t.

The second step is to define the relationship among the three endogenous variables in the model [i.e., $D(t)$, $C(t)$, and $L(t)$]. Land posits these as follows:

$$\frac{dD(t)}{dt} = f[D(t), L(t)]$$

$$C(t) = g[D(t)]$$

$$\frac{dL(t)}{dt} = h[C(t), L(t)]$$

In expository terms, we may state these relationships as follows. For the first relationship:

$$\frac{dD(t)}{dt} = f[D(t), L(t)]$$

Land writes:

> *The time rate of change in dynamic density is a function of the existing level of dynamic density and the level of division of labor.*

For the second relationship:

$$C(t) = g[D(t)]$$

he writes:

> *The level of competition is a function of the level of dynamic density.*

For the third relationship:

$$\frac{dL(t)}{dt} = h[C(t), L(t)]$$

he writes:

The time rate of change in the level of the division of labor is a function of the level of competition and the existing level of division of labor. (1970: 267)

For those with a more graphic orientation, the entire model is illustrated in Figure 2.13 as a path model.

Figure 2.13. Path diagram of Land-Durkheim model.

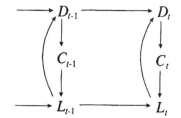

Land's model is a paragon of clarity compared with the way in which most social science models are outlined. There is a reasonable clarity of definition, and the causal paths are clearly laid out. Yet, even with the tremendous amount of effort put into this exposition by Land, several questions remain. For example, while clearly the rate of change in the division of labor is functionally related to the competition for scarce goods and the existing level of the division of labor, we are left wondering about the functional form of those relationships. Land assumes (likely for the sake of expository simplicity) that the relationships are simple linear ones. Unfortunately, Durkheim's theorizing gives us few clues about what we might expect. In practical terms, this means that it is up to the researcher to infer the functional forms from an analysis of the data by estimating several models, performing several transformations on the data, and examining the goodness of fit.

Since we are relying upon the data to generate some insight into the functional form, using the same data in a confirmatory role is not strictly legitimate. This situation is not uncommon. One solution to the issue is to employ a strategy similar to the split-half technique. Here, the data are broken into two or more subsamples. One sample is used as the constructive sample, where we perform our exploratory analysis. The other sample(s) are then used as confirmatory samples upon which the confirmatory analysis is based. This strategy is not without its limitations, however. Clearly, a reasonable amount of data is required to generate subsamples that are nontrivial. It is also supposed that the subsamples are constructed on an adequately random basis.

Further Reading

Stinchcombe A.L. *Constructing Social Theories*. New York: Harcourt, Brace & World, 1968. A solid discussion of the issues surrounding theory construction that does not get bogged down in the minutiae of formalism.

Coleman, J.S., and Ferraro, T. *Rational Choice Theory: Advocacy and Critique*. Newbury Park, CA: Sage, 1992. This collection of readings examines the strengths and weaknesses of "rational choice" models—a set of theoretical formulations that have their origins in economics but have achieved considerable following in many social sciences. Rational choice models represent an example of social theory that has a variety of expressions ranging from vague, discursive models to precise, mathematical formulations.

3

Causality

For the doctrines I am opposing here are not so much those of
Hume, but doctrines like those of Russell and Mach, or more in
our time, of Hempel and Nagel. Their philosophies admit laws of
nature, so long as they are laws of association and succession; but
they eschew causes. That seems to me to be a crazy stopping-point.
If you have laws you can get causes. . . .

—Nancy Cartwright

Causality is not a simple idea for science. It is inextricably caught up in a web of metaphysical debate that transcends time and culture. For some scientists and philosophers, the difficulties surrounding the concept are such that they have ceased to view it as a viable entity within the framework of the scientific method. Perhaps the most notable proponent of this position was Bertrand Russell, who viewed causality as a relic of a bygone age, surviving, like the British monarchy, only because of its supposed benign nature (Russell, 1929). Among contemporary scientific disciplines, the rejection of causal frameworks remains strongest in physics. Athearn, for example, espouses a framework of *scientific nihilism* for physics that incorporates the tenets of antirealism and acausality as its primary building blocks.

Yet others, such as Michael Scriven, see causality as one of the most important elements in the methodology of applied science (Scriven, 1971; also see Bunge, 1979; *Synthese,* 1986 volumes 67 & 68; Holland, 1986, 1988). Whereas Russell asserted that causal thinking offers little to modern physics, to Scriven believes that causality continues to be a fruitful framework. The disutility of causal imagery may be related to physicists' transcending what philosophers call the *narrative* basis of causal models. At the leading edge, much of what constitutes modern physics is best defined in functional or mathematical terms. There is no longer a need for the semantic discourse found in other disciplines, filling out caveats and assumptions that are not, or cannot be, expressed in functional format. As Athearn (1994: 8) states:

> "Scientific nihilism" designates an outlook or broadly shared intellectual attitude built around the core dogma, based on decisions in physics itself, that today it is no longer feasible to engage in the search for narrative causal explanations in fundamental physics. . . .

Most of the social sciences, it might be argued, are nowhere near the stage at which the narrative can be abandoned (Hoover, 1990). Instead, the best we can generate are simple functional models that rely upon a narrative background to provide context and to fill a multitude of conditions not explicitly incorporated into the functional model.

CONCEPTUAL ISSUES

Although the problems surrounding causality are many, it would appear that the importance of the difficulties varies, depending upon whether one takes a realist or an instrumentalist approach to the issue. An instrumentalist approach "only" needs to identify a set of criteria that may be agreed upon as defining a *causal relationship*. These criteria may be arbitrary in the sense that they need not reflect some inherent aspect of nature. On the other hand, the criteria must be consistent with the theoretical model or framework within which causality is defined. From an instrumentalist perspective then, causal relationships are not "true" or "natural" but are relationships that behave *as if they were causal*, where causality is defined by a set of theoretical assumptions. For instrumentalists, the ontological issue of what causality really is, is not an issue of the first degree.

Realists, on the other hand, see causality as something much more than whether empirical data meet a set of arbitrary theoretical assumptions. While not explicitly speaking within this context, Kevin Hoover (1990) succinctly expresses the realist view when he states: "Causal order is not a property of the statistically observed relations between variables. Rather it is a property of the underlying and not directly observed data-generating process." From the realist's perspective, one starts with the difficulty of coming to grips with what the term *cause* truly means. Conventional thinking often associates cause with some type of physical linking or producing mechanism, such that causes "create" effects. The notion of causality as a physical mechanism is so ingrained in our language that some observers do not believe it can be transcended unless we abandon a semantic framework. Thus, as Athearn (1994: 86) concludes, researchers are faced with "the stark options of *mechanistic* causal models or the abandonment of narrative explanation." The difficulty for realists is further compounded with the necessity of determining what properties identify *real* causal relations.

For most of us, causal thinking is so culturally ingrained that treating it in instrumentalist terms makes us feel queasy. However, I think it is best dealt in this manner for several reasons. First, causality is indeed a product of human ways of organizing the world, just as any other theory might be. Thus, imposing an ontological meaning to the concept beyond this is just another instance of reification. Second, asserting "realness" to the concept almost invariably leads to the problem of infinite reduction. That is, one soon starts on the search for the "ultimate cause" underlying the relationship of interest. Within the instrumentalist framework, it is much easier to define boundaries and to distinguish those elements that are of interest to the model at hand (endogenous relationships) from those that are outside the domain of the immediate model (exogenous relationships). Third, the instrumentalist approach allows one to avoid some unsolved (and perhaps unsolvable) philosophical problems surrounding whether causality really exists and to propose causal models of different types (e.g., strong causality, weak causality) depending upon whether some or all of one's criteria for causality are met.

This view of causation is similar to that espoused by Mario Bunge (1959: 30), who notes that causation is but one form of determinacy. Determinacy can also be expressed in other forms, such as statistical determinacy and teleological determinacy.

Regardless, the value of the causal principle is that it provides an easy way of organizing the empirical world through a familiar logical framework.

Most discussions of the fundamental properties of causality propose three identifying conditions: regularity of occurrence or covariance between causes and effects, asymmetry between causes and effects, and nonspuriousness within the cause–effect relationship. It is on those conditions that we now focus our attention.

Covariance

A fundamental aspect of causal imagery is that regularities exit in the relationship between purported causes and effects (see Cartwright, 1989; or Mackie, 1980). This assumption was so deftly argued by both Hume and Mill that it has become a basic axiom underlying nearly all current conceptualizations of causality. Identifying regularity should be a relatively easy, empirical issue to resolve. After the appropriate observations have been recorded, standard statistical techniques can be used to assess the level of empirical association between two or more variables. Pearson's r, the product moment correlation coefficient, is a prime example of a covariance measure, although many other parametric and nonparametric statistics are possible (Kendall's tau, tetrachoric r, phi, etc.). In all empirical research, however, measurement error is a problem and, as we will see in a later chapter, substantial measurement error can lead most empirical estimates of association to be biased toward zero.

Asymmetry

Inherent in causal imagery is the notion of asymmetry: causes result in effects; effects do not result in causes. Conventionally, this asymmetry has been described as temporal precedence. Causes are believed to precede effects. This simple criterion of asymmetry works for many causal models; however, it soon reaches breaking points in both theory and operationalization. Because of the ubiquity of temporal precedence as a definition of asymmetry, exploring the issue in significant detail is worthwhile.

As we have stated, it is commonly proposed that for X to be considered the cause of Y, X must precede Y in time. While conceptually simple, this requirement can be problematic when the relationship between X and Y is reciprocal or near instantaneous. The first condition creates a "chicken and egg" situation that can sometimes be unraveled through the use of lag correlations (time series analysis). However, we must be aware that the simple but common fallacy of *post hoc, ergo propter hoc* (after this, therefore caused by this) often leads to the confusion of causes with effects.[1] And, contrary to popular belief, simply extending the period of observation will not necessarily allow us to disentangle the relationship.[2] For

---

1. Again, recall the logic underlying the fallacy of affirming the consequent as outlined in Chapter 1.

2. Consider the following proposition, due to Good (1983: 224): "To explain why a physical event E occurred is to explain what caused it or tended to cause it, and this requires explicit or implicit reference to a causal chain or causal network that leads to E over some time interval of appreciable duration t. The longer the duration t the fuller the explanation."

example, it is a virtual truism in criminology that slums cause delinquency. Yet, a little thought soon suggests that delinquency may, in fact, cause slums. Therefore, the relationship may be one of reciprocal causation. To date, the ultimate starting point in this model has not been identified. One further caveat must be kept in mind: even when a temporal dimension is explicitly called for in a causal model, *temporal precedence is impossible to determine from purely cross-sectional data*.[3] This creates significant problems for much sociological research that is based on single point in time surveys.

Practically, the issue of temporal precedence is not always easy to tease out even when reliance on it is warranted. Often our observations cover a period that is too wide to allow us to see which variable comes first. Hence, observations may appear simultaneous when, in fact, they are not. A good example here is official statistics that are often available only annually, whereas the phenomena of interest may operate daily or monthly. In other instances, ongoing relationships may have achieved a state of *equilibrium* or *stationarity*, thus again assigning the issue of temporal precedence to the realm of theory rather than the realm of observation.

A second, and especially difficult issue for the requirement of temporal precedence, is embedded in the need to decide what we ought to do with *simultaneous* relationships. Formally, from a temporalist conception of causality, simultaneous relationships cannot be causal relationships. That is either the relationships we term simultaneous must be temporally related in a time duration shorter than our observation period (thus, only appearing simultaneous), or the two factors must be related through a common antecedent variable.

Excluding simultaneous relationships within the causal framework would exclude a wide range of nonrecursive structural equation models in which simultaneous reciprocal causation can easily be specified and estimated (see, e.g., Bollen, 1989: 61–67, 80–85).

Yet another difficulty with temporal precedence is found in the task of making sense of *lead* indicators. We fully expect in empirical research to observe significant *lag* relationships. That is, we expect to see situations where X or Y at some time, t, are the outcomes of changes in X or Y at $t - 1$. Still, what if the reverse is true? This may be counterintuitive for many, but it is empirically viable.[4] The situation occurs so often in economics that the concept of *rational expectations* has been introduced to explain the phenomenon (e.g., Blanchard and Fischer, 1989: 214) . In its simplest

---

3. This does not mean to imply that cross-sectional research cannot generate longitudinal data. Many examples of event history (survival) analysis are based on survey data collected at one point in time but nevertheless retaining a temporal component. See, for example, Murphy and Sullivan (1985). Also, see Trussell, Hankinson, and Tilton (1992). Such an approach does have its drawbacks, however, as respondents often forget events or misrecall specific dates (e.g., the phenomenon of telescoping or compressing perception of events in time). Still, a well-constructed questionnaire or interview schedule can often minimize these problems.

4. As for example Hubert Blalock (1964: 10), who writes: "But since the forcing or producing idea is not contained in the notion of temporal sequences, . . . , our conception of causality should not depend on temporal sequences, except for the impossibility of an effect preceding its cause."

form, rational expectations consist of our reasonable beliefs about the likelihood of future events that serve to influence our current behavior. For example, if I have good reason to believe that inflation will increase substantially in the future, I may sell my equity in the bond market and purchase gold bullion. This action is based on my knowledge that in the past, bond prices, which have fixed rates of return, have dropped precipitously in times of inflation.[5] Empirically, such behavior would likely manifest itself as a strong correlation between Y_{t-1} and X_t, with Y being the outcome variable.

One might argue that this is still not a true instance of effect producing cause, since it is the *anticipated* effect and not the *real* effect that is influencing our current behavior.[6] Granted, this may be the case. But if the *anticipated* effect leads to a behavior that results in the *real* effect (a self-fulfilling prophecy), we could argue that without reasonable probability that the ultimate outcome will occur, there would be no anticipation. Thus, it is the high likelihood of the future event that led to the anticipation, which led to the nominal cause, which led to the ultimate effect. Thus, effect has led to cause.

Unfortunately, existing nontemporal definitions (in the semantic as opposed to the mathematical sense) of asymmetry are not always easy to grasp and are often less than adequate. This, undoubtedly, is one reason many researchers have abandoned the causal framework. One popular way of describing this aspect of causality, however, is in terms of control. That is, X causes Y if control of X results in control over Y. This view is particularly attractive to disciplines that rely heavily upon traditional experimental designs in which researchers can manipulate conditions. The major weakness of the control formulation is that in practical terms, it often appears as a tautology or circularity. That is, control is identified by situations in which X is seen to influence Y—the very relationship we wish to determine.

Nancy Cartwright perceives the condition of asymmetry as "capacities." Thus, her claim that "The generic causal claims of science are . . . ascriptions of capacities, capacities to make things happen, case by case" (1989: 2–3). Capacities may also be understood as propensities or powers. Cartwright's view of causality is extremely well defended and has recently achieved a level of popularity among causal realists.

Ironically, the best view of asymmetry, especially from an instrumentalist perspective, is probably that described by the scientific nihilist, Athearn (1994: 116):

A cause neither necessitates an effect nor is a necessary condition for it in any philosophically compelling sense. If causation has an essence, it is as an *active differentiating transition* in which events or stages in a process arise out of other events or stages in a sense not further specified for the general case.

While asymmetry is difficult to define within a narrative context, defining it within a structure of linear equations is easy. We will exploit this fact in later chapters.

---

5. This brings us to the fascinating world of self-fulfilling prophecies. See Henshel (1982), Henshel and Johnston (1987), and Henshel (1993).
6. As Blanchard and Fischer (1989) note, a common notation for the expectational difference equation is: $Y_t = aE[Y_{t+1} \mid t] + cX_t$ where $E[Y_{t+1} \mid t]$ represents the expectation of Y_{t+1} at time t.

This still leaves us with the problem of how to characterize symmetrical (i.e., reversible/coextensive) relationships. If one follows the criteria of covariance–asymmetry–nonspuriousness as comprising a necessary condition for causality, then clearly symmetrical relationships cannot be causal. On the other hand, most symmetrical relationships of interest are embedded within a larger framework that includes asymmetrical relations. Instead of abandoning the good ship causality because of this issue, one might wish to distinguish between "strong" and "weak" causality: "strong" causality adhering to the classical covariance–asymmetry–nonspuriousness criteria; "weak" causality generally discounting asymmetry but allowing at least some within the broader theoretical nexus.

Spuriousness

Spuriousness is the major bugaboo of all causal research. How can we know that X is the "true" cause of Y rather than Z? In fact Z may be either a precursor to X (therefore, in some sense the "true" or "ultimate" cause of Y), or X may be coincidentally related to Y. Traditionally, scientists control for this through the use of replication and controls. Replication is based on the premise that any one experiment may produce deviant results, but in the long run, these aberrations will appear with an expected low frequency. Physical control over spuriousness is traditionally achieved through the random assignment of subjects to experimental and control conditions in planned experiments. It is believed that the application of this technique serves to mitigate or eliminate spurious or extraneous variables through the random assignment process, since these factors will be relegated to measurement error in roughly equal proportions in both groups.

Spuriousness is a much more difficult issue to address in ex post facto experiments, where the experimenter was not responsible for the assignment of subjects to treatment and/or control groups. In this instance, we often revert to the use of statistical controls or covariates, or what Bollen (1989: 45) calls "isolation."

The principal (although not exclusive) source of spuriousness in social science experiments is what we term *self-selection bias*. As Kerlinger (1986: 349) states:

> Self-selection occurs when the members of the groups being studied are in the groups, in part, because they differentially possess traits or characteristics extraneous to the research problem, characteristics that possibly influence or are otherwise related to the variables of the research problem.

It is the difficulty of dealing with the issue of spuriousness that has led some researchers, such as Holland, to argue that without manipulation (experimentation), there can be no possible imputation of causality. While it may be a necessary condition, even manipulation is not a sufficient condition for dealing with spuriousness. Let us consider some arbitrary observations Y on unit u $(Y_{(u)})$ for some treatment conditions (t) and control conditions (c). As Holland (1986: 947) notes, the *fundamental problem of causal inference* is that: "It is impossible to *observe* the value of $Y_{t(u)}$ and $Y_{c(u)}$ on the same unit and, therefore, it is impossible to *observe* the effect of t on u." This situation exists because of the Aristotelian condition that an element cannot be in two states (A and not-A) simultaneously. Since a given element cannot be in treatment and control simultaneously, we can never be certain that our results are nonspurious.[7] Thus, while experimentation may be one step up on survey research as a framework for exploring causal relationships, it is not the ultimate solution.

At present, the most sophisticated theoretical analysis of causation and spuriousness is attributable to Mackie. From the point of view of practical methodology, Mackie's most significant contribution is the observation that traditional experimental designs, while adequate in theory, pose considerable practical difficulties. Specifically, Mackie sees traditional experiments as bordering on naïve because they focus almost exclusively on main effects. Mackie's world is far more complex. Considerable higher order interactions exist that are difficult to isolate in standard designs, and much of what passes for causal knowledge is what he terms "gappy."

Mackie's exposition is presented within a deterministic framework. While the assumption of determinism is highly restrictive in most social science settings, it is sufficient for introducing the vocabulary and for gaining a basic understanding of the logic behind Mackie's argument. For those who are interested in pursuing this matter in greater detail, Cartwright (1989: ch. 1) has clearly shown that Mackie's discussion can be readily generalized to probabilistic models that incorporate nonexperimental procedures.

Within Mackie's framework, causes must be both necessary and sufficient conditions for effects. Specifically,

> "X is a necessary condition for Y" will mean that whenever an event of type Y occurs, and event of type X also occurs, and "X is a sufficient condition for Y" will mean that whenever an event of type X occurs, so does an event of type Y. (1980: 57)

Consider the nontrivial case of some outcome P, which results from a situation with elements A, B, and C, where only the complete set $\{ABC\}$ is sufficient for P. Furthermore, it is assumed that any given subset (e.g., $\{AB\}$) is not sufficient to result in P. Thus, P will follow only when all of A, B, and C are present. Now, let us assume there is a plurality of causes such that any of $\{ABC\}$ or $\{DGH\}$ or $\{JKL\}$ is sufficient for P. Again, the condition holds that P will not follow from any lesser subset (e.g., $\{AC\}$, $\{DG\}$, $\{J\}$, etc.) of the elements listed. On the other hand, if P will result only from the situations $\{ABC\}$ or $\{DGH\}$ or $\{JKL\}$ and none other, then these are also necessary conditions for P.

Thus to summarize the sets, $\{ABC\}$ or $\{DGH\}$ or $\{JKL\}$ are both sufficient and necessary conditions for P. Therefore, all ($\{ABC\}$ or $\{DGH\}$ or $\{JKL\}$) are followed by P and all P are preceded by ($\{ABC\}$ or $\{DGH\}$ or $\{JKL\}$).

Mackie defines as a *minimal* sufficient condition the fact that all elements of, say, the set $\{ABC\}$ are required to be a sufficient condition for P to occur. Thus, in elaboration:

---

7. Holland addresses this issue by proposing two solutions: the scientific solution and the statistical solution. While doubtless convincing to most people, these solutions would still not convince the profound skeptic. Holland's article and the ensuing commentaries, however, are worth studying in detail.

ABC is a *minimal* sufficient condition: none of its conjuncts is redundant: no part of it, such as *AB*, is itself sufficient for *P*. But each single factor, such as *A*, is neither a necessary nor a sufficient condition for *P*. Yet it is clearly related to *P* in an important way: it is an *insufficient* but *non-redundant* part of an *unnecessary* but *sufficient* condition: it will be consentient to call this . . . an *inus* condition. (Mackie, 1980: 62)

It is the elaboration of the "inus" condition that forms the unique basis of Mackie's contribution. If the three sets, {*ABC*}, {*DGH*}, and {*JKL*} are a complete enumeration of the causes of *P*, then they are collectively called the *full cause*. As Mackie and others have pointed out, however, it is rare for us to be able to enumerate all the elements in the full cause. Theoretical and empirical limitations often reduce both our knowledge and our interest to only parts of the full cause. Thus, as Mackie remarks, "what is typically called a cause is an inus condition or an individual instance of an inus condition" (1980: 64).[8]

How, then, does this discourse advance our formal understanding of what it means for a relationship to be spurious within a causal model? Consider the situation in which {*ABC*} may be an inus condition for two separate effects *P* and *E*. Under this circumstance we might be misled into believing that *E* is the cause of *P* for both *E* and *P* will be evident when {*ABC*} is evident.

Granger Causality

To continue working within the framework of causal imagery while trying to avoid the deeper philosophical pitfalls, some researchers have proposed limited or operational forms of causality. This gambit of proposing models of weak causality has found particular favor in disciplines characterized by a greater reliance on survey as opposed to experimental data. An example of one such approach is that outlined by Granger (Granger, 1969; Granger and Newbold, 1977). Granger's is essentially an operational definition of causality based on two conditions. First, it is assumed that causality is asymmetrical; only the past can affect the present or future and not vice versa. Thus, any observed asymmetry must be of the form of a standard, temporally evolving feedback loop. Second, Granger causality is limited to discussions of stochastic variables. Practically speaking, Granger causality is an attempt to justify standard regression models as a sufficient mechanism for assessing causal models.

Within the regression framework, *X* is assumed to be a cause of *Y* if past and present observations of *X* allow for better forecasts of the *Y* variable, ceteris paribus. To test Granger causality, a number of hypotheses need to be specified. First, there is the substantive hypothesis that the outcome variable Y_t is a function of some previous or current manifestations of *Y* and a set of causal variables, X_i. Stated more formally, it is posited that $Y_t = f$ (any Y_{t-j}, $X_{i,t-k}$, where $j = 1, 2, \ldots$, and $k = 0, 1, 2, \ldots$). If the null of this hypothesis cannot be rejected, then the specified Y_{t-j} and $X_{i,t-k}$ cannot be considered to be candidates for causality. Second, for Granger causality to

8. Mackie (1980: 64) also goes on to note that this inus condition "may be a state rather than an event"—an assertion that has important implications for much social theory.

hold, it must also be shown that the null hypothesis that Y does not have a significant effect on past and future X_i cannot be rejected.

Since tests for Granger causality invariably involve time series data, the statistical procedures for testing the appropriate hypotheses can become complex, particularly when correlated error terms are involved. Succinct reviews of appropriate statistical testing procedures can be found, however, in most standard econometrics texts (e.g., Judge et al., 1988: 767–70; Harvey, 1990: 303–309).

PRACTICAL ISSUES

Having explored some conceptual issues surrounding causality, we will now focus our attention on some practical issues of working within a causal framework.

General vs. Individual Causes

Carl Hempel (1965: 147–49) makes a distinction between what he terms general and individual causes. General causes are those that follow specific laws. Thus, for example, when paper is exposed to a sufficient source of heat (451°F) along with several other coextensive conditions (e.g., presence of oxygen), it will ignite. This process follows a general rule that can be reproduced under a variety of specific circumstances. This rule constitutes the general cause. Specific or individual causes are of the variety that consider unique factors. Thus, for example, who put a match to the paper, and why?

By making this distinction, Hempel is recognizing two situations. First, scientific explanation relies on our ability to replicate similar events (i.e., events of a given class). Second, there may be some processes (individual causes) so unique that they are not amenable to standard analysis.

Is Experimentation a Necessary Condition for Science?

It is often argued that the classical experiment is the ideal approach in the scientific method, and some researchers, such as Holland, argue that it is only through experimentation that any degree of causality can be imputed. We must ask ourselves, however, whether this is really a necessary condition for the advancement of scientific knowledge or merely a sufficient condition. For, as Holland himself has shown, there are ultimate limits to the cause–inferential viability of experiments. In principle, the answer is that the controlled experiment is only one possible approach. As Nagel states:

> It is in consequence beyond dispute that many sciences have contributed, and continue to contribute, to the advancement of generalized knowledge despite severely limited opportunities for instituting controlled experiments.

What is needed, however, is what this author terms *controlled investigation*.

Controlled investigation consists in a deliberate search for contrasting occasions in which the phenomenon is either uniformly manifested (whether identical or differing modes) or manifested in some cases but not in others, and in the subsequent examination of certain factors discriminated in those occasions in order to ascertain whether variations in these factors are related to differences in the phenomena—where these factors as well as the different manifestations of the phenomenon are selected for careful observation because they are assumed to be relevantly related. (Nagel, 1961: 452–53)

In fact, for social phenomena, a nonexperimental approach is probably a necessity, even with the possibility of controlled experimentation. This is likely the case for several reasons. First, the very act of modifying social conditions artificially (the experiment) can affect the subjects involved in the experiment. This process is akin to the phenomenon known as the Heisenberg principle in physics. Second, introducing a change in social conditions might produce irreversible changes in the relevant variables, thereby disabling our ability to replicate the situation by returning to the initial conditions. Third, it is well known that many results found in the social laboratory are difficult, if not impossible, to replicate in the field. Thus, especially for policy purposes, it is often necessary to test for complex interaction effects in the field before presuming to make firm instrumental conclusions. Unfortunately, achieving any degree of control over the relevant variables in field experiments is often difficult.[9]

Returning to our earlier discussion, it would appear that Nagel is asserting that a science can progress even when it meets only what we have termed the *weak* assumptions of causality. If this is the case, then what is the final arbiter of a theory's validity? Ultimately, it is the ability of a theory to make correct predictions. As Nagel points out, astronomy is a physical science that defies classical experimentation, yet has advanced because its models are able to make consistent and adequate predictions about the future state of the universe. Sadly, most of the social sciences have yet to produce predictive models on par with those of astronomy. Still, as all utopians would argue, it is the principle we are examining here and not necessarily its inadequate implementation.

SUGGESTIONS FOR THE IMPROVEMENT
OF CONTROLLED INQUIRY

Since controlled observation is likely the best we can aspire to in many social sciences, what can we do to improve the situation? There are some general procedures that can help.

Variance Maximization

Traditional statistical techniques and experimental designs assume that the independent variable is under the control of the researcher. The researcher attempts to provide

---

9. For an interesting discussion of the unanticipated consequences of social programs, see Henshel (1976: ch. 3).

as wide a range of values as possible to extend the external validity of his conclusions. Conclusions concerning the relationship outside this range are made at one's own risk. For example, a consumer survey of automobile ownership that focuses on consumers with family incomes of less than $100,000 per year may show that there is a positive relationship between income and the "newness" of the family automobile(s). It may be, however, that those earning more than $100,000 per year (who were not surveyed) tend to purchase automobiles with long life expectancies; therefore, their automobiles often are older than those of the middle class. Thus, anyone extrapolating the demand for new cars to the very wealthy may be disappointed in seeing a market much smaller than expected.

Generally, ex post facto research does not allow for a valid determination of the range of X. Therefore, attempts should be made to survey situations with as much variance (and as great a range) in X as possible. Practically, this often requires the oversampling of the tails of the distribution through stratification (see Chapter 6).

A Priori Positing of Hypotheses

As indicated in Chapter 1, ex post facto research conducted without the prior statement of hypotheses is of utmost danger. Conversely, this leads to the traditional "fishing expedition," where researchers dredge data for significant relationships. As classical statistics teaches us, for a given alpha level, say $\alpha = .05$, 1/20th of all true null hypotheses will be rejected by chance alone. After-the-fact explanations should be considered totally suspect, since new interpretations can always be found to fit the facts. In essence, such explanations are scientifically invalid because nullifying them is impossible. A good example is psychotherapy, which molds the explanation to fit whatever "facts" manifest themselves. It is *only* by positing the hypothesis a priori that the researcher has any chance whatsoever of *not* being able to reject a null hypothesis.

Distinguishing Proximal from Contextual Causes

It is often easy to confuse the impact of what might be termed proximal variables with contextual variables.[10] The educational example is that of "school effects." In demography, we often note a tension between contextual factors that influence fertility decisions, such as economic or cultural conditions, and proximal factors such as expectations and pressures from other family members.

In general sociology, one must distinguish between "structural" and proximal effects and decide (a) what is it that one wishes to focus upon, and (b) what is the most important factor? One published example of asking whether it makes sense to ask what factors predict exam performance when the grade distribution is set a priori (Lieberson, 1985) is a good issue. The debate has raged between "radical" and "conservative" theorists for some time about whether the real issue of analysis is the

---

10. In his fascinating little book, *Making it Count*, Stanley Lieberson (1985) distinguishes between what he terms *basic* and *superficial* causes. This is an unfortunate choice of terminology, since the search of ultimate causes soon leads to the problem of infinite reductionism. The substance of Lieberson's discussion, however, is clearly one of immediate vs. contextual causes.

social system itself, or how people behave within that system. For example, does it make sense to ask what motivates some to become criminals when the system itself constrains opportunities such that criminal behavior is the only "rational" response?[11]

Conceptual Clarity in Variables

Some variables are clearly not as subject to selection bias as others. Examples of more resistant variables include age, gender, race, and marital status. The distinction here is between what Talcott Parsons termed "achieved" and "ascribed" characteristics. Ascribed characteristics are generally those immutable factors, or at least the factors outside one's personal control, that described an individual. Age is a good example. Achieved characteristics, on the other hand, result from one's volition. Unfortunately, most ascribed characteristics are what we might term proxy variables. For example, chronological age is an irrelevant characteristic by itself.

Chronological age is often used as a proxy for many biological, psychological, and sociological factors. So too are sex, race, or any number of other "basic" dimensions. Often these factors stand in stead for such things as experience, learned culture, or social role acquisition. Even the relationship between age and mortality is really a relationship between physical decay and mortality, and exposure to risk (disease, accidents) and mortality. Thus, anything that increases the rate of exposure to a given disease (besides mere time) will increase or decrease the relationship.

Appropriate Design

Survey researchers often spend considerable time analyzing sampling questions without exploring many of the more subtle issues of design. For example, cross-sectional designs can often be combined into what we term "multiple panel" designs. This lends a longitudinal component to our research that provides one way of operationalizing the asymmetry requirement.

Once a panel approach has been chosen, it is necessary to address the issue of whether a "true" panel or "pseudo" panel design should be used. True panel studies follow the same individuals over time. These designs are often expensive to execute, since subject mortality can often be very high. Pseudopanels consist of multiple cross-sectional samples drawn independently from the same population. They are often less expensive to execute, but loss of information must be factored into the savings achieved.

A primary distinction between true and pseudopanel designs is the general inability to estimate prevalence over incidence. The distinction between these two concepts is aptly illustrated by Gottfredson and Hirschi, who speak of the problem of measuring participation in criminal activity.

> The crime rate is a function of both the number of persons in the population committing crimes (the prevalence of crime) and the number of crimes they commit. When the

11. One piece of conventional wisdom in the social sciences suggests that economics tells us how people make choices while sociology tell us why we have no choices to make.

denominator of the rate consists of the total number of people in the population, the first rate is traditionally called the prevalence rate and the second the incidence rate. (Gottfredson and Hirschi, 1990: 240)

A second example can be drawn from labor force participation. From a cross-sectional survey, we may learn that 50% of all women participate in the labor force. However, we do not know whether the same sample of women are consistently in the labor force, or more women work but only 50% are in the labor force at one point in time. It is very possible for the incidence of female labor force participation to be 50%, yet the prevalence may be close to 85%.

To address both the problems of sample mortality and differing panel samples, some surveys engage in a compromise. The Canadian monthly Labour Force Survey, for example, commences with an initial sample and proceeds to drop one-sixth of the sample each month, while picking up a new sixth at random. Thus, any one individual is sampled for a maximum of 6 months; simultaneously, the costs of finding a mobile sample are limited, since the same person has to be tracked down only for a maximum of 6 surveys.

Identifying Where Our Interests Lie

In his short methodological treatise, *Making it Count*, Stanley Lieberson (1985: 223) states: "Explanations of variation are not substitutes for explanation of the existence of the phenomenon itself." At first glance, this appears obvious. Further thought, however, suggests that the statement is very misleading. The issue is one of measurement—the difference between nominal and ratio measurement, and how a phenomenon manifests itself. Most scientists recognize that phenomena can be measured nominally (presence/absence) and, if present, in degrees of presence (ratio). Lieberson suggests that the issue of presence/absence is more important than levels of presence. This may or may not be the case, given substantive considerations. However, the two types of explanation are not exclusive by any means, and a priori, deciding purely on issues of measurement is difficult. Furthermore, there is no conceptual reason dictating why one should be exclusive of the other.

Many situations may be considered the outcome of a "two-stage" decision process. For example, how much I decide to spend on a house comes second to my decision to purchase a house in the first instance. Some factors that contribute to the first decision also contribute to the second (e.g., how much I have for a down payment; presence of a stable job; my monthly income). On the other hand, certain factors that relate to the "purchase" decision may be independent of the "how much" decision. For example, the likelihood of being transferred to another city may contribute to the "purchase" decision, not to the "how much"; the number of people in the household may determine how much can and is to be spent on the purchase price.

One example of the type of analysis that can be used to handle both existence and variance is Tobit analysis, so named after J. Tobin, an economist who looked into similar problems in the mid-1950s. Tobin's immediate problem was to determine how much people spend on automotive repairs. In this instance, Tobin realized, the question of how much is spent is determined by the presence or absence of mechanical breakdowns. Simply ignoring those who did not have repairs, however, would severely bias the parameter estimates, causing an overestimation of the amount spent in the population.

Figure 3.1 presents an example of a typical threshold effect. The response variable, Y, is at 0 until X hits some threshold value—in this case, t. Thus, for the values of X identified by the line segment AB, the phenomenon indicated by y may appear not to exist. When X achieves level t, however, the response in y commences at point C, and for values of X greater than t, the function $Y = f(X)$ follows the trajectory outlined by CD. For substantive purposes, we may wish to focus only upon a limited range in X—such as the point t where Y appears to come into "existence."

Another threshold phenomenon is illustrated in Figure 3.2. This diagram represents the phenomenon known as *catastrophe theory* (Saunders, 1980). Here we have two

Figure 3.1. An example of a threshold effect.

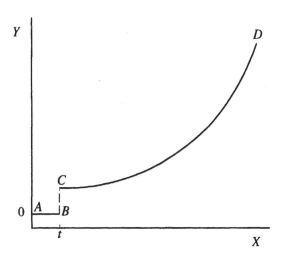

Figure 3.2. Illustration of categorical leaps.

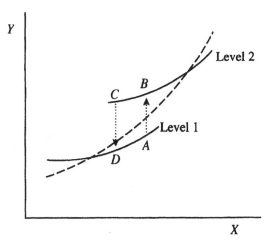

separate functions defined in the diagram as Level 1 and Level 2. At low levels of X, Level 1 defines the function relating X and Y. The function follows Level 2 for higher values of X. For part of the range, however, there is an overlap in the two functions. When the phenomenon enters the overlap range, it is assumed to be capable of making a quantum leap from one level to the other. Where that leap will take place is not determined, but often the leap from Level 1 to Level 2 (as indicated by the line segment AB) takes place at higher levels of X than the drop from Level 2 to Level 1 (as indicated by the line segment CD). The typical substantive example presented by catastrophe theorists is that of a frustrated dog. At low levels of frustration, the dog exhibits varying degrees of aggressiveness, usually in the form of snarling. At some point, however, increasing the dog's frustration level will lead to a change in the type of aggressive behavior from snarling and baring of teeth to a physical attack. The viciousness of attack, y, is determined by X along the trajectory outlined by Level 2. Ultimately, the dog will "cool down," will retreat from his attack, and return to snarling. Word has it that frustrated parents and teachers follow similar patterns of behavior.

CAUSALITY AND CORRELATION: AN ELABORATION

As we have already noted, correlation is a necessary but not a sufficient condition for causality. At some level, the identification of correlation is a simple matter: observe two variables (X and Y) over some domain of X and calculate a correlation coefficient. Unfortunately, X and Y rarely occur in isolation. Other variables may mediate the relationship in a theoretically meaningful way (in which case we call them endogenous), or they may influence the relationship outside the immediate theoretical model (in which case we call them exogenous). In most *real* research, there are often many mediating variables to consider.

The single biggest problem for empirical scientists working within a causal model framework is that several competing models can be consistent with the same data. It is the role of the methodologist to try to create test situations or procedures that can result in data that distinguish between competing models. Still, one can never be sure whether all competing models have been accounted for. To quote Mackie (1980: 66) on the matter:

> And even with any one cause, we do not know all the possible counteracting causes, all the factors the negations of which would have to be conjoined with our positive factors to make up just one minimal sufficient condition. Causal knowledge progresses gradually towards the formulation of such regularities, but it hardly ever gets there. Causal regularities *as known* are typically incomplete. . . .

Thus, again we are reminded that the inability to disprove a model does not necessarily confirm that model.

Many basic problems underlying the determination of correlation can be illustrated with the simplest scenario: that of three variables. Let us assume that the key

Figure 3.3. Varieties of causal patterns with three variables.

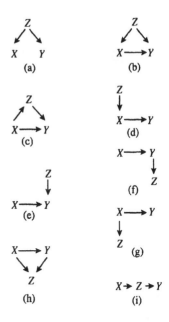

relationship of interest is that between X and Y, and that Z is the (potentially) mediating or spurious variable. Thus both X and Z conform to Mackie's inus conditions, but from a theoretical standpoint, Z is not considered to be a genuine cause. Many possible relationships exist, and these are schematically outlined in Figure 3.3. There is no "true" relationship between X and Y in Figure 3.3a. That is, ρ_{XY}, the population correlation coefficient is zero. The empirical or sample correlation, r_{XY}, is not equal to zero, however, since there is a *spurious* third variable, Z, which affects both X and Y. The variable Z is a nonproblem if we are aware of its presence, since it can be physically controlled by the investigator in experimental situations and statistically controlled in survey research. More often, we are unaware of Z and fallaciously infer a meaningful relationship between X and Y.

The issue of spurious relationships is particularly problematic when we engage in empirical fishing expeditions without strong theoretical guidance. It is also a primary pitfall underlying raw empiricism when we let "reality" alone guide our explanatory models. Put in other terms, ststements that "everybody knows" or "it is self-evident" that X causes Y do not mean that X truly causes Y. Most of what we now identify as superstitious or magical thinking likely had its origins in spurious relationships.

The relationship depicted in Figure 3.3b, on the other hand, is that of a *confounding* relationship. Depending upon the magnitudes of the correlations among the three variables, Z may act as either a suppressor variable or an augmenting variable. If the presence of Z reduces (attenuates) the absolute empirical correlation between X and Y, we call it a suppressor; if it increases the absolute empirical correlation between X and Y, it is an augmenter. In the extreme, the unknown impact of a suppressor variable can fool us into believing that there is little or no relationship between X and

Y. The unknown impact of an augmenter, however, leads to an inflated estimate of the impact between X and Y.

Exactly how r_{ZX} and r_{ZY} influence our perception of r_{XY} depends on the signs of the three correlations. Without getting into covariance algebra to any great extent, we can see this relationship if we take a close look at the familiar formula for the partial correlation coefficient. By definition,

$$r_{XY \cdot Z} = \frac{r_{XY} - r_{XZ} r_{YZ}}{\sqrt{1 - r_{XZ}^2} \sqrt{1 - r_{YZ}^2}}$$

The denominator values will always be positive, and for our purposes can be ignored. Let us consider the relationship in greater detail. The component $r_{XY \cdot Z}$ can be seen as an estimate of ρ_{XY}, or the *true* relationship between X and Y. The correlation, r_{XY}, is what we observe. Thus, the observed correlation consists of the true correlation plus the product of the correlations between X and Z, and Y and Z. That is,

$$\mathbf{r_{xy}} = \mathbf{r_{xz} r_{yz}} + \mathbf{r_{xy \cdot z}} \left[\sqrt{1 - r_{XZ}^2} \sqrt{1 - r_{YZ}^2} \right]$$

In Figure 3.3a the causal model implies that ρ_{XY} is 0; however, it is observed that $r_{XY} \neq 0$. If, in fact, all of the covariance between X and Y is a consequence of Z, then statistically controlling for Z ought to result in the partial covariance between X and Y being zero. Hence, if $\rho_{XY} = 0$, then $r_{XY \cdot Z} = 0$. The observed covariance between X and Y, therefore, is a consequence of the product $(r_{XZ} r_{YZ})$. Following through with this line of reasoning, it becomes apparent that if one or both of r_{XZ} or r_{YZ} equals 0, then $r_{XY} = \rho_{XY} = 0$. If the product of r_{XZ} and r_{YZ} is positive, r_{XY} will be positive; if the product is negative, r_{XY} will be negative.

The same reasoning can shed some light onto the confounding relationship between X, Y, and Z (Figure 3.3b). If the product of r_{XZ} and r_{YZ} is positive, then Z becomes an *augmenting* variable that produces an observed $r_{XY} > \rho_{XY}$. By calculating $r_{XY \cdot Z}$ we will obtain a reduced estimate of the causal link between X and Y. On the other hand, if the product of r_{XZ} and r_{YZ} is negative, Z will be a *suppressor* variable that leads to an observed $r_{XY} < \rho_{XY}$. Thus, $r_{XY \cdot Z}$ will be larger than the observed r_{XY}.

The remaining relationships in Figure 3.3 consist of theoretically meaningful relationships between X, Y, and Z that are both nonspurious and nonconfounding. That is, Z is an endogenous variable of substantive interest.

In Figure 3.3c, X has both a direct effect on Y and an indirect effect through Z. Sometimes this is called an interactive model, since X and Z not only have main effects on Y, but also an interactive effect based on r_{XZ}. Exactly how Z moderates the impact of X on Y depends upon the signs of the three zero-order correlations involved in the relationship. Instead of discussing the impact of the permutations of the signs of the correlations on the relationships between X and Y for each of the diagrams (Figures 3.3c–3.3i), we will simply have a quick look at the structural form of the relationships. A more general and detailed approach for examining the relationships and estimating the magnitudes of the effects is presented in the next section on path analysis.

In Figure 3.3d, Z is an antecedent variable that has an impact on Y but only through X. Empirically, then, it is only necessary to observe variations in X to predict the behavior of Y. As depicted in Figure 3.3e, however, X is a sufficient condition but not a necessary condition for Y, since Z can also affect the behavior of Y. In this instance, the behavior of Y can be predicted only by including the two main effects of X and Z into the model.

In Figures 3.3f–3.3h, Z is irrelevant to our understanding of the relationship between X and Y because in no case is Z a *causal* variable. In Figure 3.3f it is Y that affects Z; in Figure 3.3g it is X that affects Z. Knowing anything about Z, therefore, provides no information about the behavior of either X or Y. The same may be said about Figure 3.3h, where both X and Y have an impact on Z but not vice versa.

Finally, in Figure 3.3i, Z acts as a *mediating* or *intervening* variable between X and Y. In the absence of Z (i.e., $Z = 0$), X has no impact on Y.

PATH ANALYSIS

Path analysis is a technique developed by Sewall Wright in the 1920s to assist in the assessment of causal models in biology (Wright, 1921; 1934). The technique was incorporated into the social science literature after its popularization by Otis Dudley Duncan in the 1960s (Duncan, 1966). As a pedagogical procedure for delving into the intricacies of causal modeling, it is an excellent starting point. Unfortunately, as presented by Wright and Duncan, the procedure imposes constraints that are difficult to achieve empirically. Specifically, classical path analysis requires the same assumptions as ordinary least squares regression analysis. That is, for some structural equation, say $Y_i = \beta_0 + \beta_1 X_{i1} + \cdots + \beta_n X_{in} + \varepsilon_i$, we assume that the error terms, ε_i, are normally and independently distributed (of each other and the X_{ij}), with a mean of zero and some constant variance, σ^2. We also assume that the independent, or X variables, are measured without error. The reason for these OLS assumptions is that the path coefficients are essentially standardized b-values.[12] Most independent variables as operationalized in the social sciences, we would argue, are highly subject to measurement error. Furthermore, those error terms are often correlated with one another.

From a statistical point of view, then, path analysis allows for the analysis of a *structural* model, but not of a *measurement* model. That is, where we know, or have good reason to believe that these assumptions are violated, we have significant difficulties identifying and accounting for those violations within the framework of the model. As shown in Chapter 11, this limitation has been overcome in recent years with the theoretical development of generalized structural equation modeling (e.g., Jöreskog, Bollen) and the availability of software designed to estimate those models (e.g., LISREL, EQS, the CALIS procedure in SAS). Still, making those restrictive assumptions about measurement to explore the issues surrounding the structural or causal model is worthwhile.

---

12. As with ordinary regression, it is possible to estimate parameter values if these assumptions are not met. On the other hand, any inferences based on standard statistical tests (t-tests, F-tests, etc.) are of questionable validity. See, for example, Wonnacott and Wonnacott (1970: ch. 2).

Before continuing further, however, we would do well to hear the advice of Hoover (1990: 208) who reminds us that

> the analysis of causality is not a problem in statistical technique; it is a problem in the logic of empirical inference. Statistical techniques are of course important to the practice of inferring causal direction; better statistical techniques will no doubt improve causal inference; but, in order to deploy those techniques effectively, an appropriate understanding of the concept of causal order is needed.

Path Diagrams

For many of us, the great utility of path analysis is the graphical interface it provides between verbalizations of theory statements and the mathematical representations of those statements. This interface is known as the path diagram. Path diagrams consist of the proverbial "circles and arrows" that help us organize the relationships between our theory components visually. While researchers have undoubtedly used ad hoc graphical procedures for generations, path diagrams follow a set of rules that allow for the systematic depiction and interpretation of our theory statements. Some of the primary symbols are illustrated in Figure 3.4. The boxes represent manifest or observed variables or indicators. The circles, on the other hand, represent latent variables or latent factors that are not observed directly but are assumed to manifest themselves through the indicator variables. In this chapter, we will use the boxes only; the circles are presented as a prelude to the discussions of measurement models and structural equation models in Chapter 11.

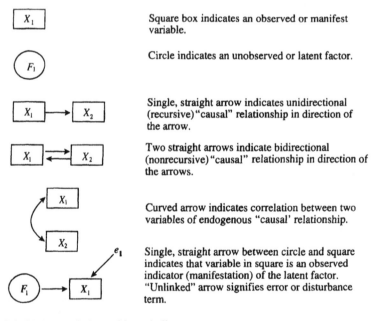

Square box indicates an observed or manifest variable.

Circle indicates an unobserved or latent factor.

Single, straight arrow indicates unidirectional (recursive) "causal" relationship in direction of the arrow.

Two straight arrows indicate bidirectional (nonrecursive) "causal" relationship in direction of the arrows.

Curved arrow indicates correlation between two variables of endogenous "causal' relationship.

Single, straight arrow between circle and square indicates that variable in square is an observed indicator (manifestation) of the latent factor. "Unlinked" arrow signifies error or disturbance term.

Figure 3.4. Major symbols used in path diagrams.

The variables are connected to each other through a series of arrows. Boxes and circles linked through arrows are assumed to influence one another either causally or otherwise. Boxes and circles not linked to one another are assumed to be theoretically independent. The *causal direction* implied in the theory statements is represented by the direction of the *straight* arrows, with the variables at the head of the arrow being considered the effects, and those at the base, the causes. The double-headed, curved arrows assume association but not necessarily causation. In the terminology of econometrics, the curved arrows represent exogenous relationships, while the straight arrows represent endogenous relationships. Boxes and circles connected by arrows that go in both directions are assumed to be reciprocal in their causation.

Path Coefficients

Path coefficients are equivalent to beta coefficients or standardized b-values obtained from an ordinary regression model. Starting with a matrix of correlations, $\mathbf{R}$, it is possible to estimate the standardized b-values. Let us assume that a correlation matrix has been partitioned into two submatrices: $\mathbf{R}_{xx}$, which consists of the $m \times m$ intercorrelations among the independent variables; and $\mathbf{R}_{xy}$ which is an $m \times 1$ matrix of correlations between the independent variables and the dependent variable. An $m \times 1$ matrix of standardized b-values or path coefficients, $\mathbf{b}^*$, may be estimated as:

$$\mathbf{b}^* = R_{xx}^{-1} R_{xy}$$

Although there are several formulations, the squared multiple correlation, R^2, is most easily determined by

$$R^2 = \mathbf{b}^{*\prime} \mathbf{R}_{xy}$$

From this, we may estimate the standard errors for each of the j path coefficients, b_j^* as approximately:

$$SE(b_j^*) = s_{b_j^*} = \frac{\sqrt{1 - R^2}}{\sqrt{r_{jj}(n - k - 1)}}$$

The r_{jj} constitute the inverse of the jth diagonal elements of the $\mathbf{R}_{xx}^{-1}$ matrix; n is the number of cases; and k is the number of slopes (independent variables) in the regression model. Individual path coefficients can be tested for statistical significance by comparing the ratio of the b_j^* s to their standard errors [i.e., $b_j^*/SE(b_j^*)$]. This ratio can be compared with the t-distribution with $n - k - 1$ degrees of freedom (df).

EXAMPLE: ESTIMATING PATH PARAMETERS

Assume that a survey is conducted in which three observations, X_1, X_2, and Y are taken on each of 50 people. Intercorrelations are calculated among the three variables resulting in:

$$\mathbf{R}_{XX} = \begin{bmatrix} 1.0 & .40 \\ .50 & 1.0 \end{bmatrix}, \quad \mathbf{R}_{XY} = \begin{bmatrix} .35 \\ .25 \end{bmatrix}$$

From this, the coefficients can be estimated as:

$$R_{XX}^{-1} \quad R_{XY} = b^*$$

$$\begin{bmatrix} 1.0 & .40 \\ .50 & 1.0 \end{bmatrix}^{-1} \begin{bmatrix} .35 \\ .25 \end{bmatrix} = b^*$$

$$\begin{bmatrix} 1.25 & -.5 \\ -.625 & 1.25 \end{bmatrix} \begin{bmatrix} .35 \\ .25 \end{bmatrix} = \begin{bmatrix} .31 \\ .09 \end{bmatrix}$$

Thus, the betas or path coefficients estimated within this model are .31 and .09. The proportion of overall variance explained, R^2, becomes $(.31 \times .35) + (.09 \times .25) = .13$. Since the diagonal elements of $\mathbf{R}_{XX}^{-1}$ are both 1.25, each r_{jj} is equal to 1/1.25 or .80. Thus, both estimates of the standard errors of the betas are given by:

$$\begin{aligned} SE(b_1^*) &= \frac{\sqrt{(1 - R^2)}}{\sqrt{r_{11}(n - k - 1)}} \\ &= \frac{\sqrt{1 - .13}}{\sqrt{.80(50 - 2 - 1)}} \\ &= .15 \end{aligned}$$

A 95% confidence interval may be determined as approximately $b_j^* \pm 1.96\,(.15)$ or $b_j^* \pm .29$. This would imply that only b_1 is statistically significant, since the confidence interval around b_2^* (.09) encompasses 0 but that around b_1^* (.31) does not. The best estimate of b_1^*, therefore, is r_{XY} or .35.

EXAMPLE: A PATH MODEL OF FERTILITY IN DEVELOPING COUNTRIES

For a more elaborate example, we will use a data set put together by Balakrishnan and Hou (1993) and presented in Chapter 13 (see Table 13.1). The model is designed to test a substantive hypothesis currently of interest in demography: that is, whether economic development has a greater impact on a country's total fertility rate than rates of female literacy. From the data set, five variables have been chosen: total fertility rate (TFR), log gross national product per capita (Log-GNP), percentage of population in agriculture (Agriculture), percent female literacy (Literacy), and the difference between the mean age of marriage between men and women (Difference). Ultimately, TFR is what we want to explain. Log-GNP and Literacy are the primary explanatory variables, and Agriculture and Difference are subsidiary causal variables. Agriculture is believed to influence TFR and Literacy, while Difference is considered an indicator of relative status. Where the difference between the average age at marriage is great, we assume that there is a large gender status differential. We also assume that this status differential is influenced by literacy among women. It is further assumed that Log-GNP and Agriculture are also correlated although not causally. Together, these relationships are outlined in Figure 3.5.

Figure 3.5. A path model of
fertility.

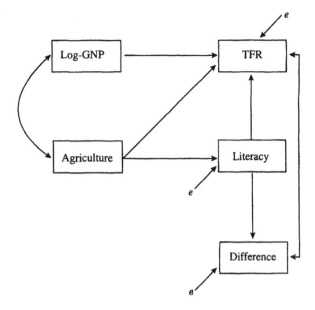

A correlation matrix was generated from the data set. Since there are values missing from the data, it was decided to estimate the correlation matrix by deleting cases that had at least one missing element. This resulted in the matrix based on a sample of 68 nations.[13] The correlation matrix is reproduced in Table 3.1.

To estimate the paths, three equations must be set up:

$$\text{TFR} = \text{Log-GNP} + \text{Agriculture} + \text{Literacy} + \text{Difference} \qquad (3.1)$$

$$\text{Literacy} = \text{Agriculture} \qquad (3.2)$$

$$\text{Difference} = \text{Literacy} \qquad (3.3)$$

Table 3.1. Correlation matrix of variables in fertility path model

	TFR	LOG-GNP	LITERACY	AGRICULTURE
TFR	1.0			
Log-GNP	−.666	1.0		
Literacy	−.742	.604	1.0	
Agriculture	.698	−.772	−.677	1.0
Difference	.579	−.442	−.611	.461

13. While ignored in this example, techniques for addressing missing data are addressed in Chapter 13. This example is based on the casewise deletion of missing data—not the best way of dealing with the problem in this instance.

For equation (3.1) we can obtain the betas or path coefficients by solving:

$$R_{XX}^{-1} \qquad R_{XY} \quad = b^*$$

$$\begin{bmatrix} 1.0 & .604 & -.772 & -.442 \\ .604 & 1.0 & -.677 & -.611 \\ -.772 & -.677 & 1.0 & .461 \\ -.442 & -.611 & .461 & 1.0 \end{bmatrix}^{-1} \begin{bmatrix} -.666 \\ -.742 \\ .698 \\ .579 \end{bmatrix} = b^*$$

Since equations (3.2) and (3.3) involve only one independent variable, the estimated path coefficient or standardized b-value is equivalent to the correlation coefficient, r. Solving the equations (3.1)–(3.3), we obtain the results presented in Table 3.2. While the parameters and standard errors can be estimated either by hand or by almost any general regression routine, we chose to conduct the analysis using LISREL8. One advantages of using a generalized structural equation package such as LISREL8 is that it will provide overall indicators of goodness of fit for the entire model.[14]

One way of measuring the entire model is to assess the degree to which it reproduces the correlation matrix, **R**.[15] Essentially, we are testing the null hypothesis that $\hat{R} = R$. In this instance, a chi-squared test can be used (see Bollen, 1989: 263–69). The estimated chi-square is 2.97 with 3 df with an associated p-value of .40. These results

Table 3.2. Regression results for fertility path model

TFR VARIABLE	COEFFICIENT	STANDARD ERROR	T-VALUE
Literacy	−.38	.11	−3.33
Difference	.16	.09	1.75
Log-GNP	−.20	.11	−1.79
Agriculture	.21	.13	1.59
$R^2 = .65$			
Literacy			
Agriculture	−.68	.09	−7.42
$R^2 = .46$			
Difference			
Literacy	−.61	.10	−6.22
$R^2 = .37$			

14. See Chapter 11 for more details.
15. Details of this technique are outlined in Chapter 11.

suggest that we ought not to reject the null hypothesis, since the expected correlation matrix closely resembles **R**; thus, using this global assessment, the model provides a good overall fit.

While the overall model appears statistically significant, an examination of the individual parameters in Table 3.2 suggests that the model is clearly not parsimonious (see also Figure 3.6). In particular, the paths flowing from Agriculture to TFR and Difference to TFR and not statistically significant. Since the Difference to TFR path is not significant, it also does not make sense to retain the path from Literacy to Difference. The path from Log-GNP to TFR is also not significant; however, we will retain this path for the moment, since it does have crucial theoretical significance. Removing the mentioned paths leaves the model specified in Figure 3.7. Reestimating this model, we note changes in some parameter values. Specifically, the path from Log-GNP to TFR changes from $-.20$ to $-.34$ and that from Literacy to TFR changes from $-.38$ to $-.53$, since the relationship between these variables is no longer modified by either Agriculture or Difference. The error term relating to TFR also changes slightly, from .34 to .37. The path between Agriculture and Literacy remains unchanged, since no other path led to Literacy. Similarly, the correlation between Log-GNP and Agriculture remains constant at $-.77$. Standard tests suggest that this model still replicates the correlation matrix reasonably well: the calculated chi-squared statistic is 4.82 with 2 df.

Just as importantly, all the individual parameter values can be judged as statistically significant, including the path from Log-GNP to TFR. Details of the path coefficients and their standard errors are presented in Table 3.3.

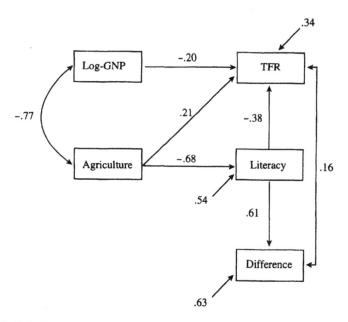

Figure 3.6. Path diagram with estimates of path coefficients for fertility model.

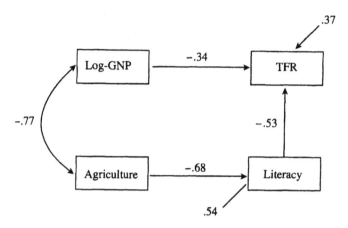

Figure 3.7. Path diagram with estimates of statistically significant path coefficients for reduced fertility model.

Table 3.3. Regression results for reduced path model

TFR VARIABLE	COEFFICIENT	STANDARD ERROR	T-VALUE
Literacy	−.53	.10	−5.61
Log-GNP	−.34	.10	−3.60
$R^2 = .63$			
Literacy			
Agriculture	−.70	.09	−7.92
$R^2 = .49$			

CAUSAL PATH MODELS

The preceding example is typical of much research that appears in the professional journals. We posited the model within a causal framework and directional arrows suggest the direction of the influences. Formally, however, the model is one of weak as opposed to strong causation because the data are not temporally asymmetrical. The data are essentially measured at one point in time.

More properly, the causal variables should be time lagged with respect to the outcome variables for the model to fulfill all the traditional requirements for "causality." As given, the example simply describes the relationships as they exist: it gives little insight into how they "got there."

Figure 3.8. Example of time-series path diagram.

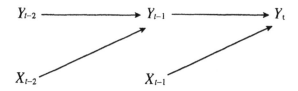

Path models can be used, however, to illustrate simple processes in time. Figure 3.8 presents one such example. For more complex models, the path framework loses its parsimony of expression and often obscures the underlying processes. Complex time-series models (typically of the econometric variety) generally use standard mathematical or statistical notation instead of path imagery.

EXPLORATORY CAUSAL MODELS

The primary focus of science as a method is that of hypothesis testing. Substantive science also involves the context of discovery. In practice, it is likely that scientists spend more time in the discovery phase than in the justification phase. This is nowhere more evident than in the enterprise of causal modeling.

Few scientists are fortunate enough to have a well-specified causal model simply waiting for empirical assessment. Typically, we have a vague model (Dumont and Wilson's theory sketch) with clear a priori linkages among some variables but not others. Typically, we have also put together a data set that reflects an operationalization of those variables. The crucial problem, then, becomes one of specifying the exact linkages that we believe are important within the model. Even models based on a few variables can generate many possible solutions: consider extending the possibilities presented in Figure 3.7 to models with "only" five or six variables.

There are many mindless and atheoretical techniques that allow for the determination of the "best fitting" model (e.g., stepwise regression; all possible regressions), but those approaches generally lead to capitalization on chance. The best overall strategy is to stick to components that are theoretically important, modify only a few, and resort to the use of verification samples. Cross-validation by using independent data sets or split-half methods is a good approach (Cudeck and Browne, 1983; Browne and Cudeck, 1989).

Further Reading

Blalock, H. *Causal Inferences in Nonexperimental Research.* Chapel Hill: University of North Carolina Press, 1964. A short but lucid discussion of elementary causal models. Requires little statistical understanding beyond correlation.

Cartwright, N. *Nature's Capacities and Their Measurement.* Oxford: Clarendon Press, 1989. An introduction to current philosophical thinking on the issue of causality.

Duncan, O. D. *Introduction to Structural Equation Models.* New York: Academic Press, 1975. This volume presents a detailed discussion of path modeling, along with several other basic techniques for conducting causal modeling.

4

Statistical Inference

> *We . . . remind the student that statistical methods are most dan-*
> *gerous tools in the hands of the inexpert. Few subjects have a wider*
> *application; no subject requires such care in that application.*
> *Statistics is one of those sciences whose adepts must exercise the*
> *self-restraint of an artist.*
> —George Udny Yule and Maurice Kendall

The primary focus of this chapter is statistical power: and how it influences our decision making regarding the acceptability of hypotheses and how it influences our choice of sample size. Before pursuing the issue in detail, however, it is necessary to digress into the logic of statistical inference.

THE LOGIC OF STATISTICAL INFERENCE

Statistical analysis gives us a vehicle for evaluating our hypotheses and theoretical models. Unfortunately, introductory statistics courses in the social sciences often focus more on technique than on the underlying theory of statistical inference. In this chapter, we discuss the basic concepts underlying statistical inference and examine what is now known as the "classical" approach—the Pearson–Neyman or PN model of hypothesis testing.

Statistical inference deals with chance events and stochastic processes as opposed to deterministic ones. It is for this reason that many statisticians consider statistics the practice of decision making in the face of uncertainty. Within a deterministic framework, where A *always* leads to B, modern statistics has no value beyond describing the observed data. On the other hand, statistics can help us assess the relative veracity of statements concerning relationships based on chance. That is, statistics helps us assess the empirical veracity of statements of the form: "There is a high probability that A will result in B" or "The likelihood of A leading to B is 75%."

We can start by asking what distinguishes a stochastic event or process from a deterministic one. Simply stated, *stochastic events* are those whose outcome on any given trial or manifestation is not strictly predictable or predetermined. Thus, for example, no one can say for certain on the flipping of a fair coin whether any specific outcome will be heads or tails.

Let us consider what we mean when we say that there has been an outcome of a stochastic process. By definition, if an outcome is stochastic, its exact nature or characteristic cannot be predicted. The event space or the range of total outcomes of that process can be defined, however. Thus, for example, with a coin it is heads or tails. Within a survey of left-handed people, the event space is a proportion within the range 0 to 1 inclusive of left-handed as opposed to right-handed people that will be captured in a randomly selected sample. What is important here is that the outcome has a range of possible values, which will form a distribution around the "true" value. In other words, while the "true" proportion of left-handed people is 10%, that exact value is unlikely to occur on any one given survey.

Now, speaking about a propensity of outcomes to some distribution sounds very metaphysical. Furthermore, the issue of how that propensity might be observed and quantified soon comes to the forefront.

One way of grounding the concept is to adopt what has come to be known as the "frequentist" perspective in statistics. By running a series of trials, it is possible to count the frequency with which the outcome occurs. In the long run, the frequency of occurrence will converge with the actual value of things. Again, the classical example is that of a fair coin. Given enough flips, the long-run probability of getting either heads or tails will be 1/2 or .5. Let us take another example. Assume for a moment that 10% of humanity truly is left-handed. To test this proposition, one might conduct a survey by drawing a small, simple random sample of, say, 200 people. The outcome of that sample may be an estimate that could range anywhere from 0% to 100%. If we draw enough such samples, say 1000, the proportion of left-handed persons will tend toward the actual proportion of 10%, or 10 out of every 100 people surveyed. This statistic may be interpreted as a probability based on frequency in the long run. On the other hand, a "large number" of researchers might decide to conduct identical surveys independently of one another but at the same time. This would not exactly be the same as in the long run, but the idea is the same: over a large number of trials, we can expect the estimated proportion of left-handed people to equate to the actual proportion in the population.

While the frequentist approach to estimating probability is a reasonable strategy for estimating some probabilities and their associated distribution, it is just one mechanism for operationalizing the inherent chance distribution of any particular outcome. Thus, as Hacking (1965: 10) notes:

> "Frequency in the long run" is all very well, but it is a property of the coin and the tossing device, not only that, in the long run, heads fall more often than tails, but also that this would happen even if in fact the device were dismantled and the coin melted. This is a dispositional property of the coin: what the long run frequency is or would be or would have been. Popper calls it a propensity of the coin, device, and situation.

Hacking (1965: 13), then, defines chance as a property of the designated chance setup and,

> A *chance set-up* is a device or part of the world on which might be conducted one or more *trials*, experiments, or observations; each trial must have a unique *result* which is a member of a *class of possible results*. (italics in original)

By viewing the matter in this context, we can take a broader perspective on probability and speak of the outcome chance or probability of unique events. For example, we might wish to consider the probability of rain later in the day as we set out to work in the morning. This day and its unique rain experience cannot be repeated; thus, the frequentist appoach of observing today over many trials is not possible. However, we still consider the specific "trial" to have a probability associated with it. It is on that basis that we decide whether taking an umbrella with us in the morning is worthwhile.

It is for this reason—that we can subjectively assign probabilities to unique events—that many statisticians perceive the frequentist approach to be too restrictive. Still, the frequentist approach covers a wide range of practical situations and offers one of the easiest mechanisms for estimating probabilities. As will be shown in a later section, however, some statisticians have been successful in exploiting the ability of people to generate subjective probabilities.

Pearson–Neyman and A Priori Testing

The Pearson–Neyman approach to hypothesis testing is based on two fundamental conditions. First, the hypothesis to be tested is stated (in null form) a priori, or before the trial (survey, experiment, etc.) is conducted. Second, the decision concerning the outcome of that trial is a binary one, resulting in either the rejection or nonrejection of the null hypothesis. Powerful in its simplicity, the PN approach has an elegance that is best seen when the issue can be truly and unequivocally expressed in either/or terms and a clear line of demarcation for either accepting or rejecting the null hypothesis can be identified.

For example, we may posit a working hypothesis that income is related to level of formal education. The null hypothesis is that no relationship exists. In operational terms, this means that after taking a random survey, we would expect the sample correlation between income and education to be zero ($r = 0$) if the null hypothesis, H_0, were "true." If the data did not support the null hypothesis (i.e., $r > 0$, or $r < 0$), then we would assume that the alternative, or working hypothesis, H_a, is "true." The crucial role of statistics is to recognize that even if the null hypothesis were true, we would not expect r to equal zero exactly. Measurement and other sources of error would serve to give us a sample estimate that might be slightly different from the true population parameter. Thus, the practical question is: How far away from zero can a correlation be and still be considered zero?

If H_0 were the true state of affairs, we could repeat the survey many times and observe how the individual sample estimates of r distribute themselves about the true population value of 0. Clearly, sample values close to 0 would occur more frequently; values far from 0 would occur less frequently. Some surveys might even generate estimates at the extreme values of $+1.0$ or -1.0, although their likelihood would be infinitesimally small. At this point, we can decide to draw a line beyond which, say, only 5% of all values fall by chance when the true population value is 0. This "critical value" helps us to decide whether any particular sample r is truly 0 (thus supporting the null hypothesis) or is not equal to 0 (thus negating the null hypothesis and leading us to give credence to the working hypothesis).

Unfortunately, as indicated in Chapter 1, given some hypothesis A, rejecting the null hypothesis, or not-A, does not always increase our credence in A because there may be many reasonable competing alternates to not-A, (B, C, D, . . . , etc.). This is particularly the case when the hypothesis A is sufficient but not necessary. Similarly, many situations are not resolved convincingly by setting a cutoff point of 5%—that is, allowing only one chance in 20 of rejecting a true null hypothesis. In fact, repeated, independent trials may lead to the rejection of several different null hypotheses (e.g., null-B, null-C, null-D), thereby raising the specter of several working hypotheses that have "statistical" if not substantive credibility.

Thus, as Hacking (1965: 75) says,

> It would be wrong to expect an absolutely sharp line between those hypotheses which should be rejected on some data, and those which should not. One can draw such a line for no hypothesis whatsoever, statistical or otherwise. One may only compare the stringency with which different hypotheses have been rejected.

Because of such insights, testing statistical hypotheses has grown beyond the a priori model first espoused by PN and has developed schools of procedures to sort among several credible competing hypotheses. While several such approaches exist, one of the more common is that attributed to the Reverend Bayes.

Bayesian Approach Based on Prior Probabilities

As with most starting points in statistics, that of the Bayesians is quite elegant, with a high level of intuitive appeal. Most of us follow some form of Bayesian decision making at some point in our lives. Consider, if you will, the instance of parimutuel betting. Bettors who frequent race tracks and see eight horses or six dogs in a lineup are rarely willing to assume that all the horses have an equal .125 chance of winning, or all the dogs have an equal .167 chance of winning. Instead, prior knowledge is used to justify the assumption that track conditions and the individual physiological and experiential differences among the animals will combine to make some contenders more likely to win than others.

Bayesians argue that we rarely enter a trial with complete indifference or ignorance among competing hypotheses. Instead, we do have some prior information or beliefs that can be brought to bear.

Bayesian statistics is based on a theorem identified by the Reverend Thomas Bayes and published after his death. The theorem is a simple explication of conditional and unconditional probabilities about which both classical and Bayesian statisticians essentially agree. The difference between these schools of statistics lies in the *interpretation* placed upon the formula.

Consider the following hypothetical example. Assume that in a particular community, 30% of criminals carry weapons while the remaining 70% do not. This information is known as the *prior distribution*. When the police are about to make an arrest, however, they must decide whether the suspect has a weapon. From the arresting officer's point of view, the crucial element is being able to make a correct prediction in the face of uncertainty. Further research into this problem indicates that when arrestees in fact have weapons, the police are correct in 70% of their judgments that a weapon is present. On the other hand, when a person is not carrying a weapon, the police assume he is carrying one 20% of the time. The question we raise is, Can we improve upon the probabilities listed in prior distribution by taking into account the judgment of the police?

Bayes's theorem suggests that by combining information—in this case, the prior distribution with the beliefs of the police about whether a person is carrying a weapon—an improvement can be made. This improvement is termed the *posterior distribution* and the probabilities associated with it are called *posterior probabilities*.

The mechanics of how prior probabilities are turned into posterior probabilities are as follows. First, the prior probabilities associated with the event space are listed according to a standard format:

Prior probabilities, $p(\theta_i)$

STATE θ_i	$p(\theta_i)$
θ_1, suspect has weapon	.30
θ_2, suspect has no weapon	.70

Second, the beliefs of the police officers are listed based on the states in the prior distribution. These beliefs are operationalized as conditional probabilities—the probability judgments of the police as to whether a suspect is carrying a weapon broken down by the actual state of affairs, θ. In this example, the conditional probabilities may be listed as follows:

Conditional probabilities, $p(X \mid \theta)$

STATE θ_i	X_1, OFFICER PREDICTS WEAPON	X_2, OFFICER PREDICTS NO WEAPON
θ_1, suspect has weapon	.70	.30
θ_2, suspect has no weapon	.20	.80

Consider now the situation of the officer who believes that a suspect is carrying a weapon and the suspect actually has one. That joint probability is

$$p(\theta_1, X_1) = p(X_1 \mid \theta_1)p(\theta_1)$$
$$= (.7)(.3) = .21$$

When the officer's prediction that the suspect has a weapon is *wrong*, we write

$$p(\theta_2, X_1) = p(X_1 \mid \theta_2)p(\theta_2)$$
$$= (.2)(.7) = .14$$

The total predicted probability that the suspect is carrying a weapon is $p_{(\text{weapon})} = .21 + .14 = .35$.

Based on this information, the posterior probabilities as to whether the suspect is carrying a weapon become

$$p(\theta_1 \mid X_1) = \frac{p(\theta_1, X_1)}{p(X_1)}$$

$$= \frac{.21}{.35} = .60$$

and

$$p(\theta_2 \mid X_1) = \frac{p(\theta_2, X_1)}{p(X_1)}$$

$$= \frac{.14}{.35} = .40$$

To summarize, we can now list these posterior probabilities as

Posterior probabilities, $p(\theta_i)$

STATE θ_i	$p(\theta_i \mid X_1)$
θ_1, suspect has weapon	.60
θ_2, suspect has no weapon	.40

What, then, is the overall likelihood that a given suspect is carrying a weapon? When the officer believes the person is carrying a weapon, the probability is raised from the .30 given by the prior probability, to the posterior probability .60 that the suspect actually has one.

Summarizing the equations above for the posterior probabilities, we may write

$$p(\theta_i \mid X_1) = \frac{p(\theta_i, X_1)}{p(X_1)}$$

and by writing out in full the joint probability, $p(\theta_i, X_1)$, we get what is traditionally termed the Bayes theorem:

$$p(\theta_i \mid X_1) = \frac{p(X_1 \mid \theta_i)p(\theta_i)}{p(X_1)}$$

The denominator component, $p(X_1)$, is a constant and, as the total of the joint probabilities, serves only to ensure that the individual posterior probabilities sum to one. On the other hand, the conditional probability, $p(X_1 \mid \theta_i)$, is an important element that appears in many applications. Most commonly, it is termed the *likelihood function*.

Neither classical nor Bayesian statisticians would have difficulty with the problem we analyzed as it was stated. Ultimately, however, what separates Bayesian statisticians from others is their use of $p(\theta_i)$. Classical statistics does not include the prior probability distribution into the decision-making process; decisions are derived only from the information at hand. Bayesians, however, view the information in the prior distribution to be crucial to the inferential process. Most classical statisticians do not disagree with this approach in principle, since the essential logic underlying Bayes's theorem is unassailable. The major point of contention, however, is that in most applications, the $p(\theta_i)$ do not have a firm empirical estimate. Under these circumstances, the Bayesians substitute "judgment" or subjective knowledge for known probabilities. It is this "guesstimation" process that irks the opposition. The Bayesians argue that this subjectivity is no different from the subjectivity that goes into deciding what is an appropriate alpha level. Further, they note that to be used fairly, the $p(\theta_i)$ need to be specified beforehand instead of after the fact.

Where the $p(\theta_i)$ can be stated with some level of precision, the Bayesian approach often has the advantage of producing smaller standard errors and narrower confidence intervals than its classical counterpart. Where the $p(\theta_i)$ are difficult to specify precisely, Bayesian analyses often differ very little from their classical counterparts. Unfortunately, in many circumstances a misspecification of the prior distribution can generate grossly misleading results.

Throughout this book we will discuss situations in which the Bayesian approach is clearly superior to that provided by classical statistics. One particularly effective application is that involving the analysis of missing data, where the ability of the researcher to bring prior knowledge to bear can result in substantial improvements in our estimates.

Likelihood Ratio Tests

Another approach to the problem of competing hypotheses that has gained many adherents in recent years is what may be termed the *likelihood* approach. This method is again referred to as an posteriori model because the judgment of acceptability is usually made after the data have been viewed rather than beforehand. Unlike the Bayesians, who focus on $p(\theta_i)$, the primary concern for likelihood theorists is the conditional probability $p(X \mid \theta_i)$. The likelihood approach starts with the assumption that while several hypotheses may be credible, in that their null forms have been rejected, some are more credible than others. For example, a criminologist may start with two "competing" working hypotheses concerning the relationship between economic circumstance and crime. Practically, the first hypothesis is based on the argument of necessity (that people steal because they are in need); the second hypotheses is based on the argument of want (that people steal because they feel unjustly deprived in comparison to others).

The criminological literature contains studies in which the null forms of both these hypotheses have been rejected. Thus, the logical conclusion is that both working hypotheses are true. Ignoring the thorny problem of contextual or interacting variables, we will assume that the researcher has to decide whether need or want is the more likely cause of crime. Under these circumstances, the researcher would probably look at the amount of variation explained by each hypothesis and assume that, while the null forms of both hypotheses have been rejected, the one that explains the most variation is most likely the correct explanation.

Thus, based on some appropriate statistic, the argument is made that one explanation has a greater likelihood of being correct than another. The likelihood approach can be extended to deal with any number of unsupported nulls and is able to provide a quantifiable assessment of relative credibility among the working hypotheses by comparing their relative likelihoods.

Within statistics, the *law of likelihood* (Hacking, 1965: 71) formally states that "if *h* and *i* are simple joint propositions included in the joint proposition *e*, then *e* supports *h* better than *i* if the likelihood ratio of *h* to *i* exceeds 1." Or put in more direct terms, "*d* supports *h* better than *i* whenever the likelihood ratio of *h* to *i* given *d* exceeds 1."

Likelihood ratio tests are most commonly found in applications of model building, where one explanation or model can often be subsumed by another. For example, when a researcher is comparing a series of logistic or log-linear models, many subsets of the model are statistically significant. The researcher, however, usually chooses to "go with" the model that generates the highest likelihood ratio in comparison to some base model. An example of the likelihood approach to hypothesis testing is outlined in Chapter 11, when the issue of assessing the goodness of fit of structural equation models is addressed.

The use of both likelihood and Bayesian approaches has increased substantially in the last 30 years and will undoubtedly become more prominent in the future. Many researchers currently see the likelihood ratio approach as an extension of the classical PN model. The Bayesian perspective has been slower to make inroads but has a great deal of intuitive appeal. One major problem with many Bayesian analyses is the lack of available software. For those not versed in Bayesian analysis, however, there is no immediate cause for alarm. Except where the various H_k can be specified with a high level of precision, the results of Bayesian and classical analyses tend not to differ by very much. Thus, while the theoretical differences are profound, the practical ones tend not to be.

Statistical Decision Making

Despite the critical problems associated with classical statistics, we will pursue the discussion of hypothesis testing within the PN approach throughout the rest of this chapter. We do this for many reasons. The pragmatic one noted in the last paragraph is probably sufficient, but there are further considerations. The primary purpose of this chapter is to explore the fundamentals of hypothesis testing, and an a priori approach is a good starting point. Besides, where one is totally ignorant of the prior probability distribution, the Bayesian approach clearly reduces to the classical one.[1] Second, the classical approach has become the received way of doing things in most circles, and where it has not, it is the starting point for the discussion of other models. Third, this approach is congruent with the simple binary decision-making process of accepting or rejecting a hypothesis and as such, simplifies the discussion of error types and statistical power.

Under the classical approach, we assume that some population parameter, θ, is given. Thus, the question becomes one of whether the sample data are drawn from

---

1. This should not be taken lightly. Contrary to the Bayesian belief that most scientists know something about what they study, many sociological articles justifying their existence with the cliché that "little or no research exists on this topic."

the population defined by θ. Once a particular null hypothesis has been formulated, it is necessary to decide whether this hypothesis is "true" or "false." Obviously, when we as researchers are faced with the available evidence, our goal is to accept true null hypotheses and reject false null hypotheses. Often, however, the wrong decision is made, and true null hypotheses are rejected and false ones accepted.

The situation faced by the researcher may be depicted as follows:

Researcher's decision

H_0 (Actual)	Reject H_0	Accept H_0
True	Type I or α-error	$1 - \alpha$
False	$1 - \beta$ or power of the test	Type II or β-error

The rejection of a true null hypothesis by the researcher leads to a Type I or α-error, while the acceptance of a false null hypothesis results in a Type II or β-error.

The α-error is directly under the control of the experimenter and is set a priori— before the analysis. This is the standard p-level for the statistical test. Since α is under direct control, so is $1 - \alpha$. The β or Type II error, on the other hand, is much more complicated, since β varies with α, the sample size, the specific statistical test used, the experimental design, and the magnitude of the effect. For a fixed sample size, as α is increased, β decreases, although the relationship is not linear or monotonic. While it is commonplace to put some thought into how small α should be, many researchers fail to realize that a very small α may have dire practical consequences. In medical research, for example, committing a Type II error may lead to failure to accept a valid treatment (H_0: the treatment has no effect), with unnecessarily high morbidity or mortality rates as a result. This could be especially worrisome for a treatment that is otherwise benign (i.e., has few or no side effects), since the practical cost of an α-error would be quite low.

Within the social sciences, concerns involving power became a major issue after Cohen (1962: 145–53) surveyed the articles published in the 1960 issue of the *Journal of Abnormal and Social Psychology*. The average power for the studies that appeared in that issue of the journal was estimated to be .48. This is an abysmally low figure, implying that if all the studies were replicated using the same procedures, only about half would result in the detection of an identifiable effect. Armed with this fact, we are not surprised by the observation that few replications are achieved in the social sciences. Interestingly, Sedlmeier and Gigerenzer (1989) examined the same journal in 1984 and estimated the average power to be roughly .50. Although these findings are based on studies published in a leading psychology journal, nonpsychology readers should not feel smug. Similar results have been found in surveys of published studies in sociology and evaluation research.

Other factors that influence the β-error are the sample size, the choice of test statistic, and the experimental design. Large Ns increase the accuracy of test statistics (ceteris paribus), thus increasing the power of the test.[2] Parametric statistics are

---

2. This fact has undoubtedly lulled many researchers who use large-scale survey samples into a false sense of security. Surely, it is often argued, a sample of 10,000 must have a power level

generally more powerful than nonparametric statistics because of the extra assumptions made about the sampling distribution of the error terms. Finally, the experimental design has a profound influence on power because it can (a) increase the accuracy of treatment effect estimates (through blocking or stratification), and (b) control for various biases affecting the internal and external validity of the study.

STATISTICAL POWER[3]

The consideration of statistical power is not simply an academic exercise. There are profound practical implications. Geoffrey Keppel (1991: 69) notes:

> Another reason for conducting a power analysis is to avoid wasting resources by performing experiments with too much power. Not only does an experiment with an excessively large sample size cost more in time and money than one with a more appropriate sample size, but also the conclusions drawn are often misleading.

As our decision table shows, the null hypothesis (H_0) may be either intrinsically true or false. Depending upon its condition in nature, a specific sample will belong to either the sampling distribution associated with a "true" H_0 or a "true" alternate, H_a. Unfortunately, the researcher has no prior way of knowing the distribution from which the sample is drawn.

Figure 4.1 presents an example of likely sampling distributions for the situations in which H_0 is true and H_a is true. Under H_0, the true population mean is μ_0, while under H_a, the true population mean is μ_a.

Figure 4.1. Sampling distributions under μ_0 and μ_α.

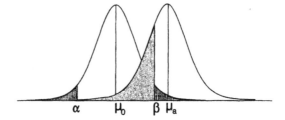

so high that it is not worth calculating. As we will see later, however, the same reasearchers often test models with 30 or 40 parameters, thereby voiding the ceteris paribus assumption.

3. Unfortunately, much statistical notation is specific to particular disciplines or authors; consequently, there little standardization. Throughout this book, we will attempt to adhere to the following rules whenever possible. Greek symbols (e.g., β, μ) are generally reserved for population parameters. Uppercase roman letters (e.g., X, Y) are used to depict population values. Thus, they are also used when variables are discussed in the abstract. Lowercase roman letters (e.g., x, y) generally refer to sample values. Boldface letters (e.g., $\mathbf{X}$, $\boldsymbol{\beta}$) denote either a matrix or a vector. A caret ($\hat{}$) above a letter also indicates an estimate.

Additional rules and definitions will be introduced when either convention dictates or confusion is possible. For example, the discussion on sampling in Chapters 5 and 6 requires an elaborated notation to avoid confusion. This is outlined in Table 5.2.

The hypothetical sampling distributions of $\overline{X} - \mu_0$ and $\overline{X} - \mu_a$ in Figure 4.1 are presented under the assumption that the $\overline{X}$ are $N \approx (0, \sigma/\sqrt{n})$ although the principle generalizes to any of the common sampling distributions (t, X^2, F, etc.). Again, the curve centered about μ_0 represents the sampling distribution given that the null hypothesis is true. The curve centered about μ_a represents the sampling distribution if the null hypothesis is false and the difference between the true population mean and the value μ_0 is greater than zero.

The symbol α, which appears in the left-hand tail of the distribution of μ_0, represents one half the α-level, or the Type I error. The symbol β, which appears in the left-hand tail of the distribution of μ_0 represents the other half the Type I error. It also represents the cumulative probability of committing a Type II error, with the Type II error probability being the area to the left of this point under the curve centered about μ_a. The area under the μ_a curve to the right of β represents the power of the statistical test.

Clearly if β is shifted to the right, the Type I or α-error will diminish but the magnitude of the Type II error will increase. Correspondingly, the power of the statistical test (assuming μ_a is true) will diminish. We can also see that the distribution under the normal curve is not constant over the entire range of X, since as the Type I error decreases (as β is moved more to the right) the Type II error increases disproportionately. To look at this from another perspective, by backing off from small α-levels in the extreme tails, disproportionate increases in the power of the test can be achieved.

The impact of the other major component of power analysis, the magnitude of the effect, is also illustrated by Figure 4.1. As the distance between μ_0 and μ_a increases, the overlap between the two curves will decrease. Clearly, as μ_a moves away from β, the probability of a Type II error will decrease and the power will increase. Ultimately, if the spread between μ_0 and μ_a is sufficiently great, the use of statistical tests becomes moot. On the other hand, where effect magnitudes are small, more sophisticated or "powerful" statistical procedures are required to detect them.

Estimating statistical power or the required sample size for a given situation generally requires either specialized software or a series of published tables. These tables present values for what are termed "noncentral" distributions (e.g., noncentral t, X^2, or F). The noncentrality parameter (usually signified by λ) represents the distance that the center of distribution under H_a (i.e., μ_a) is shifted away from μ_0. For those without access to the appropriate software, detailed tables for power analysis can be found in Cohen (1988) and Kraemer and Thiemann (1987).

In some respect, power analysis is in its infancy. Most discussions are tailored to designs in which the independent variables are fixed and the dependent variables are free, as is the case with designed experiments. Furthermore, it is generally assumed that the designs are reasonably balanced; that is, there are equal numbers of elements or subjects assigned to each condition. Situations of dependent variables that are allowed to vary (e.g., surveys) and considerable covariation among the independent variables have not been explored in significant detail. These latter situations typify research in sociology and economics. Fortunately, most sociologists and economists generally use sufficiently large sample sizes in their surveys to make the issue moot. This is not always the case, however, since even moderately complex designs can require samples in the tens if not hundreds of thousands to achieve a modicum of power.

For practical purposes, the power of a statistical test can be seen to depend on four items:

- the magnitude of the effect: that is, the difference between the value of the alternate hypothesis H_a (which is assumed to be true if H_0 is false) and the value of H_0
- the Type I, or α-error, level chosen by the researcher
- the variability in the population
- the size of the sample

The Normal Distribution

Estimating Statistical Power

The estimation of statistical power is perhaps best exemplified by the one-sample z-test. Assume, for a moment, that an instructor has given a similar introductory exam to classes of first-year students for several years. In the long run, it is noted that the mean score for this exam, μ, is 66, with a standard deviation, σ, of 12. Owing to the large number of students examined and the lengthy period covered by the exams, both quantities can be considered to be population values.

The exam is now given to a group of students who have not taken the course and wish to obtain advanced standing by challenging the course. Advanced standing will be given to students who pass the test. A group of 64 students writes the exam, and the mean score, $\overline{X}$, turns out to be 62. The instructor has two questions: Is this difference statistically significant, given a 5% chance of a Type I error? and What is the power of the statistical test?

EXAMPLE: USING THE ONE-SAMPLE Z-TEST

Since the population variance, σ^2, is known and the sample size is large ($n = 64$), it is decided that a one-sample z-test is appropriate in this instance. As a first step, the instructor estimates the standard error of μ as $\sigma/\sqrt{n}$. Thus,

$$SE(\mu) = \delta/\sqrt{n}$$

$$= 12/8 \ or \ 1.5$$

Given that the students did not actually take the course, but were attempting to obtain advanced standing, it was assumed that the group mean would be *less* than the population mean. Consequently, the instructor chose to go with a one-tailed test. Checking a table of normal deviates, the z-value corresponding to an α-level of .05 in the left-hand tail is -1.65. Thus, a one-tailed, 95% confidence interval for the mean is estimated as:

$$\mu + z_\alpha[SE(\mu)] = 66 - 1.65 \,(1.5)$$

$$= 66 - 2.48$$

$$= 63.52$$

Since the sample mean of 62 does not fall within the range of 63.5 to 66, we appear reasonable in concluding that the sample of students scored significantly lower than the overall population.

The likelihood of being incorrect in this assessment is the α-level of 5%. In this instance, however, we do not know the likelihood of a Type II error (and conversely the power). Nevertheless, the Type II or β-error can be estimated quite easily if we recognize that the lower bound chosen for μ is the cutoff for β under H_a. Under the distribution for H_a, the bound for β is:

$$z_\beta = \frac{63.52 - 62}{1.5}$$
$$= 1.01$$

The area under the curve between the sample mean and the cut point corresponding to a z-value of 1.01 is approximately .34. The area to the right of this is the β region, which is .50 − .34 or .16. Since $\beta = .16$, the power of the test is thus $1 - \beta = .84$. In this instance, the power of the test is reasonable. This is confirmed by the observation that the null hypothesis of no difference between the sample and population means was rejected.

Estimating Sample Size

In the preceding example, the issue was one of estimating the power of the test for a given α-level and sample size. We may also turn the question around and ask: For a given α-level and power, how large a sample do I need to detect a difference of a given magnitude? Thus, the course instructor in the preceding example might hypothesize that students who challenge a course will score an average of 4 points lower than the broader population of students.

Again, it is assumed that the parameters μ and σ are known. The instructor selects an α-level (say .05) and for convenience sake, is willing to accept a power level of .85. Since power is $1 - \beta$, the β-level is .15. Based on $\mu = 66$, the instructor wants to be able to detect an effect magnitude of at least 4 points; thus, the expected value for $\overline{X}$ is 62. Previously, we defined β as:

$$z_\beta = \frac{\overline{X}_L - \mu}{\sigma/\sqrt{n}}$$

where

$$\overline{X}_L = \overline{X} + z_\alpha \left[SE(\overline{X}) \right]$$
$$= \overline{X} + z_\alpha \left[\sigma/\sqrt{n} \right]$$

Combining these two equations, we get:

$$z_\beta = \frac{\overline{X} + z_\alpha(\sigma/\sqrt{n}) - \mu}{\sigma/\sqrt{n}}$$

Applying some basic algebra and rearranging a few terms, it is now an easy matter to find the required sample size, since:

$$n = \left[\frac{\sigma(z_\alpha - z_\beta)}{\overline{X} - \mu} \right]^2$$

EXAMPLE: USING THE ONE-SAMPLE Z-TEST (CONTINUED)

Following the preceding example, we note that $\sigma = 12$; $z_\alpha = -1.65$; $z_\beta = 1.02$; $\overline{X} = 62$, and $\mu = 66$. Thus, by substitution, we obtain:

$$n = \left(\frac{\sigma(z_\alpha - z_\beta)}{\overline{X} - \mu} \right)$$

$$= \left(\frac{12(-1.65 - 1.01)}{62 - 66} \right)^2$$

$$= 63.7$$

Rounding to the nearest whole number, we see that the required sample size to obtain a power level of .85 is 64 cases.

The formula above also helps us to see the relative influence of different components on either the power of the test, or the sample size. The first thing we might look at is the denominator, or the difference between $\overline{X}$ and μ. This difference is usually called the *magnitude* of the effect. All else being equal, the larger this difference (hence, the larger the magnitude), the smaller the required sample size needed to attain a given level of power. Conversely, small differences require large samples in order for us to be able to detect them.

Another factor to be considered is the alpha-or Type I error level chosen by the researcher. Small α-levels translate into large z-values; larger α-levels relate to small z-values. A small z-value (i.e., a large α-level) reduces the size of the numerator, thus again allowing for a smaller sample size for a given power level. The same functional relationship holds for the z-value corresponding to the Type II error. Small β-errors, or large power requirements, generate large corresponding z-values. Again, with all else being equal, when a large z_β is added to the numerator, the sample size will increase.

The *t*-Distribution

Estimating Statistical Power

The preceding section dealt with power estimation based on the normal distribution. The same general issues apply to other distributions such as the *t*-distribution. Unfortunately, the estimate of power under the *t*-distribution is more complicated than under the normal distribution. The difficulty arises because if H_a is true rather than H_0, the *t*-distribution will be centered over H_0 rather than H_a. This shifting of the center of t requires that we use the *noncentral t-distribution*. Because of the shift in the anchor point of this distribution, another parameter is required to identify the location of the distribution, and this is the noncentrality parameter, λ. Formally, λ is the standardized difference between the expected means μ_a and μ_0 under the alternate and null hypotheses respectively. That is:

$$\lambda = \left| \frac{\mu_a - \mu_0}{\sigma} \right|$$

Estimating the points for the noncentral t-distribution is reasonably complex; however, there are many statistical programs available, plus sources of printed tables.[4]

Where the degrees of freedom associated with the test are not too small (usually more than 10), it is possible to use a transformation of t based on the normal distribution to estimate the power of the t-test. Specifically, β is associated with the z-value found by:

$$z = \frac{t_c - \lambda}{\sqrt{1 + (t_c^2/2v)}}$$

Here, λ is the noncentrality parameter as defined above; t_c is the t-value of the central or standard t-distribution (the "critical value") with v degrees of freedom for the specified α-level.

EXAMPLE: ORGANIZING MATERIAL AND EXAM OUTCOMES

As an example, let us look at a study by Scandura and Wells (1967). These authors were interested in knowing whether exposure to organizing material before reading a 1000-word essay in mathematical topology had an impact on their performance. Fifty college students were randomly assigned to two groups of 25. One group was exposed to the "organizer"; the other group was asked to read an essay on Euler and Riemann. Each group was asked to answer several questions after having read the essay on topology. The dependent variable was the number of correct answers given to the questions. Briefly, the results were as follows:

	GROUP 1 (EXPERIMENTAL)	GROUP 2 (CONTROL)
n	25	25
$\overline{X}$	7.65	6.00
s^2	6.50	5.90

Given the small sample size, this question is clearly amenable to analysis through a two-sample t-test. Formally, we may state the null hypothesis as $H_0 : \mu_1 - \mu_2 = 0$. Selecting an α-level of .05, the test may be constructed as follows:

---

4. BMDP has kindly put a program called SOLO Calculator into the public domain. This program calculates areas under the curve and the inverse for various distributions (z, t, F, X^2, etc.) including a number of noncentral distributions. BMDP also distributes an excellent power analysis program called SOLO Power Analysis.

$$t = \frac{(\overline{X}_1 - \overline{X}_2) - (\mu_1 - \mu_2)}{\sigma_{\text{diff}}}$$

$$= \frac{7.65 - 6.00}{\sqrt{\dfrac{24(6.5) + 24(5.90)}{25 + 25 - 2}\left(\dfrac{1}{25} + \dfrac{1}{25}\right)}}$$

$$= \frac{1.65}{.704}$$

$$= 2.34$$

This value is compared with $|t_{48,.05}| = 1.68$ for a one-tailed test and $|t_{48,.05/2}| = 2.01$ for a two-tailed test. Since the calculated t-value is greater than the absolute critical t value, we reject the null hypothesis and assume that the difference between the two groups is a consequence of exposure to the treatment.

To estimate the power of this test, we must first estimate the noncentrality parameter, λ. Specifically,

$$\lambda = \left| \frac{(\overline{X}_1 - \overline{X}_2) - (\mu_1 - \mu_2)}{\sigma_{\text{diff}}} \right|$$

Again, using $\alpha = .05$ (one-tail), we can calculate the z-value for the β-error by:

$$z = \frac{t_c - \lambda}{\sqrt{1 + t_c^2/2v}}$$

$$= \frac{1.68 - 2.34}{\sqrt{1 + (1.68)^2/96}}$$

$$= \frac{-.66}{\sqrt{1.03}}$$

$$= -.65$$

The area to the left of $z = -.65$ is the β area, .26. Since the power of the test is $1 - \beta$, the power in this instance is approximately .74. If we wished to estimate the power based on a two-tailed test, the value of t_c would become 2.01 above rather than 1.68. This would produce a power estimate of .63.

Estimating Sample Size

Estimating the required sample size for a given effect magnitude, power, and α-level can be done by working backward from the preceding solution. Specifically,

$$\because z = \frac{t_c - \lambda}{\sqrt{1 + t_c^2/2v}}$$

$$\therefore v = \frac{t_c^2 z^2}{2\left[z^2 - (\lambda - t_c)^2\right]}$$

Since v (the degrees of freedom) was defined as $n_1 + n_2 - 2$, the estimated sample size should be $v + 2$. While estimating sample size by hand is possible, one is best advised to use a statistical program designed for the purpose. The main reason for this (besides reducing the likelihood of arithmetic error) is that most published tables for t and z have limited precision. Inaccurate estimates of t and z can result in relatively large errors in the estimated sample size.

The F-distribution

Few practical research problems involve simple situations in which the research merely compares a sample mean against a population mean or two sample means. More often, we are concerned with multivariate cases, where several means simultaneously, are to be compared or we wish to consider several independent variables. Analyses of this type are most often conducted with reference to the F-distribution. Two "typical" cases are discussed in this section, the first being a one-way ANOVA with four groups; the second, a regression equation with four independent variables.

One-Way ANOVA

Generally, the first statistical problem one faces in power analysis is obtaining an estimate of the magnitude of the effect. This is generally best done by examining similar research or by conducting a pilot study. Since scale makes a difference, it is generally necessary to standardize differences by dividing by the standard error of the estimate (square root of the MSE). Following Cohen's (1969, 1988) notation, (where m is used for $\overline{X}$) for the two-category situation, we may calculate the standardized difference between two means as:

$$d = \frac{m_1 - m_2}{\sigma}$$

It is clear from this formula that the value d is a z-score. The σ in the denominator is the common within group standard deviation.

In the more generalized situation with k treatment groups, where $k \geq 2$, the spread in group means is represented not by a range across means but by the variation among the means. Cohen defines this magnitude statistic as f, where[5]:

$$f = \frac{\sigma_m}{\sigma}$$

where for equal n in the groups,

$$\sigma_m = \sqrt{\frac{\sum_{i=1}^{k}(m_i - m)^2}{k}}$$

Here the m_i are the category means and m is the grand mean, or for equal ns, the mean of the means.

---

5. To avoid confusion, we will use italics for Cohen's f and present the standard f-ratio as a roman letter (f).

One advantage of using f is that it is closely related to the noncentrality parameter, λ, which defines the anchor point for the noncentral F-distribution.[6] That is, λ is the expected population value (i.e., the μ_a in Figure 4.1) about which the sampling distribution is distributed when H_a is true. The relationship between f and λ is given by:

$$f = \frac{\lambda}{\sqrt{n}} \qquad \text{and} \qquad \lambda = f\sqrt{n}$$

EXAMPLE: AN ANOVA ANALYIS OF FOUR EXAM TYPES

Here we have four test groups, G1 through G4 (Table 4.1). The groups may represent one of four exam types to which students are randomly assigned. G1 might be a multiple choice exam, G2 a short-answer exam, G3 an essay-type exam, and G4 a "mixed" exam containing elements of the other types. The null hypothesis is that there is no difference in the students' performance across exam type; the working hypothesis is that differences will exist, although at this time we are not sure of the exact outcome pattern. Each group has 8 observations; therefore, we have a simple, balanced, one-way ANOVA.

A priori, it is decided to use an alpha level of .05. These data may be analyzed in the standard fashion, with the results reported in Table 4.2.

Clearly, the F-ratio is significant at the specified alpha level; therefore, we reject the null hypothesis of no difference across the means. We might be interested, however, in assessing the statistical power of this experiment. The proportion of variance explained, η^2, is 114.375/429.875 or approximately 0.226. η is approximately 0.516.

The effect magnitude, f, can be estimated from the group means and the summary ANOVA table. The numerator, σ_m, becomes $[(22.75 - 25.44)^2 + (28.00 - 25.44)^2 +$

Table 4.1. Data on four exam types

	G1	G2	G3	G4
	25	28	29	28
	21	29	26	24
	22	30	30	27
	20	26	20	27
	26	25	25	17
	26	28	20	21
	19	30	30	30
	23	28	28	26
Mean	22.75	28.0	26.0	25.0
Grand mean	25.44			

6. It should be noted that Cohen actually uses ϕ in lieu of λ Since λ is used more commonly to denote the noncentrality parameter in the current statistical literature, we will follow that convention.

Table 4.2. Summary ANOVA table for four-exam problem

SOURCE	SUM-OF-SQUARES	DF	MEAN-SQUARE	F-RATIO	P-VALUE
Treatment	114.375	3.	38.125	3.384	0.032
Error	315.500	28.	11.268		
Total	429.875	31			

$(26.00 - 25.44)^2 + (25.00 - 25.44)^2]^{1/2} = 1.89$. The denominator, σ, is simply the square root of the mean squared error, or $\sqrt{11.268} = 3.36$. Thus, $f = 1.89/3.36 = .56$. By using either a set of tables (e.g., Cohen) or an appropriate computer program, we discover that for $\alpha = .05$; degrees of freedom $= 3, 28$, and $f = .56$; the power level is approximately .70.

Distribution of Effects

The value σ_m represents the square root of the *mean squared difference* of the column means about the grand mean m. For a particular situation, it may not make sense to use the mean deviations about the grand mean. Instead, we may wish to focus on different patterns of distributions for the m_i. Let us return to the simple case of two categories. Here, the statistic, d, was defined as:

$$d = \frac{m_1 - m_2}{\sigma}$$

For any group of k means, the values m_1 and m_2 may be replaced by the minimum and maximum values among the m_i. Thus, we may write:

$$d = \frac{m_{max} - m_{min}}{\sigma}$$

Within that range of d, however, the other means may be distributed in any number of patterns.

Cohen (1969: 270) presents three situations that he identifies as minimum, intermediate, and maximum variability. Specifically, he defines these patterns as:

- **Minimum variability**: one mean at each end of d, the remaining $k - 2$ means all at the midpoint.
- **Intermediate variability**: the k means are equally spaced over d.
- **Maximum variability**: the means are all at the end points of d.

For the first scenario (minimum variability) f relates to d as:

$$f_1 = d\sqrt{\frac{1}{2k}}$$

For the second scenario (intermediate variability) f relates to d as:

$$f_2 = \frac{d}{2}\sqrt{\frac{k+1}{3(k-1)}}$$

Finally, for the third scenario (maximum variability) f relates to d differentially according to whether k is even or odd. When k is even, we have:

$$f_3 = \frac{d}{2}$$

but when k is odd:

$$f_3 = d\frac{\sqrt{k^2-1}}{2k}$$

The distributions underlying these three patterns of variability are somewhat easier to understand in a graphic format. In Figure 4.2, the three ideal types are presented with minimum variability showing a clustering of the means around the grand mean, medium variability showing a fairly even dispersion of the means, and maximum variability illustrated by a clustering of means at the ends of the distribution.

Thus, using the preceding example, where $k = 4$, for differing distributions of the sample means, we obtain, first, for minimum variability,

$$f_1 = d\sqrt{\frac{1}{2k}d}$$

$$= \sqrt{\frac{1}{8}}$$

$$= .55$$

and for medium variability,

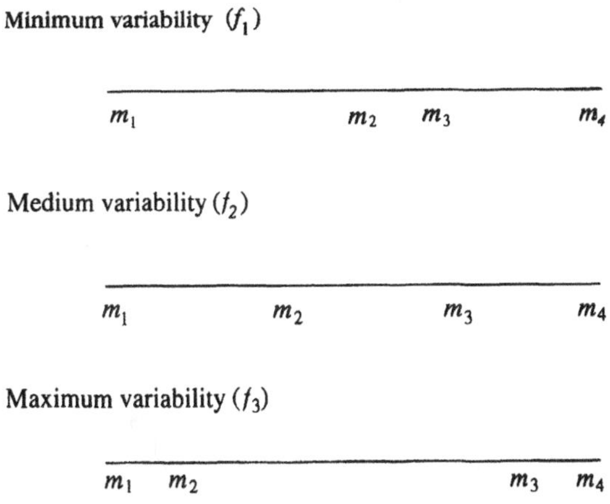

Figure 4.2. Illustrations of three classes of variability (f).

Minimum variability (f_1)

m_1 m_2 m_3 m_4

Medium variability (f_2)

m_1 m_2 m_3 m_4

Maximum variability (f_3)

m_1 m_2 m_3 m_4

$$f_2 = \frac{d}{2}\sqrt{\frac{k+1}{3(k-1)}}$$

$$= \frac{d}{2}\sqrt{\frac{5}{9}}$$

$$= d(.037)$$

whereas for maximum variability,

$$f_3 = d, \text{ since } k \text{ is even}$$

In this situation the group means of 22.75, 25, 26, and 28 appear to be reasonably evenly distributed across the entire range. Thus, f_2 would appear most appropriate. For this situation,

$$d = \frac{m_{max} - m_{min}}{\sigma}$$

$$= \frac{28 - 22.75}{3.36}$$

$$= 1.56$$

thus, $f_2 = (1.56)(0.037) = .58$. This value is only slightly higher than the original effect magnitude of .56.

Regression

For both the traditional ANOVA situation and the regression approach to the GLM, the proportion of variance explained can be estimated. In ANOVA, this term is usually identified as eta-squared, η^2; in the regression approach, we refer to R^2. It can be shown that for the general case:

$$f = \sqrt{\frac{\eta^2}{1 - \eta^2}}$$

or

$$f = \sqrt{\frac{R^2}{1 - R^2}}$$

EXAMPLE: ANOVA ANALYSIS OF FOUR EXAM TYPES (CONTINUED)

In our original ANOVA example, the value for η^2 was estimated at 0.226; therefore, $f = .60$. Again, this value of f is similar to our estimate of f based on σ_m/σ and f_2. With $\alpha = .05$; degrees of freedom = 3, 28, and $f = .60$, the power level is estimated to be approximately .77.

Estimating Sample Size

Calculating estimated sample sizes under the noncentral F-distribution is quite complex and generally involves some form of iterative procedure. There are, however, several excellent statistical programs that can do these estimations.

A feel for the relationship between sample size and required power for a given alpha level can be obtained by inspecting Figure 4.3. The main feature of the curves in Figure 4.3 is that they level out fairly quickly at a reasonably low sample size.

FINAL CONSIDERATIONS

Different statistical tests have different power functions. Some tests are relatively powerful with small Ns; others are most powerful compared with other tests with large samples. The relative power of one test to another is termed *power efficiency*. The power efficiency of a test is the power of a test compared with its most powerful alternative. In concrete terms, this implies that a test with a 90% power efficiency would require a sample of 100 cases to achieve the power level of the most powerful test with 90 cases.

Excepting broad generalities, it is difficult to rank-order tests as to their power efficiency because the power curves for a particular test can change radically with different magnitudes or sample sizes. Thus, it is possible for one test to be more powerful than another for small samples but not for large samples. Also in specific circumstances, nonparametric tests can be more powerful than parametric tests.

When considering the issue of power in planning a research design, the best strategy is to obtain a good power analysis program and explore several scenarios based on different tests, sample sizes, alpha levels, and other factors that affect power. The text by Kraemer and Thiemann (1987) is a good starting point for comparing many tests, particularly nonparametric tests. Kraemer and Thiemann's approach, however,

Figure 4.3. Power vs. sample size under the F-distribution.

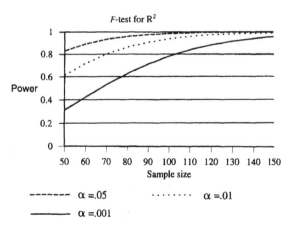

is to take advantage of normal approximations for many tests they consider. It is also possible to approach the power issue through simulation. While simulation procedures may be very computer intensive, the wholesale availability of powerful microcomputers removes many practical impediments that limited the usefulness of this procedure in the past. As Noreen (1989) has clearly shown, simulation procedures can be relatively easy to cary out, are immensely flexible, and are ideal solutions for dealing with tests for which the sampling distribution is unknown.[7]

Generally, *pure* or academic research is conservative with respect to rejecting the null hypothesis. This institutionalized conservativism is designed to limit the generation of incorrect and spurious explanations. On the other hand, it must be recognized that both society and the individual researcher expend considerable resources on social science research. Structuring a research project where a true working hypothesis has almost no chance of being considered is a tragic waste of effort. The obverse side of the coin is also true. Studies that entail too much power are a waste of resources. Too much power usually means more subjects than necessary, which incurs extra expenses and unnecessarily inconveniences people.

Ultimately, the question that might be asked is: What is a reasonable level of power? Just as with setting α-levels, setting a β-level involves many issues, not the least of which are the resources available to the researcher, the inconvenience accorded the subjects involved and the practical implications of errors of both types. Sadly, α-levels of .05 and .01 have become ritual practice throughout the social sciences, and journal editors and reviewers are often loath to accept studies with more liberal Type I error potentials—even if they do enhance the power of the study. Setting a rule of thumb for an acceptable power level is fraught with similar threats. Still, it would be encouraging to see most studies striving for a power level of .80 or greater.

Research into statistical power is expanding dramatically. Given our present understanding of the phenomenon, there is one significant stumbling block in extending power analysis to complex multivariate procedures. That stumbling block is the necessity of estimating σ^2 and the magnitude of the effect(s) a priori. In any complex design, multiple estimates of the magnitudes of the effects will exist, and likely significant difficulties will arise in estimating σ^2. While theoretical solutions to many power problems may be some time in coming, achieving practical solutions through simulation modeling is often possible.

Further Reading

Cohen, J. *Statistical Power Analysis*, 2nd ed. Hillsdale, NJ: Erlbaum, 1988. Considered to be the classical statement on power analysis for social scientists, Cohen's book contains numerous examples and detailed tables and graphs for determining power and sample size.

---

7. See, in particular, Noreen's Appendix 2A for a discussion of power considerations for approximate randomisation tests and more standard nonparametric tests.

Hacking, I. *Logic of Statistical Inference*. Cambridge University Press, 1965. This book provides a nonmathematical overview of various schools of statistics. Hacking's own bias is toward likelihood ratio procedures, which he supports quite admirably.

Kraemer, H. C., and Thiemann, S. *How Many Subjects? Statistical Power Analysis in Research*. Newbury Park, CA: Sage, 1987. A readable and practical introduction to power analysis. This is a good starting point for those who do not have ready access to a computer program for doing sample size and power analysis.

5

Sampling: Basic Statistics

The tendency of the casual mind is to pick out or stumble upon a sample which supports or defies its prejudices, and then to make it the representative of a whole class.

—Walter Lippmann

Regardless of the process used for collecting data, some strategy is required for deciding which units ought to be measured and included in a study and which ones ought to be excluded. This selection process is known as sampling. In the abstract, sampling is a simple process consisting of two components. The first component is the selection process that tells us how individual observations or elements are to be selected. The second component tells us how to make inferences from the characteristics of the chosen elements to the larger population from which they are selected. The two processes are not independent, since different selection procedures imply modifications to the inferential process, and concerns with inference instruct our selection procedures.

In this chapter the focus is on some basic statistical concepts as they apply to commonly encountered sampling strategies. We introduce a standard notation, as well as a number of elementary statistical approaches that allow for inferential conclusions. Chapter 6 will examine a number of common sampling plans and several approaches to the conduct of survey research. Chapter 7 in this sequence on sampling will address some common difficulties that arise in applied sampling.

STATISTICAL BASICS[1]

The first question one might ask is: Why should we sample? Frequently, sampling is a less desirable procedure for data collection, second to measuring the entire population. Conducting a census is either impossible or impractical for many reasons, however. Among those commonly cited are the cost involved in measuring an entire population (monetary and temporal), the logistics, the intrusiveness of the measurement procedure, and possible damage to the measured units. Ultimately, we accept sampling as a necessary compromise that may allow us to make an inferential statement about the population from which the sample was drawn.

Since sampling is a compromise based on expediency, we must first decide how good the sample needs to be. Sampling plans vary as to accuracy and, generally

---

1. Classical texts here are: Kish (1965), Hansen, Hurwitz, and Madow (1953), and Cochran (1977). Also see: Krishnaiah and Rao (1988), Thompson (1992), and Sudman (1976).

speaking, the more accurate a sample is, the more expensive it will be. In some applications such as the Canadian Labour Force Surveys, a high degree of accuracy is required to estimate worker participation and unemployment rates within a tenth of a percentage point.

On the other hand, exploratory surveys and some general-purpose surveys are "good enough" if they are accurate within ±20%, 85 or 90 times out of 100. Obviously, as researchers, we want results that are accurate enough to be worthwhile, but we do not want to waste resources in attempting to obtain more accuracy than a project requires. It must also be kept in mind that measurement is generally an intrusive enterprise and people have a right to their privacy. Surveys that are needlessly at the extremes of the accuracy continuum present unwarranted intrusions in people's lives and as such, ought to pose an ethical problem for the researcher. If a high level of accuracy is required but the resources are not available, the researcher should either consider an alternate strategy (such as downscaling the project) or put off the project until a later date. As Sudman (1976: 9) states: "Almost all researchers will agree that a small study well-designed and executed is superior to a large study that has been botched." Sudman also rather poignantly continues, "Frequently, research is labeled as 'exploratory' merely to protect it from criticism directed against a poorly designed or executed sample."

Before starting any survey then, the researcher should seriously consider the ethical issues surrounding his or her proposed intrusion. This consideration can be helped a great deal if the researcher provides a clear statement of the objectives and implications of the study, identifies the required level of accuracy, and clearly lists the resources that are available for getting the job done. If, having considered this information, the researcher still agrees that the project is warranted, this information will greatly help in developing the most appropriate sampling strategy.

Inference

One of the first issues raised when a sample is to be drawn is that of how the sample ought to be selected. In our day-to-day lives we continuously come across applications of sampling. At a grocery store, for example, we might select one grape from a bunch to judge the sweetness of the whole. The sampling procedure we use is judgmental, based on convenience, fortuitousness, or selectivity. We might, for example, choose the smallest grape on the bunch based on the assumption that it is likely the least developed and consequently, the least sweet. Or, we might pick a grape in the middle of the bunch on the assumption that it is "most typical" of the remaining grapes. Outside the grocery store we might be accosted by a "market researcher" soliciting opinions on sour grapes. The surveyor's selection of respondents is based on a convenience sample—whoever is willing to respond is included in the sample. Unknown to us, the solicitor may have been asked to select a quota sample, in which a fixed number of men or women or people of another identifiable characteristic were to be chosen for the survey.

While this approach *may* produce usable results for the surveyor, such judgmental sampling procedures are not open to quantitative assessment. That is, there is no way to assess the validity of the inferences drawn from such samples, nor is it possible to estimate their precision. It is only by conducting a scientific sample that we can have any measurable confidence in the estimates and conclusions we draw from the sample.

For a sampling procedure to be minimally scientific, it must be based on a random sampling procedure that is independent of the volition or wishes of the sampler or the respondents. Furthermore, the likelihood of selection for each element in the population must be known (or at least knowable) and nonzero. These conditions lead to the selection of what is termed a *probability sample*. When all the elements and all combinations of elements in the population of interest have an equal probability of inclusion in the sample, the sample is known as a *simple random sample*, or srs. Normally, such a sample is selected by using a random number generator.

Many sample surveys that come to our attention are not probability samples. For example, readership surveys by magazines that ask readers to respond with a mail-in form are not probability samples. It is not possible to know what the probabilities of selection are among those who choose both to read a particular magazine and to respond to its queries. Thus, certain readers' attitudes toward their spouses, their sex lives, space aliens, or the president of the United States give us little insight about how the general population views these phenomena.

Within a true srs, each element has an equal probability of selection. This, however, is not a prerequisite for a probability sample. Elements may have unequal probabilities of selection if the selection probabilities are *known*. For example, for a consumer survey of cosmetics, one might wish to oversample women in comparison to men. If the women in the sampling frame are twice as likely to be selected as men, then for the tabulation of the results, the sampled womens' responses should be weighted by one half. When responses are weighted by the inverse of the selection probabilities, the sample results can be corrected to the respondent's actual distribution within the population. Samples in which the sampled elements are likely to be selected in the same proportion as they appear in the population are known as self-weighting samples. Samples with differential likelihoods of selection for the elements are known as weighted samples.

The use of a probability sample allows us to estimate the precision of whatever statistic we wish to estimate—such as a mean, proportion, or total. The bases of the determination of the precision of an estimate are the *law of large numbers* and the *central limit theorem*. Thus for any nontrivial sample (nonsmall ns), the central limit theorem (CLT) allows us to form a confidence interval around a sample estimate that will likely include the population parameter with a specifiable or known chance of error. Convenience sampling and other judgmental approaches cannot appeal to the CLT and, consequently, the precision of any statistic that might be generated from the results cannot be estimated.

The selection of a scientific sample does not necessarily mean that the results we obtain will be useful—the resulting estimates may simply be too imprecise for our purposes. For example, a survey that estimates the proportion of women in the United States as 51% plus or minus 10% is of little practical use. However, the selection of a probability sample enables us to make that determination. Nonscientific samples are not open to such an assessment. Researchers who rely on nonscientific samples are like the proverbial ostrich who puts faith in the adage that ignorance is bliss.

Basic Notions

As with any scientific endeavor, it is essential to start by defining the basic terms. Sampling is best understood as relationships between sets. In set theory, the primary unit of analysis is the "element." An element is the simplest, most basic observational unit. Elements could represent anything from human beings to grapes to grains of sand on the beach.

It is useful, however, to consider different aggregations of elements (sets) and to look at the relationship among those aggregations. In sampling, we often refer to three hierarchical and subsuming sets: universes (or superpopulations), populations, and samples.

- **Universe or superpopulation**: a theoretical infinity of all elements that might exist throughout all time–space coordinates; "all humanity."
- **Population**: the set of all elements bounded by a particular set of time–space coordinates; for example, all people living within the geographical boundaries of Uganda on July 1, 1991. The observation and measurement of an entire population is called a census.
- **Sample**: a subset of a population chosen according to some procedure that allows for the observation and measurement of elements fewer than the population.

For all practical purposes, there should be a close correspondence between the universe and the population. The two concepts should not be taken as identical, however, since the universe defines a theoretical concept while the population defines an operational entity.

The relationship between the universe and the population parallels the discussion in Chapter 2, where our attention was drawn to the relationship between a theoretical model and its empirical referents. An understanding of the distinction between the universe and the population does allow for greater understanding of the problem some researchers face when deciding how statistics based on populations should be treated.

Some researchers argue that statistical analysis performed on population data should be limited to descriptive statistics alone. The essence of the argument is that if the data are truly population data, then any characteristics calculated from the population data constitute "real" relationships (point estimates, differences, correlations, etc.) and are not subject to sampling variation. Often this argument is invoked when official statistics that purport to measure the entirety of events are analyzed, or when the population under analysis is small. By appealing to the concept of the universe or superpopulation, it is possible to recognize that what we believe to be a population is but one possible manifestation of a broader possible set of theoretical outcomes—that is, outcomes that might be observed on different occasions (other than on census day, or at the end of the fiscal year) or in different places. From this perspective, it makes sense to conduct statistical tests on data that may be defined as constituting a population.

A more compelling reason for *not* doing statistical analysis on population data stems, not from the idea that any data set designated as a population provides a "true" parameter measure, but from the practical problem inherent in large numbers. If an empirically defined population is large (such as the population of the United States on census day), then any estimate of the standard error will lead to values that are so trivial as to be of no practical value. The normal formula for the standard error of the mean is $s/\sqrt{n}$. Consider how small this value would be if n were the size of a city (possible of a million inhabitants) or a country (of 50–200 million inhabitants). Clearly, conducting inferential statistics on population data makes practical sense only if the population is relatively small.

Other important concepts that are central to the understanding of basic sampling include the following:

- **Sample frame**: a complete listing of the population from which the sample of interest is to be drawn. If there is no preexisting frame, it is impossible to determine the probability of selection for any given element; hence, the precision of our statistics cannot be estimated.
- **Sampling units**: the basic observational units on which upon which the measurements are taken. Sampling units contain elements and are used for selecting elements into the sample. If there is one element per unit, we use the term "element sampling." Where natural groupings of elements occur, such as in a household or in a school classroom, the sampling units are called "clusters."

Drawing a Sample

To reiterate, two sets of rules are needed when we conduct research with samples: one for drawing a sample and another for making inferences back to the parent population. For "scientific" samples, the first set of rules generally implies that the primary sampling units are drawn on some probabilistic basis using impartial rules. That is, they are drawn independent of the researcher's volition by some "impartial," mechanical procedure following some predetermined probability distribution (see Box 5.1). *Where every element in a population has an equal probability of selection, and every combination of elements has an equal likelihood of selection*, a special form of sample known as a simple random sample (srs) is produced.

The second set of rules corresponds to the rules of statistical inference, which should be familiar to readers through their exposure to statistical techniques.

The basic principles behind drawing an srs apply whatever actual procedure is used to collect the data (e.g., telephone surveys, face-to-face interviews, mail). Essentially, in drawing an srs there are four steps to follow:

- List all of the elements in the population from 1 to N.
- Decide on the required sample size (see Chapter 4).
- Using either a table of random numbers or a random number generator, select n uniform random numbers between 1 and N.
- Select the elements indicated by the n random numbers and conduct the survey.

Simple random samples come in two variants: sampling with replacement and sampling without replacement. In sampling with replacement, any selected elements are returned or *replaced* in the original frame for further possible selection. This may lead

■ **Box 5.1**

RANDOM NUMBERS

Traditionally, researchers used published lists of random numbers to draw a random sample. Today, researchers use "random number generators" that are included with most statistical software. These utilities generate uniform random numbers between 0 and 1. Most will also generate numbers based on some other sampling distribution, such as the normal (z), the F, or the χ^2 distribution.

Most computer-generated numbers are not *true* random numbers but what we term *pseudo*random numbers. The algorithms that generate these numbers are deterministic, since the same seed or starting value will reproduce the series. The generated numbers are called random numbers because they behave *as if* they were truly random. That is, they pass certain statistical tests for the overall shape of the distribution, the number of runs in the series, and so on. Typically, pseudorandom number generators are based on the random rounding error that occurs when calculations are performed at or beyond the precision of a computer.

Most pseudorandom number generators are good enough for practical purposes, although problems can arise when small samples are generated. A common problem, for example, is that a small series of random numbers will have longer sequential runs of numbers (e.g., 1,2,3, . . . ; 23,24,25, . . .) than would generally occur by chance alone.

Some statistical packages can select a random sample simply by specifying the proportion of elements or the exact number to be chosen. Most packages, however, allow the researcher control over the distribution from which the random numbers are generated and the actual selection of the sample.

to selected elements being chosen subsequently, in which instance the duplicated case is simply counted or weighted by the number of times it is chosen. The advantage of sampling with replacement is that the probabilities of selection remain constant over all selections. In sampling without replacement, the probabilities of selection for later selected elements increase. For example, consider a population with five elements. On the first selection each element has a .20 probability of selection. If the first element is not replaced, the second selection is based on the remaining elements, each having a .25 probability of selection, and so on.

For extremely large populations from which a modest sample is to be selected (such as a market survey of a sample of 1000 from a population of 100,000), the issue of sampling with or without replacement becomes moot; however, for small populations, it may be crucial. Occasionally, sampling with replacement is impossible, even from small populations. Consider our problem of testing the sweetness of grapes on a bunch. The measurement process leads to the destruction of the sampled elements. In these instances, the analysis may be carried out; however, we must correct the primary variance term, which is s^2/n for an srs. The correction term is known as the *finite population correction factor* (fpc) and is $1 - f = 1 - n/N$, where n is the number of elements in the sample and N is the number of population elements.

Essentially, the common variance estimate is weighted by $1 - f$. The impact of the fpc can easily be seen if a couple of hypothetical examples are considered. First, assume that a sample of 250 is drawn from a population of 1000. In this instance, the fpc $= 1 - n/N = 1 - 250/1000 = .75$. If the same sample of 250 is drawn from a population of 10,000, however, the sampling fraction becomes $1 - 250/10,000 = .975$. In the first example, the variance estimate s^2/n will be reduced by .25; in the second example, it is reduced by .025—a relatively trivial amount.

EXAMPLE: DRAWING A RANDOM SAMPLE

An introductory statistics and methods class has 200 students enrolled. Those students might be considered a *population*, and the complete listing of the students would constitute a *sample frame*. After the fourth week of the semester, the instructor distributes a questionnaire to all the students. Among the questions asked are "How many hours did you spend studying last week?" and "Do you work part time?" The results of the survey are presented in Table 5.1. The first 70 students (as indicated by the boldface numbers) are males and the remaining 130 students are females. The second column represents the students' answers to the question of how many hours they worked in the preceding week; column 3 tells whether they work part time ($1 =$ yes, $2 =$ no).

The instructor decides to select a 20% random sample for detailed analysis. Normally, if the instructor were interested only in a sample of students, information would not be available on all the remaining elements (students) in the population. For pedagogical purposes, however, it suits us to have information on the entire population.

There are several ways in which the sample could be chosen. Thus to select this 20% sample, the instructor might generate a list of 200 uniform random numbers between 0 and 1 corresponding to the 200 elements in the population. If the random number had a value of less than .2, the corresponding population element would be included in the sample. Here, 41 of the random numbers have a value of less than .2; therefore, the sample size is higher than the exact value of 20% by one. Since each element within the population can be chosen only once, this procedure is a variant on sampling without replacement.

As suggested, this procedure can result in more or fewer than an exact number of expected elements. If generating an exact number for some reason is necessary, the procedure can be modified to do this (Bebbington, 1975).

Alternate ways of selecting the sample do exist. A common procedure is to generate a list of 40 random numbers between 1 and 200. One possible outcome of this approach is the same number being generated more than once, forcing us to address the issue of sampling with or without replacement. If we are willing to accept duplicate entries (sampling with replacement), then the 40 random numbers will be sufficient. If we wish to have a sample of 40 unique individuals from the population, then we probably

Table 5.1. Population of 200 students[a]

CASE	H	J	S	CASE	H	J	S	CASE	H	J	S	CASE	H	J	S
1	13	0	0	**51**	11	0	0	101	14	0	1	151	12	0	0
2	8	0	0	**52**	9	1	1	102	12	0	0	152	16	0	0
3	11	0	1	**53**	8	0	1	103	13	0	0	153	17	0	0
4	5	1	1	**54**	8	0	0	104	16	0	0	154	14	0	0
5	9	0	0	**55**	8	1	0	105	15	0	1	155	9	0	0
6	11	0	0	**56**	6	0	0	106	16	0	0	156	14	0	1
7	5	1	0	**57**	7	1	1	107	13	0	0	157	11	0	0
8	8	0	0	**58**	6	0	0	108	14	0	1	158	14	0	0
9	8	0	0	**59**	9	0	0	109	12	0	0	159	13	0	0
10	7	0	0	**60**	10	0	0	110	10	0	1	160	11	0	0
11	7	0	0	**61**	5	1	0	111	21	0	0	161	12	0	0
12	7	0	1	**62**	11	0	0	112	14	1	0	162	13	0	0
13	10	1	1	**63**	10	0	0	113	12	0	0	163	13	0	0
14	6	0	1	**64**	9	1	0	114	14	0	0	164	14	0	0
15	7	0	0	**65**	6	0	0	115	15	0	0	165	12	0	0
16	11	0	1	**66**	11	0	0	116	14	1	0	166	14	0	0
17	11	0	0	**67**	9	0	0	117	14	0	1	167	18	0	0
18	7	0	1	**68**	8	0	0	118	16	0	0	168	16	0	1
19	8	0	0	**69**	5	0	0	119	14	0	0	169	11	0	0
20	13	0	0	**70**	9	0	0	120	13	0	0	170	16	0	0
21	7	0	0	71	14	0	0	121	14	0	0	171	15	0	0
22	10	0	0	72	14	0	0	122	15	1	1	172	14	0	0
23	8	1	1	73	17	0	0	123	11	1	0	173	11	1	0
24	10	0	0	74	13	0	0	124	12	0	0	174	12	0	1
25	7	0	0	75	11	0	0	125	14	0	0	175	15	0	0
26	12	0	1	76	13	1	0	126	13	0	1	176	12	0	1
27	9	0	1	77	10	0	1	127	14	0	0	177	16	0	0
28	7	0	0	78	16	1	0	128	13	0	0	178	13	0	0
29	9	0	0	79	14	0	1	129	16	0	0	179	16	0	0
30	14	1	0	80	15	0	0	130	13	0	1	180	17	0	0
31	10	1	0	81	13	0	0	131	15	0	0	181	16	0	0
32	10	0	0	82	13	0	0	132	11	0	0	182	11	0	0
33	9	0	0	83	15	0	0	133	14	0	0	183	13	0	0
34	8	0	0	84	16	0	0	134	16	0	0	184	15	0	0
35	6	0	0	85	14	0	0	135	16	0	1	185	15	0	0
36	8	1	0	86	11	0	0	136	16	0	1	186	15	0	0
37	11	0	0	87	16	0	0	137	13	0	0	187	17	0	0
38	11	0	0	88	16	0	0	138	16	0	0	188	15	0	0
39	8	0	0	89	15	0	1	139	14	1	1	189	13	0	0
40	9	1	1	90	10	1	0	140	15	0	0	190	14	0	1
41	10	1	0	91	13	0	0	141	15	0	1	191	15	0	0
42	8	0	0	92	13	0	0	142	16	0	0	192	16	0	0
43	12	0	0	93	13	0	0	143	16	0	0	193	18	0	1
44	8	0	1	94	15	0	0	144	15	0	0	194	11	1	0
45	9	1	0	95	15	0	0	145	15	0	0	195	15	0	0
46	9	1	0	96	13	0	0	146	14	0	0	196	12	0	1
47	7	0	0	97	16	0	1	147	13	1	1	197	15	0	0
48	8	0	0	98	13	0	0	148	14	0	0	198	13	0	0
49	4	0	0	99	15	0	1	149	12	0	0	199	15	0	1
50	7	0	0	100	15	1	0	150	14	0	0	200	16	0	0

[a]Boldface numbers, male students; H, hours studied; J, part-time job (1, job; 0, no job); S, randomly selected sample (1, member of sample; 0, not selected).

will have to generate more than 40 random numbers, since it will be necessary to skip numbers that have already occurred.

In Table 5.1, the fourth column is coded 0 or 1 with a "1" indicating membership in the sample.

Sampling Notation

One of the biggest problems faced by students entering the sampling literature is the apparent lack of consensus in the field over notation. In this text, we will parallel that used by Kish (1965). Box 5.2 presents the basic notation used throughout this discussion to identify various sample components and their population counterparts. Complementing this material, we may usefully review some basic statistical concepts and notational conventions that impinge directly on our future discussion of sampling.

■ Box 5.2

BASIC SAMPLING NOTATION

Population	**Sample**
N = number of elements in a population	n = number of elements in the sample
Y_i = value of y variable for the ith population element	y_i = value of y variable for the ith sample element
$Y = \sum Y_i$ or the population total	$y = \sum y_i$ or the sample total
$\bar{Y} = Y/N = (1/N) \sum Y_i$ or the population mean	$\bar{y} = y/n = 1/n \sum y_i$ or the sample mean
$S^2 = (1/N) \sum (Y_i - \bar{Y})^2$ or the population variance (sometimes σ^2), with S being equal to the standard deviation	$s^2 = 1/(n-1) \sum (y_i - \bar{y})^2$ or the sample variance, with s being equal to the standard deviation
	In EPSEM (equal probability of selection method) samples, $\bar{y}$ is used to estimate Y and $N\bar{y}$ is used to estimate Y (the population total)
	$f = n/N$ or the sampling fraction

As indicated, $\overline{Y} = Y/N = (1/N)\sum Y_i$ is the "true" or population value. Sometimes this is represented in the literature as μ. Since this parameter is generally unknown, the sample mean, $\overline{y} = y/n = (1/n)\sum y_i$ is used to estimate the population parameter. Because the sample mean is a random variable, it will have a sampling distribution that is the theoretical distribution of all possible values of an estimate (statistic), each with its own probability of occurrence. The standard deviation of the sample means about the population mean is known as the standard error of the estimate.

Unfortunately, the standard error (SE) is known only theoretically, since we usually only have a single point (sample). It can be shown (by the CLT), however, that for an srs with replacement, the standard error is $\sigma_y/\sqrt{n}$. Since σ^2 cannot be estimated from the sample, we use s^2 as an estimate. Therefore, the standard error of the mean (say) can be given as[2]:

$$SE(\overline{y}) = \frac{s}{\sqrt{n}}.$$

At this point, it makes sense to provide a more precise definition of the central limit theorem.

> If all possible random samples of size n are drawn from a population with a mean μ and a variance of σ^2, then as n increases, the sample means will be approximately normally distributed, with mean μ and variance σ^2/n.

Notice that this theorem does not make any assumptions about the shape of the population from which the samples are drawn. The original data may be normally or uniformly distributed, or even distributed as a cross section of the Rocky Mountains. The key notion is that despite the distribution of the original data, the distribution of a statistic such as $\overline{y}$ will be normal. It is this very powerful and critical assumption that allows us to make inferences about sample statistics. It should also be noted that the accuracy of the approximation increases with n.

Sampling Errors

Assume for a moment that an extremely large number of nontrivial samples are drawn at random from a population. The CLT assures us that the estimated means of each of those samples will form a distribution about the true population mean $\overline{Y}$ and eventually, $E(\overline{y}) = \overline{Y}$, as illustrated in Figure 5.1. For any given sample, it is unlikely that $\overline{y}$ will equal $\overline{Y}$ exactly. This difference, $\overline{y} - \overline{Y}$, is called *sampling error*. As indicated, the sampling error can be computed by the researcher through the calculation of the standard error. Occasionally, sampling bias can be introduced. This difference, is $E(\overline{y}) - \overline{Y}$ (the long-run difference between the mean of the sample means and the population mean) and is generally a consequence of either errors in statistical

---

2. Note that if n is used in the calculation of s^2, we divide s by $\sqrt{n-1}$, not $\sqrt{n}$ in calculating the standard error. This is often a source of confusion, since there is a lack of consistency among statistics texts.

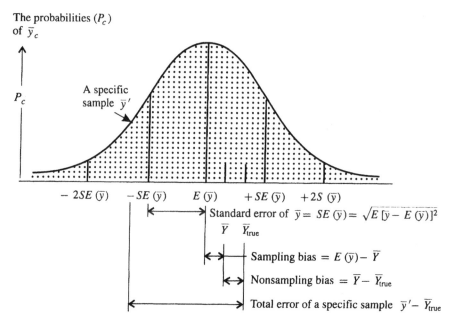

Figure 5.1. A Typical Sampling Distribution. Taken from: Kish (1965: 12) figure 1.3.I.

computation (e.g., using n as opposed to $n-1$ in the denominator) or assuming the wrong sample design (e.g., assuming an srs when the design is, in fact, complex).

There are, however, other sources of error that creep into our design. These are called *nonsampling errors*. Some of these errors are random and cancel themselves out; others are systematic and result in systematic bias. Nonsampling errors are typically a consequence of some systematic bias in the collection of the data. In this situation, it is the case that $\bar{Y} \neq \bar{Y}_{\text{true}}$. For example, the tendency of some questionnaires to generate response sets produces a systematic directional bias in the results. Other sources of nonsampling error include selectivity bias that results when some classes of elements are not included in the sample frame, unwillingness among certain groups to participate in the survey, interviewer biases, or systematic mistakes at data entry. This combination of sampling and nonsampling error is known as the total error of a sample.

Since all sources of error contribute to variations over samples, decomposing this variation into its constituent components is possible. Thus, the mean squared error of the sampling distribution is related to the variance in the $\bar{y}$ values. That is:

$$\text{MSE}\,(\bar{y}) = \text{var}\,(\bar{y}) + \left[E(\bar{y}) - \bar{Y}\right]^2$$

When the latter term, $\left[E(\bar{y}) - \bar{Y}\right]^2$, is not zero, the estimate is biased. In well-designed samples, however, the bias is generally very close to zero.

Estimates from Simple Random Samples

The standard formulas for point estimates such as sample means and standard errors presented in introductory statistics courses generally assume that the data are collected through an srs with replacement. Thus, the standard formulas for estimating the sample mean $(\bar{y} = \sum y_i/n)$ and the standard error of the mean $(\text{SE}[\bar{y}] = s/\sqrt{n})$ readily apply.

The situation is somewhat different, however, when the selected sample is srs but *without replacement*. The traditional formula for the mean, $\bar{y} = \sum y_i/n$, remains appropriate. The standard error for $\bar{y}$, however, requires modification, especially when the sample is drawn from a relatively small population. In this situation, the standard error of $\bar{y}$ is defined as:

$$\text{SE}(\bar{y}) = \sqrt{(1 - f)\frac{\sum_{i=1}^{n}(y_i - \bar{y})^2}{n(n-1)}}$$

or

$$\text{SE}(\bar{y}) = \sqrt{(1 - f)\frac{s^2}{n}}$$

For proportions, the corresponding formula for the standard error is:

$$\text{SE}(p) = \sqrt{(1 - f)\frac{pq}{n-1}}$$

with $q = 1 - p$. When the standard error of a population total must be estimated, the formula $\text{SE}(Y) = N\,\text{SE}(\bar{y})$ or $N\,\text{SE}(p)$ can be used.

Although we have used the finite population correction factor $(1 - f)$ in these formulas, it should be again noted that its impact becomes negligible when the sample size is small compared with the overall population. For example, if a sample of 500 is to be drawn from a population of 100,000, the fpc essentially becomes 1. In this instance, whether one uses the fpc formula for estimating $\text{SE}(\bar{y})$ noted above, or the more familiar $s/\sqrt{n}$ is irrelevant.

EXAMPLE: ESTIMATING THE AMOUNT OF TIME STUDENTS SPEND STUDYING

If we focus our attention on the number of hours reportedly spent studying by the 41 students in the sample, we can calculate $\bar{y}$ as $\sum y_i/n = 12.0$. The total sum of squares is 434; hence, the variance is estimated by:

$$s_y^2 = \frac{\sum_{i=1}^{n}(y_i - \bar{y})^2}{n-1}$$

$$= \frac{434}{40}$$

$$= 10.85$$

Since the sample was drawn without replacement, the estimate of the standard error thus becomes:

$$SE\ (\bar{y}) = \sqrt{(1 - f)\frac{s^2}{n}}$$

$$= \sqrt{\left(1 - \frac{41}{200}\right)\frac{10.85}{41}}$$

$$= .46$$

Having calculated $SE(\bar{y})$, it is possible to calculate a confidence interval around the estimate of the mean, $\bar{y}$. For a 95% confidence interval, we would estimate:

$$\bar{y} \pm 1.96\ SE(\bar{y})$$

$$12.0 \pm 1.96(0.46)$$

Thus,

$$11.10 \le \bar{y} \le 12.90$$

A corresponding calculation can be made for proportions. Again, from the sample, we can estimate that the proportion of students with a part time job is $p = 9/41 = .22$. Therefore,

$$SE\ (p) = \sqrt{(1 - f)\frac{pq}{n - 1}}$$

$$= \sqrt{\left(1 - \frac{41}{200}\right)\frac{(.22)(.78)}{40}}$$

$$= .06$$

Having now calculated $SE(p)$, we can calculate a confidence interval around the estimate of proportion, p. For a 95% confidence interval, we would estimate:

$$p \pm 1.96\ SE(p)$$

$$.22 \pm 1.96(.06)$$

Thus,

$$.10 \le p \le .34$$

Stratified Samples

Often, simple random sampling (srs) schemes lead to very large estimates of the standard error of the estimate. Sometimes, exceedingly large SEs can result in estimates of little practical value. Fortunately, it is often possible to reduce the SE of an estimate at minimal or no cost to the sampler. One procedure that is frequently employed is *stratification*. Typically, stratification increases the *efficiency* of the sample. Efficiency, it will be recalled, is the relative size of the sampling error of a sample to other samples of the same sample size and the same cost of execution.

In stratified samples, the parent population is divided into more homogeneous segments according to some criterion variable. By "homogeneous" it is meant that on average, any two items chosen at random within a stratum or segment are more alike than any two elements chosen at random from the total parent population. Essentially, stratification increases efficiency through the loss of between-strata variance. The key to success in stratification is to find a variable that is strongly related to the estimate or outcome variable. Thus, for example, if income is strongly related to geographical region, then region could serve as a stratification variable.

To obtain unbiased results in stratified samples, the elements within each stratum must be selected as an srs. That is, we select the stratum elements independently from each other and from the elements in the other strata and at random.

How this increase in efficiency is gained can be shown through a trivial example. Assume for a moment that a hamlet consists of two blocks. An srs of four houses is selected from *within* each block, and the number of occupants or household members is recorded.

STRATUM	HOUSEHOLD MEMBERS	STRATUM MEANS
Block 1	1 2 2 4	$\bar{y}_1 = 2.25$
Block 2	6 6 8 7	$\bar{y}_2 = 6.75$

The overall mean, $\bar{y}$, is 4.5. The total sums of squares, $\sum(y - \bar{y})^2$, is 48; thus, the estimated variance across all the households (which is what we would estimate for an srs) is $s^2 = 48/7 = 6.857$. The corresponding sums of squares and sample variances for stratum 1 are 4.75 and 1.583, and for stratum 2 are 2.75 and 0.913, respectively. Since the elements within each stratum were selected independently of one another and of the elements in each other stratum, the overall variance, s_{st}^2, is simply the sum of the variances within each stratum. Thus, $s_{st}^2 = s_1^2 + s_2^2 = 1.583 + 0.917 = 2.50$. By stratifying the hamlet by block, we have reduced the estimated sampling variance by $[(6.857 - 2.500)/6.857]100$, or 64%.

This procedure is analogous to performing a one-way ANOVA. Within the ANOVA framework, the total sum of squares is equal to the within-group sums of squares (which is an element of the error variance) plus the between-groups sums of squares. If there is no group effect (in this case, stratification effect), then the total sum of squares is equal to the sum of the within-group sums of squares. On the other hand, if the grouping (stratifying) variable is related to the outcome variable, the within-group sum of squares is reduced by the size of the sum of squares attributable to the grouping variable.

In stratified sampling then, the worst that can happen is that the stratifying variable has no effect and the estimate of s_{st}^2 becomes no worse than s_{srs}^2. On the other hand, finding an effective stratifying variable can reduce the estimate of the error variance considerably.

Estimating the Standard Error

Let us assume that a sample is divided into H strata, with each stratum having N_h elements in it out of a total, N. The relative sizes of the strata will be W_h, where $W_h = N_h/N$ and $\sum W_h = 1$. The population mean becomes a weighted mean calculated across all H strata. Consequently, $\overline{Y}_{st}$, is defined as:

$$\overline{Y}_{st} = \sum W_h \overline{Y}_h = \frac{\sum N_h \overline{Y}_h}{N}, \qquad h = 1, \ldots, H$$

This can be estimated from the sample data by using the analogous formula:

$$\overline{y}_{st} = \frac{\sum n_h \overline{y}_h}{n}, \qquad h = 1, \ldots, H$$

Estimating the sampling error of $\overline{Y}_{st}$ is more complex than for the mean of an srs. The complexity, however, is more an issue of bookkeeping rather than any major conceptual distinction. First, apply the formula for sample variance within each stratum.

$$s_h^2 = \frac{\sum (y_{ih} - \overline{y}_h)^2}{n_h - 1}$$

Once the individual stratum estimates have been obtained, the overall variance of the estimate of $\overline{Y}_{st}$ becomes:

$$V(\overline{y}_{st}) = \sum W_h^2 \frac{s_h^2}{n_h} (1 - f_h)$$

$$= \sum \frac{N_h}{N} \frac{s_h^2}{n_h} \frac{(N_h - n_h)}{N}$$

$$= \frac{1}{N^2} \sum N_h (N_h - n_h) \frac{s_h^2}{n_h}$$

where again, the fpc becomes negligible for large samples. An estimate of the standard error is thus

$$SE\left[V(\overline{Y}_{st})\right] = \sqrt{V(\overline{Y}_{st})}$$

Standard Errors of Population Totals

An estimate of the population total, Y, is given by $N\overline{Y}_{st}$ (i.e., $\sum_{h=1}^{H} N_h \overline{Y}_h$). The estimated variance of $N\overline{Y}_{st}$ becomes $N^2 V(\overline{Y}_{st})$ or:

$$N\overline{y}_{st} = \sum N_h^2 \left(\frac{N_h - n_h}{N_h}\right) \left(\frac{s_h^2}{n_h}\right)$$

An estimate of the standard error is thus

$$SE(\overline{Y}_{st}) = \sqrt{V(N\overline{Y}_{st})}$$

EXAMPLE: STRATIFYING STUDENTS BY GENDER

An example of the impact of stratification on an estimate can be obtained by considering our earlier project involving study time spent by students. In the original sample of 200, it was known that the first 70 students were males and the remaining 130 students were females. Thus, the sample frame contains two strata defined by sex.

Intuition tells us that the male students are less conscientious and spend less time, on average, studying. This suspicion is borne out when we calculate the mean number of hours spent studying by the two strata. For the first stratum, $\overline{Y}_{males}$ is 8.47 and for the second stratum, $\overline{Y}_{females}$ is 14.04. The weighted mean for the whole sample is calculated as follows:

$$\overline{Y}_{st} = \sum_{h=1}^{H} W_h \overline{Y}_h$$

$$= \left(\frac{70}{200}\right) 8.60 + \left(\frac{130}{200}\right) 14.04$$

$$= 12.14$$

Our primary interest, however, resides in the estimation of $\overline{y}_{st}$ and $SE(\overline{y}_{st})$ from the random sample of 41 students. The weighted sample mean for the stratified sample becomes:

$$\overline{y}_{st} = \sum_{h=1}^{H} w_h \overline{y}_h$$

$$= \left(\frac{26}{41}\right) 14.04 + \left(\frac{15}{41}\right) 8.47$$

$$= 12.0$$

Again, the sample was drawn without replacement; consequently, the standard error, $SE(\overline{y}_{st})$ is estimated as follows:

$$SE(\overline{y}_{st}) = \sqrt{\sum_{h=1}^{H} \frac{w_h^2 (1 - f_h) s_h^2}{n_h}}$$

$$= \sqrt{\frac{(.65)^2 \left(1 - \frac{26}{130}\right)(3.36)}{26} + \frac{(.35)^2 \left(1 - \frac{15}{17}\right)(3.84)}{15}}$$

$$= \sqrt{.04 + .02}$$

$$\doteq .26$$

If the samples within each stratum had been drawn with replacement, the fpc $(1-n/N)$ would be dropped from the formula. Regardless, a 95% confidence interval may be estimated as $\overline{y} \pm 1.96(.26)$.

It is readily apparent that this estimate of the standard error is almost half the corresponding srs standard error of .46. Thus, it seems that our original objective of increasing the efficiency of the estimate has been successful.

Corresponding estimates may be made for proportions. If we consider the proportion of students with part time jobs, P may be estimated as follows:

$$P_{st} = \sum_{h=1}^{H} W_h P_h$$

$$= \left(\frac{70}{200}\right).23 + \left(\frac{130}{200}\right).09$$

$$= .14$$

For the sample of 41 students, the sample proportion, p_{st}, and $SE(p_{st})$ have estimates equivalent to those for continuous data. Thus,

$$p_{st} = \sum_{h=1}^{H} W_h p_h$$

$$= \left(\frac{15}{41}\right).40 + \left(\frac{26}{41}\right).12$$

$$= .22$$

and for the standard error,

$$SE(p_{st}) = \sqrt{\sum_{h=1}^{H} \frac{w_h^2(1 - f_h)p_h q_h}{n_h - 1}}$$

$$= \sqrt{\frac{(.65)^2\left(1 - \frac{26}{130}\right)(.40)(.60)}{14} + \frac{(.35)^2\left(1 - \frac{15}{17}\right)(.12)(.89)}{25}}$$

$$= \sqrt{.0014 + .0016}$$

$$= .06$$

In this instance, nothing is gained through stratification, since the srs estimate of the standard error is also approximately .06.

A Caveat

When well executed, a stratified sampling design can be highly effective. Unfortunately, it is not the panacea that some would believe. Stratifying works best with simple surveys designed to measure only a few variables. Basically, what may be a good stratifying variable for one measure may not be so for another. Thus, in complex, multipurpose surveys, identifying strata that work with more than a few variables is very difficult. The last word on the matter is probably best left to Sudman (1976: 108):

> Naive researchers with high anxiety levels will often be concerned that a sample using probability methods will yield very strange results. . . . To ensure against this, they insist that the sample be stratified so that age, race, sex, occupation, income, education, household size, and other variables are guaranteed to be perfectly represented. . . . If the request is taken literally, there is simply no way to comply with it. The census data that would be necessary for strata controls would not be available in such detail . . . the cost of perfectly matching these in the field would be prohibitive . . . [and] . . . the effects on the data of this tortuous process would probably be undetectable.

Cluster Sampling

In the discussion so far, it has been assumed that the primary sampling units (psus) consist of the individual elements as listed in the frame. In many situations, the psus are not individuals but some other element containing a bunch or cluster of individuals, such as a household or a school. In this situation, the sample frame consists of a listing of clusters (e.g., households), not individual elements. Common psus that make up clusters are road locations for random roadside checks for drinking and driving ("spot checks"); work groups; city blocks; industrial organizations, and classrooms.

More so than with other sample designs, the notation for cluster samples can become complicated. Figure 5.2 illustrates the notation we will employ for simple cluster samples. Within the population, it is assumed that there are A clusters. Any given cluster will be indicated by the subscript α, where $\alpha = 1, \ldots A$. Inside a given cluster, it will be assumed that there are B elements, subscripted by β, where $\beta = 1, \ldots, B$. From the population of A clusters, a sample of size a may be selected. Similarly, within a particular sampled cluster a subset of b elements may be chosen from the total, B. If it is considered desirable to stratify the clusters, then the strata would be indicated by the previous notation where h signified the hth stratum and $h = 1, \ldots, H$.

Equal Sized Clusters

It is rare for clusters to be of equal size; however, the basic concepts of cluster sampling are best identified by using that configuration as a starting point. Let $Y_{\alpha\beta}$ represent the Yth variable associated with the βth individual in the αth cluster. In total, there are A clusters with B individuals in each, therefore, $N = A \times B$. For each cluster, we may calculate a cluster mean as follows:

$$\bar{y}_\alpha = \frac{1}{B} \sum\nolimits_{\beta=1}^{B} y_{\alpha\beta}$$

For a clusters out of A, the overall cluster mean (i.e., the mean of the clusters) is:

$$\bar{y}_{cl} = \frac{1}{a} \sum\nolimits_{\alpha=1}^{a} \bar{y}_\alpha$$

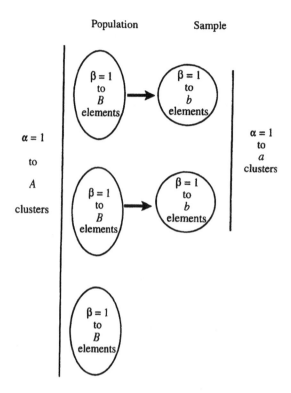

Population   Sample

Figure 5.2. Notation for cluster samples.

and the equivalent formula for the variance among the clusters is:

$$\text{var}\left(\bar{y}_{cl}\right) = (1 - f)\frac{s_a^2}{a}$$

where

$$s_a^2 = \frac{1}{a - 1}\sum_{\alpha=1}^{a}\left(\bar{y}_\alpha - \bar{y}_{cl}\right)^2$$

Do note, however, that for $\text{var}(\bar{y}_{cl})$ the variance is among the clusters and not the individuals.

Unequal Sized Clusters

In most practical situations dealing with "natural" clusters, the number of elements varies from cluster to cluster. Furthermore, whenever we deal with a probability sample of clusters that are unequal in size, the ultimate sample size that results is itself a random variable.[3] From a statistical point of view, this is an anomaly, since

---

3. For example, surveys of drinking drivers consist of probability samples of clusters because the number of cars that drive by a given site is not fixed.

we generally treat the sample size as fixed. Thus, in traditional samples where we are trying to estimate the proportion of some phenomenon, the numerator is a random variable, but the denominator is fixed. Where the sample size is itself unknown, the proportion is estimated by the ratio of two random variables. This complicates the math somewhat, and exact estimates become difficult to generate.

Assume, for a moment, the outcome variable, Y, is coded 0,1. Where both numerator and denominator are random variables, the estimated proportion is termed a *ratio mean (R)*, which may be defined as follows:

$$R = \frac{Y}{X} = \frac{\sum_{\alpha=1}^{A} \sum_{\beta=1}^{B} Y_{\alpha\beta}}{\sum_{\alpha=1}^{A} X_{\alpha}}$$

In other words, the ratio mean is the ratio of cluster totals to the total sample size.

For a random subset of clusters then, the sample ratio mean, *r*, is:

$$r = \frac{y}{x} = \frac{\sum_{\alpha=1}^{a} \sum_{\beta=1}^{b} y_{\alpha\beta}}{\sum_{\alpha=1}^{a} x_{\alpha}}$$

Because the sample mean is a ratio, it is subject to some bias [i.e., $E(r) \neq R$]. In large surveys, this bias is usually quite small, being in the order of $1/x^2$.

While estimating the ratio mean is reasonable straightforward, estimating the variance of the ratio mean is more complex. Specifically,

$$\text{var}(r) = \frac{1-f}{x^2} a \left(s_y^2 + r^2 s_x^2 - 2r s_{xy} \right)$$

where f is the sampling fraction, a is the number of clusters, and r is the ratio mean (not to be confused with Pearson's r). If f is reasonable small (as often happens in large-scale surveys), then the first component may be reduced to $1/x^2$. The individual variances and covariances for the numerator and denominator are:

$$s_y^2 = \frac{\sum_{\alpha=1}^{a} \left(y_\alpha - \bar{y}_{\text{cl}} \right)^2}{a-1}$$

$$s_x^2 = \frac{\sum_{\alpha=1}^{a} \left(x_\alpha - \bar{x}_{\text{cl}} \right)^2}{a-1}$$

and

$$s_{xy}^2 = \frac{\sum_{\alpha=1}^{a} \left(y_\alpha - \bar{y}_{\text{cl}} \right) \left(x_\alpha - \bar{x}_{\text{cl}} \right)}{a-1}$$

Cluster sampling is often used when it is impossible to put together a frame of all individual elements or when the random selection of individual elements is extremely expensive or ineffective. The roadside survey example suggests a prime situation in which element sampling procedures are simply unworkable. It is impossible to list all drivers on the road at a particular time and to draw a random sample; drawing a random sample of road locations is, however, possible.

While cluster sample designs are often much more practical and cost-effective than element samples, they are not without their associated costs. Usually, the standard errors of cluster samples are much larger than element samples of the same size (n). Sometimes this problem can be mitigated by stratifying the clusters. For example, if it is known that urban drivers are more likely to be driving intoxicated than rural drivers, the roadside clusters could be stratified along a rural/urban dimension.

EXAMPLE: ESTIMATING THE PROPORTION OF DRIVERS OVER THE LEGAL BLOOD ALCOHOL CONCENTRATION (BAC) LIMIT IN A CLUSTER SAMPLE

In one typical application of cluster sampling, random roadside surveys are conducted to estimate the proportion of drivers who have a blood alcohol level above the legal limit. This example entails a number of sites chosen from the 1986 random roadside survey conducted in Ontario, Canada. The original survey consisted of 298 sites selected at random throughout the province. The actual sampling design consisted of a two-step affair.

The province's census tracts and enumeration areas were stratified by population, and site selection was conducted proportionate to population size. The underlying assumption here was that vehicle registration and more importantly, traffic volume, would be proportionate to the population of the census area. Census tracts and enumeration areas were randomly selected within each stratum. Once that selection had been made, grids were laid over the census area and sections were drawn at random until a suitable survey location had been selected.[4]

Site suitability was judged on the basis of whether there would be sufficient traffic flow, whether there was a location at which the survey could be conducted, and other logistical issues, such as whether the safety of the survey crew could be assured.

For the current example, 42 sites have been selected from the original 298 (see Table 5.2). Two variables have been included: the total number of vehicles stopped at each site and the number of vehicle drivers who had blood alcohol concentrations (BAC) over the local limit of 80 mg %. To simplify matters, the weights and sampling fractions have been omitted.[5]

From the sample data, the mean number of over the limit drivers, $\bar{y}_{cl}$, is estimated to be 2.143 and the mean number of drivers stopped, $\bar{x}_{cl}$, is 40.310. The corresponding totals are $y_{cl} = 90$ and $x_{cl} = 1693$, and sample variances are $s_y^2 = 3.686$, $s_x^2 = 280.902$, and $s_{xy}^2 = -2.143$.

Thus, the estimate of the proportion of drivers over the legal BAC limit of 80 mg % is the ratio mean:

---

4. This survey was designed in accordance with a set of rules outlined by the Organization for Economic Cooperation and Development (OECD). Methodological details of those surveys have been discussed in a number of sources including Stroh (1974), Government of Ontario (1988), and Maxim (1989).

5. Analysis of the original data indicate that the impact of the fpc is minimal, since it has a value close to 1. The utility of weights is also mooted, since our primary interest here is in estimating a proportion rather than a total.

Table 5.2. Roadside sites data for estimating proportion of drivers over the legal limit[a]

CLUSTER	y_α	x_α	CLUSTER	y_α	x_α	CLUSTER	y_α	x_α
1	0	32	15	5	29	29	2	30
2	3	37	16	6	40	30	2	33
3	1	47	17	3	41	31	2	20
4	1	35	18	1	46	32	1	66
5	0	60	19	1	23	33	2	59
6	7	17	20	0	52	34	1	40
7	1	44	21	5	26	35	3	57
8	3	29	22	0	23	36	1	43
9	4	36	23	0	13	37	5	45
10	2	26	24	0	9	38	1	46
11	0	65	25	2	55	39	0	33
12	2	65	26	0	49	40	6	49
13	5	31	27	1	28	41	4	42
14	3	90	28	2	19	42	2	63

[a] y_α, number of drivers over the legal limit at site α; x_α, number of drivers surveyed at site α.

$$r = \frac{y}{x} = \frac{90}{1693}$$

$$= .053$$

The variance of r (omitting the fpc) is estimated as:

$$\text{var}(r) = \frac{1}{x^2} a \left(s_y^2 + r^2 s_x^2 - 2r s_{xy} \right)$$

$$= \frac{1}{(1693)^2} 42[3.686 + (.053)^2 280.902 - 2(.053)(-2.143)]$$

$$= .69 \times 10^{-4}$$

Consequently, the standard error of r is the square root of the variance, $\sqrt{[\text{var}(r)]} = .0083$.

Based on these results, it is possible to form a 95% confidence interval around $r(.053)$ as $r \pm 1.96(.0083)$, or

$$.036 \le r \le .069$$

DESIGN EFFECTS

The differences in the variances produced by different sampling schema for a sample of a given size are termed *design effects*. Formally, the design effect (DEFF) is the ratio of the variance of a particular sample to the variance of a simple random sample of the same size. That is:

$$\text{DEFF} = \frac{\text{var}(\bar{y})}{(1 - f)s^2/n}$$

Harkening back to the student example, it will be recalled that the standard error for the stratified design was .26, while that for the srs design was .46. In this instance, the design effect is:

$$\text{DEFF} = \frac{(.26)^2}{(.46)^2}$$

$$= .32$$

Design effects of less than 1 suggest improvements in efficiency of a particular design over its srs counterpart and are consequently considered more cost-effective. DEFF values greater than 1, suggest a relative loss of efficiency compared with an srs of a similar sized sample and are considered less cost-effective than a simple random sample.

Design effects for cluster samples are almost always larger than 1, even with the judicious use of stratification. Typical design effects of three for cluster samples are not uncommon. This implies that a given cluster sample is about 1/3 as efficient as an srs of the same sized sample, or conversely, an srs would require only 1/3 the sample of the cluster sample to achieve a similar efficiency. In the roadside example illustrated above, the variance of the ratio mean is estimated as $.69 \times 10^{-4}$. The estimated variance for an srs with the same number of sample elements would be $pq/n = [(.053)(.947)]/1693 = .30 \times 10^{-4}$. Thus, the approximate design effect is $\text{DEFF} = (.69 \times 10^{-4})/(.30 \times 10^{-4}) = 2.3$.

Cluster samples generally produce DEFF values greater than 1 because the intra-cluster homogeneity is greater than the intercluster homogeneity. Consider the example of measuring religious affiliation within households. Generally, all members of a household have similar religious affiliations. Thus, knowing the affiliation of one person in a household suggests the affiliation of all the other household members.

Because DEFF is based on a ratio of variances instead of standard errors, Kish suggests that it is sometimes convenient to use DEFT, where $\text{DEFT} = \sqrt{\text{DEFF}}$.

Since homogeneity is such an integral concept of DEFF, it makes sense to present a statistics that represents this phenomenon directly. Hansen, Hurwitz, and Madow (1953) were the first to explore this issue of homogeneity within clusters in detail. They offer a statistic designated as ρ that Kish (1965: 161) prefers to call roh, or the *rate of homogeneity*. Roh is derived from DEFF as follows:

$$\text{DEFF} = \frac{s_{cl}^2}{s_{srs}^2} = 1 + \rho(\bar{n}_\alpha - 1)$$

By isolation,

$$\rho = \frac{s_{cl}^2 - s_{srs}^2}{(\bar{n}_\alpha - 1)s_{srs}^2} = \frac{\text{DEFF} - 1}{\bar{n}_\alpha - 1}$$

In the formula above, $\bar{n}_\alpha$ represents the mean cluster size. The formula is not exact, but it is reasonably accurate if there is not too much variation in $\bar{n}_\alpha$. With equal size clusters, this value would be replaced by b.

For the sample of 42 roadside clusters, the mean cluster size is $1783/42 = 42.5$. Thus, roh is estimated as

$$\rho = \frac{\text{DEFF} - 1}{\bar{n}_\alpha - 1} = \frac{2.3 - 1}{42.5 - 1} = .031$$

Theoretically, roh has a range of -1 to $+1$; however, roh is usually greater than zero. Negative values of roh occur only when the elements within the clusters are more heterogeneous than the randomly selected elements across clusters.

Roh will be revisited in the next chapter, when we address the issues of cost and optimal cluster size.

One of the major limitations of using DEFF and roh to depict the relative impact of one design over another is that both measures often vary according to the variable upon which the estimate is based. In multipurpose surveys, DEFF can vary radically depending upon which variable is considered. In these situations, it is usual practice to base DEFF on the primary variables identified when the objectives of the study are initially established. Where DEFF is relatively consistent across a number of indicators, the mean DEFF is sometimes used both for planning purposes and for generating approximate standard errors for complex statistical analysis, where corrections for the design cannot be directly incorporated into the calculations.

A NOTE ON STATISTICAL SOFTWARE

Although the need to correct for design effects and to introduce the fpc into the analysis of samples drawn from small populations without replacement has been known for most of this century, few software packages incorporate these dimensions into their standard routines. Most of the major statistical analysis programs assume that the data are gathered as an srs and generate results on that basis. In fact, many packages do not even allow for the use of fractional weights in the analysis and require the researcher to recode the weights into integers. Weighting is then done by the "case duplication" method, where a given case is generated I times. Depending upon the magnitude of the integer weights, this can be a very cumbersome and time-consuming process, even on modern computers.

Currently, the researcher has three options. The first, or traditional, approach is to use the available software to produce intermediate results, such as stratum variances and cluster means, and to finish calculating the required estimates by hand. The second approach is to use specialized software, such as PC-CARP, to conduct the analysis. This is certainly a major improvement over the by-hand approach, since difficulties in keeping track of the arithmetic for complex surveys can easily lead to computational errors. Unfortunately, these specialized packages are often limited in the types of analysis they can perform. A third approach is to use a major package that incorporates into its general toolkit the ability to analyze designs other than the srs type. At present, the only major package that includes a reasonable range of survey design options is STATA.

Further Reading

Cochran, W.G. *Sampling Techniques*, 3rd ed. New York: Wiley, 1977. More advanced than
    Scheaffer, Mendenhall, and Ott, this book by Cochran is considered one of the classical

texts on modern sampling techniques. Cochran explores the basic issues raised in this chapter in much greater detail while still using elementary mathematics.

Kish, L.T. *Survey Sampling*. New York: Wiley, 1965. This is an extemely "packed" text that covers a great deal of theoretical and applied material. Kish's strength is in the wide variety of examples provided and in the wealth of practical suggestions for addressing difficulties researchers face in the field.

Scheaffer, R.L., W. Mendenhall, and L. Ott. *Elementary Survey Sampling,* 5th ed., Boston: Duxbury, 1996. An elementary sampling text, directed toward the undergraduate market. Easy to read, it has a wealth of basic examples.

Sudman, S. *Applied Sampling*. San Diego, CA: Academic Press, 1976. As the title implies, this text is light on the sampling theory but heavy on practical advice. It offers a wealth of excellent information, especially for those considering original data collection for a thesis.

6

Sampling: Designs

Perhaps believing in good design is like believing in God, it makes you an optimist.

—Sir Terence Conran

Many sampling strategies can produce acceptable probability samples. The basic criteria of acceptability are that a strategy must produce reasonably unbiased estimates (or estimates with calculable bias); it must allow for the calculation of errors in estimates (standard errors), and it must allow for inferences back to a known population. Within these general rules, countless strategies may be employed. Ultimately, however, the individual elements in the sample must be drawn through some form of randomized procedure.

Beyond the issue of statistical acceptability are issues of practical acceptability. A good sample design must be able to address the problem under consideration, and it must do this accurately and economically. Before discussing the merits of particular designs, we examine these additional requirements.

CRITERIA FOR SAMPLE DESIGN SELECTION

Several criteria must be taken into consideration when selecting a sampling plan or design. These are divided into four categories.

- **A Statement of Objectives**. GIGO (garbage in, garbage out), the acronym that used to adorn the walls of computing centers, is particularly applicable to sampling. If the researcher is unclear as to the objectives of the study, the data will be useless, no matter how many are collected. In deciding upon the appropriate sampling design, it is essential to know what data need to be collected and why. Having some idea of what statistics the sample is expected to generate is also essential. Is the objective to generate point estimates such as a mean or a total for a particular variable, or are the data to be used to test a multivariate relationship? It is important to know, because a design that could probably generate precise and economical results for a point estimate will not necessarily do so if several variables are of equal interest.

  Specifying the objectives of the study also refers to specifying the unit of analysis for the objective at hand. For example, is the focus on individuals, households, enumeration areas, or what? Clusters require one form of strategy, element samples another.

- **Measurability**. Measurability is what distinguishes probability samples from all others. The researcher must know the probability of selection of every element of the population from which the sample is to be drawn. In the absence of this information, drawing inferences within estimable credibility limits is not possible. Measurability then, requires a complete and accurate sampling frame.

- **Practicality**. The sample design must be doable. From the outset, it can be determined that some plans cannot be executed. Questions that require overly precise answers ("I want to know what percentage of the population has hangnails within one tenth of 1 percent, 99 times out of 100.") are not practical. When considering whether the design can be executed, it is essential to specify the resources that are available, the period in which the study needs to be conducted, and whether the phenomenon under consideration can be measured by means of the proposed techniques.

  A key issue of practicality is whether the research ought to be done at all. If a lot is known about a topic, yet another survey might add nothing further to our understanding. Often the most that can be expected from such enterprises is a congressional "golden fleece" award. All research activity carries with it an opportunity cost. This opportunity cost may be as funds that could be diverted into a more worthwhile project or as time wasted by the researcher.

- **Economy**. Cost is a major factor in any survey. Cost may be measured in many ways, such as money, time, or other nonmonetary resources (e.g., available personnel). A primary objective of a sampler is to achieve the highest precision possible per unit cost. Two elements of exactitude may be differentiated: precision and accuracy. Precision refers to the inherent variability of the phenomenon in the population while accuracy takes into consideration the inherent variability plus any included bias.

  Formally, precision and accuracy may be defined as follows:

  $$\text{precision} = \frac{1}{\text{var}(\overline{y})}$$

  and

  $$\text{accuracy} = \frac{1}{\text{MSE}(\overline{y})} = \frac{1}{\text{variance} + \text{biases}}$$

  Practically, this means that the researcher either (a) fixes the desired precision and then determines the sampling design that would yield it for the minimum cost, or (b) fixes the cost and attempts to achieve the maximum precision within that cost constraint.

Some of these issues can be addressed by the researcher, spending some time at a desk and thinking through the process step by step. Yet other issues are best dealt with through a pilot study. A trial run on 30 to 50 cases can usually pinpoint the major weaknesses of a study. Except for extremely rare populations of interest that may not be captured in a small sample, pilot studies identify failings in the measurement instrument and provide valuable feedback on the data collection mechanism. Furthermore, a pilot study can often provide a rough estimate of the sampling variance, which can be used to fine-tune a sample size estimate. Conducting a pilot study is no guarantee of success; however, not doing one is a harbinger of failure.

SAMPLE SELECTION PROCEDURES

As Kish (1965: 21) tells us, "Simple random sampling (srs) is the basic selection process, and all other procedures can be viewed as modifications of it, introduced to provide more practical, economical, or precise designs." The basic elements of srs sampling were addressed in Chapter 5. What is important to note about all probability samples, however, is that whatever the approach taken, at the ultimate stage the elements must be selected randomly.

Sampling with or Without Replacement

The issue of sampling with and without replacement also was broached in Chapter 5. Sampling with replacement assures that the probability of selection stays constant. Sampling without replacement results in higher selection probabilities for items chosen later in the sampling procedure. On the other hand, sampling without replacement can often produce more efficient estimates, especially when sampling with replacement results in many duplicate selections. The issue of which approach to take (where a choice is available) is moot if the sampling frame (the eligible population) is sufficiently large, since the fpc becomes so small that the results are indistinguishable from one another. Clearly, sampling with replacement has some advantages in that it simplifies the statistical calculation of the standard error; however, this strategy is not always available to us, especially when the sampled element is somehow modified through the measurement process. For small samples without replacement, the sampling distribution best approximates a hypergeometric distribution.

Although several formulas are applicable to simple sampling without replacement plans, as we saw in Chapter 5, it is not always an easy task to calculate the correct estimates. Thompson, for example, notes that without-replacement designs are often difficult to carry out when selection probabilities are required to be exactly proportionate to unit size or to another variable of interest (Thompson, 1992: 53).

EPSEM (Equal Probability of Selection Method) vs. Unequal Probabilities Methods

In equal probability of selection method samples, the population elements have equal probabilities of inclusion into the sample. EPSEM samples are essentially self-weighting, thus allowing for the simple and direct estimation of parameters such as the mean. EPSEM samples may also be achieved through compensating unequal probabilities at several stages. The opposite to EPSEM samples are unequal probability samples, usually corrected by using inverse weights. Unequal probability samples are often used when the selection frame is not complete or has problems, or when it is necessary to oversample some class of elements. Oversampling is often useful when a given class of interest is a rare event. In these situations, an srs would generally not produce enough cases to yield reliable estimates.

Random vs. Systematic Selection of Elements

Random sampling involves the independent random selection of elements within a stratum. A common variant for selecting elements from a population or a particular stratum is what is known as systematic selection. This approach is worthy of some consideration because it appears quite often in practice and, under most circumstances, produces results that would occur if the sample had been drawn as srs.

Systematic selection first involves a determination of the sampling fraction, n/N. For the sake of example, let us assume that this is 1/100. As a second step, a uniform random number between 1 and 100 is generated. This random number (say 39) is used to select the first element from the sample frame—in this case, the 39th element. After the first element has been selected, each successive 100th element is chosen for sample inclusion (i.e., 139, 239, 339, . . .) until the total sample has been chosen.

Systematic selection is extremely practical when the sample frame does not include a discrete listing of all elements in the population. Aerial sampling that uses map grids as frames is a good example of such a case. Another application the author came across some years ago involved the auditing of a selection of professional case files. No complete listing of the case files existed; however, the files were arrayed on a series of shelves and the total number of files was known. In this circumstance, a random start number was generated and every fth file corresponding to the sampling fraction was selected for examination. Since several thousand files were involved, this procedure saved considerable time and expense over having to create an initial listing or frame from the population of case files.

Clearly, systematic selection has its uses. In some situations, however, bias can be introduced. One danger is that *periodicities* may exist in the implicit frame, with the result that the selection of every fth element produces a very nonrandom sample. The traditional example used to illustrate periodicity is that of houses on uniform blocks. Through bad luck, the researcher may generate a start number that results in almost every selected house being a corner house. Periodicities also are highly probable when elements must be selected within a time frame. Using systematic selection to examine retail sales patterns over time may result in the selection of sales on a specific day of the week or, if the units are months, on a seasonal basis, such as months in which there are holidays.

Another problem that might arise is that of linear trends. Here, the values associated with the population elements increase or decrease across time or distance. From a statistical perspective, this situation results in serial correlation among the selected elements.

Overall, however, periodicities and linear trends are rare in most social science sampling applications. Where they might exist, the researcher can still use systematic sampling, although with some modifications. For example, it may be possible to "shuffle" the frame if it is known to be sorted in some specific, periodic order. It may also be possible to stratify the frame and to generate a new start number from each stratum. Where linear trends exist but little can be done to alter the sampling plan, the best solution may be to acknowledge the situation and correct for the serial correlation during the statistical analysis.

Stratified vs. Unstratified Sampling

Unstratified selection implies that the sample is drawn from the entire population in one stage (or a single stratum). Stratified samples require the population to be segmented into homogeneous subpopulations, with random samples drawn independently from each segment. As indicated in Chapter 5, effective stratification can result in a greatly reduced estimate of the sampling error. At worst, ineffective stratification generates results similar to those for an srs.

The most general form of stratified sampling is what is known as *disproportionate stratified sampling*. Two subtypes are often discussed in the literature, and these are *proportionate stratified sampling* and *optimum sampling*. In disproportionate stratified sampling, the sampling fraction is allowed to differ across strata. Thus, in stratum 1, the sampling fraction might be 1/100 and in stratum 2 it might be 1/25. Disproportionate sampling fractions are generally used when the strata differ substantially in size or the costs of measurement are different across strata. When conducting a labor force participation study, for example, it might be worthwhile to stratify by sex and by class of worker. Since salaried work is the norm for both men and women, it would likely be more efficient to stratify by class of worker—for example, salaried, self-employed, unemployed, and not in the labor force—and to use a lower sampling fraction for the salaried workers than for the remaining groups.

Disproportionate stratification poses little difficulty for analysis if the analyst remembers to weight the data by the sampling fraction for each stratum. Thus, if $f_h = n_h/n$, then the appropriate weight for all elements in stratum h would be f_h. To obtain an estimate of the sample total, one would obtain the product $n\bar{y}_{st}$. When it is necessary to estimate a population total, the strata elements should be weighted by the corresponding population values. Therefore, the corresponding fraction would be $W_h = N_h/N$, and the total would be estimated by $N\bar{Y}_{st}$.

Proportionate stratified sampling is the special situation of all f_h being equal and, as such, requires no further comment.

Optimum allocation, however, is a procedure used to allocate more of the total sample to those strata with the largest variances. That is, as s_h^2 increases so does n_h^2. Optimum allocation is achieved when $\sum_{h=1}^{H}(s_h^2/n_h)$ is minimized.

An estimated optimal sample size for the hth stratum may thus be determined by

$$n_h = n \frac{N_h S_h}{\sum_{h=1}^{H} N_h S_h}$$

Optimum allocation requires reliable existing information on the strata variances. Consequently it is a procedure that is normally applied when the same survey is to be conducted repeatedly. For example, monthly labor force surveys, repetitive political attitude surveys across several regions, and periodic market trend surveys are prime candidates for optimum allocation; as a rule, "one-shot" surveys are not. A further difficulty with optimum allocation is that what might be optimal for one variable is not likely optimal for another. Thus, multipurpose surveys rarely incorporate optimum allocation. Where the researcher obtains a copy of a survey based on optimal allocation, the analysis is conducted in the same manner as a survey based on disproportionate stratified sampling.

Element vs. Cluster Sampling

Element sampling implies that the primary sampling unit (psu) contains only one element. Cluster samples generally assume more than one element per psu. The distinction between element and cluster sampling should not be confused with the issue of level of analysis. A household, for example, could be considered either an element or a cluster depending upon whether the household itself is to be the unit of analysis. Cluster samples come in a variety of designs, with one- or multistage samples and equal or unequal clusters being some options. Generally, cluster sampling reduces the accuracy of an estimate for a given sample size.

Cluster samples probably occur more often than is generally realized. In the random roadside traffic survey, for example, the site location is actually a cluster. Cluster samples should also not be confused with "snowball" samples.[1] The standard error of a cluster sample can be estimated; the same cannot be done for a snowball sample.

Generally cluster samples are employed when the psus occur in natural groupings, when it is too costly or logistically impossible to list all the elements in a sample frame, or when selecting them at random is impossible. Occasionally, cluster samples consist of clusters within clusters. For example, a survey of schools might consist of a multistage cluster sample. Here, the first clusters chosen (the primary sampling units) would be the schools; within each school, the researcher could select secondary sampling units or classes at random. Within the classes, one might wish to survey all students or simply choose a random sample of students from the class list.

As pointed out in Chapter 5, one cost associated with cluster samples is the increase in the estimate of the sampling error as compared with an srs of the same size. This comes about because the variance is based more on the number of psus (clusters) than on the total number of elements surveyed. To offset this loss, cluster samples are usually stratified.

Single-Phase vs. Multiphase Samples

Single-phase sampling refers to a process whereby the entire sample is drawn in a single operation. Multiphase sampling, however, involves drawing the sample in two or more stages. The second phase of a multiphase sample involves selecting a subsample from a larger preselected sample. The advantage of multiphase samples is that the first phase can often provide detailed information for improving upon the final selection.

The general procedure in multiphase samples is to conduct a less costly general or screening interview for the first phase and then revisit a selected subsample for more detailed interviewing in the second phase. This type of strategy might be employed in

---

1. The use of snowball samples will be discussed in Chapter 7.

a fertility survey. Here, a general interview schedule could be presented to all women included in the sample. As a second phase, one might wish to conduct more detailed interviews with women who have had miscarriages or who, based on the initial results, may appear to be infertile.

Often multiphase samples are multimodal. That is, a less expensive telephone interview procedure might be used at the first phase, while more expensive in-person interviews might be reserved for the second phase.

Effectively designed sampling strategies may employ different combinations of the foregoing dimensions. As a practical endeavor, sampling involves a trade-off between costs, "doability," and statistical considerations.

Sampling Proportionate to Size

It often happens in practice that the psus vary considerably in size but the researcher wishes to select a sample of a fixed overall size, n, and of similar sizes within each of the primary units. For example, a criminologist may wish to estimate how much violence takes place in schools. It is decided that the overall sample size should consist of 1100 students out of the total regional population of 220,000. Furthermore, to maintain consistency in the size of the variance of the estimates, the criminologist decides that approximately 50 students be selected from each school. This suggests that 22 initial psus (schools) are to be selected. If the schools are of approximately equal size, it would be a simple matter to randomly select 22 schools from the study region and then further select a random sample of 50 students within each school. In practice, the schools in a given region vary considerably in size from, say, 600 students to 2000 students. Thus, an srs of schools would be biased against students in the larger schools. That is, the probabilities of selection for students in the larger schools would be less than for the smaller schools.

To address this problem, it is common practice to select the psu with probabilities proportionate to their size. Thus each student in the region has a constant overall probability of selection.

The situation can be illustrated by examining the selection probabilities separately at the two stages. Again, f is the overall sampling fraction n/N. Let N_α be the number of students in cluster α; let b represent the number of students to be selected within each cluster, and consider F as $1/f$. In essence, F is N/n. Since the sample to be selected within each cluster is fixed at b, the probability of selection for the second stage is b/N_α. Now we need to determine the probabilities of selection for primary sampling units. Since the overall sampling fraction is fixed at f, the solution may be achieved by substituting the appropriate values in the equation

$$\frac{N_\alpha}{Fb} \frac{b}{N_\alpha} = \frac{1}{F} = f$$

Thus, the appropriate probabilities of selection for the clusters at stage one are N_α/Fb. Since the denominator, Fb, is a constant, the selection probabilities are proportionate to the cluster's sizes, N_α.

Occasionally, the exact cluster sizes are not known. In these situations substituting a measure that proxies N_α is often possible. For example, if in a study of manufacturers' employees, reliable data on the number of employees per firm were not available, it might be possible to substitute a reasonable proxy such as annual total sales, or amounts paid by the firms in benefits. This proxy for the number of employees per firm is known as a *measure of size* and is usually designated as Mos_α. By substituting Mos_α for N_α, we obtain the equation for the two-stage selection probabilities as

$$\frac{Mos_\alpha}{Fb}\frac{b}{Mos_\alpha} = \frac{b}{Fb} = f$$

Again, the probability of selecting the αth psu should be equal to Mos_α/Fb. Some consideration might prompt us to ask how the population total, N, can be determined if the exact sizes of the individual psus are not known. Occasionally, this information is available from selected industry or census documents. All is not lost, however, if the information is not available. If it can be assumed that Fb is again fixed, with a psus, then we can substitute

$$Fb = \frac{\sum_{\alpha=1}^{A} Mos_\alpha}{a}$$

What is important here, however, is that if Mos_α is used for the calculation of the selection probabilities for the primary units, it must also be used for the calculation of the selection probabilities for the secondary units. That is, Mos_α cannot be used for one and N_α for the other.

A Caution

Why should we bother selecting clusters proportionate to size when the frame could just as easily be stratified according to size and psus chosen on that basis? The answer is that these are two very different processes, and while both are statistically "legitimate" things to do, the procedures address two very different problems. In sampling proportionate to size, we assume that the units of interest are the elements within the clusters. In the preceding example, that would be the students within the schools. Stratifying the psus by size and then conducting an srs selection within the strata implies that the unit of interest is the cluster itself. Thus, the focus would be on the characteristics of the school as a unit, not the individual students, or on the firm as opposed to the individual employees. The distinction is one of units of analysis. Hence, it is again essential that the person designing the sample be fully aware of the objectives it is supposed to serve.

Poststratification

Occasionally, a researcher has prior knowledge of a distribution of a population on some criteria in conjunction with the survey. These data may be obtained from analyses of census files or from larger, multipurpose samples. Where minor differences exist between the distribution of characteristics in one's sample and the known distribution of the characteristics in the population, it may be appropriate to reweight the sample. When used judiciously, this reweighting, known as *poststratification*, can lead to improved estimates in samples that have succumbed to the vicissitudes of chance.

Some researchers use poststratification as a procedure for correcting for nonresponse in the survey. This is a much more tenuous enterprise and one that should not be engaged in lightly. The use of weighting to correct for nonresponding or missing cases may be a viable approach to the problem. However, weighting is but one possible way of addressing the issue. The researcher should be aware that there are many approaches to the missing data problem, and the advantages and disadvantages of each. This issue will be dealt with in greater detail in Chapter 13.

SAMPLE SIZE AND DESIGN EFFECTS

The issue of estimating an appropriate sample size for testing hypotheses was addressed in Chapter 4. Here we examined the simple relationship between the size of a sample, the variance of the estimate, and the impact of DEFF and roh for cluster samples.

The Simple Random Sample

The relationship between n and the standard error can be illustrated as follows. First, recall that the variance of an estimate such as a proportion is

$$\text{var}(p) = (1 - f)\frac{s^2}{n} = \frac{s^2}{n^*}$$

It is possible to solve for n^*:

$$n^* = \frac{s^2}{\text{var}(p)}$$

and for n:

$$n = \frac{n^*}{1 + f} = \frac{n^*}{1 + n^*/N}$$

EXAMPLE: ESTIMATING SAMPLE SIZE FOR AN SRS

From a previous survey s^2 is estimated to be .2491 and the population, N, is known to be 10,000. The researcher wants a standard error of no more than 1%. By substitution,

$$n^* = \frac{.2491}{(.01)^2} = 2491 \quad \text{and} \quad n = \frac{2491}{1 + 2491/10,000} = 1994$$

There are two significant points of note here. First, n^* is very sensitive to the size of var(p), and as var(p) becomes smaller, n^* increases geometrically. Second, except where f is very large, the fpc has only a small impact on the required sample. These two points are well illustrated in Table 6.1, where the researcher considered how sample size varied with differing values of the standard error of p. To illustrate the impact of the population total on n, two cities have been assumed: one with a population of

10,000 and the other with a population of 100,000. Where f is small, n remains similar whether the population from which the sample is to be drawn is 10,000 or 100,000. This pattern, illustrated by the estimates reported in Table 6.1, appears counter-intuitive to many people, who assume that if a sample is to stay "representative," sample size must increase as the population increases. In fact, for a given sample size with negligible fpc, the precision of a sample is essentially the same whether the sample is drawn from a population of several thousands or several millions.

Table 6.1. Relationship between SE(p) and n for selected SE(p)

			n	
STANDARD ERROR	var(p)	n*	N=10,000	N=100,000
0.01	0.0001	2491	1994	2430
0.015	0.000225	1107	997	1095
0.02	0.0004	623	586	619
0.025	0.000625	399	383	397
0.03	0.0009	277	269	276

Estimating Sample Size Where s^2 Is Known

In this and the following sections, it is assumed that a researcher is interested in obtaining a point estimate rather than testing a hypothesis. Consequently, the issue of statistical power (which was addressed in Chapter 4) can be ignored.

Following the logic of the preceding section, estimating the required sample size for an srs is relatively straightforward. Prior to being able to estimate an acceptable sample size, however, the researcher needs to know three things. First, some estimate is required of the variance of the variable or phenomenon under investigation. Second, an acceptable level of error needs to be specified. That is, for some parameter, θ, to be estimated, it must be decided how large an error limit, L, is acceptable, where $|\theta - \hat{\theta}| < L$. Third, the probability $1 - \alpha$ needs to be stated to specify the expected proportion of the times the estimate must be less than L. Typically, if $\alpha = .05$ were acceptable, L would be 1.96 SE($\hat{\theta}$).

Under these circumstances, we know that

$$ L = z\frac{s}{\sqrt{n_0}}, \quad \text{thus} \quad L^2 = z^2\frac{s^2}{n_0} $$

Solving for n_0,

$$ n_0 = z^2\frac{s^2}{L^2} $$

EXAMPLE: SAMPLING FOR VOTES

The basic principles are easiest to illustrate where the statistic of interest, θ, is a proportion. Suppose that in the last elections held in a particular jurisdiction, 35% of the voters cast their ballots for the Democratic candidate. Before deciding to run again, the candidate wishes to estimate the likely proportion of votes she would receive, plus or minus 2.5%, with a 95% level of confidence that the estimate falls within that range.

From the previous election, the variance (s^2) is estimated as pq or $(.35)(.65) = .2275$. The candidate wishes to estimate $p \pm z\ SE(p)$, where $z\ SE(p) = .025$. To simplify notation, let L represent the acceptable limit of $z_{\alpha/2}\ SE(p)$. Furthermore, it can be assumed that the candidate is running in a jurisdiction with a large population (say several million), so the fpc factor is moot. By substitution, we have

$$n_0 = (1.96)^2 \frac{.2275}{(.025)^2}$$
$$= 1398$$

In other words, a sample of 1398 voters is required to estimate the proportion of votes the candidate might receive within ±2.5% 19 times out of 20.

Where the population from which the sample is to be drawn is finite, the preceding formulas can be used if they are adjusted for the fpc. If the jurisdiction in which the candidate is running is a town of 5000, the following adjustments can be made:

$$L = z\frac{s}{\sqrt{n}}\sqrt{1 - \frac{n}{N}}, \qquad \text{thus} \qquad L^2 = z^2 \frac{s^2}{n}\left(1 - \frac{n}{N}\right)$$

Solving for n, we obtain

$$n = \frac{\dfrac{z^2 s^2}{L^2}}{1 + \dfrac{1}{N}\left(\dfrac{z^2 s^2}{L^2} - 1\right)}$$

This formula is somewhat unwieldy. However, it will be noticed that the term $z^2 s^2 / L^2$, which appears in both the numerator and the denominator, is the estimator for n_0. By substituting n_0, n can be expressed more manageably, as follows:

$$n = \frac{n_0}{1 + \dfrac{1}{N}(n_0 - 1)}$$

EXAMPLE: SAMPLING FOR VOTES (CONTINUED)

Again, substituting the appropriate values, n is determined as follows:

$$n = \frac{1398}{1 + \dfrac{1}{5000}(1398 - 1)}$$
$$= 1093$$

Since the population is now considered finite, the fpc results in a reduction of the necessary sample size by 22% from 1398 to 1093.

Estimating Sample Size Where s^2 Is Unknown

In some situations, s^2 either is not known or is of questionable reliability. Under these circumstances, one must generate an estimate of s^2. There are three ways in which this is typically done. First, the researcher can search the available literature for similar studies conducted elsewhere. As indicated previously, the estimate of s^2 need not always be very precise, especially when one is dealing with proportions. In other situations, it is possible to conduct a sensitivity analysis by using the best estimate of s^2 and then generating several estimated ns by varying the value of s^2. For example, the desired formula for n can be entered into a spreadsheet. A first expected n can be generated by means of the best estimate of s^2, and subsequent values for n can be obtained by increasing s^2 by 25%, 50%, . . . , 100%, and so on.

A second approach to obtaining an estimate of s^2 is to conduct a pilot study. Where possible, pilot studies are highly recommended for many reasons. Not only is it possible to obtain an estimate of s^2, but the measurement instrument can be assessed, and any research assistants or interviewers involved in the study can get firsthand experience with both the instruments and the design procedure. Unfortunately, quality pilot studies can be difficult to execute. When the design costs of doing the research are very high compared with the cost of collecting the data (e.g., conducting face-to-face interviews in the Himalayas), doing a pilot may not be economical.

A third approach that can be used is generally attributed to Cox and Stein. The Cox–Stein procedure involves estimating the final sample size "on the fly." This approach has the advantage of combining the pilot and the actual study into a single process. Its primary disadvantage is that the final sample size is not known until after the study has started; hence, the final cost is not known at the start. This contrasts with the pilot approach, where the cost usually can be fixed and the results from that study allow a fixed cost estimate to be produced for the final study.

The Cox–Stein approach includes the following steps (Cochran, 1977: 78–80).

1. Select an initial subsample of size n_1, and estimate s_1^2.
2. Calculate n_2 as follows:

$$n_2 = \frac{s_1^2}{V}\left(1 + \frac{2}{n_1}\right)$$

   where V is the level of precision required.
3. Calculate n as follows:

$$n = \max\left[n_1, \left(n_2 \frac{1}{\left(\frac{n_2}{N}\right) + 1}\right) + 1\right]$$

4. Take $n - n_1$ additional observations.

EXAMPLE: ESTIMATING THE PERCENT OF TWO-PERSON HOUSEHOLDS WHERE s^2 IS UNKNOWN

Assume that a researcher wishes to estimate the percentage of two-person households, plus or minus 2% in a retirement community of 5000 households. An initial sample, n_1, of 20 households is selected for an srs telephone survey. It is determined that 8 of the surveyed households contain two people. Thus, $p = .4$ and $s_1^2 = (.4)(.6) = .24$. In this case, the variance, V, is $(.02)^2 = .0004$, consequently,

$$
n_2 = \frac{s_1^2}{V}\left(1 + \frac{2}{n_1}\right)
$$

$$
= \frac{.24}{.0004}\left(1 + \frac{2}{20}\right)
$$

$$
= 660
$$

and

$$
n = \max\left[n_1, \left(n_2 \frac{1}{\frac{n_2}{N}+1}\right)+1\right]
$$

$$
= \max\left[20, \left(660\frac{1}{\frac{660}{5000}+1}\right)+1\right]
$$

$$
= \max\ \{20, 584\}
$$

$$
= 584
$$

Therefore, the researcher needs to take a further sample of $584 - 20 = 564$ residents.

Cluster Size and Sampling Error

The preceding chapter introduced the concepts of DEFF and roh with respect to clustering, the point being that the expected homogeneity of clusters reduces their effective standard error in comparison to an srs based on the same number of elements. The loss in precision can also be seen to depend on the size of the clusters. In Chapter 5 we showed that $\text{DEFF} = [1 + \text{roh}(\bar{n}_\alpha - 1)]$ and consequently, $\text{roh} = (\text{DEFF} - 1)/(\bar{n}_\alpha - 1)$.

For the random roadside survey, roh was estimated to be .031. By assuming that roh is reasonably constant in such surveys, the relationship between cluster size and DEFF can be illustrated. In Table 6.2, DEFF has been calculated for roh of .031 and cluster sizes from 10 to 100 (assuming either a constant b per cluster or a stable $\bar{n}_\alpha$). Clearly, as the cluster size increases, DEFF increases and the effective sample size relative to an srs decreases correspondingly. If achieving the smallest sampling error

Table 6.2. DEFF and Effective Sample Sizes for Different Sized Clusters

CLUSTER SIZE	DEFF	EFFECTIVE SAMPLE WHERE srs = 1783
1	1	1783
5	1.124	1586
10	1.279	1394
20	1.589	1122
30	1.899	939
40	2.209	807
75	3.294	541
100	4.069	438

for a given n were the only consideration, the smallest cluster size possible should clearly be selected. Unfortunately, other factors come into play, complicating one's task in establishing an optimal cluster size.

For example, in the roadside surveys, the proportion of drivers with BAC levels over the legal limit was estimated to be about 5%. Thus driving in a state of statutory intoxication is a relatively rare event; and with small clusters, it is likely that few (if any) drivers over the limit would be captured at any given site. With an average cluster size of 20, we could expect only one driver to be over the limit. Clearly, reasonable sized clusters are required in this instance to capture the point estimate, p. Even with $\bar{n}_\alpha = 42$ (as here), only two drivers on average can be expected to be over the legal limit.

Cost is another significant factor that must be considered with cluster samples. Often, it costs 20 to 50 times as much to identify and reach the cluster as it does to measure the elements in the cluster. Surveying students in classrooms across a state or province illustrates this problem. The costs of travel and of the interviewer's time to appear on location are substantial. At each site, however, the cost of surveying a classroom of 20 to 30 students is negligible.

Since cost is a major factor in determining how much data can be collected, it is worth turning our attention to this issue.

SURVEY COSTS

Collecting data is expensive. The costs may be measured directly in monetary terms, as is done when a for-profit agency is hired to conduct a survey, or they may be indirect, as they are when doctoral students invest time in collecting their own data. In the latter case, the data are not "free." There is an opportunity cost involved, since time the doctoral candidate puts into data collection could be used for other activities—writing the thesis, spending time with one's family, or working full time.

Determining the cost of data collection is an iterative process. Initially, sample size requirements are based on how precise one would like the estimate to be. This may be based on a practical motive, such as a political candidate's wanting to be able to estimate with a reasonable degree of certainty how many voters are likely to be captured, or it may be based on theoretical criteria, such as the desire to be able to estimate DEFF or another important parameter. These demands for accuracy, however, are tempered by the resources available. If the cost of collecting the desired sample is prohibitive, then the sample size may be scaled back (consequently decreasing the precision of the estimate), or the enterprise may be abandoned. Usually when we collect data, we wish to know how much the exercise will cost, but we also work within the confines of a predetermined budget.

Thus, sampling is the art of compromise, and the key question is, Can we satisfy our desire to generate an estimate having an acceptable level of precision for an acceptable cost? The issue of precision, which varies with the sampling error, has been examined in some detail. The next step is to examine the factors that enter the cost equation.

The total cost of data collection can be broken into two components: fixed costs and variable costs. The fixed costs are those associated with aspects of data collection that are somewhat independent of the size of the sample. For example, in executing a survey, the cost associated with developing the questionnaire is the same whether the instrument is presented to 10 people or 10,000 people. The variable cost components are the items driven by the number of elements. In a telephone survey, this would include items such as the per-interview cost for the interviewer. Some items may cross categories depending upon the situation. For example, the cost of phone calls in telephone surveys may be fixed if the surveyor is making local calls on a flat-rate billing system, but it may be variable if per-call or long-distance charges apply.

Kish (1965: 263–72) presents a four-component cost model that works well in the main. Specifically, Kish's model for total costs, C_t, is defined as follows:

$$C_t = C_k + C_{kv} + nc + nc_v$$

In this equation, C_k represents fixed costs that apply despite the size of the survey or the specific design chosen. These include such elements as the process of deciding upon the survey design, the per-diem expenses of a consulting statistician, the development of the measurement instrument, the performance of the data analysis, and the cost of publishing and distributing the final report.

C_{kv} are design-dependent cost factors that do not vary with the sample size. Hence, they are independent of n but they do depend on the strategy selected. These factors may include differential costs of training and supervising interviewers to collect data in a cluster as opposed to an srs survey.

The third component, nc, consists of variable costs related to the sample size but independent of the design. Typically these costs are the per-unit cost of collecting data (interviewing or another form of measurement), the incremental costs of supervising the data collection, and some elements of overhead (e.g., cost of renting more office space or a fixed office space for a longer time). One issue that may be overlooked is the tendency of large samples to take longer to collect than smaller samples, thereby imposing an opportunity cost by delaying the analysis and publication of the results.

The fourth component, nc_v, consists of items that vary with both the number of elements sampled and the design of the sample. Thus, a cluster sample sometimes requires regional offices to reduce the cost of traveling to the sites, and the cost of supporting those regional offices is proportional to the number of clusters and the number of elements sampled.

Because of the fixed costs, larger surveys tend to cost less per element than small surveys. On the other hand, increases in precision often have a steeper incremental cost function (because of the geometric requirement for data) than the per-unit savings function associated with a larger sample size. As with most human activities, the cost–precision relationship is one of marginal incremental returns to scale. Initially, significant increases in precision are obtained as more resources are put into increasing the sample size. After a point, however, the costs per unit increase in precision become prohibitive.

Optimal Strata Sizes

Without considering costs, it has been suggested that the optimal strategy for allocating elements over a stratified sample is to allocate disproportionately to strata that have either the largest variance or the largest N_h. If the total cost is fixed, this approach can be modified so that the strata with the largest variances get the largest proportion of elements and those with the highest associated costs receive a smaller proportion of the overall sample.

Different models can be used to estimate the total cost of carrying out different sampling designs. Some of these can be defined analytically, while others are based solely upon field experience. The simplest model, however, is a linear cost model that assumes constant incremental unit costs as the sample size increases or decreases. Thus, the assumption is made that the total cost, C_t, is composed of a fixed cost component, C_k, and a variable stratum-dependent component, C_h, associated with each element in the hth stratum. That is, $C_t = C_k + \sum_{h=1}^{H} C_h n_h.$[2] Cochran (1977: 96–99) shows that under these criteria, the lowest variance is obtained when the stratum sizes are proportionate to $N_h S_h / \sqrt{C_h}$. Thus, for a fixed overall cost for the sample, the best estimate for the total sample size is given by

$$n = \frac{(C_t - C_k)\left(N_h S_h / \sqrt{C_h}\right)}{\sum_{h=1}^{H} N_h S_h \sqrt{C_h}}$$

Once the total sample size has been estimated, the stratum allocations, n_h/n, may be estimated by

$$\frac{n_h}{n} \doteq \frac{W_h S_h / \sqrt{C_h}}{\sum_{h=1}^{H}\left(W_h S_h / \sqrt{C_h}\right)} = \frac{N_h S_h / \sqrt{C_h}}{\sum_{h=1}^{H}\left(N_h S_h / \sqrt{C_h}\right)}$$

In this instance, it has been assumed that the cost is fixed. Cochran also provides a discussion on estimating n_h based on the requirement that var$(\overline{y}_{st})$ be fixed and the total cost be allowed to vary instead.

---

2. Remember that cost need not always be estimated in dollar terms. C_t may represent some other finite commodity, such as the total number of person-hours available for conducting the data collection phase of the study.

Optimal Cluster Size

When the size of a cluster increases (all other things being equal), the DEFF increases and the effective sample size decreases. Consequently, the following question is often posed: What is the optimal cluster size?

The answer to this problem is best addressed in two steps. The first step is to decide the optimal sample size for an srs of an acceptable precision. Once determined, n is multiplied by the design effect to compensate for the fact that the effective sample size is less than the nominal sample size. Needless to say, the difficulty here lies in obtaining reasonable estimates of both s^2 and DEFF. Based on this exercise, however, the researcher can often determine roughly whether the available budget can support the research. For a cluster sample, the basic cost model may be defined as follows:

$$C_t = ac_1 + nc_2 = ac_1 + \bar{n}_a ac_2$$

where again, C_t is the total cost, a is the number of clusters, c_1 is the cost associated with the cluster, and c_2 is the unit cost associated with the elements. By knowing roh, it is possible to estimate the optimal cluster size, $\bar{n}_{opt}$, as

$$\bar{n}_{opt} = \sqrt{\frac{c_1}{c_2}\left(\frac{1-\rho}{\rho}\right)}$$

After $\bar{n}_{opt}$ has been determined, the number of required clusters becomes $a = n/\bar{n}_{opt}$.

A side benefit of this formulation is that the actual values of c_1 and c_2 need not be known to calculate $\bar{n}_{opt}$. It is sufficient to know the approximate ratio between these two elements to estimate the optimal cluster size.

Where the total cost, C_t, is fixed, however, a may be estimated within that constraint as follows:

$$a = \frac{C_t}{c_1 + \bar{n}_{opt}c_2}$$

Further Reading

See the selections presented at the end of Chapter 5, especially the books by Kish and Sudman.

7

Sampling: Special Problems

Surveys vary greatly in their complexity. To take a sample from 5000 cards, neatly arranged and numbered in a file, is an easy task. It is another matter to sample the inhabitants of a region where transport is by water through the forests, where there are no maps, where 15 different dialects are spoken, and where the inhabitants are very suspicious of an inquisitive stranger.

—William G. Cochran

Applied sampling schemes rarely turn out as neatly as specified in the sampling texts. Perhaps more than any other part of the research enterprise, sampling is the area that illustrates Murphy's law: if anything can go wrong, it will. This chapter addresses some of the more common problems and suggests some possible solutions.

Most problems faced by the researcher in applied sampling result in a decrease in sampling accuracy. This occurs because bias is introduced into the sample estimates.

SAMPLING BIAS

While bias may be introduced into sampling estimates through many sources, these are commonly grouped into three broad categories.

- **Statistical Bias**. The primary cause of statistical bias is the use of n as opposed to $n-1$ in the calculation of s or s^2. Neglecting the inclusion of sampling fractions in small samples and treating complex samples, such as stratified cluster samples, as srss may also lead to similar problems. Except in instances of failure to include the appropriate weights in a data set, statistical bias can be corrected easily through a reanalysis of the data. Other sources of bias, however, tend to be correctable only before or during the data collection phase.

- **Frame Bias**. Bias can be introduced by using improper or imperfect selection frames. For example, transients are often undersampled, or not sampled at all, in labor force participation studies. Frame biases are a primary source of bias in sampling. The difficulty of putting together an adequate frame is nowhere better illustrated than in the problems faced by the U.S. Bureau of the Census in conducting a "census" of the United States. Doing a census may be seen as an effort of putting together a population frame; the execution of the census also requires some existing frame, such as an aerial depiction of housing units. Because of the difficulty of capturing transients and illegal immigrants in the

1990 census, some major centers like New York City have sued the bureau for the loss of transfer payments from the federal government. New York argues that it must provide services to such groups but receives less than its full share of financial aid in this matter because of the census undercount.

- **Observation Bias**. Missing observations due to missing cases or missing values on particular variables can also lead to considerable bias. Data go missing for many reasons, including inattentiveness by the persons taking the measurements, and the inability to find certain elements within the sample frame. The resulting bias varies with the degree to which nonrespondents differ from respondents. As will be shown in Chapter 13, to ignore or delete missing cases is to implicitly assume that the missing cases are equal to the mean of the observed cases. If that assumption is valid, fine. If it is not, then one has to confront the problem directly.

The issues addressed in this chapter are related to bias-generating aspects associated with inadequate sample frames or observational bias.

FRAME PROBLEMS

The sampling frame consists of a listing or enumeration of all elements in the population. Occasionally, preformed lists exist that act as a handy frame. Examples include municipal directories, telephone directories, and membership rosters from professional associations. Often, however, complete frames do not exist and alternate strategies are required for their construction.

One common alternative to the use of itemized frames is area sampling. To conduct area sampling, one needs aerial maps over which a standard grid can be placed. Grid sections are then selected at random. For large geographical areas, it may be necessary to use multistage selection—that is, to place selected areas under ever smaller grids, with random selection taking place at each successive stage.

A frame is considered perfect if every element is listed separately, once and only once, and nothing else appears on the list. Often, however, frames are plagued with duplicate and incomplete listings. In these situations, the researcher has at least three alternatives.

- **Ignoring and Disregarding the Problem**. This may be a viable alternative if the error in the listing is known to be small compared with other errors. It may also be a reasonable option if the missing cases are known to be randomly distributed. The problem with duplicate listings and missing cases in the frame is that the probability of element selection is not equal to what it is in the population.

- **Redefining the Population to Fit the Frame**. If the frame is complete on some segments of the population but not on others, restructuring the target population to include only elements that are members of the complete listing may be worthwhile. For example, a study of professions may find that sample frames are complete for physicians and lawyers (who must belong to professional societies to maintain their professional status) but incomplete for accountants (for whom membership may be voluntary). Upon completion of the analysis, however, the researcher must be careful not to generalize the findings beyond the redefined target population.

- **Correcting the Entire Population List**. For duplicate listings, this may not be an onerous task, especially with the assistance of computerized listings and search routines. Care must be taken, however, not to eliminate different people with the same name. A good example of duplicate listings is found when telephone directories are used as frames for households. Many households have more than one line (teenagers' phones, home business lines) and consequently, may have two, three, or more entries.

Completing an incomplete population frame, on the other hand, can be a very time-consuming and expensive proposition. It may be a worthwhile exercise, though, if the unenumerated cases represent a particularly important group in the study. Sometimes, elements that are missing due to noncoverage or an incomplete frame can be included in a separate stratum.

RESPONSE RATES AND SURVEY TACTICS

Decreasing response rates are becoming an increasingly important problem in the social sciences, particularly in survey research. Professional survey firms are finding it more and more difficult to maintain the response rates of previous years, despite constant improvements in survey technology. In a review of more than 500 face-to-face interviews, telephone surveys, and mail surveys, Goyder (1987) reports mean response rates of 67, 60, and 58%, respectively, Groves and Lyberg (1988) show a long-term decline in response to telephone surveys. In their review of surveys conducted primarily by academics as opposed to private research firms, Hox and DeLeeuw (1994) suggest that over the period 1947–92, responses to telephone and face-to-face surveys have converged with those of mail surveys.

Variations in response rates and how they might be dealt with depend upon the survey procedures employed. Some people are difficult to locate (thus necessitating callbacks or setting of appointments), and some are reluctant to participate in surveys of any kind. Telephone surveys were very successful tools before direct-dial marketers latched onto the procedure and succeeded in souring the level of consumer cooperativeness. Ever more people are now perceiving any form of telephone soliciting as harassment and an infringement on their privacy.

Because response rates are declining universally, it is even more important that researchers use whatever procedures are available to maintain the overall response rate. Fortunately, there are some tried and true techniques at our disposal if we are willing to make the effort to use them.

In-Person Interviews

In-person surveys generally involve house-to-house interviews with area residents. This has been the traditional procedure used to collect information for censuses and large-scale surveys. Recently, however, in-person interviews for large-scale projects have fallen out of favor. They are exceedingly costly, and there is some evidence that both response rates and data quality can be improved through other procedures, particularly telephone surveys.

Still, in-person interviews do offer some advantages over other techniques. They allow for ancillary information to be gathered through on-site inspection. Thus, for example, the interviewer can later provide qualitative assessments of the condition of the respondent's residence or the physical condition of the interviewee. The interviewer can also perform quick validity checks on such items as the apparent age of the interviewee or the apparent standard of living maintained in the household. Furthermore, it is possible to cross-check some aspects of the sample frame through direct observation. This may be particularly useful in canvasses of dwelling units that have been subdivided and not reported to municipal authorities (as happens with illegal suites).

The negative aspects of in-person interviewing generally relate to cost. This type of research is very expensive in terms of personnel, time, and travel. Not only are interviewer costs high, but the costs of training interviewers are high as well. Other difficulties relating to in-person interviews involve quality control. Unlike mail or telephone interviewing, supervisors generally do not have firsthand contact with interviewers in the field. It must be assumed, therefore, that these employees are conducting the interviews as expected and that the sessions are essentially consistent across interviewers.

Procedures for increasing response rates for in-person interviews revolve around the traditional callback. Unfortunately, a dozen or more tries may be necessary to achieve an interview with one person. Indeed, many interviewees feel little obligation to honor their commitment to keep appointments arranged over the telephone. Given the travel costs associated with in-person interviews, this unreliability can force the researcher to select a lower overall sample size than might be warranted.

Occasionally, an interviewer who has been stood up by the person who made the appointment can interview another household member who may have similar characteristics or may be knowledgeable about the objectives of the survey. Also, some pertinent data may be collected through direct observation that might either suffice per se or supply data for an analysis of missing cases.

The use of interviewers with characteristics similar to those of the interviewees (e.g., ethnic affiliation, gender) may also increase response rates, although dissimilarity in such respects does not appear to be a major problem. These issues are addressed in greater detail in Chapter 12.

Telephone Interviews

Telephone survey techniques are quickly replacing in-person interviews in survey research. The primary advantages of the former are reduced cost and the timeliness of data collection. In some automated teledialing centers, the data are entered directly into microcomputers, thereby allowing for both internal consistency checks on answers and virtually instantaneous analysis. Advances in random digit dialing also allow for simple random samples as opposed to the heavy reliance on stratified samples for in-person interviews. Because of travel costs, in-person interviews often made heavy use of clustering and stratifying which, in turn, complicated the sample design (DEFF).

Other advantages of telephone interviews generally relate to the degree to which supervisors have control over the interviewers. It is possible to monitor interviewers to make sure that standards are adhered to at least at minimum levels and that each expected interview is both conducted and conducted as it ought to be.

Telephone interviews are not without costs, however. While almost universal coverage exists in many parts of the world, not everyone has a telephone. In fact, for some surveys, the target population might be the one whose members are least likely to have private telephone service. Validity checks are much more difficult to make, and the relative anonymity of the telephone (which may be an advantage for some things) makes it difficult to uncover lies or misleading answers from respondents. Furthermore, some individuals in the sampling unit may be less accessible by telephone than through in-person interviews. Overall, however, the telephone interview is becoming the technique of choice for more and more surveyors.

Calls around supper time are most likely to find people home, but are also likely to find people most upset about intrusions. Precalling to set up interviews (especially with professionals, etc.) is one way to schedule a more convenient time for the interviewee. Also helpful is affiliation with a high profile institution (such as a university or well-known polling agency).

Mail Surveys

The researcher's traditional response to the expense of the in-person interview has been the mail survey. Certainly for lengthy, national surveys, this procedure is less expensive than even the telephone survey. The mail survey is fraught with problems, however. It generally has the lowest response rate of all survey techniques; there is no control over the sequencing of questions; there is no opportunity for internal consistency checks, and no control over the return time for the survey. The telephone interview is also much more timely. Another disadvantage of the mail survey is that the interviewee has no opportunity to ask for an explanation of difficult-to-understand questions. Ultimately, of course, mail surveys require respondents to be functionally literate.

Unsolicited commercial mail surveys are often considered successful if the response rate is beyond 20%. Since the response rate for this procedure has generally been among the lowest, more techniques have been devised to increase response here than with any other procedure. As Hox and DeLeeuw suggest, those improvements in mail survey methods have led to general increases in response rates over the last few years. Much of this is undoubtedly due to Dillman's (1978, 1991) four-step "total design method." This process, which has engendered variants in recent times, essentially encompasses the following. First, an initial mailing is sent out with a questionnaire, covering letter, and postage-paid return envelope. Second, a postcard reminder is sent out a week or two later. Third, after another couple of weeks, a second mailing similar to the initial mailing is sent out. Finally, a special mailing is sent out.

Among the other useful techniques for increasing mail response are:

- precalls by phone to provide notice of incoming surveys
- offers of small gifts in the survey (e.g., pens to complete it or nominal amounts of cash)
- offers to donate small tokens to charity if the survey is returned completed
- pointing out the procedure's lack of intrusion in comparison with other survey techniques (in-person or telephone)

Notes on "Nonscientific" Samples

Within the universe of sampling plans, probability samples are only a small segment. In many situations, nonprobability procedures may be more than acceptable, particularly if a wealth of supporting evidence exists.

Convenience samples of the type found in shopping malls and supermarkets are a good example of nonscientific sampling strategies that often "work." These procedures typically target the user population of a particular good and provide adequate indicators for marketing purposes. As an indicator of population preferences, however, they can be suspect. A classical example here is the flawed procedure Ford Motor Company executives used to assess demand for the Edsel, which was introduced in the mid-1950s.

Snowball sampling is another procedure that has its uses. Snowball samples are particularly good at identifying sample frames. Working on the basis of "birds of a feather flocking together," this procedure requires the location of an individual of a given characteristic; then that person is asked to provide names of other suitable subjects. Initial research into AIDS was based on snowball sampling procedures. This approach is very useful when (a) there is no preexisting sampling frame, or no obvious alternative to one, and (b) the issue in question is a rare probability event that tends not to be (near) randomly dispersed throughout the population. Snowball samples may appear to be cluster samples, but they are not. Unlike cluster samples snowball samples are not probability samples.

Another commonly used nonscientific sampling procedure is the quota sample. Quota samples as originally conducted, appeared to parallel stratified samples. Again, unlike true stratified samples, quota samples are not probability samples. Original quota samples were essentially convenience samples directed at subpopulations. A more recent use of the term is what Sudman calls "probability sampling with quotas."

RARE AND HARD-TO-LOCATE ELEMENTS

Some particularly interesting populations often constitute rare events or hard-to-locate individuals. For example, the proportion of drunk drivers on the roads, those infected with AIDS, Americans of Danish ancestry, and persons with incomes over $1 million would likely be missed in a typical general-purpose survey. The cost of identifying and surveying hard-to-find elements through normal sampling techniques can be prohibitive. Consequently, we turn to alternate strategies.

Before examining those strategies in detail, we focus briefly on the issue of why the elements of interest might be difficult to find. Spreen distinguishes between what he terms "rare" and "hidden" populations. Essentially, difficult-to-locate populations may possess the trait either because they are small or, as Spreen (1992) terms them, "insufficient" proportions of the population, or because they wish to remain hidden. Diagrammatically, the situation may be depicted as follows:

	EASY TO REACH	HARD TO REACH
Sufficient proportion	Sufficient subpopulations	Large hidden populations
Insufficient proportion	Rare populations	Small hidden populations

Naturally, sufficient subpopulations comprise the group most often captured in standard survey sampling. Rare populations are easy to reach (i.e., once identified, they pose no greater problem than sufficient populations) but pose a problem of high unit cost because of the many ineligibles that need to be screened to identify a single element of interest.

Hard-to-reach populations, however, may or may not be rare events. They are difficult to locate because the trait being investigated is socially sensitive. Studies that focus on drug use, tax evasion, or pedophilia and other nonmainstream sexual practices will find the target population difficult to find. Generally, members of "hidden populations" are reluctant to cooperate and, when they do agree to participate, often provide unreliable responses.

At one level, the techniques we employ to capture these difficult-to-locate samples differ. Easy-to-reach but rare populations require techniques that either reduce the per-unit screening cost for large populations or increase the likelihood of selection for the rare elements relative to the sufficient ones. Hard-to-reach or "hidden" populations require an approach that will induce the respondent to cooperate. As Spreen (1992: 37) notes, "It will take a lot of time to gain the confidence of the respondents for getting reliable answers and low nonresponses. Clearly, this will be a very time consuming and expensive way of sampling."

At another level, the same techniques used to identify rare elements can often be used to gain an entrée into a hidden population. Link-tracing designs, for example, use informants to direct the researcher to other members of the target population.

Frame Location

Occasionally, finding specialized lists that can act as sampling frames for normally hard-to-locate populations is possible. This is particularly the case with easy-to-reach but rare populations. Surveys of professionals fall into this category. A general survey would likely capture few if any physicians, accountants, or lawyers. On the other hand, persons in those occupational groupings tend to belong to their respective professional associations, and those membership lists are potential frames. The same can be said for other rare groups, such as volunteers, persons with unique hobbies, or individuals with rare diseases of certain types. Depending upon the circumstances surrounding the study, these specialized frames may be made freely available to the researcher by the agency or organization holding the list, or the list may be purchased. Before relying on a special list, however, the researcher should explore the likelihood of duplicate entries and rates of inclusion and exclusion. A list of physicians provided by the American Medical Association is likely a good census of all licensed physicians. A list of members of a local philatelic society would likely underestimate the total number of stamp collectors in that community; it is also possible that some persons on the list are no longer collectors.

The issue of duplicate listings can be alleviated sometimes by using computerized sort and search programs, although the outcome might be frustrating to someone who has purchased the list on a cost-per-entry basis. How much inclusion or exclusion exists can often be "guesstimated" based on one's knowledge of the organization owning the list. As always, the crucial dictum is Know thy field—statistical acumen is no substitute for substantive knowledge of one's area of study.

Use of Existing Multipurpose Surveys

Many government and private organizations conduct large-scale surveys regularly. The National Opinion Research Center's General Social Survey (GSS) or the monthly labor force surveys, contain data on thousands of respondents. Often a sufficient sample can be drawn from one or more existing general-purpose surveys. This is particularly the case with large surveys conducted frequently with nonoverlapping samples.

In other situations it is possible to use large multipurpose surveys as screening mechanisms for locating rare populations. The sponsoring agency may collect a small charge per question for each element; however, that cost is likely to be only a small fraction of the cost of constructing one's own screening survey. Once the rare elements have been located, they may be asked a series of questions added to the multipurpose survey, or they may be followed up on a subsequent occasion.

Correlated Factors

Occasionally, it is possible to find rare elements by knowing that they are correlated with some readily identifiable indicator. Heavy drinkers, for example, are more likely to be captured by conducting "exit interviews" at a randomly selected sample of liquor outlets than by means of a random digit dialing telephone survey.

Again the crucial element is researcher familiarity with the behavior under study. The more knowledge one has of the correlates of the trait of interest, the more likely it is that one will be able to specify a correlate that can be used to identify the target population.

Large Clusters

We have already noted the relative cost advantage of many cluster samples. For reasonably common events, cluster samples impose a high cost because of the adverse impact they have on the variance. For rare events, however, even extremely large clusters may not invalidate a sample, since only a few elements will be found per cluster. The problem of locating drinking drivers is a good example of the value of large clusters.

Some studies that have focused on the prevalence of rare genetic disorders have found clusters as large as a village to be cost-effective. The key here, of course, is the relative cost of traveling to the cluster site and setting up the screening mechanism compared with the cost of surveying the elements within the cluster. Where the fixed costs are high, but the variable cost of surveying individual elements is low, samples with large clusters hold a particular advantage.

Disproportionate Stratified Sampling

The key to disproportionate stratified sampling is to find small strata with a large proportion of rare elements. Usually, we look for special lists that identify the trait in question or have a highly correlated variable. Occasionally, specialized frames such as aerial census data will serve to identify areas with a high proportion of a target population.

Link-List Procedures

The procedures discussed above work well with rare but easy-to-reach populations. For hard-to-reach or hidden populations, it is often necessary to use something other than general screening procedures.

One technique that has received considerable attention lately is the use of link-lists. This technique is an umbrella term for several related procedures variously known as snowball samples and adaptive sampling techniques; other specialized approaches are included, as well. Once an individual of interest has been found, he or she is asked to identify others with the same trait of interest. As Spreen (1992: 35) defines the term, link-tracing is "a sample design in which the respondent is asked to mention other persons, according to some inclusion criterion defined by the researchers."

For example, early AIDS research used a classical snowball procedure and asked known AIDS sufferers to list all their intimates. Those individuals were contacted and asked to provide a list of their intimates, and the procedure continued, pyramid style, until no more unique individuals were identified.

Link-list procedures have proven effective in putting together sampling frames of rare and hidden populations. Once the frame has been constructed, all the individuals in the frame, or a selected sample of the frame, may be included in the study. Unfortunately, link-list frames are not without their share of problems. One set of problems is strictly methodological and relates to the issue of inclusion and exclusion. Specifically, "popular" elements are more likely to be included on the list than "loners." That is, link-list procedures generate better frames among groups that are highly social and interactive. Furthermore, link-tracing procedures are based on the assumption that there is a clear structure in the target population. Thus, if the individuals within the target population are largely unknown to each other, frame construction will not be very successful. For example, link-list procedures are not very good for identifying pedophiles, who tend to be loners.

A second set of problems surrounding link-tracing procedures involves statistical inference. Most standard statistical applications using data collected through link-tracing are biased. The seriousness of this problem depends on several factors. Techniques have been developed to generate reasonably unbiased estimates when the initial respondents are selected at random. Clearly, this is a less worrisome problem when one is trying to identify simply rare as opposed to hidden populations. Most ethnographic approaches that identify the initial respondents based on their quality as "informants" produce biased results, since the informants are generally more widely known individuals. How much bias is involved is unknown. Given the extensive base of "qualitative" and ethnographic research in the social sciences, it is perhaps surprising that more attention has not been focused on this issue. Snijders (1992: 68) made the intriguing suggestion of an approach through a series of simulation experiments.

For those interested in using snowball or link-tracing methods to estimate population parameters, it should be noted that these procedures are similar to what are known as adaptive sampling designs. These designs have been studied extensively and under many conditions are known to give unbiased (albeit sometimes inefficient) estimators. An accessible review of these procedures is given in Thompson (1992: pt. VI). One advantage of the estimators discussed by Thompson is that they are often design based, opposed to model based. That is, one need not make any assumptions about the distribution of the estimable parameters.

PROBLEMS WITH PANEL SURVEYS

Increasingly, social researchers are turning to panel surveys to monitor social trends and to test theoretical propositions. Unlike cross-sectional surveys, panels provide for the collation of data across a series of slices in time. From a theoretical perspective, panel data provide more opportunity to address issues of causality than do static, cross-sectional surveys.

While allowing the researcher to address a wider range of questions than their point-in-time cousins, panel surveys pose a few unique problems, not the least of which is tracing respondents across panels. Most survey respondents, however, can be traced using at least one of three basic techniques, namely, *retrospective, forward,* and *reverse tracing.*

Retrospective tracing simply involves trying to find a respondent for a follow-up by revisiting the interviewee's previous address. If the respondent is found at that address, the interview is conducted as planned. If the respondent has moved, attempts are made to trace him or her. Typically, the interviewer would contact the current resident or immediate neighbors to start the tracing procedure. The important point relating to retrospective tracing is that it is reactive as opposed to proactive. That is, the surveyor is only concerned about the possibility of having to trace a respondent once the person has moved. If the population of interest is not very mobile, retrospective tracing may be less expensive and less time-consuming than other tracing procedures. The obvious disadvantage is that for highly mobile populations, this approach can be extremely expensive and cumbersome.

Forward tracing essentially involves a procedure for obtaining more recent addresses before the follow-up is conducted. In forward tracing procedures, the onus for identifying the respondent's location is often placed on the respondent. For example, the researcher may give the respondent several cards, with instructions to mail one in at every change of address. Other approaches to forward tracing call for the researcher to take the initiative in following the respondent—for example, the following up of college graduates by searching alumni records. The forward tracing of certain professional groups is simplified because members are required to keep their professional associations up to date with respect to their whereabouts.

Whether forward tracing is more cost-effective than retrospective tracing is related to the type of target population one is following and the length of time between surveys. Proactive forward tracing may be expensive, but over time, the advantages accrued through the ease of location and decreases in the amount of missing data may make this technique worthwhile.

Reverse tracing is a specialized technique used to construct retrospective data. In some censuses, for example, respondents are asked where they resided 5 years ago. This information allows the researcher to reconstruct the respondent's residential history. Reverse tracing works best with census-type data, where exhaustive micro-level information is available and the researcher has some hope of retrospectively constructing one or more panels.

Effectively tracing individuals is an art as much as a science. Locating respondents, particularly after a substantial period between surveys, requires ingenuity, perseverance, and resources. Of course if sufficient resources are available, contracting a company that specializes in tracing people may be possible. Most researchers are not blessed with such a surfeit of riches, however, and must rely on their own initiative. Several articles on the topic provide both case studies and general suggestions on effective tracing (Crider, Willits, and Bealer, 1971; Hogan, 1983; Booth and Johnson, 1985). Box 7.1 reproduces a collation of ideas presented in a review article on the subject by Burgess (1989).

Spacing Panels

One issue that has not received much attention in the literature is that of spacing panels. The timing of existing panel studies varies widely, from labor force surveys that are mandated monthly, to ad hoc surveys that are executed irregularly every 2 to 3 years.

As with all sampling problems, the timing of panel surveys involves trade-offs between resources and accuracy. Generally, for a given period, the shorter the duration between surveys and the more frequent the surveys, the more expensive the enterprise becomes. On the other hand, increasing the duration between panels increases the likelihood of error resulting from telescoping and forgetting. Furthermore, conducting surveys too frequently may be a waste of resources because of the reduced likelihood that any significant change has taken place in a brief period. That is, the information across such surveys is highly redundant. On the other hand, panels spaced too far apart risk being insensitive to fluctuations in the outcome measures.

■ **Box 7.1**

SOME BASIC TRACING INFORMATION SOURCES

Reference

Telephone directories
Telephone directory assistance
City/suburban directories
   Numerical, reverse, street

General public/Companies

Neighbors
Apartment managers
Banks and trust companies
Credit bureaus
Real estate companies
Social clubs, cultural centers
Landlords
Employers

Government

Post office
City/municipal records
   Land titles
   Assessment/tax records
   Motor vehicle/driver license records
Civil records
Department/agency records
Voter lists

Others

Utility companies
School, college, university records
Subscription/mailing lists

Source: Burgess (1989: 60).

In a survey article on panel surveys, Bailar (1989) reviews several major U.S. panels and finds a remarkable lack of consistency over the issue of spacing. She reports that spacing for several American panel surveys ranges from monthly to durations as long as three times in 10 years. In her review, however, Bailar notes that duration between surveys can have a considerable impact on the accuracy of the point estimates. For example, it is noted that in a U.S. Survey of Residential Alterations and Repairs conducted in the 1960s, extending the recall period from 1 to 3 months resulted in a 40% dropoff in reports of minor repairs. Reports of major or more costly repairs, however, did not suffer a similar decline.

The U.S. National Criminal Victimization Survey was the subject of several pretest experiments in the mid-1970s. Researchers discovered that reported rates of monthly victimization differed substantially depending upon whether the respondents were asked to use 3-, 6- or 12-month reference periods. In short, victimization rates for a 3-month reference period were 10 to 20% higher than for a 6-month reference period, which in turn were 10 to 15% higher than rates reported for a 12-month reference period.

At the other extreme, Bailar notes that the San Jose [California] Health Survey generated reported daily rates of illness four times higher when a one-day recall was used as opposed to a one-month recall period.

Clearly, recall duration is significant. Unfortunately, too little research is available in this area to generate firm recommendations about optimal spacing. What literature does exist suggests that the loss of recall is not the same for events of all kinds. Events judged less significant by the respondent (i.e., less costly or less serious) appear to have a greater loss rate than events judged by respondents to be more significant or more important.

Sudman and Bradburn (1974) have addressed the two main sources of time-related error in surveys—telescoping, and omissions or forgetting—by suggesting a functional formula for both problems. These authors suggest that for telescoping (in which events are reported as taking place more recently that they actually do), the error rate is defined by

$$r_t = \frac{\log(ct)}{t}$$

Where, r_t is the error rate as defined by the difference between the actual and reported dates for an event in some reference period t. The parameter c represents the impact of telescoping as calendar time is transformed into subjective time.

For omissions, Sudman and Bradburn suggest that recall can be defined as

$$r_0 = a\exp(-bt)$$

The quantity r_0 consists of the number of events reported in period t as a proportion of the events occurring during the interval. The parameter a is a scaling parameter that likely varies with the social desirability of the events under study, and b is the "omission" parameter that relates the proportion of reported events to the duration t. The key feature of both models is their exponentiality, as opposed to linearity. Both imply a "clumping" effect, whereby greater importance is attached to one segment of the reference period than to another.

Suggestions have been made to address both recall problems. For telescoping, it has been suggested that errors can be reduced by using a technique known as the bounded interview. A bounded interview starts by reminding the respondent of his or her answers at an earlier interview; then the person is asked to report all subsequent events. Clearly, bounded interviews are directed toward second and subsequent surveys. While intuitively appealing, bounding has been the subject of little systematic research. We do not know, for example, whether it is best to bound all previous panels or if using only the first one as a bound will suffice. Bounding all waves adds to the complexity and the cost of the interviews—a cost that may not be warranted if little is gained by bounding interviews beyond the initial session. We also know very little about the context of bounding. With which types of issue does it work best? Is it counterproductive in some situations?

The problem of omission or forgetting has been addressed by various techniques generally called "aided recall." Most aided-recall procedures involve the use of prompting cues such as the interviewer identifying several possible events or giving the respondent checklists or cards.

As noted earlier, estimating the cost of a survey is relatively straightforward. However, because of the lack of systematic research into the accuracy problems due to telescoping and forgetting, identifying the optimum cost–accuracy trade-off for any particular study is difficult.

Panel Conditioning

Survey researchers have noticed that responses tend to change across panels. Specifically, responses change according to the length of time respondents stay in the panel. For example, it is common for respondents to victimization surveys to indicate fewer victimizations per unit time the longer they remain in the panel. Labor force surveys often generate higher monthly rates of unemployment, the greater the number of follow-up waves. Those changes may result in greater accuracy or more error, depending upon the substantive focus of the research. Several candidates have been put forward as the specific cause of those changes; however, all are encompassed under the term *panel conditioning*.

The phenomenon of panel conditioning raises two immediate issues. The first relates to our ability to decide which panel estimates are the most accurate. Should we accept the results from the first interview or are the results of the later panels more accurate? Few studies have been conducted that included cross-validation of survey responses with other data sources. So far, the results appear inconclusive.

The second issue relates to our ability to identify the specific factors that produce the conditioning in the first instance. The potential candidates often parallel those raised in applications of test–retest methodologies for estimating test reliability. Briefly, we may classify those conditioners into two general categories: intrinsic factors and extrinsic factors. Intrinsic factors consist of items related to the interview itself. For example, some researchers have suggested that panel conditioning is a consequence of learning and memory effects—the respondents' acumen increases as they become more familiar with the test instrument and the interviewing process. Other factors intrinsic to the interview process include an increasing loss of interest or commitment to the task, an increased comfort level with the test situation (thus resulting in more responses to less socially desirable questions and fewer "don't knows"), and a lack of memory aids, such as bounding, on the first interview.

Extrinsic factors relate to components outside the specific instrument. Attrition, for example, might lead to increased respondent bias as the remaining respondents in the panel become ever more selected. Where the unit of analysis is the household, the respondent may change. Other factors are attributable to the implementation of the research. That is, the researcher may use different modes on follow-up interviews. In the Canadian Labour Force Survey, for example, it is common for the first interview to be a face-to-face meeting, to allow the respondent to become "familiar" with the interview and the interviewer. Subsequent interviews, however, are usually conducted over the telephone.

The researcher may also use slightly different versions of the questionnaire over time, with subtle changes in the wording of key questions. Often, the interviewer will change, resulting in the confounding of the interview results with interviewer bias. These and likely many other factors not yet identified can contribute to varying degrees of bias and error in survey results.

How great a problem panel conditioning poses is an empirical question. If panel conditioning were constant or additive, the difficulties could be mitigated by means of appropriate statistical controls. Unfortunately, if the biases that form panel conditioning do not follow these conditions (and it is likely they do not), their identification and amelioration become much more difficult. Where those biases affect the estimated amount of change across surveys, they undermine the reliability and validity of any inferences we might draw.

Appending Durations: The "Seam" Problem

In some circumstances, we may wish to join sets of responses that cover different reference periods. Because of problems relating to telescoping, forgetting, and conditioning, we may find "spikes" at the points where the two data sets are joined. Specifically, it is not uncommon for the last period of the first survey and the first period of the last survey to overestimate the rates of occurrence. This is because the month closest to the survey often generates more event recollections than months further away.

Where exact point estimates are needed to estimate absolute numbers of events (totals), spiking creates problems for the investigator, who must then decide whether the spikes or the valleys represent the more accurate estimates. Where our interest is directed toward trends (such as average rates per month), the spiking problem can be addressed through the application of some form of smoothing (see Chapter 14).

Attrition and Nonresponse

The discussion of problems associated with panel surveys started with the inherent problem of following up respondents. Where that follow-up fails, the researcher is left with missing data. Attrition has already been mentioned as a possible source of difficulty in panel conditioning. The overall difficulties posed by attrition are generally more extensive, however.

Most panel surveys, even the best designed and executed, experience some attrition. Over a series of five interviews, a panel that experiences a 10% dropout rate after each interview will end with a retention rate of only 66% at the end of the fifth period. Matters are made worse when attrition is lumped with ordinary nonresponses to create a generic "nonresponse" or "missing" observation.

Of course, actual panels vary in their attrition experiences. Kalton, Kasprzyk, and McMillen (1989) review several panel surveys generally respected for their "quality" and find considerable variability in rates of attrition. For example, they report that the U.S. National Medical Care Utilization and Expenditure Survey generated a nonresponse rate of 9.9% on the initial wave that increased to 22.1% on the fifth wave. The waves were spaced at 3-month intervals.

The U.S. Panel Study of Income Dynamics reportedly generated a cumulative nonresponse rate of 50% after 17 years, and the British National Child Development Study, which followed a cohort of young people from age 7 to age 23, produced a 76% response rate at age 23 (after exclusion of respondents who had died or emigrated). While it might be argued that the retention of 76% of respondents over 16 years is commendable, the missing data still pose a substantial problem.

As we will see later, if both the cases lost to attrition and those lost to traditional nonresponses were random, the problem could be solved relatively easily. However, addressing the problem when the data are not missing at random is much more difficult.

Where attrition or nonresponse is systematically related to the outcome variable, the missing data can cause substantial bias in the results.

The difficulties inherent with systematic attrition are well documented by Singer's (1986) discussion of how the relative effectiveness of drug treatment programs might be evaluated. Wainer (1986) also provides an example of the difficulties involved in the temporal assessment and interpretation of SAT scores.

Statistical Analysis and Panel Data

The statistical analysis of panel data presents a series of problems not found in connection with cross-sectional surveys. Obviously, database management problems are associated with matching cases across waves. The sheer volume of data, and the decision about whether the cross-sectional aspects as opposed to the longitudinal aspects ought to be one's primary focus, also contribute to the complexity. Those issues might be considered to be exogenous, however, in that they do not necessarily influence either the content of the questionnaire or interview, or the manner in which the data are collected.

More germane to the scope of methods, is the impact of measurement error on our ability to estimate unbiased and efficient parameters. Two central concerns in the analysis of any temporal data are the impacts of measurement error associated with the independent variables (often referred to in econometrics as "errors in measurement") and the impact of model misspecification. Misspecification in this context refers to the exclusion of key "causal" and control variables from the model, and the inclusion of extraneous indicators.

Classical regression approaches to the analysis of panel data can easily generate inaccurate estimates when either the model is misspecified or the independent variables are susceptible to measurement error. The error need not be systematic: even random measurement error can have a deleterious impact upon our results. The problem can be addressed partially by respecifying the model in terms of the dependent variable. Analyzing difference scores across waves (i.e., $\Delta Y = Y_{t+1} - Y_t$) as opposed to raw scores helps to mitigate the problem of overall model misspecification. On the other hand, in the absence of misspecification, estimates based on raw or cross-sectional data are often far more accurate than those based on differences. For applied researchers, classical regression poses a Hobson's choice, with neither solution being completely palatable.

A better but technically more complicated solution to the problem is to analyze the data within a structural equation model framework (see Chapter 11 for an introduction). In this approach, both the structural model of interest and the measurement model are addressed explicitly. To address the measurement model, however, multiple indicators or measures of the concepts are required. Thus, for example, a single question asking whether a respondent supports "abortion on demand" cannot be used to estimate the impact of measurement error on the structural parameters. At least two, and occasionally several more, indicators are required to allow for an analysis of the measurement model.

We address measurement error in greater detail in the chapters relating to measurement. At this point it is important to note that before a given study is conducted, the researcher should have some inclination about how the data might be analyzed. If it is expected that the analysis will be limited to classical regression approaches, then single indicators will suffice. On the other hand, the expectation that the data will be analyzed within a structural equation framework requires a questionnaire structured to include multiple indicators. Prudence would also suggest that those indicators be subjected to rigorous pretesting to assess their overall reliability before the actual survey is begun.

ESTIMATING MOBILE POPULATIONS

Most sampling procedures devised for human populations assume that the population is relatively immobile. That is, dwelling units are fixed locations and people have an attachment to those units, at least for the duration of the survey. For certain subpopulations, these assumptions are simply untenable. The homeless in big cities and nomads in parts of Africa and other areas of the world are highly mobile. Thus, for example, standard enumeration and sampling techniques for estimating the number of prostitutes, drug addicts, or "street people" tend not to work very well.

Many procedures have been devised to address this problem, but one technique that appears to be gaining in popularity is the *capture–recapture* approach. Capture–recapture methods grew out of biologists' attempts to estimate the size and distribution of animal populations (Seber, 1982). If the underlying assumptions are met, the estimation algorithms are simple. Assume, for example, that Y_c roaches are captured, marked with a dot of red paint, and released. Subsequently, y roaches are recaptured and y_c are discovered with a red dot. If both the Y_c and y roaches were captured at random and without replacement, then the total population of roaches can be estimated by

$$Y = Y_c \frac{y}{y_c}$$

The corresponding estimate of the variance of Y, S_Y^2, is given as follows:

$$S_Y^2 = \frac{y^2}{y-1} \frac{Y_c}{y_c} \left(\frac{Y_c}{y_c} - 1\right)\left(\frac{y}{y_c} - 1\right)$$

Elaborations on these formulas have been developed, but these two equations stand at the heart of those developments.[1]

While conceptually very simple, the capture–recapture technique stands or falls on how well its underlying assumptions are met. The essential assumptions may be defined as follows[2]:

---

1. It should be noted that while consistent, Y is a slightly biased estimate of the population total. The intuitive explanation is to see the parallel between the estimate y_c/y and the discussion of the estimate of the ratio mean in the section dealing with cluster sampling. As with the ratio mean, both the numerator and the denominator in y_c/y are random variables.
2. See Seber (1982: 59) for an enumeration of these conditions as they apply to animal populations.

- The population is closed so that N is constant
- All individuals have the same probability of being selected in both surveys.
- Measuring (observing, interviewing) the individuals in the first survey does not affect the likelihood of inclusion in the second survey of this set of individuals.
- We can identify which individuals are included in both surveys, and all individuals canvassed in the first survey are indicated as such in the second survey.

Unfortunately, it is extremely difficult to ensure that these assumptions are met in actual field conditions. Consider the first assumption. The homeless population of most major cities is constantly in flux, with people moving both into and out of the big urban areas. The difficulty of framing a population suitable for analysis by means of capture–recapture techniques can be mitigated to some degree by reducing the duration between surveys. While those point estimates might be relatively accurate at the time of the study, estimates for narrowly defined areas with high rates of migration will soon be outdated.

The second assumption is likely the most difficult to meet in practice. Many studies of drug addicts, for example, rely for their basic estimates on appearances and reappearances at street clinics. This approach is highly unreliable, since both initial and subsequent appearances at a clinic are not at all likely to be random events. Taking an aerial approach and randomly selecting certain street segments or dwelling units in areas generally known to have high concentrations of the target population would theoretically produce better results. Without some form of "impersonal" selection procedure, near equal likelihood of selection is almost impossible with human populations because of the high variation in behavioral patterns related to selection.

Although of less importance than the second assumption, the third assumption also raises major concerns. It is possible that those who are successfully observed or interviewed in the first survey are also more likely than their compatriots to be selected in the second survey. This may be a consequence of a personal relationship built up in the first interview; alternatively, fear that the observer poses a personal threat may have been lessened.

Unwarranted reliance on the third assumption is most likely to pose a problem when the individuals in the surveys are merely observed rather than interviewed. However, many mobile populations, such as indigents, are elusive and reluctant to be identified. Thus, determining whether someone in the "recapture" survey was observed in the initial survey may be easier said than done.

The analogous conditions for animal surveys are also rarely met. Thus, when complementary estimates are available against which to compare survey results, the population total is almost invariably found to be underestimated. Statistics concerning the relative distribution of the target population, on the other hand, seem to fare better (Cormack, 1968).

Despite the difficulties in ensuring that the appropriate assumptions are met, variations on the capture–recapture theme have been carried out in several areas, including the estimation of drug addicts (Bloor et al., 1991; Brecht and Wickins, 1993; Larson, Stevens, and Wardlaw, 1992) and homeless mentally ill people (N. Fisher et al., 1994). Theoretical progress is also being made on circumstances under which some basic assumptions, such as that of population homogeneity, do not hold (Darroch et al., 1993).

S-Night: Counting the Homeless

One of the most systematic and best-documented attempts to count a transient population is the "Shelter and Street Night" (S-Night) surveys conducted by the U.S. Bureau of the Census to augment the 1990 census. The S-Night survey was conducted on March 20–21, 1990, in an attempt to count people in emergency shelters and street locations in five major U.S. cities: Chicago, Los Angeles, New Orleans, New York, and Phoenix. Martin (1992: 419) describes the plan:

> Street enumeration was implemented from 2 to 4 A.M., March 21. For the street phase, enumerators were to interview all people visible and awake, who were not in uniform or engaged in money-making activities, in preidentified nighttime street sites and all-night places of commerce. Sleeping persons were not to be wakened for an interview, but they were to be counted and their age, race, and sex estimated by observation. The sites—city parks, areas under bridges, bus and train stations, hospital emergency rooms, and other locations where homeless people were thought to stay at night—had been identified prior to the census by local governmental units, police, groups working with homeless persons, and Census Bureau district office personnel.

To assess how well the enumeration procedure was executed, teams of 60 observers (120 in New York) were assigned to selected street sites. Ideally, the observers would be counted by the enumerators as they went about their appointed task. According to Martin (1992: 419), "The observers were instructed to stay in the open to enable census enumerators to see and enumerate them. They were to observe whether enumerators came to the sites, and if so, when they arrived, how long they stayed, and how they conducted the enumeration."

The variation in the number of observers captured by the enumerators was astounding. The percentage of observers interviewed by the enumerators ranged from a high of 67% in New Orleans to a low of 7% in Chicago. Some observers were not interviewed but were either clearly or probably counted. That proportion ranged from a high of about 29% in New York to a low of 6% in Los Angeles. The percentage of observers who did not see an enumerator or were not counted ranged from 15% in New Orleans to 75% in Chicago. Overall, the variability was such that in one city, approximately 85% of the observers were apparently captured by the enumerators while at the opposite end of the spectrum, only about 25% were captured.

The ex post facto construction of an explanation for why so many observers were not counted reads like a litany of what can go wrong in applied sampling. Among the more important factors identified were the following:

- Some enumerators arrived at their sites early or left late. Observers' field notes showed that "enumerators typically stayed at each site only 15 minutes, on average" (Martin, 1992: 423).

- Some enumerators apparently chose to drive by the sites in their cars rather than inspect them on foot, as they had been instructed. In drive-by situations, it is possible that the observer might have missed the enumerator, or vice versa.
- Despite substantial work put into identifying sites beforehand, many instructions regarding site locations were vague or ambiguous. More than 90% of the enumerators reported difficulties in finding their sites. At some sites, enumerators reported conflicts between street numbers and building names on the official lists and in the actual neighborhoods.
- Many sites posed intrinsic difficulties. They either were dark or had "visual barriers" that made observation difficult.
- While the obvious falsification of data ("curbstoning") was ruled out as a significant factor, it did appear that some enumerators simply chose not to expend much energy in locating and counting the people at their assigned sites.

While the researchers evidently faced substantial problems with enumerators in certain instances, difficulties were also experienced with the observers. Like many of the enumerators, some observers apparently had difficulties finding sites. Some observers also chose not to spend the entire duration at the site. Furthermore, the observers were tired when asked to fill out questionnaires at the end of their shift, and some appeared to be functionally illiterate or not fluent in English. Consequently, many follow-up questionnaires were of questionable value.

It is commendable that the Bureau of the Census has been so open and has allowed for so many detailed descriptions of the S-Night experiment to be published.[3] The practical difficulties faced in the S-Night survey are clearly an eye-opener, and given the professionalism and expertise of bureau personnel, one inevitably is much more inclined to suspect surveys conducted by less experienced researchers. Undoubtedly, some major lessons have been learned from the S-Night experience. Clearly, many problems with S-Night related to the difficult conditions surrounding this type of survey—at night, often in less desirable parts of town, and with a highly transient population. However, many of the other problems are endemic with large-scale, face-to-face interview projects that require many interviewers and offer little opportunity for on-site supervision.

Further Reading

Dillman, D.A. *Mail and Telephone Surveys: The Total Design Method.* New York: Wiley, 1978. Dillman's book did a great deal to revive the flagging fortunes of mail surveys. It presents detailed, practical instructions for improving the quantity and quality of responses in mail surveys.

Evaluation Review, 16, vol. 4, 1992. Interesting and varied accounts of S-Night surveys for tracking the homeless in each of the target cities. The S-Night study was part of an attempt to address issues relating to the 1990 census undercount.

---

3. See volume 16, number 4 of *Evaluaton Review* (1992) for detailed accounts of S-Night experiences in each of the target cities. Numerous U.S. Bureau of the Census publications have also appeared on the S-Night study. See the references in Martin (1992) for a partial listing.

Groves, R.M. Biemer, P., Lyberg, L.E., Massey, J.T., Nicholls, W.L., and Waksberg, J., eds. *Telephone Survey Methodology*. New York: Wiley, 1988. A series of papers given at a 1985 conference on telephone survey techniques. Presents the state of the art in telephone surveying and deals with a broad range of issues from problems of nonresponse to the estimation of standard errors.

8

Experimental Designs

Statistical designs always involve compromises between the desirable and the possible.

—Leslie Kish

THE DESIGN OF EXPERIMENTS

According to Darryl Bock (1975: 14), "The investigator's objective in a behavioral experiment is to demonstrate that, by manipulating the conditions to which subjects respond, he can alter their behavior in a predictable manner." The primary idea behind experimental designs is the notion of control. The more control the experimenter has over the allocation of subjects or elements to the various conditions and over the conditions themselves, the more power can be squeezed out of the inferential process.

Two primary reasons exist for developing experimental designs. The first, as Bock contends, is to increase our assurance that any change in the outcome of a behavior is a consequence of our intervention and not some spurious factor. This, you will undoubtedly recall, harkens back to our discussion of causality in Chapter 3.

The second reason for employing experimental designs is to make sure that the subjects assigned to the treatment and control groups do not differ systematically on any variables except those under consideration. Since perfectly matched subjects can be found only rarely, the next best strategy is to employ random assignment, so that any differences between the groups will be nonsystematic. Thus, in the end, any differences between the groups on factors other than those introduced by the experiment will fall within the realm of expected statistical variation. All nonexperimental designs (and some experimental designs) suffer from the threat of self-selection. That is, we cannot rule out the possibility that the study elements differ systematically because of some factors other than those imposed by the experimental design.

As with all research endeavors, the decision about which design to use depends on several elements. As Winer (1971: 150) notes, "A major problem in planning an experiment is to find or develop that design which is most efficient per unit of experimental effort in reaching the primary objectives of the experiment." Some designs may be considered ideal in a given situation, but the expense in time, money, and other resources may make them unworkable. Cost, in the broadest sense, is always a major consideration in conducting any research. While we are often aware of the direct cost associated with experimentation, forgetting the many indirect costs is easy. Most social research also entails several hidden costs, such as inconvenience to the subjects, loss of status, and the "contamination" of subjects for future research.

The convergence of experimental design with modern statistical practice, particularly analysis of variance (ANOVA), took place in the 1920s with the work of

R. A. Fisher. Although most of Fisher's substantive applications were in agriculture, the marriage proved fruitful in nearly all scientific fields. Thus, contemporary discussions of experimental designs are usually integrated into a general discussion of ANOVA.

BASIC DESIGNS

The purpose of the basic experimental design is to estimate how much change (if any) is attributable to an experimental intervention.[1] Using a standard notation, where O_i represents a set of observations and X some form of intervention, several alternatives can be examined. In Fisher's early agricultural experiments, the design was simply:

$$X \quad O_1$$

$$O_2$$

a design that Campbell calls the static group comparison. Here, two groups are observed. One that is exposed to some intervention or treatment, and a second that is not. This design makes the strong assumption that the subjects are identical on all relevant characteristics before the experiment is conducted. Since this identity is assumed rather than subjected to explicit observation, Campbell asserts that this design is merely a "reference point" for purposes of explicating more advanced designs. Yet, the design works well in many agricultural and natural settings, where the underlying assumption may hold.

In practical social settings, the design is also employed when it suffices to compare some sample statistic with a known value or population parameter. The "one-shot" design is the basis underlying many one-sample tests, such as the one-sample t-test. In this situation, it is sufficient to know whether the group under consideration differs from some value considered important. As suggested, this value may be a population parameter, a theoretically important value, or a criterion based on performance guidelines. One may, for example, suspect that the participants in a particular class are outstanding on their examination performances. This hypothesis can be tested by comparing the students' test scores with previous norms. The value or applicability of this design is limited, however, by our inability to make any inference about what mechanism led to the group's enhanced performance. We cannot know, for example, whether it is due to self-selection, some administratively based selection procedure, superior effort in teaching, or simple random chance.

Another related design often used in the natural sciences is the "one-group pretest–posttest" design consisting of

$$O_1 \quad X \quad O_2$$

---

1. For an overview of experimental designs in the social sciences, see: Campbell and Stanley (1966) and Winer (1971).

This design implicitly assumes that any control group at time 2 would be equivalent to O_1. Again this design holds well in the natural sciences, since most inanimate elements are stable over time. The traditional experimental design of high school chemistry classes fits into this format. Unfortunately, human (and some animal) subjects are influenced by extraexperimental events such as history, maturity, learning, instrument decay, and a myriad of other issues such as, in epidemiological research, competing risks of infection. Further, the longer the time between O_1 and O_2, the greater the chance that these factors will have a confounding influence with the effects of X. From a statistical point of view, this design is a classical one-sample test–retest situation in which the observations are not independent of one another. Care must therefore be taken *not* to use independent sample t-tests or ANOVA in the analysis of the data.

A variation on this test–retest design is to compare a sample of subjects who have been exposed to treatment X and a sample who have not. Graphically, we have:

$$X \quad O_2$$

$$O_1$$

This design combines some strengths and weaknesses of the two previously mentioned designs. Here, O_2 is assumed to be adequately measured before X by another sample, O_1. Unfortunately, without measuring O_2 before X, we have no firm basis for knowing whether O_1 and O_2 were equivalent in the first instance. It is quite possible that subjects were self- or otherwise selected into the treatment group. Typically, such designs would be analyzed using independent sample t-tests or simple one-way ANOVA. As to statistical mechanics, one would normally test to see whether the variances across O_1 and O_2 were equal before conducting a difference of means t-test. If there were unequal variances, then Welch's variant would be appropriate. On the other hand, the inequality of variances across O_1 and O_2 could be an indication that O_1 and O_2 were not equal in the first instance.

The realization of the confounding influences in the preceding designs led to the development and adoption of the classical "pretest–posttest control group" design around the turn of the century, especially by psychologists. Formally, this design is defined as:

$$O_1 \quad X \quad O_2$$

$$O_3 \quad\quad O_4$$

As Campbell (1975) notes, "this design so neatly controls for the main effects of history, maturation, testing, instrument decay, regression, selection and mortality." While the design is very powerful, some important issues remain to be considered. As Campbell suggests, it is usual in this type of design to make the comparison of the differences D_1 with D_2 where $D_1 = O_2 - O_1$ and $D_2 = O_4 - O_3$. If $D_1 \neq D_2$, it is assumed that any differences are attributable to the intervention.

This model also assumes that the subjects at O_1 and O_3 are equivalent. The assumption is generally justified by pointing out that subjects are randomly assigned to the treatment and the control group and that the random assignment process negates the possibility of any systematic bias. This assumption may be checked, of course, by testing the null hypothesis $H_0 : O_1 - O_3 = 0$. If H_0 is rejected, then the difference between D_1 and D_2 must be statistically greater than D_2 plus or minus $O_2 - O_1$. This modification in testing does not negate some of Campbell's situational problems (which will be discussed in detail later), such as the issue of simultaneous testing of control and experimental groups.

Among some uncontrollable confounding influences in this type of design are experimenter effects (where the uniqueness of the experimenter interacts with the treatment, as often happens in counseling experiments), contamination effects between experimental and control groups (often the case in field experiments such as family planning), and the so-called *Hawthorne effect* (Roethlisberger and Dickson, 1939). Naturally, all these factors can (in principle) be overcome by means of multiple experiments or multiple experimenters, greater separation between groups, or the use of multiple treatments and double blinds. Unfortunately, the practicalities of actual experiments, especially when conducted in the field instead of the laboratory, often rule out these precautions.

A further problem arises in dealing with subjects who become *test-wise* or *experiment-cynical*. In the first situation, the subjects are drawn from a population that is constantly under experimental or treatment surveillance. Good examples include prison inmates, welfare recipients, and people in third-world study villages. These people are tested so often that they become unique subjects, and any results are difficult to generalize to a nontested population. Experiment-cynical subjects are direct products of researchers' attempts to hide the true purpose of experiments through ruses. Subjects who have become cynical as a result of such treatment constantly attempt to second-guess the experimenter and perform according to how they think they ought to perform. Again this leads to major difficulties with external validity.

A fifth basic type of design identified by Campbell is the Solomon four-group control design. Formally, this design may be depicted as:

$$O_1 \quad X \quad O_2$$
$$O_3 \qquad\quad O_4$$
$$\quad\; X \quad O_5$$
$$O_6$$

The power behind this design is that it allows the researcher to control and measure both the main and interaction effects due to experimentation and the influences due to maturation and history. Conceptually, this design is about as good as is practical. Its practicality is often toward the limits of acceptability, however, because of the high cost of implementation. The design is complex and requires many subjects. Thus, outside small-scale social psychological experiments conducted in laboratory settings, few practical examples exist.

Moreover, the most appropriate comparisons for statistical analysis are not obvious. That is, a single specification that encompasses all of what we would expect to see is difficult if not impossible to identify, making this design all the more challenging to put to proper use.

The basic comparisons for all the designs discussed here are summarized in Table 8.1. Looking at the last cell, we see some possible comparisons for the Solomon design. At a minimum, we would expect the following hypotheses not to be rejected:

$$\frac{O_5 + O_2}{2} > O_4$$

$$O_1 = O_3 = O_6$$

$$\frac{O_5 + O_2}{2} > \frac{O_1 + O_3 + O_4 + O_6}{4}$$

As suggested, other reasonable comparisons may be made. Unfortunately, it is not obvious which among the many comparisons are sufficient and which are necessary for generating a valid inference. Clearly, the different components we might test provide different pieces of information. How important those components are depends largely upon the substantive questions we are asking.

TABLE 8.1. Effect comparisons for five experimental designs

DESIGN	SCHEMATIC			EFFECT COMPARISONS
"One-shot" case study	X	O_1		$O_1 - k$
One group pretest/ posttest	O_1	X	O_2	$O_2 - O_1$
Pretest/posttest control group design	O_1	X	O_2	$(O_2 - O_1) - (O_4 - O_3)$
	O_3		O_4	
Pretest/posttest nonequivalent control group design	O_1			$O_2 - O_1$
		X	O_2	
Solomon four-group design	O_1	X	O_2	$(O_2 - O_1) - (O_4 - O_3)$ or,
	O_3		O_4	$\dfrac{O_2 - O_1}{2} + \dfrac{O_5 - O_6}{2} - (O_4 - O_3)$ or
		X	O_5	
	O_6			$\left(O_2 + \dfrac{O_5}{2} - O_1\right) - \left(O_4 + \dfrac{O_6}{2} - O_3\right)$ or
				?

Experimental designs remain our strongest procedures, however, and are the ideal to which we strive. They are strong on internal if not external validity, and they offer a degree of elegance not found in other methods. One weakness of most experiments, however, is the brevity of the period covered, in practice, by the posttest evaluations. Thus, the possibility of decay or delayed-reaction effects is rarely considered. Decay occurs through mechanisms such as memory deterioration and the loss of enthusiasm and vigilance. The delayed-reaction effect is often spoken about in education but is rarely examined in experimental situations. For example, we justify the value of a liberal arts education for its supposed value "down the road," but rarely, if ever, do we attempt to measure this dimension.

STATISTICAL CONSIDERATIONS

Fixed vs. Random Effects

In selecting treatment and control or comparison conditions, the experimenter has two fundamental options. Specific selections may be made where one specific treatment is compared with another. This allows one to infer that a particular treatment does not differ from a particular control. In the literature, this is known as a *fixed effects* or Model I design. An alternate approach is to select randomly one or more treatments from a group of treatments and to make a contrast with a control similarly selected. This allows for the inference of differences back to a general class of treatments. This is known as the *random effects* or Model II design.

As an example, consider comparing Montessori and regular public schools. We may choose to compare a particular Montessori school with a particular public school, or we may randomly select one or more Montessori schools and compare them with one or more public schools. Taking the latter approach, we can generalize back to the experimental and control populations from which the samples were drawn. In the first example, our inference is limited to the schools in the study, not the general population from which they are drawn.

Often, in the statistical literature, fixed effects designs are called Model I, and random effects designs are called Model II. The distributions underlying the respective models are presented in Figures 8.1 and 8.2. As we can see, the fixed effects model treats each group as a separate subpopulation. Each subpopulation has a distribution associated with it centered about a group mean, μ_i. The overall mean, μ, is the weighted average of the three subpopulation means. The substantive hypotheses we are testing relate to the effects, a_i, which represent the difference between each $\mu_i - \mu$. If there are no differences between the treatments, all a_i will be functionally zero. Put another way, the null hypothesis is one of equality among the treatment or subpopulation means; thus, $H_0 : \mu_1 = \mu_2 = \cdots = \mu_j = \mu$.

Analogously under Model II, the variation among the subpopulation means, σ_a^2, will be zero if there are no differences among the subpopulations (see Figure 8.2); hence the null hypothesis $H_0 : \sigma_a^2 = 0$.

The difference between the models is subtle but important regarding the overall generality of the conclusions we might wish to draw. Sometimes, random and fixed effects can be mixed to create what is known as a Model III design.

Subpopulations

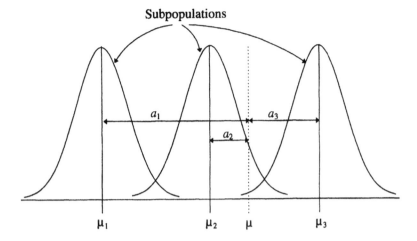

Figure 8.1. Random effects model.

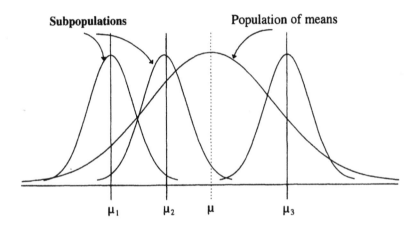

Figure 8.2. Fixed effects model.

Generally, the calculations relating to the sums of squares are identical with both models (Keppel, 1991: appendix C; or Hays, 1988: ch. 13). The major difference, however, is in the components of the variance estimates, especially the treatment variance. Briefly, for a one-way ANOVA, the differences in the variances may be outlined as follows:

SOURCE	MODEL I	MODEL II
Treatment	$\sigma^2 + \dfrac{\sum_{i=1}^{I} J_i \alpha_i^2}{I-1}$	$\sigma^2 + k\sigma_a^2$
Error	σ_e^2	σ_e^2

Thus, for the random effects or Model II case, the expected mean squares between the treatments is:

$$\sigma^2 + k\sigma_a^2$$

with

$$k = \frac{1}{I-1}\left[\frac{\sum_{i=1}^{I} J_i - \sum_{i=1}^{I} J_i^2}{\sum_{i=1}^{I} J_i}\right]$$

When all J treatments have equivalent sample sizes, then $k = J$. Given this information, obtaining an unbiased estimate for σ^2 from the summary ANOVA table is possible. Specifically, since

$$\text{MST} = \sigma^2 + k\sigma_a^2$$

the treatment variance is estimated by:

$$\sigma_a^2 = \frac{\text{MST} - \text{MSE}}{k}$$

Assumptions Underlying Most Practical Applications of Planned Experiments

Over the years, researchers who use the regression approach to the general linear model have been aware of the possible impact of violations to the assumptions underlying such models. Anomalously, this is not always the case for ANOVA. Many researchers believe ANOVA, or more precisely, the F-tests employed in assessing ANOVA models, to be robust to violations of the underlying statistical assumptions. This is definitely not so. ANOVA results are just as susceptible to problems with non-independence, heteroscedasticity, nonnormally distributed error terms, and outliers as are regression results. Therefore, it makes sense to review some basic assumptions that underlie the analysis of variance.

- **Statistical Assumptions**. Experiments are assessed based on their statistical merits—generally, the performance of the F-test. For valid inferences to be made from the results of a statistical test, certain assumptions about the observations are necessary. First, it is essential that the subjects be selected and assigned randomly and that the selection process produce elements whose selection is statistically independent. Failure to establish these conditions results in a lowering of statistical power at best; at worst, any credence we might have in the inferential process is totally undermined. Many situations conspire to undermine the researcher's ability to meet the independence assumption. One common situation, often overlooked, is that of matched pairs in which the subjects are selected at random but the observations may not be completely independent. Fortunately, this situation often can be dealt with by taking differences across observations and adjusting the degrees of freedom.

Another fundamental statistical assumption is that the *error* terms are normally distributed with a mean of zero and a constant variance, σ^2 [i.e., $N \approx (0, \sigma^2)$]. This latter assumption is the homoscedasticity assumption and can often be tested directly. The appropriate procedures for doing so are discussed in most statistics texts. Do note, however, that *the characteristic of interest does not have to be normally distributed in the population* if the error terms are normally distributed. In many situations, the data can be transformed to meet these requirements. The analysis of much sensory and attitudinal data, for example, will not typically meet the assumptions unless they are log-transformed beforehand.

- **Measurement Assumptions.** The basic model for one-way ANOVA is $Y_{ij} = \mu + \alpha_j + \varepsilon_{ij}$; where μ is an overall mean or scaling parameter; α_j is the effect of being in the jth treatment, and ε is a random measurement error distributed $N \approx (0, \sigma^2)$. Variance among subjects is thus composed of variance due to belonging to different treatments and variance due to exogenous error (ε). Consequently, the total intersubject variance (σ_t) can be decomposed as variance to treatment effects and random error, that is, $\sigma_t = \sigma_b - \sigma_e$. Obviously the greater the differences between treatments (generally the point to be illustrated), the larger σ_b will be compared with σ_e. Therefore, the F-ratio is $F = \sigma_b / \sigma_e$, which with $n_1 - 1$ and $n_2 - 1$ degrees of freedom is compared with a standardized table to discover what is critically large.

The object of experimental designs, therefore, is to develop circumstances that lead to an increased σ_b relative to σ_e. Put another way, the design can often be used to maximize the magnitude of the effect which, as has been discussed, is one way of enhancing statistical power. In some circumstances, it is less expensive to enhance the likelihood of a large effect magnitude by using an appropriate experimental design (thereby increasing the power) rather than increasing the number of subjects or observational units.

QUASI-EXPERIMENTAL DESIGNS

It is arguable that the single most important historical contribution to methods has been the development of the classical experimental design. While not perfect, the classical experimental design controls for unforeseen factors that could have led to systematic differences between the control and the study groups before the experimental intervention. Through random assignment, any potential biases that may result from self- or other forms of selection are assumed to be relegated to statistical error.

Unfortunately, it is not always possible for our research to proceed within the classical design framework. For example, a true experimental procedure for studying the impact of broken homes on the propensity toward juvenile delinquency would require the random "breakup" of selected families and the maintenance of others, whatever the motivations and intentions of the families involved. Not only would such experimental manipulations raise profound ethical questions, the practical considerations would likely undermine any attempt to carry out the design.

176 Quantitative Research Methods in the Social Sciences

In certain circumstances, however, the *form* of the classical experiment appears to occur. That is, one group may be subject to some form of intervention while another, apparently equivalent group, is not. This situation differs from the classical experimental design in lacking a random assignment of subjects to conditions in the sense that the researcher has control over the randomization process. When these situations take on the outward appearance of true experimental designs, they are often called *quasi-experimental designs*. The terminology of quasi-experimental designs was introduced into the literature by Campbell and Stanley (1963). Campbell also went to great lengths to expound upon the strengths and weaknesses of these approaches (Campbell and Boruch, 1975; Cook and Campbell, 1979).

Unfortunately, many researchers have overlooked the limitations mentioned by Campbell and Stanley and have come to view the idea of quasiexperimental designs as sufficient justification for any form of pseudoexperimental approach. This is particularly the case in evaluation research, where typically, true experimental conditions are either difficult to achieve or expensive to carry out. Before we explore this issue in greater detail, you are warned that the use of quasi-experimental designs is clearly a case of caveat emptor—buyer beware! Quasi-experimental designs are inevitably a second-best approach to testing hypotheses and should be used only where true experimental designs are clearly impossible to carry out.[2]

It is worthwhile starting the discussion of quasi-experimental designs by examining in more detail what distinguishes quasi-experiments from true experiments on the one hand, and survey or correlational research on the other. Briefly, the two key components of a true experiment are the randomized allocation of subjects by the researcher, and the controlled application of some form of treatment or intervention. We have already noted that randomized allocation is not possible in some circumstances: but what about controlled intervention? Generally, when the investigator does not have control over the intervention, or no apparent intervention occurs, the design is considered to be some form of survey design. Quasi-experimental designs, then, are limited to situations allowing for some control over the application of the treatment.

For example, the use of legislation to control the distribution and ownership of guns, and the decision to conduct a crackdown on drinking and driving by a local police force are planned interventions. They are clearly definable events, implemented at certain points in time and in certain geographical locations. Occasionally, it is proposed that natural events (catastrophes such as floods or tornados) might substitute for a planned intervention. While appearing similar in form to quasi-experiments, these situations are perhaps best viewed as another class of designs such as *natural experiments*. Making this distinction is important because in planned interventions, controlling the application and subsequent retraction of the intervention is at least theoretically possible.

Thus, America's experience with prohibition might be considered a quasi-experiment in the sense that the application and retraction of prohibition were controlled

---

2. For an inventory of true experimental designs in field settings see Boruch, McSweeny, and Soderstrom (1978).

events. The eruption of Mount St. Helen, on the other hand, was a natural event over which humans had no control. This would be considered a natural experiment.

Interrupted Time Series

A time series consists of several observations taken in chronological order over a specified period. Typical time series include daily stock market quotations, annual reports of crime rates, monthly unemployment figures, and annual counts of publications. Often time series data follow specific patterns such as linear trends, seasonal variations, or long-term trends that become apparent only over decades (e.g., Kuznets cycles in economics). Occasionally, we intervene in these cycles to effect some desired outcome. For example, people typically consume larger quantities of alcohol and are more prone to drinking and driving during holiday seasons. To counter this trend, police forces often increase the number of roadside checks (spot checks) during peak seasons to dampen the bulges in the seasonal trend.

Other examples of intervention in existing time series include the attempts by central banks to modify money supplies and interest rates either to stimulate or to restrict economic growth. Once the monetary authority has acted, the question becomes one of whether the intervention had the desired impact. That is, did the trajectory of the time series change in the expected direction? The statistical literature on time series analysis is extensive, and we shall not review it in detail. Students interested in pursuing this literature might look to Harvey (1990), Makridakis, Wheelwright, and McGee (1983), or Nelson (1973) for guidance.

The principles of interrupted time series analysis, however, are reasonably simple. Consider a series of observations $O_1, \ldots, O_5$, some intervention X, and a further series of observations, $O_6, \ldots, O_{10}$. If the intervention, X, is deemed to have an impact, then we would expect the linear pattern of $O_6, \ldots, O_{10}$ to be different from the initial five observations. The basic principle can be seen in Figure 8.3. Here, Y is an outcome measure (say traffic accidents), X is time, and I is the point when some intervention takes place. The trend line to the left of I illustrates a monotonic increase in traffic accidents over time. We can assume that without some form of intervention, the trend line, a, would continue its trajectory with a constant slope over the entire range of X. However, in this instance, the intervention I has taken place (perhaps the introduction of photo radar on highways) and the trend line changes its trajectory. The new trend, b, is now observed.

Figure 8.3. Regression discontinuity design.

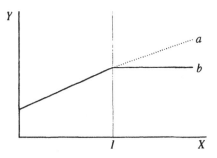

Normal regression procedures can now be used to test whether the slope of the line segment before *I* is similar to the line segment, *b*, which is observed after *I*. It is for this reason that the design is often called the *regression discontinuity design*. If the slopes are significantly different, one might draw the conclusion that the intervention had the expected impact. But should one? In Figure 8.3, it would be extremely coincidental for the change in slope coinciding with *I* to have taken place independent of the intervention. Unfortunately, interventions, no matter how radical they might be, rarely have an immediate impact.

Consider the pattern in Figure 8.4. Here again is a clear monotonically increasing pattern before *I*. As often happens, however, the intervention does not have an immediate impact. Instead, there is a delay before patterns of behavior change, and the line follows trajectory *b*. The observer might again assume that it is *I* that is responsible for the change in trajectory. However, several possibilities come to mind. Without intervention, the pattern might have continued along trajectory *a*, as previously assumed. On the other hand, another unforeseen factor might have occurred slightly after *I* that affected the change in slope producing line *b* (the introduction of air bags, say). A further possibility is that without the intervention, the trend might have peaked and produced trend line *c*, which shows an even more drastic temporal reduction in traffic accidents. In this instance, the intervention is actually counterproductive.[3]

In some circles, there is a tendency not to acknowledge that interventions may produce results that are worse than the status quo ante. This belief, often called *Parieto optimality*, may be stated as follows: if an intervention works, at worst some are somewhat better off, while at best, everyone is better off. That is, there is a net gain. On the other hand, the belief that if an intervention has no impact, no one will be worse off than before is clearly naïve in many circumstances. It is quite conceivable for an intervention to have unanticipated consequences, resulting in conditions being worse for some, if not all concerned. It is also possible for some to gain but for the group as a whole to experience a net loss.

Occasionally, interventions only produce the appearance of an impact. That is, the target phenomenon might have corrected itself despite any planned activity. A typical

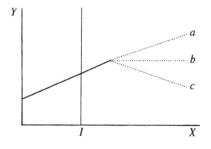

Figure 8.4. Regression discontinuity with delayed impact.

---

3. It is conceivable that with the coming implementation of photo radar and its expected impact, engineering safety measures even more stringent than air bags would be introduced.

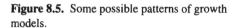

Figure 8.5. Some possible patterns of growth models.

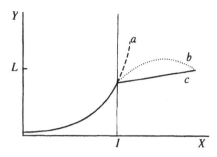

example is illustrated in Figure 8.5. The trend line before *I* is that of the exponential growth curve, *a*. Unfettered, rabbits appear to reproduce at a rate producing a growth curve illustrated by *a*. In fact, rabbit reproduction increases exponentially only to a point. Eventually, the environment becomes saturated with the beasts and can no longer support the ever increasing rabbit population. Food supplies and available territories diminish, and predators switch over to a new and increasingly available food supply, thereby increasing the population of predators. Ultimately, the rabbit population will level off, following the S-shaped line, *b*.

Our intervention at *I*, on the other hand, produces pattern *c*. If one assumes that the rabbit population would continue along the exponential growth curve, *a*, then clearly *c* represents a victory over rabbit reproduction. On the other hand, comparing *c* with *b* suggests that the "victory" is largely illusory, since the rabbit population would have leveled off anyway. Many policy makers refuse to acknowledge that many social problems are self-correcting, or at least self-regulating, if left alone. This is a major philosophical difference between liberal and conservative economists. Simplifying, it is still fair to say that conservative economists recognize that most market aberrations are self-correcting with time. Liberal economists, on the other hand, are prone to believe that without direct intervention, aberrations will continue ad infinitum.

Does this mean that the regression discontinuity pattern is not useful? The answer is an unequivocal, "not necessarily." As with Figure 8.3, an immediate change in the trend line that is caused by something other than *I* would be highly coincidental. Our faith in the intervention is further strengthened if we have good theoretical reasons for believing in its effectiveness, or if similar interventions have worked in another place or at another time. The intervention's credibility is further enhanced if it is retracted at some future date and the pattern continues along the trajectory established before *I*.

Their clear limitations notwithstanding, regression discontinuity designs have many desirable statistical properties, such as producing unbiased estimates of treatment effects, that make them very attractive in practice. Where interventions can be identified with a specific point in time, and where traditional experimental procedures are practical nonstarters, the regression discontinuity design has much to recommend it.[4]

---

4. Good discussions of the regression discontinuity design are to be found in Marcantonio and Cook (1994) and Trochim (1984). For a useful examination of relevant software, see Harrop and Velicer (1990).

Interrupted Time Series with a Nonequivalent Control Group

The inferential power of quasi-experimental designs can often be enhanced by providing a quasi-control group. In the true experimental design, the random assignment of subjects to experimental and control conditions assures us that there is a statistical equivalence between the two groups on all relevant dimensions. That is, the randomization process provides a certain level of statistical credibility that the two groups do not differ on dimensions that, being uncontrolled in the design, might affect the outcome variable. Where factors are known to affect the outcome, we usually the design along those factors. This stratification process increases the power of the experimental design by reducing the error variance. A possibility always exists, however, that the outcome is affected by other factors that are unknown to the researcher.

Where subjects select one group over another, that selection process (self-selection) is often related to the characteristics that influence the outcome. For example, self-selected experimental subjects are often more ambitious, more able, or sometime simply more desperate than control subjects. In this situation, we can never be sure that such factors have not influenced the outcome of the intervention.

Sometimes, the application of an intervention to one group as opposed to another is purely fortuitous. In these situations, we are more likely to believe that any difference is due to the intervention than to either self-selection or other confounding factors. For example, mandatory seat belt legislation might be imposed in one state but not another. If the states are reasonably similar in most other aspects, then the state without the intervention might be considered a control of sorts. Since the control state is not assigned to the control condition at random, we cannot be assured of its equivalence to the experimental state in the statistical sense. Therefore, the control state is more properly called a *nonequivalent control*. Still, the underlying assumption here is that what happens in the nonequivalent control would likely happen in the state with the intervention *if the intervention did not take place*.

The fundamental design of an interrupted time series with a nonequivalent control group is outlined in Figure 8.6. The line marked E is the trend for the experimental group; the line marked C represents the control. Before the intervention, I, both trends ran parallel. After I, the lines are no longer parallel, suggesting that the intervention has had some impact. Again, the caveats concerning simple interrupted time series designs apply to designs with a nonequivalent control group. We can never be certain that the

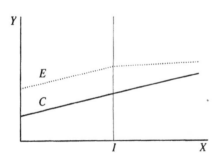

Figure 8.6. Intervention with a nonequivalent control group.

Figure 8.7. Intervention and retraction with a nonequivalent control group.

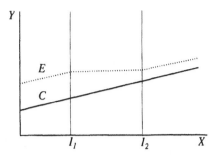

change in the experimental group would not have taken place despite the intervention. In fact, it is possible that the factor that underlay the decision to intervene would have led to a change in the behavior of the experimental group regardless. Thus the trend might have remained unchanged in the control group because the control group was not truly equivalent to the experimental group. Ultimately, some systematic factor might have been the basis for deciding to carry out the intervention in one group over the other.

The power of our inference can be enhanced, however, if we follow the strategy suggested previously and remove the intervention at some future date. Figure 8.7 illustrates what we would expect to see under such circumstances. Even with a delay in the intervention effect, the experimental group trend changes between the application of the intervention at I_1 and the removal of the intervention at I_2. After the intervention has been removed, the trends for both experimental and control groups continue along similar trajectories.

EXAMPLE: THEFTS FROM PARKING METERS

The first example is taken from an analysis conducted in connection with a civil case seeking compensation for theft from New York City's parking meters by several employees working for Brinks, Inc. The Brinks security firm had been given the contract to clear the city's parking meters. Through an anonymous tip, it was learned that some Brinks employees were skimming from the daily collections. Those employees were prosecuted and found guilty in the criminal courts. Subsequently, the City of New York sought damages from Brinks for negligence and breach of contract involving the thefts (Fairley and Glenn, 1986).

In the civil trial both the City of New York and Brinks used statisticians as expert witnesses and presented statistical evidence to support their respective positions. At stake were restitutive and punitive damages running to millions of dollars.

The Case

Following the discovery of the thefts, the contract to empty the parking meters was given to the CDC Company. Within the first 10 months, CDC collected almost $1 million more than Brinks had in any 10-month period during which it was under contract. The situation is illustrated in Figure 8.8, where average daily revenues per parking meter are plotted over a 22-month period. Months 1 through 10 represent the period of the Brinks contract; months 13 through 22 represent the commencement of the CDC contract. Visually, a substantial difference appears to exist in average revenues per meter during the two contract periods. The analysis by the plaintiff's expert statisticians also suggested that the difference in revenues between the two periods was statistically significant. However, as we have noted, it is possible that other factors might emerge to explain the change in revenue. To identify such competing explanations, the city hired an expert on parking meter revenues (see Box 8.1). Fairley and Glen suggested that any competing factor would have to explain four issues: (a) the *suddenness* of the upward shift over the two-month gap between contracts; (b) the *sizableness* of the difference in the amount of the collections—a shift of more than 8.5%; (c) the *uniqueness* of the shift—its occurance at the point of contract transition and at no other period; and (d) the *uniformity* of the shift, in as much as it occurred in every borough in the city. After examining several possibilities, Fairley and Glen (1986: 236) concluded that "In sum, no evidence was presented that demonstrated that specific causal factors other than theft would account for the jump in level between the two periods."

Rejoinder

The convenient aspect of court cases (at least from a pedagogical point of view) is that they present two sides to a story. While evidence presented in the criminal case showed that employee theft had taken place, the crucial issue in the civil case was the size of the damage award. The federal district court jury awarded the city compensatory damages of $1 million for loss of revenue and punitive damages of $5 million. The latter figure was reduced to $1.5 million by the trial judge.

As noted, Brinks also presented statistical evidence at the trial, and a defense witness suggested that the size of the loss was grossly overestimated (Box 8.2).

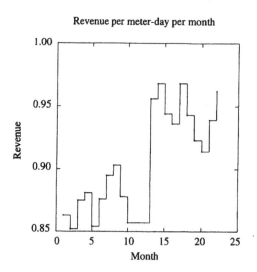

Revenue per meter-day per month

Figure 8.8. Monthly revenue from parking meters—version 1. [Drawn from data in Fairley and Glenn (1986).]

■ **Box 8.1**

DISCOUNTING OTHER FACTORS INFLUENCING METER REVENUE

The city also hired a nationally known expert in the analysis and design of security systems for parking meter plants and parking garages. . . . When he identified over 40 possible causes of change in parking meter revenues, the analysis seemed doomed. When he was able to conclude that many of these variables were either not present in the New York area during the comparison period, such as the opening or closing of a unique shopping site, were equally present during the Brinks and CDC periods, such as the incidence of legal holidays, or were incapable of making a significant difference, such as the fact that snow emergency streets had parking bans for one more day in the Brinks period than in the CDC period, the picture brightened considerably.

Source: Fairley and Glenn (1986: 228).

■ **Box 8.2**

ALTERNATE EXPLANATIONS FOR REVENUE TRENDS

I have criticized two aspects of Fairley and Glen's analysis. First, the methodology used to address the question of trend is defective because the time intervals they study are too narrow to accurately guage the trend effect, and because their method of seasonal adjustment artifactually produces a pattern which is improperly interpreted as a meaningful signal in the data. Second, the attribution of period revenue differences entirely to theft remains largely speculative due to the presence of uncontrolled systematic biasing factors and substantial month-to-month variability. Reasonable alternative explanations for the revenue differences are presented that are unrelated to theft and that cannot be easily dismissed.

Source: B. Levin (1986: 246).

Specifically, Bruce Levin, the statistician hired by Brinks, argued that the primary evidence presented by the city neglected to indicate that there had been a long-term upward trend in collections throughout the term of the Brinks contract and that trend had continued throughout the CDC contract (Levin, 1986). Furthermore, Levin suggested that the increased variance in total dollars collected per day after CDC took over the contract strongly suggested that factors other than theft had produced the differences in the total amounts collected.

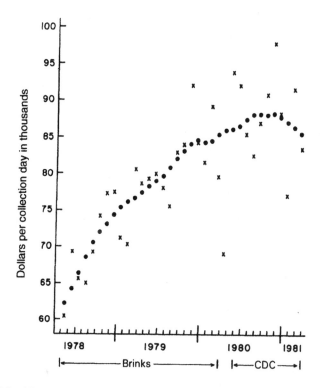

Figure 8.9. Monthly revenue from parking meters—version 2. [From Levin (1986).]

The core of Levin's argument is illustrated in Figure 8.9, which shows both the average monthly revenue per collection day and a superimposed smoothed trend line. Neither the original trial jury nor the appeals court was convinced by Brinks's rejoinder. However, the evidence presented in Figures 8.8 and 8.9 suggests that the evaluation of trends using quasi-experimental designs is far from unequivocal.

EXAMPLE: THE BRITISH BREATHALYSER STUDY

An oft-cited example of an interrupted time series design with nonequivalent dependent variables is the analysis of the British Breathalyser crackdown of 1967 by Ross, Campbell, and Glass (1970). The objective of the program under study was to reduce serious traffic accidents believed to be related to drinking and driving. A primary locus of alcohol consumption in Britain is the pub, which has limited opening hours. If the crackdown were effective in deterring drinking and driving, we would expect a significant reduction in the accident rate during the hours in which pubs are open. The researchers examined the number of serious accidents (including fatalities and serious injuries) for the period January 1966 to December 1968 inclusive. The crackdown was carried out in October 1967. Three accident series were examined—those during all hours, those during the hours in which the pubs were closed, and accidents on weekend nights. Implicitly, the series for all accidents despite time of day is the control group, since any historical effects unrelated to the intervention should be reflected in this series. The basic results are reflected in the graph reproduced in Figure 8.10.

As Figure 8.10 shows, the impact of the crackdown on the number of serious accidents during closing hours was virtually nonexistent. On the other hand, the serious accident rate during weekend nights dropped precipitously at the point of implementation. As might be expected, the trend line across all hours and days showed only a marginal decrease after the application of the crackdown. The accompanying statistical analysis by Ross et al. confirmed the visual pattern.

One aspect of the weekend night trend is the decay that takes place over time; that is, the accident trend converges back toward that for closed hours over time. A supplemental commentary by Ross (1973) examines this phenomenon in considerable detail. Among the author's major points is the failure of the British courts to follow through on charges levied under the legislation. Although Ross's analysis of the situation was thorough, he did not consider that even with a crackdown, the absolute likelihood of apprehension under the tightened conditions was probably quite small. Since certainty of apprehension is a major factor related to the determent of antisocial behavior, it is not surprising that the deterrent effect of the crackdown would diminish as drivers gained more firsthand experience with the actual probabilities of

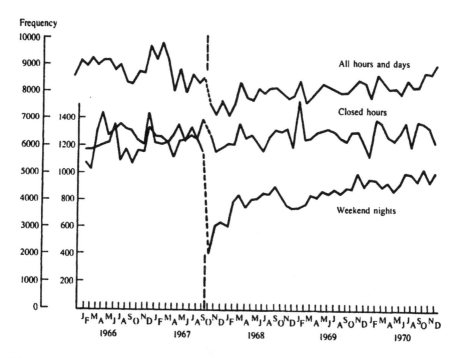

Figure 8.10. British fatalities plus serious injuries before and after the breathalyser crackdown of October, 1967, seasonally adjusted. [From Ross, Campbell, and Glass (1970: 500).]

apprehension (Keene, Maxim, and Teevan, 1993). Still, the intervention clearly had a significant impact on the accident pattern—at least in the short run. What is not clear, however, is the detailed causal model that produced the observed effect.

Internal Validity Threats in
Quasi-Experimental Designs: A Checklist

Donald Campbell, who has perhaps done most to develop and publicize the formalization of quasi-experimental designs, has developed what he terms an inventory of threats to experimental validity (Campbell, 1969; Cook and Campbell, 1974). As Campbell has noted, these items may or may not apply to any given design. Furthermore, the inventory is not intended to be exhaustive: it is merely a guide to some more common factors that affect designs. Broadly, such threats fall into one of two categories: threats to internal validity and threats to external validity. As for internal validity threats, Campbell has outlined the following.

- **History**: events other than the intervention that might affect the outcome. For example, government may impose a tax on a commodity to deter consumption. Simultaneously, however, a substitute product of lesser price and higher quality is developed that has an independent suppressive impact upon consumption.

- **Maturation**: processes that take place within the observational unit (persons, organizations, etc.) that affect behavior over time. People grow physically and evolve socially and intellectually over the life course; organizations often become more complacent and less competitive over time. Sometimes fatigue becomes a factor.

- **Instability**: the measurement process may become less reliable over time, and outside factors may influence the collection of data. For example, press reports of obscene phone calls might reduce response rates in telephone interviews. Subjects may selectively drop out of the study.

- **Testing**: the repeated use of a particular instrument with the same study group may influence the responses to that instrument. For example, employees whose expense accounts are being audited, may change their spending and recording habits.

- **Instrumentation**: the "calibration" of a testing instrument may change over time, or there may be changes in the observers or recording procedures. An example is provided by the recent renorming of SAT scores.

- **Regression artifacts**: it has been known since the time of Galton that extreme scores and observations regress toward the mean over time. In education, for example, students' test scores will move toward the group mean despite any change in the students' behavior or that of the teacher.

- **Selection**: selection bias is a major problem in all research in which subjects are not randomly assigned to situations. Individuals who self-select for experimental programs may be more energetic, more informed, or maybe even more desperate than those who do not. Similarly, researcher-selected study groups may contain people who are more amenable to treatment or are perceived to "have nothing to lose anyway."

- **Experimental mortality**: participants may drop out of the treatment or control groups at different rates or on selective bases.
- **Selection–maturation interaction**: biases may exist that result in the differential growth of subjects who opt for treatment or control conditions. For example, signaling theory in economics suggests that people who choose to pursue higher education are inherently more productive than those who do not. Therefore, the innate ability of those people to develop and become more productive is said to account for their success, rather than anything substantive learned in the education process.

Campbell also identifies several threats to external validity. These issues affect the generalizability of the experimental results to other situations.

- **Interaction effects of testing**: pretests, in particular, may raise the saliency of issues of certain types that alter the respondents' outlook or behavior. For example, surveying employees regarding the incidence of harassment or discrimination may heighten awareness of those issues such that employees perceive and report incidents that they would not have identified previously.
- **Interaction of selection and experimental treatment**: this may result when subjects are aware that they are assigned to either a treatment or a control group. Control groups may become demoralized ("We aren't good enough to be in the treatment group"), or they may engage in compensatory behavior to "show those researchers" that they are as good as the experimental group. This problem is often dealt within true experimental designs through *double blinds*: that is, neither the respondents nor the immediate researchers know to which group each subject is assigned.
- **Reactive effects of experimental arrangements**: the so-called the *Hawthorne effect*.[5] Sometimes the measurement process itself or the knowledge that one is part of a study group seems to alter performance.
- **Multiple-treatment interference**: sometimes subjects are exposed to multiple treatments. This may lead to outcomes that are unobserved when a person is exposed to only one treatment. Inmates in prisons are often exposed to a variety of rehabilitation programs, making it difficult to decide whether any one program has a significant impact.
- **Irrelevant responsiveness of measures**: many measurement instruments are complex and contain "filler." Data produced in response to such items may indicate apparent effects that are in fact totally spurious.
- **Irrelevant replicability of treatments**: many interventions or treatments are complex, and replications may fail to incorporate those aspects of the intervention that are actually responsible for the effect.

---

5. Interestingly enough, there is some question as to whether the original Hawthorne effect actually existed (Jones, 1990, 1992). Clearly, however, it is a concept that has found intellectual credence independent of its empirical veracity (e.g., Adair, Sharpe, and Huynh, 1989).

CORRELATIONAL DESIGNS

Many social scientists such as sociologists, economists, and anthropologists rarely work with experiments but often use correlational or survey data collected during a particular interval. Thus, the survey may be considered a "cross-sectional" or "slice-in-time" design. The primary weakness of survey designs stems from researcher's lack of control over the allocation of subjects to various conditions. Consequently, the potential for selection bias is always possible when subjects allocate themselves to one condition or another according to some systematic influence (intelligence, motivation, interest, sociocultural background, etc.). The standard response of survey researchers has been to introduce "control" variables that act as statistical, rather than physical controls for potentially confounding or biasing effects. Unfortunately, as Lieberson (1985: ch. 2) points out, controls can have just the opposite effect, producing greater bias than the simple examination of zero-order correlations.

Furthermore, there is the issue of how many controls to include. The exercise may soon degenerate into reductio ad absurdum (the shotgun approach), with the imposition of layer after layer of control. Too many controls soon lead to immense data requirements, and even large data sets soon yield expected cell frequencies close to zero when 8 to 10 control variables (and interaction effects) are included. This leads to the compounding problem of unreliable parameter estimates.

Yet another problem of including multitudinous controls lies with the α-level conundrum. In essence, the more controls (particularly in exploratory work), the more implicit hypotheses or parameters one is testing. The more parameters, the greater the likelihood that one or more will be statistically significant by chance alone. This does not apply to testing an overall model, but it does apply to testing the significance of individual parameters.[6]

Corrections for Sample Selection Bias

The problem of sample selection bias has been long recognized by social scientists, but most have simply treated it either as a nonexisting phenomenon or as a feature that can be corrected with the inclusion of a few more control variables. A different approach to the problem has been proposed by James Heckman (1979). Heckman suggested that the problem of selection bias be modeled explicitly and that that modeling process be used to correct estimates in the substantive model. The following example illustrates the applicability of the process.

Let us assume that a sociologist wishes to examine the impact of years of education on women's income. Simply regressing the income of women in the labor force on their level of education will probably introduce a bias in the overall estimate, insofar as women not in the labor force are likely to differ systematically from those in the labor force. A priori, women not in the labor force may have other attributes that lead them to earn less on average than the average female labor force participants, even at

---

6. There are several solutions to this problem, the simplest and most common being Bonferroni's approach of setting a p-value for testing individual parameters as $p = \alpha/k$, where α is the overall α-level and k the number of parameters to be tested.

the same level of education. In fact, it may be the awareness of this possibility that convinces nonworking women to stay at home. If these women did enter the labor force, the parameter estimates of the education–income relationship would be lower that otherwise projected.

By modeling the process, it should be possible to correct for this inherent bias. Heckman, among others, has suggested that the participation/nonparticipation distinction be analyzed using a probit analysis. If this model is significant, the inverse Mill's ratio is generated and saved in the data set with the variables of interest. It is then included as an independent variable in the income estimation model.[7]

While Heckman's approach has gained significant acceptance in economics and is encroaching into sociology, it does have its limitations. Monte Carlo studies by Stolzenberg and Relles (1990), for example, shows that Heckman's method does well under some circumstances but can produce worse estimates in other circumstances. Heckman's approach appears to work best when the selection equation explains a high proportion of the variability in the selection process. In other words, just as we require a high R^2 value in the substantive model, we also expect a high R^2 in the measurement model. The issue is still an active area of research, however, and many articles continue to appear suggesting alternate procedures. Readers are directed toward the econometrics periodical literature (*Econometrica* and *Journal of Econometrics*) for further references.

DATA STRUCTURES IN SURVEY DESIGNS

The stylized form of planned experiments often imposes a fixed structure upon the data. Traditional approaches to ANOVA, for example, are not so much statistical procedures as ways of organizing one's data. In quasi-experimental and correlational designs, however, the manner in which the data are structured is far more arbitrary. By imposing a structure upon a set of data, we often presuppose the analysis we are about to conduct. That is, certain layouts or data structures are more amenable to certain types of analysis than others. Restructuring a data set often enables us to see it in a different light and, consequently, to see the data as addressing different questions. The issue of data structures was once the sole domain of computer scientists and database managers. Ever more, however, researchers are beginning to recognize that how the data are structured can have a significant impact on how we conduct the analysis. The sections that follow examine some common data structures; the list, however, is not exhaustive.

Cross-Sectional Designs

Cross-sectional designs are the most commonly used data structures found in survey research. These designs consist of data collected at one point in time, usually over several observational units. The complexity of cross-sectional designs comes from the

---

7. See Greene (1990: ch. 21). For another approach (the pattern–mixture model), see Little and Rubin (1989–90).

manner in which observational units are distributed in space, with researchers usually trying to maximize the observational variation across units. While cross-sectional designs can provide a great deal of descriptive information on social phenomena, they have the fundamental weakness of not allowing for true causal analysis. Specifically, most cross-sectional data structures do not allow for the determination of temporal sequencing.

At this point it is prudent to note that there is a difference between cross-sectional data structures and cross-sectional surveys. Cross-sectional data structures relate to data limited to one observational period. Cross-sectional surveys, while they may be conducted in a specified period, can potentially generate time series data either by asking people to reconstruct a sequence of events from memory or by initiating a search for records of the events in question. Data typically recorded in a census or reported in an annual statistical yearbook, instruments that report events for a given day or year, are typical of cross-sectional data structures.

The great advantage of cross-sectional data structures is that they are easy to handle, being limited to two dimensions (as a data matrix). The great disadvantage, as previously noted, is the impossibility of making true causal imputations. Occasionally, researchers will argue for what is known as the *stationarity assumption*. Under conditions of stationarity, we assume that any cross-sectional relationship discovered is time-invariant or Markovian. Thus, for example, we might argue that the relationship between education and income does not change over time. If this is the case, then any parameter value estimated from cross-sectional data (e.g., b or r) should remain constant (within normal sampling variation) over time.

From one point of view, invoking the stationarity assumption may not be as tenuous as first it appears. Time, like age and many other variables we routinely consider, is often used as a proxy variable for other, unobserved processes. Understood from this perspective, time is irrelevant *if* the variable for which it stands in stead can be measured. For example, if time is used as a proxy for industrial development (or modernization), then it might be possible to measure industrial development directly, without concern for the time dimension. Often, however, the assumption of stationarity is made for the sake of convenience rather than on well-considered theoretical grounds.

While clearly susceptible to the validity threats due to unique historical factors, the usual sampling bias considerations in cross-sectional data structures result from inappropriate sampling within the spatial domain: that is, across observational units. Thus, the general problem of sampling bias in cross-sectional data structures stems from the failure of the researcher to put together an adequate sampling frame or from self-selection bias, where some observational units willfully refuse to participate.

Censorship and Truncation

Truncation refers to the deliberate limiting of a sample within a fixed range. Specifically, values above or below a fixed point are ignored. Thus, the decision to survey only persons below the so-called poverty line involves truncation. The decision to exclude only immigrants to Sweden from other Scandinavian countries is also a form of truncation. Censoring, on the other hand, is the process of ignoring certain values whose existence in the sample is known. Thus, excluding observations because of missing values involves censorship. The primary difference between the two concepts is that truncation relates to population-based exclusion while censoring involves sample-based exclusion. Hence, self-selection bias is a consequence of self-*censorship*.

Aggregation Effects or the "Ecological Fallacy"

A chronic difficulty researchers face with survey research concerns the question: What is the appropriate level of analysis? Often, surveys are conducted with individuals as the unit of response. It is possible, however, to aggregate across individuals and to generate group characteristics. For example, one might aggregate respondents by income, ethnicity, or geographical area. From a large census data set, respondents may be aggregated by geographical area, such as Consolidated Metropolitan Statistical Areas to generate CMSA level characteristics such as the percentage of visible minorities or the mean income. Often, we want to ask whether there is a relationship between aggregate level correlations between two such variables and correlations at the individual level.

In a classical article, W. S. Robinson (1950) showed that when counties were used as the unit of analysis, a strong correlation between could be shown proportion of African-Americans in a county and rates of literacy. This correlation, however, was not apparent when individual level data were used to address the issue. The error of blindly inferring from one level of analysis to another became known as the "ecological," or aggregation, fallacy. Robinson's research created a substantial conundrum for many researchers, who were unsure what the appropriate level of analysis ought to be.

While this issue will not be pursued in detail, making a couple of observations at this point is sufficient. First, the appropriate level of analysis is determined by the substantive question being asked. If one's theory addresses individual level issues, then, in general, individual level data ought to be used. If the theory is one of aggregates (such as urban or political district characteristics), then aggregate level data ought generally to be used. Inferring results from one level to another is often a recipe for disaster, as anyone who has observed the often disjunctive results between popular votes and electorial district distributions in parliamentary systems will quickly recognize.

Second, it is not always the case that results at one level have anything valid to say about results at another level. Occasionally, however, the upper and lower bounds in relationships can be estimated across levels of analysis. Recent studies suggest that, depending upon the problem, the ability to infer across levels of analysis may not be as difficult as many researchers believe (King, 1997).

Third, techniques do exist for the valid integration of data across levels of analysis that allow for the combining of individual level results and group or structural results. The problems with all these issues are not primarily statistical ones. Rather, the fault generally lies with inadequate theoretical conceptualization in the first instance. Good theorizing not only alerts us to the possible mechanism that is at work, but also considers the appropriate unit of analysis.

Means vs. Variances

Correlating group means is common for aggregate level analyses. For example, a common research question in criminology is whether income relates to rates of homicide. The typical data used to address this issue give rate of homicide correlated with GDP per capita or mean personal income. While there is nothing intrinsically incorrect about focusing on points of central tendency, it may often be of greater utility to use measures of dispersion (such as variance or some index on inequality, such as the Gini index) in one's analysis. Aggregate level data consist of distributions, and there are often more interesting facets to distributions that their means. Still, the final arbiter of what are the most appropriate statistics to consider should be theory. However, much research is exploratory and looking at more than one aspect of a relationship can be insightful.

Time Series Designs

Time series designs involve the observation of one or more units over several periods (Kish, 1987). While firmly entrenched in economics, time series designs in various guises are making inroads in other social science disciplines as ever more data are becoming available.

Sampling in the Time Domain

As the term suggests, time series data consist of multiple observations within the time domain. Substantively, the collection of time series data should simply be a logical extension of collecting cross-sectional data with an added dimension. Often, however, it is not. One prime example of the deviation in strategies lies in the tendency of cross-sectional data to be randomly sampled within the spatial domain. Time series data, however, are rarely sampled randomly. Nearly all time series consist of convenience samples within a fixed temporal domain, thus raising a fundamental question: How representative are these data? Often, the answer is: Not very.

Under these circumstances, the appropriateness of statistical testing might be raised. Within a classical framework, valid statistical inferences require the random selection of data points. Obviously, the purposeful selection of a period undermines the issue of randomness. Many researchers, however, still feel a need to calculate p-values to lend further credence to their descriptive findings. The naïve fail to recognize the issue of nonrandomness; the sophisticated argue that such estimates can be used as *information statistics* that enhance our *feel* for the goodness of fit. If conducted appropriately, random permutation tests may be useful in this situation (see Chapter 15). Another view on this issue is that such practices do little to further our belief or disbelief in the null hypothesis. At best, this type of purposeful sampling is a form of quasi-experimental design and is subject to all the validity threats to which such designs are normally heir. Honesty is perhaps best served by avoiding appeals to inferential theory and relying solely upon quantal measures of effect. That is, it is sufficient to present the reader with an estimate of R^2 or some similar summary measure of fit and skip the appeals to F, t, or z distributions. To do otherwise is to engage in scientism as much as science.

Panel Designs

Panel designs are essentially a series of cross-sectional slices arrayed in sequence. Usually this designation (i.e., panel) is used instead of "continuous time" when the duration between the surveys is "long." Thus, monthly or annual surveys (such as the ongoing labor force surveys in most industrialized countries) are generally considered to be continuous time surveys. Five- or ten-year intervals, or intervals of unequal duration, generally result in the application of panel nomenclature.

A further distinction can be made between *true panels* and *pseudopanels*. True panels consist of responses from the same observational units across panels, while pseudopanels consist of responses from different random samples taken from the same sampling frame across panels. True panels allow for the analysis of individual level changes across the panels, while pseudo designs allow only for the analysis of aggregate differences. Because of the costs involved in tracking down the same individuals over several survey periods, most practical panel designs are either pseudopanels or some type of hybrid. Even when cost is not a factor, true panel designs generally suffer from mortality as subjects either refuse to continue, cannot be unlocated, or die. Unless the design includes a mechanism for generating replacements, normal motality will result in a continual decrease in sample size across panels. A typical strategy for maximizing the benefits of true and pseudopanels is commonly termed the rotating panel, as typified by many monthly labor force surveys. Here some fraction of the panel is purposefully dropped each month (usually 1/6 or 1/12) and replaced by a similar fraction randomly selected from the same frame. Under this schema, it is necessary to find and interview each person on only 6 or 12 successive occasions. The practical problem in rotating samples stems from the mechanical difficulties involved in linking records across panels.

Censorship and Truncation

As with simple cross-sectional surveys, panel designs often suffer from problems of censorship and truncation. Within the panel framework, censorship relates to the issue of establishing arbitrary spatial and temporal cut points for the panel. Deciding to survey only residents of Harlem within the broader framework of New York City, or only the years 1990, 1994, and 1998 within the decade of the 1990s, constitutes censorship. Using respondents only within those spatial–temporal points because the data were not recorded by the authorities is truncation.

Both issues are problematic in panel designs, since patterns may exist in the excluded data that are different from those in the data collected. With censorship, it is up to the researcher to be able to justify the decision to select certain space–time coordinates from all the possible ones available. A justification based on random sampling is much easier to defend than one based on simple expediency. Truncation may be a more difficult issue to address, since systematic external forces may have been the cause of the missing data.

Continuous Time

Traditionally, continuous time panels have been extremely rare. The most common forms of these data structures are to be found in population registers collected

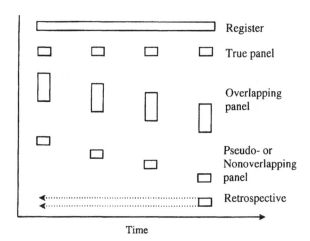

Figure 8.11. Cross-sectional data structures within a time domain.

in many European countries. In Denmark, for example, population registers are maintained which record such aspects as residency and labor force participation. Samples extracted from these registers can provide ongoing lines of information about a group of individuals. Population registers are continuous time panels because data are recorded as events unfold, as opposed to being tapped at fixed survey points.

Continuous time data structures are rare for two primary reasons. First, collecting such data is expensive. Unlike point-in-time surveys, continuous time data structures require an ongoing commitment of personnel and organizational resources. Second, continuous time data structures are often voluminous, requiring massive storage. Further, these large and often complex data sets pose serious difficulties for analysis. The statistical tools that allow us to take reasonable advantage of the nature and quantity of data collected in continuous time models were developed only recently.

Because of the costs associated with collecting social data in continuous time, many researchers have turned to retrospective models designed to "reconstruct" social processes in continuous time. Retrospective studies are usually conducted either at an arbitrary point in time or at the end of a process. Participants are then asked to delve into their memories and personal records to reconstruct a past sequence of events.

With the fuller development in recent years of survival models (or life history methodology, as it is often called), continuous time data structures have attracted increasing attention.

As with discrete time panel studies, continuous time data structures face problems of truncation and censorship. Typically, truncation in continuous time data structures results from a limiting of the time within which the data are recorded. For example, one may decide to record (or reconstruct) only data for a fixed period—say, January 1, 1970, to December 31, 1995, inclusive. Censorship in such models consists of missed periods or unrecorded events. For example, a switch in computer systems in February 1988 may have meant that no events taking place in that month were being recorded. Similarly, individual respondents may have lost or forgotten records for certain periods.

Constructing several thematic variations based on elementary panel designs is possible. Two of the more common themes are explored in the next two sections, which present age–period–cohort designs and life history models in greater detail.

Age–Period–Cohort (APC) Designs

A common longitudinal design is the cohort design. Lewis Terman's study of "gifted" children in California is generally considered to be the first major cohort study in modern times. Terman's study, which was started in the 1920s, is what we call a *prospective* cohort study, since the cohort members were identified at a young age and followed over time. *Retrospective* cohort studies identify a group of people who were born during some selected period and reconstruct their career histories from official records or self-reports. The advantage of prospective studies is that observations can be made of pertinent factors as they manifest themselves. Retrospective studies, however, rely on data or reconstructions of data (e.g., memories) that someone other than the researcher decided to record. For reasons of time and costs, however, most cohort studies are retrospective.

Briefly, cohort studies can be placed into one of two general groups. They are either true cohort studies or studies of *synthetic* cohorts. True cohort studies involve the identification of a specific group of individuals who are examined over time. Synthetic cohort studies, on the other hand, do not generally require the identification of individual group members. Instead, the cohort's characteristics are inferred by following a specific age group over time.

Age, Period, and Cohort Effects: What Is a "Cohort Effect"?

Because of the cost associated with following true cohorts, some researchers have turned to alternate approaches in an attempt to answer cohort-related questions. One technique is to use official data, broken down by age, over a long time. This procedure is used extensively in demography (Hagenaars and Cobben, 1978; Hobcraft, Menken, and Preston, 1982). Demographers often use a Lexis diagram to depict cohorts (see Figure 8.12). The Lexis diagram shows how a cohort consists of a diagonal series of observations in an age–period table. For example, Figure 8.12 illustrates how cohort 4 (C_4) can be followed through the table, starting with those who are aged 30–34 in 1930–34 through to ages 45–49 in 1945–49. Cohort 8, on the other hand, are ages 10–14 in 1930–34 and can be followed through to age 45–50 in 1960–64. Beside cost considerations, synthetic cohort studies have the advantage of allowing for comparisons across multiple cohorts. For those studying true cohorts, the capture of two or three groups is considered a remarkable feat (for two examples within criminology, see Shannon, 1988, and Tracy, Wolfgang, and Figlio, 1990), but analyses of synthetic cohorts often encompass 20 or 30 groups (Glenn, 1976).

The prime weakness of synthetic cohorts, however, is that specific individuals cannot be identified, and thus distinguishing prevalence from incidence is virtually impossible. Also, in- and out-migration cannot be controlled, since some individuals leave over time and others join the group.

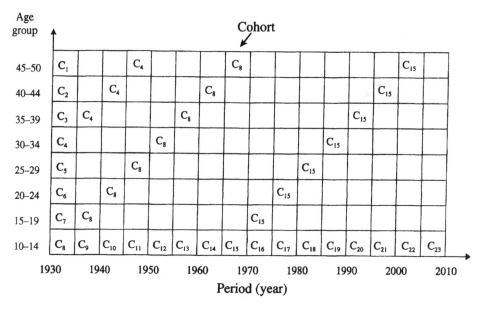

Figure 8.12. Synthetic cohorts.

A major debate surrounding the analysis of synthetic cohorts entails the implications of the term itself. Many studies have attempted to separate out age from period and cohort effects. Some have argued that this is a futile quest, since mathematically, if any two of these effects are identified, the third is implicit. While proponents of the three-effect position do not deny the mathematical relationship, they do argue that the interaction effect has a valid substantive interpretation (Rogers, 1982; Maxim, 1985).

Mathematical Problems Inherent in Estimation

Using a small example, it is possible to show how a design matrix can be constructed to estimate age, period and cohort effects. Let A_i represent the ith age group; P_j represent the jth period, and C_k represent the kth cohort. While the rows and columns can represent any of the three effects, it is common to represent the rows as ages and the columns as period effect, with the cohort effects along the diagonals. Typically, then, we would have:

$$
\begin{array}{cccc}
 & P_1 & P_2 & P_3 \\
A_3 & C_1 & C_2 & C_3 \\
A_2 & C_2 & C_3 & C_4 \\
A_1 & C_3 & C_4 & C_5
\end{array}
$$

Allow Y_{ij} to represent the dependent variable of interest (e.g., crime rates, fertility rates). Substituting the Y_{ij} into their proper locations, the APC matrix can be rewritten as follows:

	P_1	P_2	P_3
A_3	Y_{11}	Y_{12}	Y_{13}
A_2	Y_{21}	Y_{22}	Y_{23}
A_1	Y_{31}	Y_{32}	Y_{33}

Viewed in this way, the APC design takes on the form of a traditional ANOVA design with age as the row effects and period as the column effects. Such a framework makes it easier to see the cohort effects as interaction effect between A and P. Just as with an ANOVA design, it is possible to reparameterize the model as a general linear model by aligning the Y_{ij} observations as a column vector and relating the APC effects through a design matrix. While many patterns can be used, the following represents one possible option. Here an "effect-coded" matrix is used to impose the traditional ANOVA constraints $\Sigma A_i = 0$; $\Sigma P_j = 0$; and $\Sigma C_k = 0$.

	P_1	P_2	A_1	A_2	C_1	C_2	C_3
Y_{11}	1	0	−1	−1	1	0	0
Y_{12}	0	1	−1	−1	0	1	0
Y_{13}	−1	−1	−1	−1	0	0	1
Y_{21}	1	0	1	0	0	1	0
Y_{22}	0	1	1	0	0	0	1
Y_{23}	−1	−1	1	0	−1	−1	−1
Y_{31}	1	0	0	1	0	0	1
Y_{32}	0	1	0	1	−1	−1	−1
Y_{33}	−1	−1	0	1	−1	−1	−1

As usual, one of each of the P and A vectors is dropped out to avoid singularity in the $X'X$ matrix. It is also necessary to delete two of the C vectors for the same reason. In this instance, we have chosen to delete C_4 and C_5, which is tantamount to assuming that C_4 and C_5 are equivalent.

Once the design matrix has been constructed, we can write the structural equation:

$$Y = \Sigma b_i A_i + \Sigma b_j P_j + \Sigma b_k C_k + e$$

and estimate the appropriate parameters. By partitioning the various effects, one might also determine the proportion of variance explained (R^2) that might be attributed to each component.

Issues of Immigration, Emigration, and Confounding with Mortality

A major problem with any panel design is the "dropout" issue: that is, the difficulty associated with maintaining the same target sample from one panel to another. In pseudo- or nonoverlapping panels (and partially in overlapping panels) the issue is mooted because the design does not intend to capture the same sample over time. With a true panel, however, the problem may be significant. Original panel members are often lost to the researcher for such causes as emigration, mortality, or a simple refusal to continue participating. Occasionally, participants in early panels may return or decide to participate again in later surveys. In other circumstances, such as those entailing the use of official statistics, later panels may increase in size because of immigration. The problem here, of course, is how this often complex pattern of censorship should be handled. To make matters more complex, the censorship issue may affect both the specific sample and the sample frame or base population.

For example, assume one wanted to conduct an APC analysis based on rates of criminal events. Not only may there be censorship in the numerator, that is, among those who commit crimes (again, due to in- or out-migration and also mortality), but there may also be censorship in the denominator or the base population. For common events within a large base population, this potential for censorship may pose no serious problem. For rare events in which the risk factor is not homogeneous across the population, however, the problem may be extreme.

Censorship and Truncation

APC designs are just as subject to problems of censorship and truncation as any other design we have examined. The most obvious sources of censorship surround the start and finish points for the age and period categories. It is also evident from Figure 8.12 that the cohorts in the upper and lower corners of the data matrix will be incomplete. In fact, the issue of whether the incomplete cohorts should be estimated, and if they are, how the related coefficients should be interpreted, is an important one. To date, it has not been addressed satisfactorily.

Life History Models

The term "life history model" encompasses several procedures, such as survival analysis, that have a common underlying statistical model. Life history models generally attempt to model qualitative outcomes as a function of a series of fixed and time-dependent covariates. The outcomes are often defined as a state space and can consist of two or more outcomes or events or categories. For example, a study of labor force participation might consider a three-dimensional state space: employed, unemployed, and outside the labor force. Certain fixed covariates, such as gender, level of formal education, race, or physical ability, might influence the likelihood that an individual will be in one employment category or another. Similarly, time-dependent covariates, such as age, and number and ages of children, may also influence the likelihood that a given person will be in one employment category or another. The objective of a life history model is to be able to combine both the fixed and time-varying covariates into a single model that can make reasonably accurate predictions of state space membership at some particular time.

A typical example of how life history data are distributed is presented in Figure 8.13. Here labor force participation is the outcome state space and age is the covariate.

The two basic aspects of life history models—the state space and the temporal dimension—pose two of the primary difficulties in life history analysis. The first issue, of course, is the appropriate definition of the outcome state space. The second issue is one of identifying the duration or interval between time-varying covariates. That is, on what axis do we measure durations between changes in level of education, marital status, or job experience (seniority) that may, in turn, affect the outcome variable?

Time-Dependent Covariates

In cross-sectional research, the predictor variables are usually static or fixed. Thus, for example, a person's gender is usually time independent, and so often is education once adulthood has been achieved. Some variables, such as employment status and number of children, may change over time. In demography, these variables are termed time-dependent covariates.[8] Few social processes remain static over a lifetime. Focusing

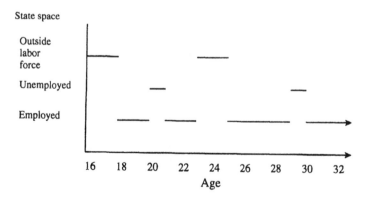

Figure 8.13. Sample employment history.

---

8. For an elementary introduction to the analysis of time-dependent variables, see Rutherford, and Choe (1993: ch. 9). More advanced introductions can be found in Blossfeld (1989) and Courgeau (1992).

only upon static characteristics misses many of the dynamic factors that influence behavior.

CONCLUSIONS

The issue of design is fundamental to research. The design we choose determines both the internal and external validity of any conclusion that might be drawn. At best, poor designs result in low power; at worst, they lead to invalid and spurious inferences. While classical experimental designs are held up as the ideal, they are not perfect. In fact, under some conditions, well-executed alternative designs can be more valid and powerful than poorly executed classical experiments.

As Nagel noted, some sciences (such as astronomy) have developed successfully despite their inability to invoke random designs. Since there is no single perfect or ideal design, it is incumbent on the researcher to assess the broader context of the research and select the best possible design among the available options. As Kish tells us, statistical designs *are* a compromise between the desirable and the possible.

When we choose a design strategy, no matter how good it appears, we should be aware of its limitations. By identifying and addressing a design's limitations directly, it is easier to determine whether those disadvantages pose minor or insurmountable restrictions on its internal and external validity.

As Lakatos argued regarding the evolution of theory, it makes sense to view design and testing as part of a coherent research program. No one sample and no one test will provide an unequivocal assessment of the null hypothesis. By testing different data relating to different aspects of our substantive hypothesis, we accumulate knowledge about our problem. By being critical and identifying flaws in our strategies, we can subsequently use approaches that rest on different assumptions.

Further Reading

Cook, T.D., and Campbell, D.T. *Quasi-Experimentation: Design and Analysis Issues for Field Settings*. Chicago: Rand-McNally, 1979. This book, which provided for many researchers the legitimation for quasi-experimentation, is generally the starting point for discussions of quasi-experimentation. It is worthwhile to read it in detail.

Cook, T.D., and W.R., Shadish. "Social experiments: Some developments over the past fifteen years." *Annual Review of Psychology*, 45: 545–80, 1994. This short article provides an excellent overview of the literature since the appearance of Cook and Campbell's book in 1979. Critics and supporters are given equal consideration. The literature reviewed in this article also provides interesting insights into some of the political fads and fashions that arise over time.

9

Measurement Theory

Measurement is a sine qua non of any science.
—George Bohrnstedt

MEASUREMENT TYPOLOGIES

Measurement is one of the most important aspects of the research enterprise. Nancy Cartwright even asserts that "science is measurement." Measurement involves the process by which empirical events are linked to our basic theoretical concepts. Without sound measurement, empirical science is a vacuous endeavor. Unfortunately, while measurement is central to the research process, it is often treated as an afterthought because it lacks the glamour associated with problems of experimental design, sampling, or data analysis.

Formally, measurement is the process of mapping empirical phenomena onto a system of numbers. Often, we say that the empirical phenomena we are interested in studying exist in an *event space*. This event space is also known as the *domain*. Measurement involves the linkage of the events in the domain to events or points in another space called the *range*. Most often the range consists of points on a scale. The process is illustrated in Figure 9.1.

Differences exist in the mapping rules (also known as rules of correspondence) that link the domain to the range, thus leading to differences in the kinds of arithmetic and mathematical operations that can be performed. Because of the differences in these mapping rules, typologies of scales have been produced by various authors (Stevens, 1946; Pfanzagl, 1968; Anderson et al., 1983). In the social sciences, we tend use a modified form of S. S. Stevens's typology and speak of nominal, ordinal, interval, and ratio level scales. It should be noted, however, that no consensus exists among methodologists about what is the most appropriate typology. As an example, Mosteller and Tukey (1997) suggest that a sixfold typology, based on grades, ranks, counted fractions, counts, amounts, and balances, might be useful. Since Stevens's typology is the basis for much of the discussion of measurement in the social sciences, however, it is worthwhile for us to use it as a starting point and to look at it in more detail.

Nominal Measurement

Nominal measurement is the process of assigning numerals to categories. These categories need not be in any special order or relationship to one another. The numbers on football or hockey jerseys provide a good example of numerals that stand for names.

Domain

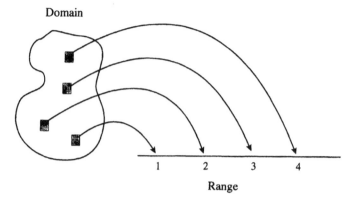

Range

Figure 9.1. Mapping the domain onto the range.

Even this example is not perfect, however, since the number a player is assigned is often related to a subsidiary dimension such as the position to be played.

We might graphically depict the mapping process for nominal measurement as follows:

$$
\begin{array}{cccccc}
1 & 5 & 6 & 2 & 3 & 4 \quad \leftarrow \text{range} \\
\uparrow & \uparrow & \uparrow & \uparrow & \uparrow & \uparrow \\
\blacksquare & \blacksquare & \blacksquare & \blacksquare & \blacksquare & \blacksquare \quad \leftarrow \text{domain}
\end{array}
$$

The symbols associated with the range are numerals onto which the objects in the domain (here black squares) are related. Notice, however, that no particular order exists in the sequencing or ordering of the numerals.

At this point, you may be wondering why the symbols related to the range are called numerals and not numbers. The term *numeral* refers to the set of symbols 0 through 9. These symbols take on meaning as *numbers* only when they are related through some type of measurement model. When we refer to nominal level measurement, the numeric symbols are indistinct from other symbols or sets of symbols that we use to identify an object. Thus, identifying football players by the designations 10, 15, or 30 is no different from calling them Jim, Bill, or Sue. When further assumptions are made regarding the meaning of the numerals and the relationships among the numerals, then they become numbers.

Most constructed typologies in the social sciences are forms of nominal level measurement, with each type forming a category. Traditional discussions of typologies held that the categories needed to be mutually exclusive as a condition for logical adequacy (Gregg, 1954; Tiryakian, 1968: 177–86). This may be a sufficient condition but it is not a necessary one; there is no inherent reason nominal categories cannot have "fuzzy" or overlapping boundaries.

Ordinal Measurement

In ordinal level measurement, the nominal scale is ordered monotonically through some process (*P*) such as precedence or preference. Thus, *aPb* (*a* precedes *b*) and *bPc* (*b* precedes *c*) logically imply *aPc*. There is no indication of "by how much"—only an indication of "greater than" or "less than."

Thus, to present the situation graphically, we have:

Unlike the case of nominal measurement, the range in an ordinal scale is always sequenced, but the spacing among the points is arbitrary. When numerals take on the added assumption of ordinality, they are generally called numbers. Some authors, however, like to create a crude dichotomy and refer to measurements at the nominal and ordinal levels as "qualitative" and scales with yet further assumptions as "quantitative" measurement.

Interval Measurement

Interval level scales introduce another assumption or dimension to the measurement process and order the mapped values on equally appearing intervals. In interval measurement, there is no absolute zero point, so the scale can start and end at any arbitrary position. Centigrade and Fahrenheit thermometers are traditional examples of interval measurement. Obviously, 20°C is not twice as warm as 10°C (unlike the Kelvin scale which does have an absolute zero point). In the social sciences, many scales start from some arbitrary point such as a minimum threshold (e.g., a minimum wage, the poverty line) or a midpoint.

Following through on our graphical presentation, interval level measurement may be depicted as follows:

Most of the items in attitude scales that social scientists construct are assumed to be of this interval type. If the numbers represented in the range are designed to reflect an individual's level of satisfaction with some phenomenon, then we can see that they have the properties of being correspondence mapped (nominal), of being rank-ordered (ordinal), and of being distributed with equal distances between the points (interval). We cannot assume that a person who responds to a question with a 6, however, is twice as satisfied as a person who responds with a 3.

Ratio Measurement

Ratio measurement implies that a scale not only incorporates all the assumptions above but has an absolute zero point, thus allowing for the construction of meaningful ratios. If how much money one possesses is considered a ratio level scale, then the implication of having $200 in one's pocket is that one has twice as much as someone who has $100.

Thus, the mapping relationship may be illustrated:

Generally, ratio level measurement is the goal to which we aspire, since ratio numbers contain more information than lower level scales.

Other Classes of Measurement

While Stevens's typology is almost universally referred to in undergraduate methods and statistics texts, it is not without its detractors. A major criticism levied against this typology is that it is not exhaustive. Mosteller and Tukey's suggestions have already been noted. Some demographers have also argued that it is necessary to add at least one more scale—the absolute scale—to the measurement typology. Absolute measurement consists of a determined isomorphic relationship between the things being observed and the number system. Counts, such as censuses and sample sizes, represent absolute measurement. The difference between ratio and absolute measurement is best typified by the realization that a phenomenon such as weight can be ratio but not absolute. That is, weight can be mapped onto a system of kilograms or pounds without losing any meaning. Counts, on the other hand, have meaning only when a direct one-to-one correspondence exists between the domain and the range.

Stevens also discussed a logarithmic interval scale that appears to have major applications in psychophysics. Subjective intensities of light and sound (lumens and decibels) are prime examples of this type of measurement. Here the unit increases are exponential, but are unreliant on any specific zero point. That is, any arbitrary starting point would be sufficient—all points above and below the starting point are increments or decrements in powers of 10.

The distinction between simple interval and log-interval scales raises an important issue in social research that is the subject of much controversy and misinformation. The controversy surrounds the meaning of the term *linear*. Nonnumerate critics of quantitative research often point to what they perceive as a fundamental limitation in much quantitative analysis in that we rely heavily on *linear models*. And indeed, until about 20 years ago, estimating nonstraight line models was difficult. Somehow, the term "linear" was assumed to mean "straight line," when in fact any graphical representation of a curve is a line.

More properly, that which is often called a linear model should really be called a straight-line model. Nonlinear models, on the other hand, should be called non-straight-line or curve models.

Stevens's measurement typology is itself an ordinal scale. The ordinality is in terms of the subsumption of assumptions, with higher level scales subsuming all the assumptions of lower level scales and then adding some. Stevens's hierarchy of scales is irreflexive in that lower level measures cannot be transformed into higher level ones, but higher level ones can be transformed into lower level ones.

Since this process of "scaling down" is so common, examining the issue in some detail is worthwhile. Reducing quantitative or magnitude measures to a series of categories is popular in some areas. One typical example is that of age. Rather than asking respondents to report their actual age to the nearest year, researchers often provide a series of categories, such as less than 15, 15 to 24, 25 to 34, 35 to 44, 45 to 64, and 65 and over. Justifications for this practice are many but generally fall into one of two categories. The argument is either that the asking of a specific age as opposed to a category will reduce response rates, or that the variable is "really" a nominal or ordinal level variable in the first instance and to treat it otherwise is a methodological sin.

Generally, the needless collapsing of a quantitative variable is not a good strategy. Again, the reason revolves around issues of power. Consider the example presented in Figure 9.2. Here, a hypothetical relationship is drawn between age and relative disposable income. The "true" underlying function is that of a quadratic, with the young and the elderly having larger amounts of relative disposable income than the middle-aged. To take the extreme instance, age is dichotomized into two categories—young and old. In Figure 9.2, the mean income levels of the two groups are signified by horizontal bars. When this convention is adopted, however, the quadratic nature of the relationship is lost: one is merely left with a comparison of mean income across two categories. In this instance, the slight difference in category means (the horizontal bars) is not statistically significant, given the large variances within the two age categories. Unfortunately, lost information by collapsing into a lower level of measurement cannot be regained at a later time.

Certainly, circumstances exist under which collapsing is justified. The issue of nonresponse is significant. Trading off an increase in response rates for a loss of information through the judicious use of categories may be reasonable. The problem also becomes less severe as the number of categories increases. A lesser justification is that prior research has shown the relationship to be stepwise, with certain category limits forming threshold boundaries. Using categories on a questionnaire may some-

Figure 9.2. Categorizing a continuous function.

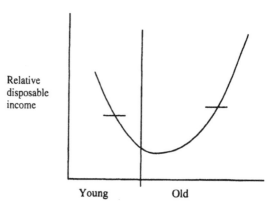

Relative disposable income

Young   Old

how be seen as saving time that otherwise would have been devoted to coding and analysis. A minimal defense is that people are more likely to answer fallaciously when asked to choose a specific number as opposed to checking a category. Ultimately, this is an empirical question. Demographers have long known that age heaping or spiking is commonplace. Still, by asking an exact age, this problem can be dealt with by smoothing, imputing—and yes—through informed and judicious collapsing. Other arguments, however, ranging from "everyone else does it" to "it looks better on a questionnaire," are bogus and do not warrant our attention.

OTHER CONCEPTUAL ISSUES

As indicated, Stevens's measurement typology came under criticism from statisticians and methodologists from the outset (e.g., Lord, 1953. For a more contemporary view, see Borgatta and Bohrnstedt, 1980, and Luce et al., 1990). Stevens (1951: 26) himself recognized that a too inflexible invocation of this typology could be counterproductive. Unfortunately, many introductory statistics and methods texts have adopted Stevens's fourfold typology as gospel truth, as opposed to a pragmatic organizational framework. This misleading trend, combined with an increase in computer software supposedly based on "artificial intelligence," led at least two authors to rail against a mechanistic adherence to a rigid fourfold framework. In a review of Stevens's work, Velleman and Wilkinson (1993) point out that criticisms of Stevens's typology focus on three issues:

> First, restricting the choice of statistical methods to those that "exhibit the appropriate invariance for the scale type at hand" is a dangerous practice for data analysis. Second, his taxonomy is too strict to apply to real-world data. Third, Stevens's prescriptions often lead to degrading data by rank ordering and unnecessarily resorting to nonparametric methods.

Much of the debate over the appropriate organizational principles for measurement scales is a consequence of one's starting point. Mathematical social scientists and theoretical methodologists often approach the issue from a formalist perspective where the *generative* mechanism underlying the numbers is assumed to be known. Thus, for these researchers, measurement is strictly a mapping problem. Statisticians and data analysts, on the other hand, usually start with the numbers and are either uncertain about which specific theoretical mechanism generated the data or approach the task as one of trying to discover the generative mechanism. Thus, for most empirical researchers, the elegance of formal mapping rules becomes obscured in the muck of everyday research.

As an example of how difficult deciphering the underlying process that generated the observed numbers might be, Velleman and Wilkinson (1993) present the following scenario:

> At a reception . . . consecutively numbered tickets, starting with a "1," were allotted at the door as people entered so that a raffle could be held. As the winning number, 126, was

selected and announced, one participant compared it to her ticket to see if she had won, thus interpreting the "126" correctly as a nominal value. She then immediately looked around the room and remarked that, "It doesn't look like there are 125 people here," now interpreting the same value, again correctly (but using the additional information that tickets had been allotted consecutively starting with 1), as a ratio-scale value. One of the authors compared his ticket number (56) to the winning value and realized that he had arrived too soon to win the prize, thus interpreting the values ordinally. If additional data about the rate and regularity of arrivals had been available, he might have tried to estimate by how much longer he should have delayed his arrival from the 70-ticket difference between his ticket and the winner, thus treating the ticket number as an interval-scale value.

The example may seem a bit fanciful, but it does get the point across.

DISCRETE VS. CONTINUOUS MEASUREMENT

Practicing social scientists regularly face major difficulties in the area of measurement. This is particularly so for those working in the cognitive sciences, where many of our most fruitful concepts are deemed *unobservable*. It is because of these difficulties that we cannot avoid addressing the assumptions underlying our measurement schema. Coming to grips with the formalities of measurement may not be the most exciting part of the research enterprise for most substantive researchers; however, it is time well spent.

For example, it is worthwhile considering that most social science measurement is discrete, although we may be dealing with an underlying ratio or interval metric. This situation is primarily the fault of our measurement and counting instruments, which can often detect only cardinal values, not fractional ones. Thus, we rarely observe a 3.78 on a seven-point scale. The respondent is forced to round either up to 4 or, less likely, down to 3. Because of these limitations in instrumentation, we must rely heavily upon the assumptions of measurement to make valid interpolations between the observed points. This process may be problematic (especially in attitude scaling) when it is unclear whether the underlying metric is interval or merely ordinal. Likert-type scales suffer from this problem, since we are often unsure about whether the differences between given points are constant or variable. Many items included in scales of this type are log-interval, and many are exponential from some midpoint. By coming to grips with this problem, the researcher can try several transformations on the scale items in an attempt to decide what the most appropriate metric might be (Draper and Smith, 1981: ch. 5).

Sociologists, for example, generally use Likert-type scales as strict ordinal or interval level scales; yet most economists assume that within a utility framework, perceptions of worth follow a power function.

How well we manage to link the domain of social phenomena onto the range of the number system is a primary research problem in methods. The two major problems surrounding the mapping process involve the *validity* of the mapping and the stability or *reliability* of the process—two issues we now explore in greater detail.

VALIDITY

A variable is *valid* when it measures what it is supposed to measure. For example, IQ tests are supposed to measure intelligence; victimization surveys are supposed to tell us how much crime exists in a community. While reasonably easy to define, validity becomes far more nebulous when we attempt to operationalize it. The reason for this difficulty is that validity refers to how closely operational definitions are linked to nominal definitions. Thus, returning to an earlier discussion, the measurement of validity is the quantitative equivalent to the logical rules of correspondence that supposedly link operational and nominal definitions.

The process of recording observations is known as measurement: the linking of operational indicators to a theoretical concept involves the invocation of a measurement model. In the literature dealing with structural equation models, the nominal definition of a concept is often called a latent variable. Measurement models link or connect the latent variable to one or more operational measures or observed variables.

Validity, then, addresses whether operational indicators are true indicators of the latent variable. That is, does a variable measure what it is supposed to be measuring? The problem of validity has received most attention from psychologists, who have developed four categories: content validity, criterion validity, construct validity, and convergent and discriminant validity.

Content Validity

Content validity reflects subjective judgment about whether an indicator references that which it is supposed to reference. The researcher makes a judgment on whether a given item includes the appropriate theoretical or substantive domain. Often, this process is called arriving at "face validity." Here, one attempts to decide whether an item substantively falls within the conceptual domain of the nominal term. Thus, for example, the question "Do you feel that your life has meaning?" might be judged as a valid indicator of anomie; the question "Do you like carrots?" likely will not pass that judgment. The assessment of content validity is largely an exercise in theory.

Generally, researchers assess content validity by circulating scale items among panels of judges who are deemed to be experts in the substantive area being investigated. A high interrater concordance does not necessarily mean that the items have content validity, however. The debate over whether scores on currently constructed IQ tests truly reflect intelligence is a prime example of many researchers accepting the content validity of a pool of items while many others do not.

A further problem with content validity is the issue of whether a pool of questions covers the entire domain of the concept one is attempting to measure. Assessment of performance in many undergraduate classes, for example, is often based on multiple-choice exams. Frequently, however, students argue that the items presented covered merely a small portion of what they think they know about the topic area. If the instructor had included a broader range of items, then a student's "true" range of knowledge would come to the forefront. Generally, this problem is known as an inadequate sampling of the domain.

Ultimately, the test of content validity is dependent upon a disciplinary consensus. How well an item meets the criterion of content validity is based on the degree to which the underlying concept is defined theoretically. Except for an interjudgmental consensus, there are no objective indicators of content validity.

Criterion Validity

Criterion validity is the correspondence between an operational indicator and its latent factor or nominal definition. For example, one might ask a group of individuals to report their ages. If those verbal reports were then corroborated with a search of birth registrations, the correlation between these two items would be considered to represent criterion validity. The assumption here, of course, is that no errors exist in the recorded birth registrations. In the realm of job satisfaction, one might look toward productivity or the number of days absent as criteria with which a job satisfaction scale ought to be correlated.

When the "true" measure coexists with the operational indicator, the correlation between the two is termed *concurrent* validity; when the "true" measure appears in the future, the correlation is called *predictive* validity. Thus, for example, LSAT or GRE scores are assumed to have predictive validity because it is believed that performance on those instruments anticipates how well one will do in law school, or even later, in professional practice.

Criterion validity is not an unproblematic issue. Typically no obvious criterion measures are available with which our indicator can be correlated. Furthermore, the concept begs the question of why the criterion variable is not being used in the analysis instead of the operational indicator. Kenneth Bollen (1989: 186–88) has also shown that the traditional measure of criterion validity—the absolute correlation coefficient between a measure and its criterion—has several undesirable characteristics.

Construct Validity

Construct validity consists of the correlation between two or more separate notions of the same construct. Ultimately, this measure is based on a set of theoretically based predictions as to the direction of the relationships between several separate instruments. Construct validity relates primarily to measures for which there is no apparent "real-world" counterpart. Examples abound in the social sciences and range from the concepts of anomie and alienation in sociology to intelligence and personality characteristics (e.g., need for achievement; introversion/extroversion) in psychology. Because the concepts are hypothetical, the assessment of construct validity is not easy. As Bollen states (1989: 189): "No one empirical test determines construct validity. Establishing construct validity is a long process, with each test providing information and suggesting revisions that can aid the next empirical test." To put this matter into context, researchers have spent close to 100 years attempting to verify the concept of intelligence, yet still debates rage over whether the concept truly exists.

The issue of how we identify construct validity is a methodological minefield in which many researchers have found substantial grief. While discussions concerning construct validity can still be found in the literature, perhaps the best statements of the issue and problems surrounding it are to be found in the classical articles by Cronbach and Meehl (1955), and Bechtoldt (1959).

Convergent and Discriminant Validity

Campbell and Fisk (1959) introduced a technique for deciding validity that they termed the *multitrait, multimethod* technique. Here, a correlation or covariance matrix comprising at least two different constructs measured by at least two different techniques is estimated. An example of a multitrait, multimethod matrix is presented in Table 9.1.

The basic premise behind this model is that two (or more) different measures of the same concept ought to be highly intercorrelated. This Campbell and Fiske called *convergent* validity. Further, the correlation between the two (or more) methods designed to measure the same trait ought to be higher than the correlations among the traits. This Campbell and Fiske called *divergent* validity. In other words, unless constructs are more dissimilar than the techniques used to measure them, they can no longer be considered separate entities.

With specific reference to Table 9.1, X_1 and X_3 represent a matched pair of constructs (or one trait), and X_2 and X_4 represent another pair (the second trait). The correlations r_{31} and r_{42} are the convergent validity measures. According to the theory behind this method, these two correlations should be higher than r_{32} and r_{41}. The convergent validity measure (r_{31} and r_{42}) should also be higher than the correlations of the different constructs (traits) measured by the same method. Thus, r_{31} and r_{42} should also be higher than r_{21} and r_{43}.

The multitrait, multimethod approach assumes that the measurement methods used to gather the data are equally good, and this is a major problem within the classical test theory. The question of whether different measurement techniques provide similar results has been long debated. An issue raised more recently is that of whether telephone interviews are equivalent to person-to-person interviews (Groves, 1988). Combined with this issue, it is required that the measurement methods be independent (uncorrelated) of the traits.

A second problem with this approach is that Campbell and Fiske did not initially specify the type of statistical criterion that should be used to evaluate the model. Many authors have put forth suggestions: the soundest may be the use of structural

Table 9.1. Multitrait, Multimethod Matrix

	METHOD 1		METHOD 2	
	X_1	X_2	X_3	X_4
Method 1				
X_1	1			
X_2	r_{21}	1		
Method 2				
X_3	r_{31}	r_{32}	1	
X_4	r_{41}	r_{42}	r_{43}	1

equation modeling, or confirmatory factor analysis (Jöreskog, 1971). Since this is the substance of Chapter 11, we will leave the detailed discussion of this issue for the present.

In summary, the convergent–discriminant approach to the problem appears to provide the most stringent test of validity available. Naturally, it is the one least likely to be achieved in practice.

OPERATIONALIZING INDICATORS

In this section we will look at some examples of how items are constructed. Students interested in conducting survey research should search the relevant literature to see how existing studies have addressed the issue at hand. As a starting point, and certainly as a source of good examples, there are many compendia of existing scales and instruments available in most college and university libraries. These volumes often provide summaries of scale reliability, validity indices, and references to specific applications (Bonjean, 1967; Shaw and Wright, 1967; J. P. Robinson, Rusk, and Head, 1968; J. P. Robinson, Athanasiou, and Head, 1969; J. P. Robinson and Shaver, 1973; Brodsky and Smitherman, 1983).

Single-Item Indicators

Indicators in the social sciences come in one of two variants—single-item indicators and multi-item indicators or scales. Usually, we employ single indicators to measure simple concepts (such as sex, age, or fecundity) and scales to measure more complex concepts (such as job satisfaction, locus of control, or alienation). Historically, single indicators have posed problems for classical measurement models, since their reliability cannot be assessed. Thus, researchers attempted, whenever possible, to construct scales to operationalize their concepts. As common sense would also tell us, a single indicator assumes that the underlying concept we are attempting to operationalize is unidimensional. Multi-item indicators, or scales, however, also allow for the operationalization of multidimensional phenomena.

An example of typical single item indicators is presented in Figure 9.3. The excerpt presented in Figure 9.3 is taken from a demographic and health survey (DHS) conducted in Tanzania. While this example is directed toward the Tanzanian situation, the same survey has been carried out in many different countries.

The items in the questionnaire represent a wide range of measurement levels. Question 101, for example, identifies the starting time of the interview. Later, space is provided for the time at completion. By taking the difference between these two recordings, a ratio level variable—length of interview—can be created. Question 102 relates to place of residence when the respondent was less than 12 years of age. At first glance, the response options appear to provide a nominal trichotomy, since three mutually exclusive geographical areas are listed. On a second viewing, however, the responses—Dar es Salaam, other urban area, and rural area—may be considered to form an ordinal scale based on population density.

NO	QUESTIONS AND FILTERS	CODING CATEGORIES	SKIP TO
101	RECORD THE TIME.	HOUR . . . . ⬚⬚ MINUTES . . . . ⬚⬚	
102	First I would like to ask some questions about your background. For most of the time until you were 12 years old, did you live in Dar es Salaam city, another urban area, or in the rural area?	CITY (DAR ES SALAAM) . .1 OTHER URBAN AREA . . . .2 RURAL AREA/VILLAGE . . .3	
103	How long have you been living continuously in (NAME OF CURRENT PLACE OF RESIDENCE)?	YEARS . . . . ⬚⬚ ALWAYS . . . . .95 VISITOR . . . . .96 → 105	
104	Just before you moved here, did you live in Dar es Salaam city, another urban area, or in the rural area?	CITY (DAR ES SALAAM) . .1 OTHER URBAN AREA . . . .2 RURAL AREA/VILLAGE . . .3	
105	In what month and year were you born?	MONTH . . . . ⬚⬚ DK MONTH . . . . .96 YEAR . . . . ⬚⬚ DK YEAR 96	
106	How old were you at your last birthday? COMPARE AND CORRECT 105 AND/OR 106 IF INCONSISTENT.	AGE IN COMPLETED YEARS . . . . ⬚⬚	
107	Can you read and write kiswahilli easily, with difficulty, or not at all?	EASILY . . . . .1 WITH DIFFICULTY . . . . . . .2 NOT AT ALL. . . . . .3 → 109	
108	Do you usually read a newspaper or magazine at least once a week?	YES .1 NO 2	
109	Have you ever attended school?	YES .1 NO . . . . .2 → 111	
110	What is the highest formal school you completed?	LESS THAN 1 YEAR. . . . . .00 STANDARD 1 . . . . .01 STANDARD 2 . . . . .02 STANDARD 3 . . . . .03 STANDARD 4 . . . . .04 STANDARD 5 . . . . .05 STANDARD 6 . . . . .06 STANDARD 7 . . . . .07 STANDARD 8 . . . . .08 FORM 1 . . . . .09 FORM 2 . . . . .10 FORM 3 . . . . .11 FORM 4 . . . . .12 FORM 5 . . . . .13 FORM 6 . . . . .14 UNIVERSITY . . . . .15 OTHER_____16 (SPECIFY)	

Figure 9.3. Examples of unidimensional indicators taken from *Tanzania: Demographic and Health Survey, 1991/1992* (Macro International, Inc., Columbia, MD, 1993, p. 222).

Questions 103 and 106 (relating to how long one has lived in one's current place of residence and age at last birthday) appear as interval or ratio level variables. Question 107, which deals with literacy, is ordinal, although it could be treated as a nominal trichotomy. Questions 108 and 109 (concerning, respectively, newspaper readership and school attendance) are clearly nominal dichotomies, while question 110 (level of formal education) is most likely an ordinal level indicator, although some might argue it could be used as an interval level one. The education issue is very interesting, since it is not clear what completed years of schooling actually represent. Presumably, increased years involve incremental learning, so that a person with 3 or 4 years has more "learning" than someone with only 1 or 2 completed years. If we can assume that the curriculum is evenly spread over several years, then the indicator would clearly be an interval level one. On the other hand, one might argue that the more one learns, the more capacity one has to learn, so that the increase in knowledge forms some type of geometric progression (say, a log-linear or power function) over time. Some researchers, however, have argued that "years of education" refers not so much to amount of knowledge acquired but to credential acquisition. In this instance, it is probably better to look for significant "thresholds" such as completion of "standard" levels (primary education), forms (secondary), or university. If the thresholds are what is important, it would be worthwhile viewing level of education as a series of ordered categories instead of an incrementally continuous variable.

It is not possible to estimate the reliability of these items as single-item indicators. While it is likely the responses to these items are *probably* more reliable (and valid) than answers elicited by some of our more esoteric scales, they are not infallible. For example, demographers have long known that surveys such as this one often produce "age heaping" on questions relating to age. That is, people often round their age up or down to the nearest number finishing in a 0 or a 5. Some people simply do not know their age and guess. Furthermore, older people, especially in societies where advanced age confers increased status, often exaggerate their age and present highly inflated responses.

Similar problems relate to estimates of level of education. Responses to other questions, even nominal dichotomies, can be subject to memory effects such as telescoping (i.e., underestimation of how long ago an event took place). The fact is, even seemingly simple indicators such as questions relating to age can be problematic.

Sometimes validity and reliability checks can be built into the questionnaire. For example, in a different section in the Tanzanian survey, several questions are asked relating to childbearing. Separate questions relating to the ages of one's children and the years of their births (and deaths) are asked. These answers can be cross-checked for consistencies. Modern telephone survey techniques that use computer-based data entry programs allow these programs to "flag" inconsistent answers to such sets of questions. The telephone interviewer then has the option of pursuing the reason for the inconsistency with the respondent.

Ideally, for nominal level indicators, whether they are dichotomous or polytomous, the categories should exhaust the domain and should be mutually exclusive. The issue of response exclusivity, however, is a thorny one. Some instruments allow for only one response; others allow for multiple responses. Allowing respondents to choose only one category (usually "the best" or "most frequent") makes subsequent statistical analysis easier. On the other hand, multiple responses are sometimes more meaningful—usually when the scale is inherently multidimensional or a degree of "fuzziness" occurs in the category boundaries. With respondent complaints to responses restricted to nominal dichotomies, it is likely that the latent response into which the researcher is tapping is of an inherently higher level of measurement. That is, consideration should be given to revising the response categories either to increase the number or to rework the measurement to allow for a magnitude response.

It is also worthwhile pointing out that nominal level indicators can often be transformed into measures of magnitude. For example, by aggregating or counting categorical responses across respondents, it is possible to generate proportions, rates, and ratios—all of which are generally treated as quantitative measurements. Once converted into such higher order measurements, the data are amenable to any number of linear and nonlinear transformations, such as power and log functions, and nth-order roots.

It is also common practice in linear modeling to treat nominal level indicators as a special case of interval level scaling. The justification for "dummy" or "effect" coded design matrices is that the categorical indicators are special cases of interval level scaling. One way of conceiving this is to think of the typical binary indicators 0,1 as defining the end points of a single interval.

To more effectively deal with questions of reliability and validity, researchers often resort to the construction of multi-item indicators or scales. It is to these that we now turn our attention.

Multi-Item Indicators and Scales

Nominal Level Scales

A cursory review of the literature will make it evident that a variety of scales can be constructed, even based on nominal or ordinal response categories. Most often, categorical scales are coded on a yes/no, true/false basis and are subsequently recoded on a 0,1 or dummy coding scheme. Two examples of nominal level items designed to produce a scale are presented in Figure 9.4. The entire scales have not been reproduced, only representative items; readers interested in exploring these instruments in more detail are referred to the source references.

In Rotter's Internal–External Locus of Control Scale, the respondent is asked to select one of a pair of statements. Presumably, agreement with one statement reflects an internal locus of control while agreement with the other reflects an external locus of control. In the two sample questions provided, the italicized items are believed to show external control. The scale has many such dyads, and the respondent is asked to respond to all items. The overall score for the scale is the sum of the items selected. The higher the score, the more externally oriented one is; the lower the score, the more internally oriented one is assumed to be.

The Katz, Attitude Toward the Law Scale is typical of a binary outcome scale: that is, a respondent either agrees or disagrees with each item. As with Rotter's scale, the number of agreements or disagreements is summed to produce a final scale score.

Many scales are constructed in this manner, and the scale items are summed to form a count. Most students, of course, are familiar with traditional class exams where

---

Rotter's Internal-External Locus of Control

Each item consists of a pair of alternatives lettered a or b. Select one and only one that you consider to be the case as far as you're concerned.

2a. *Many of the unhappy things in peoples lives are partly due to bad luck.*
 b. People's misfortunes result from the mistakes they make.
3a. One of the major reasons we have wars is because people don't take enough interest in politics.
 b. *There will always be wars, no matter how hard people try to prevent them.*

Rotter, J.B. (1966) "Generalized expectations for internal-external control of reinforcement." *Psychological Monographs*, 80: 1–28.

Katz's Attitude Toward the Law Scale

Place a ✔ if agree with an item; an X if you disagree

---

1 We have too many laws.
2 Law is the greatest of our institutions.
3 The law is just another name for tyranny.

Figure 9.4. Examples of Nominal Scale Items. Reproduced in Thurstone, L.L. (1931) *Scales for the Measurement of Social Attitudes*. Chicago: University of Chicago Press.

questions are marked as "right" or "wrong" and one's score is simply the number (or percentage) of "right" answers. For attitude scales, where there are no necessarily correct answers, the final count is used as an indicator. For items designed to measure a "quantity" of knowledge (i.e., when there are right and wrong answers), the problem of guessing comes into play. With binary response items, an individual has a 50% chance of selecting the correct answer by chance alone. Thus, the expected base for such a scale is not 0, but half the number of items (50%). In these situations, where one wishes to estimate the respondent's actual quantity of correct information, it is commonplace to introduce a correction factor. With binary response items, the number of incorrect responses is often subtracted from the number of correct responses. Where the number of possible responses to an item increases, the correction formula changes to reflect the possibility of scoring a correct response by chance. Thus, where there are four alternatives, the probability of guessing the right answer is 25%. Thus, only one-quarter of the incorrect responses is subtracted from the correct ones.

By simply summing the items, however, the researcher is assuming that each item contributes equally to the final scale value. That is, each item is an equally good (or bad) measure of the underlying concept. With many scale items, this is probably not a bad assumption, since there would have to be a large discrepancy among the items to warrant the introduction of differential weights to the items. On the other hand, scales with only a few items might generate less reliable overall scores if the items were inherently unequal in their worth as indicators.

Traditional techniques for deciding the weights for multi-item scales have varied considerably, although two approaches predominate. The simpler approach has been to look at the distribution of overall scale scores. The items are then discriminated according to what proportion of respondents in the highest 50% or the highest quartile answer "yes" or "correctly" to the item. Those proportions are then used as weights in future applications of the scale. The second most commonly used approach is to generate a correlation matrix of all the items and conduct some type of factor analysis on them. The factor loadings are then used as item weights (see Kim and Rabjohn, 1979, for an application to binary data). While used extensively in the research literature, exploratory factor analytic techniques are not satisfactory. The primary problem is that since the estimated solutions are indeterminate, many different solutions may be generated from the same data matrix. Add to that the issue of the number of factors to be extracted and problems relating to rotation, and one could clearly spend most of one's career simply deciding the appropriate weights for a single scale. Also, the indeterminacy of factor solutions probably contributes to difficulties researchers face in reproducing scale results.

If weighting is needed, a far more useful approach is to employ some form of confirmatory factor analysis. This issue will be dealt in considerable detail in Chapter 11.

Ordinal Level Scales

Ordinal level scales have not been as popular as scales constructed from categorically or continuously scored items. The primary reason for this is the relative lack of progress in research on ordinal level statistics. Algorithms for estimating ordinal level scales are also quite complex. Often, researchers have found that the results obtained from ordinal level scales do not differ very much from results tallied from the scale items that were treated as categorical (nominal level) items, or as continuous (interval, ratio level) items.

A secondary reason for the scarcity of ordinal-type scales is the complexity of responding to the scale items. Consider, for example, the items reproduced in Figure 9.5. The respondent is asked to rank-order each of 15 food items about preference for a series of scenarios. While most people can complete this task with little difficulty, it is time-consuming. The question of how to deal with tied ranks (indifference among items) is also left open. Still, several gallant attempts have been made to deal effectively with preference and rank order scales (Coombs, 1964; Green and Rao, 1972). Ordinal scaling based on a sorting procedure seems to have made its greatest inroads in marketing research.

Interval Level Scales

Most multipoint scales have either 3, 5, 7, or 10 points. Other forms are possible and do appear in the literature, but are less evident. Multipoint scales associated with verbal descriptors are often called Likert-type scales—particularly when multiple items are summed. If practice counts for anything, seven point items may be the optimum that can be used with verbal descriptors since these predominate in the literature. Typical of seven-point items is the following list of responses.

1 - Extremely dissatisfied
2 - Very satisfied

3 - Satisfied

4 - Neither satisfied nor dissatisfied

5 - Dissatisfied

6 - Very dissatisfied

7 - Extremely dissatisfied

Breakfast Food Preference Scale

Breakfast items:
1. Toast pop-up
2. Buttered toast
3. English muffin and margarine
4. Jelly donut
5. Cinnamon toast
6. Blueberry muffin and margarine
7. Hard rolls and butter
8. Toast and marmalade
9. Buttered toast and jelly
10. Toast and margarine
11. Cinnamon bun
12. Danish pastry
13. Glazed donut
14. Coffee cake
15. Corn muffin and Butter

.. [W]e would like to get some idea of your personal preferences for each of the food items under various types of eating occasions or menus. In each case merely place the stimulus number of the item you most prefer, next most prefer, and so on, in each of the rank positions under each eating occasion/menu description.

a. Overall preferences

(Highest)	Rank		
		1 ( )	9 ( )
		2 ( )	10 ( )
		3 ( )	11 ( )
		4 ( )	12 ( )
		5 ( )	13 ( )
		6 ( )	14 ( )
		7 ( )	15 ( ) (Lowest)
		8 ( )	

b. When I'm having a breakfast consisting of juice, bacon and eggs, and beverage

(Highest)	Rank		
		1 ( )	9 ( )
		2 ( )	10 ( )
		3 ( )	11 ( )
		4 ( )	12 ( )
		5 ( )	13 ( )
		6 ( )	14 ( )
		7 ( )	15 ( ) (Lowest)
		8 ( )	

Figure 9.5. Examples of Ordinal Level Scales. Green, P.E. and V.R. Rao (1972) *Applied Multidimensional Scaling*, New York: Holt, Rinehart and Winston.

Examples of some typical interval level scales are presented in Figure 9.6. In the first example (perception of significant others) the respondent is asked to show where these "others" lie along several bipolar dimensions. Each item allows for one of five possible responses. Traditionally, a scale such as this is scored on a 1–5 basis, or, if the valences of the items have some a priori significance, the scoring might be −2, −1, 0, 1, 2. The very presentation of this scale implies that the middle category represents something akin to "neutral," "typical," or "average." One difficulty with these items, however, is that one's self-rating (e.g., where "I" falls on the careless–careful scale) may change according to circumstances. Clearly situations may arise in which I, or someone important in my life, am careful, as well as other situations in which one or both of us are careless.

The second example presented in Figure 9.6, Weston's Attitudes Toward Government Workers Scale, is a similar type, but in this instance, the respondent has a clear verbal indication of the meaning of the responses, and the number of options is increased. Scale items of the second type might be more useful from a statistical point of view in that they *may* be more likely to produce greater item variances and thus allow for greater degrees of discrimination in the final scale.

Of course, all the issues relating to item weights discussed previously also apply to scales of these types. Several other issues, however, are also open for consideration. One difficulty arises when one attempts to attach verbal descriptors to the

---

Perception of Significant Others Scale

"I am"

Complicated	____:____:____:____:____	Simple
Insane	____:____:____:____:____	Sane
Tense	____:____:____:____:____	Relaxed
Careless	____:____:____:____:____	Careful

Chang, D.H., Zastro, C.H. and Blazicek, D.L. (1975) 'Inmates' perception of significant others and the implications for the rehabilitation process." *International Journal of Criminology and Penology*, 3: 85–96.

Attitudes Toward Government Workers

1. Do you think firemen do a good job?

Strong yes				Neutral				Strong No	
100	90	80	70	60	50	40	30	20	10

2. Do you think game wardens do a good job?

Strong yes				Neutral				Strong No	
100	90	80	70	60	50	40	30	20	10

3. Do you think teachers do a good job?

Strong yes				Neutral				Strong No	
100	90	80	70	60	50	40	30	20	10

Weston, P.B. (1965) "The attitudes of offenders toward occupation in the administration of justice." *Criminology*, 6: 83–96.

Figure 9.6. Examples of Interval Level Scale Items.

numerical values. Many researchers who typically use these types of scales find that beyond seven points, the descriptors start to lose sense, although the increased numerical range might be useful. As suggested previously, one very useful step is to recode these types of scales on a −3 to +3 scale with 0 representing neutral. This helps to relate the positive or negative substantive valence of the scale to a more intuitive numerical scale. There is also the issue of assuming equal distances between the points—one of the theoretical assumptions underlying interval level measurement. For example, if the elements in the domain are truly interval and are correctly mapped on an interval domain, we would expect the functional form of the mapping to be linear. This is illustrated by the dashed line in Figure 9.7, where the scale item X is depicted as a seven-point, symmetrical scale with the range −3 to +3. For illustrative purposes, the specific numbers assigned to X are irrelevant and could just as easily be 1 to 7; what is important here is the shape of the relationship between the latent and manifest responses. On the other hand, it is conceivable that the functional form of the mapping exercise is misjudged. That is, the latent response may actually be curvilinear as opposed to linear. Such an example is represented by a solid line in Figure 9.7. Here, we have drawn the arbitrary function $Y = X^2$ although any number of interesting relationships can be imagined.

The issue, of course, is: What does this misjudgment imply for our analysis? Besides the obvious fact that we will misunderstand the true functional intensity of the latent response, we are also left with the possibility that statistical power will be lost when we attempt to test any hypothesis in which the observed outcome, X, is included. Specifically, unless some functional form that comes close to including an X^2 transformation is identified, the likelihood of rejecting the null hypothesis is less than it ought to be.

Figure 9.7. Mapping of linear and nonlinear latent response on a seven-point scale.

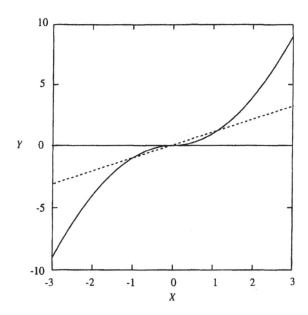

How significant a problem is this? The answer is unknown. Likely, the problem differs by discipline. Some fields, such as psychophysics, make this issue a central element of the discipline; fields that focus on attitude research seem to emphasize it less.

There are at least two good ways to decide whether a transformation is warranted: (a) plot the response function (although this may only show the distribution of responses and not the perception of the meaning of the scale) and (b) conduct a cross-modal verification (as is done in psychophysics). One must also be careful not to make the assumption that all respondents understand and interpret the underlying metric of the number or scoring system the same way. Experience shows, for example, that even many college students do not understand the basic assumptions underlying the use of ratios. Also, illiteracy (verbal and numerical) is not an uncommon phenomenon.

Ratio and Magnitude Scales

Some attempts have been made to construct ratio or magnitude scales that allow the estimation of true ratios across the scale items. Two examples are presented in Figure 9.8.

The first example asks the respondents to estimate how old they will be when certain events will likely take place. Clearly, someone who visits a foreign country at

	Future Events Test	
	If you think it will not happen Circle "Never"	If you think it will happen Guess Age
1. Finish college	Never	_____
2. Visit a foreign country	Never	_____
3. Have a new car	Never	_____
4. Get a job you really want	Never	_____

Stein, K.B., Sarbin, T.R. and Kulik, J.A. (1968) "Future time perspective: Its relation to the socialization process and the delinquent role." *Journal of Consulting and Clinical Psychology*, 32: 257–64.

Sellin-Wolfgang Seriousness Index
The offender steals a bicycle which is parked on the street = 10.
1. The offender stabs a person to death
8. The offender robs a person of $1000 at gunpoint. The victim is shot and requires hospitalization.
19. The offender robs a person of $5 at gunpoint. No physical harm occurs.
53. The offender enters an unlocked car, forces open the glove compartment, and steals personal belongings worth $5.

Sellin, T. and M.E. Wolfgang (1964) *The Measurement of Delinquency*. New York: Wiley.

Figure 9.8. Examples of Ratio Scale Items.

age 40 is twice as old as someone who does so at age 20. Thus, it would appear that the items are scored on a true ratio basis.

The second scale, the Sellin–Wolfgang Crime Seriousness Scale, is also an attempt to construct a ratio level scale. In the original version of the scale, respondents were presented with a series of items like those presented in Figure 9.8 and then asked in an open-ended fashion to provide a numerical value about how serious they perceived the item to be. Later versions gave respondents an "anchor" against which to compare how seriously they perceived subsequent items. Commonly, respondents were told to assume that a simple bicycle theft is worth 10 points and to score the other scenarios accordingly. Beyond that, however, the allowable scores are open-ended.

The Sellin–Wolfgang scale has been explored extensively, and the consensus is that perceptions of crime seriousness follow a power function of the form X^p. Consequently, researchers commonly calculate the geometric mean of the item responses to create the final scale magnitudes.

Some interesting measurement issues are raised by the *Risk Perception Scale* reproduced in Figure 9.9. At first glance, the items might be scaled as ratio level items, since the respondent is presented with several equally spaced percentages. The full range from 0% to 100% is not provided for each item, only the four limited categories. Here, the scale is more closely related to the interval level scaled items

---

1. *Murder*—killing a person on purpose. For instance: A man plans to kill his wife. He buys a gun, takes it home, and shoots her. What percent of murders end up with someone being arrested for the crime?
   - ☐ 62%
   - ☐ 72%
   - ☐ 82%
   - ☐ 92%

2. *Negligent manslaughter*—killing a person without wanting to, but because of some carelessness. For instance: A man throws a can out the window without looking. Someone is passing on the street. The can hits him on the head and kills him. What percentage of negligent manslaughters end up with someone being arrested for the crime
   - ☐ 63%
   - ☐ 73%
   - ☐ 83%
   - ☐ 93%

4. *Robbery*—taking something from another person by means of force. For instance: A man stops another man in an alley. He makes him hand over his wallet by telling him he'll get hurt if he doesn't hand it over. What percent of robberies end up with someone being arrested for the crime?
   - ☐ 8%
   - ☐ 18%
   - ☐ 28%
   - ☐ 38%

Figure 9.9. Risk Perception. Claster, D.S. (1967) "Comparison of risk perception between delinquents and nondelinquents." *Journal of Criminal Law, Criminology and Police Science*, 58: 80–6.

presented in Figure 9.6. The other interesting characteristic of this scale is that the range of responses obviously seeks to assess the respondent's knowledge about the magnitude of a series of events, yet the range of responses in limited. While the ranges (i.e., 62–92%, 63–93%, and 8–38%) likely incorporate the "true" percentage of events in the population, they do restrict how much error that could appear in a respondent's answer.

Other Issues

Labeled Response Categories

To anchor response categories, numerical scales are often linked to lexical response categories. These have the advantage of adding a "quality" to the numerals that may be missing if they are presented only as elements of a number system. Although many variations on this theme exist, Sheatsley (1983) itemizes some of the more popular. Among these are:

- excellent—good—fair—poor
- approve—disapprove; favor—oppose; good idea—bad idea
- agree—disagree
- too many—not enough—about right; too much—too little—about right amount
- better—worse—about the same
- very—fairly—not at all
- regularly—often—seldom—never
- always—most of the time—some of the time—rarely or never
- more likely—less likely—no difference

As Sheatsley points out, the primary advantage of these descriptors is that they are reasonably standard as formulations, widely applicable, and easily understandable. The fact that they are used so often allows one to assume a certain level of cultural acceptance and understanding. Furthermore, by combining lexical descriptors with numerical assignments, the researcher probably elicits the best aspects of both dimensions. Still, one should not overestimate the value of lexical descriptors, no matter how wide their applicability. Unlike numbers alone, lexical descriptors carry varying degrees of connotative meanings and also denotative meanings. As such, there is a greater likelihood that there will be systematic individual and subcultural differences over the meanings of the terms—in terms of valence, ordinality, and interval spacing. The attachment of lexical intermediate indicators (i.e., indicators for values other than the end points) may also result in an interval level scale item reverting to simple ordinality. Also, attempts to extend lexical descriptors to more than four or five categories are often difficult because of the inherent limitations of the English language (or any other for that matter).

Vague Quantifiers

An ongoing debate in item construction is whether one ought to use vague quantifiers (e.g., "sometimes," "often," "frequent") or request an estimate of an exact frequency. For reasons discussed earlier regarding the problem of "scaling down," the ideal from the perspective of measurement theory is to use an estimate of an exact frequency. Researchers continue to use vague quantifiers, however, for many reasons. First, it is assumed that the exercise is difficult for most people, and many respondents, when confronted with the need to recall an exact number, simply refuse to answer. Second, it is often argued that recall errors are so great that asking for an exact estimate is simply an exercise in false precision—the actual response is only roughly interval and more likely ordinal in nature. Third, the use of vague quantifiers has simply become common practice in some areas, and breaking with convention carries perceived risks of professional derision and rejection.

The crucial question here involves the degree to which vague quantifiers correspond to respondents' frequency estimates and to actual frequencies of occurrence. Of lesser, although significant importance is the question of whether other elements of response error are introduced by using vague quantifiers. Some insight into the latter issue is obtained though an example. Nora Schaeffer (1991) opens an article entitled "Hardly Ever or Constantly?" with a recitation of a sequence from the movie *Annie Hall*. The example is a classical one and bears retelling:

> In the movie Annie Hall there is a scene with a split screen. On one side Alvie Singer talks to his psychiatrist; on the other side Annie Hall talks to hers. Alvie's therapist asks him, "How often do you sleep together?" and Alvie replies, "Hardly ever, maybe three times a week." Annie's therapist asks her, "Do you have sex often?" Annie replies, "Constantly. I'd say three times a week."

Clearly, the use of vague quantifiers introduces a set of modifiers beyond the issues of recall and scaling down.

Unfortunately, little systematic research on the relative merit of vague quantifiers over direct frequency estimates exists. The best review to date is a paper by Schwartz (1990). Overall, however, the results seem to show that absolute frequencies are more difficult to generate than relative frequencies; that bias in the use of relative frequencies varies by characteristics of the respondent (such as age, education, and race); and that context is an important consideration. Furthermore, if absolute frequency estimates are cross-validated, considerable regression to the mean appears, with rare events being overestimated and frequent events being underestimated. Social desirability also seems to play a considerable role, with desirable behaviors (such as voting) more likely to be overreported and socially undesirable behavior more likely to be underreported (P. V. Miller and Groves, 1985).

Likert Scales

The origins of attitude scaling can be identified with the work of Thurstone and Likert that appeared in the late 1920s and early 1930s (Thurstone, 1928; Likert, 1932).

While achieving early popularity, Thurstone's binary (generally yes/no) procedure was crude and cumbersome and these primitive traits had a dampening effect on its acceptance. The summated ratings scale of Rensis Likert, however, continues to be one of the most commonly used scale applications. This procedure has attracted the imagination of researchers over the last seven decades for many reasons. The combining of many individual items to generate an aggregate score has substantial intuitive appeal; the scale is simple to use; it seems to work well in a wide range of circumstances; and it appears to be fairly robust. Although originally considered an interval level scale, the procedure can be justified under conditions of unidimensional ordinality (Andrich, 1985; Masters, 1985). In fact, Likert scales can be considered a subset of the more general Rasch Rating-Scale model (Rasch, 1966). Because of their popularity, the Likert-type scales have generated considerable attention in the methodological literature. Several more important issues deserve further consideration.

Optimal Number of Categories in Likert Scale Items

Soon after Likert's article on scaling appeared, researchers began to want to know the optimal number of categories for scaling the individual items. Historically, the research literature can be divided into two periods: before the mid-1950s and afterward. The early literature focused primarily on the ability and willingness of respondents to make discriminations and to use the full range of categories. Although many researchers concluded that the optimal number was really an empirical issue, related to the content of the scale and the context of the application, some investigators identified specific point levels (Ghiselli and Brown, 1948; Guilford, 1954). For example, Symonds (1924) suggested that seven-point items were optimal for subjects versed in the procedure but fewer items probably were optimal for "untrained" or "uninterested" respondents. Champney and Marshall (1939), on the other hand suggested that for "trained" raters, nine-point scales would be optimal, with few points being reserved for untrained raters.

From the mid-1950s onward, the issue of the optimal number of scale items was placed in the context of overall scale reliability and validity. Matell and Jacoby (1971) examined items scaled with as many as 18 points and concluded that the number of categories was independent of overall reliability. This view that the number of item categories is independent of overall scale reliability and validity has been echoed in subsequent studies (Boote, 1981; Brown, Widing, and Coulter, 1991). On the other hand, literature can be found to support the achievement of optimal reliabilities from three- or four-point scales (Bendig, 1954a, 1954b), five-point scales (Lissitz and Green, 1975; Jenkins and Taber, 1977) and seven-point scales (Finn, 1972; Ramsay, 1973; Cicchetti, Showalter, and Tyrer, 1985). It is perhaps because of this confusion and because the results seem to "work" empirically that most researchers stick to items with five or seven points.

While identifying an optimal number of item points may be impossible, some literature suggests that there is a limited, empirically workable range. Research by Alliger and Williams (1992) notes that as the number of scale points increases, the likelihood of obtaining response sets increases. This outcome often increases the homogeneity in the results and has the side effect of increasing most measures of reliability. The issue has been explored further by Chang (1994), who notes that while the problem of response sets increases as the number of items increases, the problem of artifactual increases in reliability is solvable. According to Chang's work, scale reliabilities are inflated only when reliability estimates are based on similar methods. The problem does not arise, however, when reliabilities are estimated using different methods. Thus, Chang's solution is to use a multitrait, multimethod approach to address the issue. Akin to the problem of response sets is the tendency of some respondents to skip the more extreme categories, such that they end up collapsing categories (e.g., "strongly disagree" and "disagree").

On the other hand, care must be taken not to reduce the number of response options too much. Matell and Jacoby (1971) have reported that as the number of item categories increases, the proportion of "uncertains" decreases, thus improving overall item variances.

An interesting issue that has recently arisen in the literature involves the question of whether one ought to use an even or odd number of categories. The problem arises because odd-numbered scales (e.g., five-point or seven-point) often have a natural "neutral" value at the mid- or central point of the scale. Even-categorized scales (e.g., four-point or six-point scales) have no such "neutral" point, however, and often force a response of a definite positive or negative valence. The inclusion of the midpoint as a "neutral" value has been shown to result in multidimensionality occasionally (Nunnally, 1970; Goldberg, 1981; Chang, 1994).

The issue of dimensionality is an important one for traditional Likert-type scales. Each item in a scale is assumed to identify a respondent's position on some underlying or latent continuum. Summated ratings scales are perceived to be an advancement over single-item indicators because they provide for a greater sampling within the domain of the latent continuum. In other words, aggregating over many similar items produces a final score that is assumed to result in a better estimate of where an individual is located. If the scale items are not all measuring the same underlying phenomenon, (i.e., if the scale is multidimensional), then the scale gives at best, a biased estimate of a person's location on that continuum and, at worst, a meaningless result.

It is easy to understand why dimensionality may have been perceived as a problem in the past, when the statistical analysis of multidimensional scales was a daunting task. As we suggested, the great appeal of summated ratings scales is their inherent simplicity. Given recent advances in confirmatory factor modeling (see Chapter 11) and the near ubiquity of personal computers, however, it is difficult to understand why the use of multidimensional scales should be considered objectionable. If a series of items of empirical or theoretical merit turns out to be multidimensional, then procedures for dealing with that condition can be employed. Indeed, artificially forcing a multidimensional scale into unidimensionality does a major disservice to our understanding of the phenomenon under study. Not only do we lose an opportunity to understand the richness of the issue, but we likely contribute to substantial measurement error by forcing respondents to make an "unnatural" choice. In today's research environment, the costs associated with constructing, validating, and applying complex scales are probably minor compared with the benefits to be accrued from having sensitive, reliable instruments.

Valence—The Problem of Directional Wording

Traditionally, commentaries on Likert-type scale construction have suggested that the valence of the questions be alternated to produce a "balanced scale." Typically, the researcher is told to word half the items positively ("Carrots are good for you.") and half the items negatively ("Rutabagas are not good for you."). Recently, some authors have suggested that achieving the desired balance is not as easy as it seems.

Factor analysis of several scales with items of positive and negative valence revealed that negative valence items often cluster together (load on one factor), while the positive valence items form a separate cluster (load on a second factor) (Nunnally, 1970; Goldberg, 1981; Chang, 1994). Whether this finding turns out to be real or artifactual remains to be seen. Most of the research purporting to show this outcome uses exploratory rather than confirmatory factor analysis; hence, the results may turn out to be a methodological artifact. Still, as Trott and Jackson (1967) point out, some items are far more amenable to reversal than others. The idiosyncrasies of discursive language make successful reversal highly dependent upon grammar and context.

INDICES

It is the practice in many disciplines to construct an index to summarize a multidimensional concept. Most of these indices are assumed to be interval or ratio level scales.

An index with which most people are familiar is the Consumer Price Index. Essentially, the Consumer Price Index presents the percentage change in the estimated cost of a basket of goods over two or more points in time. Substantively, the key issues are determining which items ought to be included in the basket and in what quantities. Statistically, the primary issue is one of determining the actual costs of those items.

Formally, a price index (PI) can be defined as follows:

$$PI = \frac{\sum \left(Q_{i,t_0} \times P_{i,t_1} \right)}{\sum \left(Q_{i,t_0} \times P_{i,t_0} \right)}$$

where t_0 is the base year[1]
    t_1 is the reference year
    Q_{i,t_0} is the quantity consumed in the base year, t_0
    P_{i,t_0} is the price per unit in the base year, t_0

Consider the following table. The basket consists of three commodities: potatoes, chicken, and broccoli. Each ith product is consumed in some quantity, Q_i, and each has a specified price, P_i, associated with it at some time, t.

---

1. Price indices that use consumption quantities from the base year are known as Laspeyres indices; those that use consumption quantities based on the reference year are known as Paasche indices. Whether base year or reference year consumption profiles are theoretically advantageous is debatable and is a question of substantive rather than statistical or methodological importance.

COMMODITIES IN BASKET	PRICE PER UNIT AT t_0 (P_{i,t_0})	PRICE PER UNIT AT t_1 (P_{i,t_1})	QUANTITY CONSUMED AT t_0 (Q_{i,t_0})	COST AT t_0 ($Q_{i,t_0} \times P_{i,t_0}$)	COST AT t_1 ($Q_{i,t_0} \times P_{i,t_1}$)
Potatoes	2.00	2.50	20	40.00	50.00
Chicken	5.00	6.00	10	50.00	60.00
Broccoli	10.00	11.00	15	150.00	165.00
Total				240.00	275.00

Based on the information provided in this table, the price index for year t_1 may be determined as follows:

$$
\begin{aligned}
PI_{t_1} &= \frac{\sum \left(Q_{i,t_0} \times P_{i,t_1} \right)}{\sum \left(Q_{i,t_0} \times P_{i,t_0} \right)} \\
&= \frac{275}{240} \times 100 \\
&= 115
\end{aligned}
$$

For year t_0, the numerator would be the same as the denominator; thus, the price index for the base year is 100. Therefore, the percentage increase from the base to the reference year is recognized to be 15%.

Price indices are intuitively appealing to the public: they combine several items (a "grocery basket") into a single index that is weighted in proportion to people's actual consumption patterns.

Problems

A primary difficulty with price indices is that they are deterministic and do not consider measurement error. Empirically, there is substantial variability in the quantities of items actually consumed in a community as well as in the prices consumers pay for the items. Consumers are not homogeneous. Consequently, while many may see the index as market relevant, it is not always consumer relevant. For example, market prices for new rents, or new homes, may increase substantially, but perhaps only a small proportion of the population is in the housing market at any given time. The overwhelming proportion are likely to be on longer term leases or property owners who are locked into longer term mortgages. Thus, the CPI is not relevant to all consumers in the market.

It should also be noted that items are not constant over time. Personal computers, for example, are standard consumer durables in the 1990s but did not exist in the 1960s as consumer items. Television existed in the 1950s but the receivers sold then are not at all technologically comparable to the sets currently available. Furthermore, consumers often substitute items with lower prices that serve the same function. This substitution takes place over time and across cultures. For example, the price of wheat, which has been so important as an indicator of the cost of living in Europe and North America, is largely irrelevant in Asian societies, where rice serves as the staple carbohydrate.

CPIs also can be poor indicators where there is a substantial underground economy. Several studies have estimated the size of the underground economy in various countries. Dallago (1990: 21–23) summarizes a few key studies, focusing primarily on the late 1970s and early 1980s. For the United States, estimates of the size of the underground economy range from a low of about 2% of GNP to a high of 27% of GNP, with a median close to 15%. Estimates for Italy range from a low of approximately 10% to a high of about 30%, with most estimates in the mid-20% range. Estimates in the mid-teens and low twenties are also provided for Hungary, Poland, and the former Soviet Union while they retained Soviet-type economies. Black markets in goods and services can contribute substantial bias to official estimates of consumer prices.

Complex Indices: The Human Development Index

The consumer price index is a relatively simple index to construct and interpret. The Human Development Index (HDI), on the other hand, both is more complex to construct and has less intuitive appeal. While including few variables (certainly many fewer than most CP indices), the HDI includes a "utility-corrected" item and then combines all through differential weighting. The HDI is worth examining in detail because it illustrates how a number of theoretically relevant factors can be incorporated into a single measure. Despite the advantages of the HDI's theoretical richness, however, it retains most of the limitations of other deterministic indices.

The HDI incorporates three dimensions of "human development": life expectancy, educational attainment, and income. Life expectancy is the number of years a person can be expected to live at birth. The range of this variable is truncated to 25 years at the low end and 85 years at the upper end. Education consists of two indicators, the proportion of adults in a nation who are literate, and the combined enrollment ratios of students who are in primary, secondary, or tertiary education. Both subindicators have a range of 0 to 100%. The educational attainment factor is constructed by weighting the literacy indicator by two-thirds and the enrollment indicator by one-third. The income indicator consists of a nation's gross domestic product (GDP) per capita in U.S. dollars and discounts it using Atkinson's formula for the relative utility of income.

As an example, consider the following data for the United Kingdom and Uganda. These countries currently represent the extremes of development, with the United Kingdom near the top of the distribution and Uganda near the bottom.

COUNTRY	LIFE EXPECTANCY AT BIRTH	ADULT LITERACY	COMBINED ENROLLMENT RATIO	GDP PER CAPITA (U.S., $)
United Kingdom	76.7	99	86	18,620
Uganda	40.2	61.1	34	1,370

In creating the overall HDI, three subindices are created. Each index is defined by the formula

$$\text{index} = \frac{\text{actual } x_i \text{ value} - \text{minimum } x_i \text{ value}}{\text{maximum } x_i \text{ value} - \text{minimum } x_i \text{ value}}$$

The HDI Subindices

Life Expectancy Index For each country, the life expectancy index can be determined as

$$\text{U.K.} = \frac{76.7 - 25}{85 - 25} \qquad\qquad \text{Uganda} = \frac{40.27 - 25}{85 - 25}$$

$$= .86 \qquad\qquad\qquad = .25$$

Educational Attainment Index The educational attainment index is the weighted average of two components. The first measures adult literacy; the second measures school enrollment.

Adult Literacy

$$\text{U.K.} = \frac{99 - 0}{100 - 0} \qquad\qquad \text{Uganda} = \frac{61.1 - 0}{100 - 0}$$

$$= .99 \qquad\qquad\qquad = .61$$

Combined Enrollment Index

$$\text{U.K.} = \frac{86 - 0}{100 - 0} \qquad\qquad \text{Uganda} = \frac{34 - 0}{100 - 0}$$

$$= .86 \qquad\qquad\qquad = .34$$

Education Attainment

$$\text{U.K.} = .99 \times \tfrac{2}{3} + .86 \times \tfrac{1}{3} \qquad\qquad \text{Uganda} = .61 \times \tfrac{2}{3} + .34 \times \tfrac{1}{3}$$

$$= .95 \qquad\qquad\qquad\qquad = .52$$

Income The income component of the HDI is much more complex than the other two. Initially, the income index corrects for the notion that the utility of income is not linear but declines incrementally. In other words, a fixed increase (say $1000 U.S. per year) has a much greater impact on one's quality of life if the base income is $3000 per year instead of $15,000 per year. There are several ways to correct for the marginal utility of income, the easiest and most common being a logarithmic transformation of the amount considered. The authors of the Human Development Report, however, use a more complicated transformation that corrects for income based on multiples of the world average.

In 1994 the world average income was $5835 U.S. This is defined as a threshold value, Y^*. According to the HDI's authors, utility adjusted per capita income thus becomes

$$Y_{adj} = Y^* \text{ for } 0 \leq Y \leq Y^*$$

$$= Y^* + 2\left[(Y - Y^*)^{1/2}\right] \text{ for } Y^* \leq Y \leq 2Y^*$$

$$= Y^* + 2\left(Y^{*1/2}\right) + 3\left[(Y - Y^*)^{1/3}\right] \text{ for } 2Y^* \leq Y \leq 3Y^*$$

$$= Y^* + 2\left(Y^{*1/2}\right) + 3\left[(Y - Y^*)^{1/3}\right] + n\left\{\left[Y - (n-1)Y^*\right]^{1/n}\right\}$$

$$\text{for } (n-1)Y^* \leq Y \leq nY^*$$

The average GDP per capita for the United Kingdom is the equivalent of $18,620 U.S., or between three and four times the world average. Thus, the U.K. adjusted income may be calculated as follows:

$$Y_{adj} = Y^* + 2\left(Y^{*1/2}\right) + 3\left[(Y - Y^*)^{1/3}\right] + n\left\{\left[Y - (n-1)Y^*\right]^{1/n}\right\}$$

$$= 5835 + 2(5835)^{1/2} + 3(18,620 - 11,670)^{1/3} + 4(18,620 - 17,508)^{1/4}$$

$$= 6068$$

Recall that the minimum and maximum accepted values for GDP per capita were $100 and $40,000 respectively. Using the transformation on the maximum value, the corresponding adjusted per capita income is calculated to be $6154. The income index for the United Kingdom therefore becomes

$$\text{U.K.} = \frac{6068 - 100}{6154 - 100}$$

$$= .99$$

For Uganda, on the other hand, the average GDP per capita is below the world average of $5835. Since this amount does not require deflating for marginal utility, it is possible to calculate the income index directly as

$$\text{Uganda} = \frac{1370 - 100}{6154 - 100}$$

$$= .21$$

The HDI is now obtained by averaging the life expectancy index, the education index, and the adjusted GDP index for each country. Thus, for the United Kingdom, HDI $= (.86 + .95 + .99)/3 = .93$, and for Uganda, HDI $= (.25 + .52 + .21)/3 = .33$.

Evaluating the HDI

As with the price index, the HDI rests on several crucial assumptions. First, it is assumed that the individual component indices are additive. This assumption may be valid. It can be argued, however, that the three subindices are not independent (i.e., income affects life expectancy and education; education affects life expectancy and income), and thus a multiplicative function might be more appropriate.

Second, the three subindices are granted equal weighting, while the education subindex components are weighted differentially (literacy being weighted twice combined school enrollment). Whether this is the appropriate weighting schema is again an issue that could be the subject of empirical and theoretical debate.

Third, the HDI is a deterministic index. Therefore, it is assumed that no measurement error is involved in the individual components. In fact, the data underlying all three subindices are estimates that are subject to substantial correction. The problems posed by underground economies for validly assessing price indices are an even thornier problem for determining GDP.

CONCLUSIONS

Overall, good scale construction is no easy matter, and at times, it is more art than science. Experience and familiarity with one's substantive area are very important in the construction of good scale items. Also, we can state unequivocally that one can never have too much pretesting. Even the best crafted instrument by the most experienced researchers will contain unforeseen "bugs." Each instrument has an element of uniqueness, and any attempt to produce an exhaustive checklist would likely go on for too many pages; however, a few practical pointers should be keep in mind when putting together an instrument:

1. Allow enough choice in the responses to tap subtleties but not so much that the distribution becomes meaningless or difficult to use.

2. Consider the general level of intelligence and literacy of the prospective interviewees. Decide whether the target population is to consist of children, native speakers, college-educated individuals, or people familiar with the substance of the scale (e.g., professional groups knowledgeable about the issues), and structure the language accordingly. Avoid jargon for general audiences; however, the use of jargon may be required to attain a certain level of "professional credibility" with some groups.

3. Consider the meanings of the numbers attached to the scale (intensity) and consider whether they make sense. Consider the use of verbal descriptors instead of numbers and vice versa. Numbers, for example, may suggest symmetry that cannot be expressed in words.

4. Check for response patterns. Change the valence of questions fairly frequently to avoid response patterns and to make interviewees think about the questions before answering. Make sure, however, that the respondents indeed respond to the changes in valence and do not simply assume a constant valence across all questions. Make sure that changing the valence does not change the meaning of any items.

5. Be aware that interaction effects may occur between the target population and commitment to respond. Some scales may be boring (resulting in inattention) to some populations but very salient to others. For example, issues relating to gun control may have more meaning to victims of robberies than nonvictims.

6. Even experienced researchers rarely start from scratch. For best results review the literature for existing instruments that can be used in toto or can be easily modified. There are many compendia of scales and measurement instruments that can serve as convenient sources.

7. Pretest.

8. Pretest again.

Further Reading

DeVellis, R.F. *Scale Development: Theory and Applications*. Newbury Park, CA: Sage, 1991. An elementary discussion on item and scale construction. Contains some good suggestions for improved item development.

van der Ven, A.H.G.S. *Introduction to Scaling*. New York: Wiley, 1980. Aimed at the intermediate audience, this book has a discussion of scaling that is far broader and in greater depth than the DeVellis book. Several aspects of scaling not covered in the present text (e.g., Guttman scaling and Coombs general theory of scaling) are addressed, along with probabilistic and deterministic scaling models.

10

Classical Test Theory

Yet what are all such gaities to me
Whose thoughts are full of indices and surds?

$$x + 7x + 53 =$$

$$\frac{11}{3}$$

—Lewis Carroll

RELIABILITY

The earliest approach used to investigate reliability and validity in the social sciences is generally known as classical test theory (Torgerson, 1958; Magnusson, 1966; Zeller and Carmines, 1980; Ghiselli, Campbell, and Zedeck, 1981). This model was first discussed by Spearman (1910) and achieved reasonably full development with the publication of Gulliksen's text 40 years later (Gulliksen, 1950). The basic elements of this model are few. We start with some observation, Y, a hypothesized true score, T, and an error component, e. With these components, the underlying model is defined as follows:

$$Y = T + e$$

It is from this simple model—that all observations are composed of a true score and an error component—that classical test theory derives both nominal and operational definitions of reliability and validity. To obtain a tractable solution to the estimation of the reliability and validity of a measurement instrument, classical test theory makes several assumptions about the error component. These include:

Assumption 1. $E(e) = 0$.
Assumption 2. $r_{(T,e)} = 0$.
Assumption 3. $r_{(e_i, T_j)} = 0$.
Assumption 4. $r_{(e_i, e_j)} = 0$.

That is, the expected value of the error terms across a series of observations is zero; the true score is uncorrelated with the error component either within a given observation or across observations; and over a series of observations, the errors are uncorrelated with one another.

Combined, these assumptions will result in error terms that are normally and independently distributed with a mean of zero and a constant variance, σ^2 [i.e.,

$e \approx \text{NID}(0, \sigma^2)$], thus allowing for the conclusion that the expected observed score will be equal to the true score, or,

$$E(Y) = E(T)$$

Practically, this implies that the mean of a series of observations approaches the true score as the size of the sample increases. It is important to recognize that at this point we make the assumption that the error components, e, are *random errors*; thus, situations that include systematic bias (e.g., the tendency for certain groups to understate their age) are not considered within this framework. And it is this assumption that poses a great limitation for the classical test theory model, but more on that later.

To derive a formal definition of reliability, it is necessary to consider the implications of assumptions 1 to 4 on the respective variances of the component terms in our measurement model. Following Zeller and Carmines (1980: 8), we may note that since

$$Y = T + e$$

it follows that

$$\sigma_Y^2 = \sigma_{T+e}^2$$

By expansion, we can write

$$(T + e)^2 = T^2 + 2Te + e^2$$

and therefore,

$$\sigma_Y^2 = \sigma_T^2 + 2\sigma_{Te} + \sigma_e^2$$

But, according to assumption 2, $\sigma_{Te} = 0$, thus the component $2\sigma_{Te}$ drops out and we are left with

$$\sigma_Y^2 = \sigma_T^2 + \sigma_e^2$$

That is, the variance of the observed score is equal to the sum of the variances of the true score plus the error score. Within this framework, *reliability* is the proportion of the observed score accounted for by the true score. Or,

$$\text{reliability} = \rho = \frac{\sigma_T^2}{\sigma_Y^2} = 1 - \frac{\sigma_e^2}{\sigma_Y^2}$$

The reliability coefficient, ρ, can range from 0 to 1, with 0 being achieved when all the observed variance is accounted for by error ($\sigma_T^2 = 0$; hence, no reliability at all), and 1 being achieved when the entire variance in Y is attributable to T ($\sigma_e^2 = 0$, or perfect reliability).

To estimate the reliability coefficient (hence, variance), it is necessary to have at least two measures of the same phenomenon. This is usually achieved by giving what are known as parallel tests. Parallel tests are tests having identical true scores and equal error variances.[1] By considering Y to be the original score and Y' to be its parallel, this situation may be represented as follows:

$$Y = T + e \qquad \text{and} \qquad Y' = T + e'$$

with $\sigma_e^2 = \sigma_{e'}^2$, and $Y = Y'$.

Parallelism in testing can be achieved through several techniques; however, the most common are variations on the test–retest method and the parallel but not equivalent technique. Test–retest, of course, involves giving the subject the same test more than once, preferably subject to a limiting time constraint. While the strengths and weaknesses of this method will be discussed in detail later, it is clear that in some situations the scores will not be independent and equivalent, but will be corrupted by such factors as salience and learning. Parallel tests, on the other hand, do differ from one another but are supposed to be equivalent in all important respects. For example, in a questionnaire relating to capital punishment, one might be asked to respond to the following (and supposedly equivalent) items (Jurow, 1971):

1. I am opposed to capital punishment under any circumstances.
2. I could not vote for the death penalty regardless of the facts and circumstances of the case.

If two tests are equivalent, then it can also be assumed that both the following would hold.

1. $E(Y) = E(Y')$.
2. $\sigma_Y^2 = \sigma_{Y'}^2$.

These equivalences can be exploited by drawing upon the concepts underlying statistical correlation. For example, by definition, Pearson's correlation coefficient is:

$$r = \frac{s_{XY}}{s_X s_Y} = \frac{\text{cov}(X, Y)}{\sqrt{\text{var}(X)}\sqrt{\text{var}(Y)}}$$

By substituting Y and Y' for the components X and Y, we may write:

$$r_{YY'} = \frac{\sigma_{YY'}}{\sigma_Y \sigma_{Y'}}$$

Expanding the Y terms, we further note that,

$$r_{YY'} = \frac{\sigma_{YY'}}{\sigma_Y \sigma \delta_{Y'}}$$

$$= \frac{\sigma_{(T+e)}\sigma_{(T+e')}}{\sigma_Y \sigma_{Y'}}$$

$$= \frac{\sigma_T^2 + \sigma_{Te} + \sigma_{Te'} + \sigma_{ee'}}{\sigma_Y \sigma_{Y'}}$$

---

1. This assumption can be relaxed to what we call tau [τ] equivalence, in which case only the true scores are equal.

Given the assumptions that the error terms are uncorrelated and that the error terms are not correlated with the true scores, three of the terms in the numerator drop out and this latter equation reduces to:

$$r_{YY'} = \frac{\sigma_T^2}{\sigma_Y^2}$$

which is the same as the reliability coefficient.

In conclusion, the *correlation* between two parallel items can be considered a *reliability coefficient*. Because of the definition of ρ, however, it can be a positive value only (except in rare instances with few cases, and where σ_e is very large) within the range 0,1. This conceptualization also allows us to estimate the variance of the true scores, σ_T^2, from the observed scores by:

$$\sigma_T^2 = \sigma_Y^2 r_{YY'}$$

VALIDITY

Classical test theory had a fair amount to say about reliability but very little concerning validity. According to the classical model, *validity* is defined simply as the correlation between two parallel measures, X and Y. For example, a criminologist may assess the validity of a self-report questionnaire on amount of time spent in prison by comparing it with actual prison records. Within this framework, validity may be formally defined as the correlation between these two indicators, or:

$$r_{XY} = \frac{\sigma_{XY}}{\sigma_X \sigma_Y}$$

Logically, then, it can be seen that validity is equal to reliability with respect to parallel measures. This statement is not very enlightening and begs the question about whether reliability and validity are distinct concepts. Since no one to date has argued for the exclusion of either concept, we can only conclude that a way must be found to transcend the manner in which validity has been defined within the classical framework. As we will see in the next chapter, some attempts have been made in this direction, but as with many problems, this is a task that is easier identified than accomplished.

Staying with classical test theory, however, it can also be shown that validity and reliability are related such that,

$$r_{XY} \leq \sqrt{r_{YT}^2} \quad \text{or} \quad r_{XY} \leq \sqrt{r_{YY'}^2}$$

In other words, the validity of a test with respect to a second measure cannot be greater than the square root of its reliability (Zeller and Carmines, 1980: 10).

EXTENSIONS OF CLASSICAL TEST THEORY

Following the discussion to this point, clearly classical test theory has two major limitations: it cannot deal with nonrandom error, and it tells us very little about the issue of validity. Regarding nonrandom error, it is often the case in applied research that some systematic bias creeps in. Sometimes this manifests itself as "response sets" where the respondent has a preference for "yes" or "no" answers, sometimes it is due to "memory effects," and sometimes it results from the presence of an indicator that might be interpreted to refer to more than one underlying concept. In all these cases the correlation between errors on distinct measures is not zero and the estimate of validity provided by classical theory is inaccurate. This can create far-reaching problems for many forms of analysis, as Box 10.1 illustrates. Some attempts have been made to rectify these problems and, fortunately, advances in one area have led to advances in the other.

To reformulate our classical model, let us consider the case in which some systematic bias, S, is included in the measurement process. The measurement model is then defined as follows:

$$Y = T + S + R$$

$$\underbrace{\qquad\qquad}$$

Disaggregation of e

where Y is again the observed score, T is the true score, S is the systematic bias, and R is a random measurement error component. In this situation, the expected value of

---

■ **Box 10.1**

RELIABILITY AND BIAS IN REGRESSION

What implications does low reliability have for many of our standard data analytic techniques such as regression analysis? The issue is complex, but a flavor can be obtained by considering the impact of low reliability on b_{yx} in the case of simple regression. Classically, it is assumed that x is measured without error. But what happens when this assumption is violated?

The formula for b_{yx} is:

$$b_{yx} = \frac{s_{yx}}{s_x^2}$$

As we have shown, however, $s_x^2 = s_t^2 + s_e^2$.

Reduced reliability implies an increase in the error variance in s_x^2; hence, s_x^2 will be inflated. This, in turn, results in a sample estimate of b that is closer to 0 that β. As mentioned, the situation is more complex because we not only have error in the x variable in the denominator, but we must introduce it into the covariance term in the numerator. Furthermore, the assumptions of independent errors and independence between the true score of x and the errors may not hold. Hence, those terms need to be taken into account.

See Aiken and West (1990: ch. 8) for an elementary discussion of the matter, or Fuller (1987: ch. 1) for a more developed discussion.

the observed scores will no longer be simply the expected value of the true scores, but will also include the expected value of the bias. That is,

$$E(Y) = E(T) + E(S)$$

By extension, the expected variance of the observed scores is no longer the simple sum of the variances of the expected true scores plus the random error, but is a combination of these factors plus the expected variance of the systematic bias and the covariance of the true score and the bias. Formally,

$$\sigma_Y^2 = \sigma_{(T+S+R)}^2$$

Expanding this, we obtain

$$(T + S + R)^2 = T^2 + TS + TR + TS + S^2 + SR + TR + SR + R^2$$

Hence,

$$\sigma_Y^2 = \sigma_T^2 + \sigma_{TS} + \sigma_{TR} + \sigma_{TS} + \sigma_S^2 + \sigma_{SR} + \sigma_{TR} + \sigma_{SR} + \sigma_R^2$$

Since we retain the assumptions of independence for random errors, (assumptions 2 and 3 above), it is possible to drop all of the terms that equal zero (σ_{TR}, σ_{SR}) and write:

$$\sigma_Y^2 = \sigma_T^2 + \sigma_S^2 + \sigma_R^2 + 2\sigma_{TS}$$

While perhaps better reflecting reality, this reconceptualization does introduce a major complication. The variance of Y is not just the simple sum of the true score, the systematic error, and the random error; it is, instead, the sum of these elements plus twice the covariance of the true score and the systematic bias. Furthermore, unlike estimates of variance, which are invariably positive, it is possible to have a negative covariance term to complicate the matter further.

Yet another issue of concern is the need to make several subsidiary assumptions, if it is required to estimate anything other than the total variance σ_Y^2 and the "pure" error variance σ_R^2. The covariance term and the variances of the true scores and the systematic error are not readily decomposable. Conceptually we might start to appreciate the issue by asking the question: How is it possible to know how many underlying factors make up σ_S^2? Purely statistical considerations cannot hope to differentiate among the possible unknown factors.

On the other hand, theory-guided assumptions can help in the estimation process. These will be dealt with later. For now, however, the definition of reliability may be broadened as follows[2]:

$$\text{reliability} = \frac{\sigma_T^2 + \sigma_S^2 + \sigma_R^2 + 2\sigma_{TS}}{\sigma_Y^2}$$

$$= \frac{\sigma_Y^2 - \sigma_R^2}{\sigma_Y^2}$$

and

---

2. Note that if σ_{TS} is large and negative, something can be valid but unreliable under this model.

$$\text{validity} = \frac{\sigma_Y^2}{\sigma_{Y'}^2}$$

In considering these formulas, Zeller and Carmines (1980: 13–14) note:

> Reliability is the consistency or repeatability of measurements; validity is the degree to which a set of indicants measures the concept it is intended to measure. These formulations imply not only that systematic error is separable from true score variance but that these two components may be correlated with each other. Most important, these expressions make clear that the difference between reliability and validity is entirely dependent upon systematic error. If a set of indicants contains no systematic error— that is, it measures only the concept of interest with random fluctuations—then validity will equal reliability and both will differ from 1.00 by the amount of random error. Conversely, if measurements contain a substantial amount of systematic error, validity can be significantly less than reliability. In the unusual circumstance when *all* observed variance is represented by systematic error, reliability would be perfect but validity would be zero. Thus, systematic error produces reliable but invalid measurements.

CLASSICAL ESTIMATES OF RELIABILITY

Practically, reliability may be assessed as stability (test–retest methods) or equivalence (split-half methods). Once an appropriate correlation matrix has been generated, based on the preceding formulas, or on another correlation statistic, generating several estimates of reliability is possible. While classical test theory has spawned several measures over the years, a few dominate the literature. Traditionally, the most commonly employed estimates were based on the test–retest method, parallel tests, split-half techniques, and the Kuder–Richardson approach. More recent additions to the classical test theory toolbox are Cronbach's alpha (which is an extension of the Kuder–Richardson approach) and some statistics derived from exploratory factor analysis.

The test–retest method involves administering the same test twice. As one might imagine, its validity can be problematic if the test is readministered within a short period. Significant memory effects are likely to occur, resulting in inflated estimates of reliability. The longer the period between tests, however, the more likely it is that exogenous factors will affect the true test scores.

Parallel tests, on the other hand, involve constructing two versions of the same instrument that are as alike (parallel) as possible. Parallel tests are generally administered within the same interval, thus alleviating the memory problem inherent in the test–retest cycle. The disadvantage of the parallel test approach is that constructing one good version of a test is often difficult, never mind two! If this can be done, however, care must be taken not to space the test administrations too much, since exogenous factors can again influence the true test score.

While the test–retest and parallel test approaches are still employed in some disciplines, in their classical guise, they are appearing less frequently in the literature. This is largely because of the problems just described, plus the availability of more general techniques for dealing with problems of separating out and estimating memory and other forms of systematic error from true error (issues discussed in the next chapter).

Among the classical reliability estimates, one is most likely to come across in the general social science literature are the split half, Cronbach's alpha (α), theta (θ), and omega (Ω). We will discuss each of these measures in turn and provide an illustration of each estimate.

EXAMPLE: CREATING A SCALE OF JOB SATISFACTION

As an example of a typical problem, let us consider a one-dimensional scale designed to assess level of job satisfaction. The scale is assumed to contain one underlying factor operationalized through nine items. Table 10.1 presents the results of an unpublished study that, in part, addressed this issue. The actual data for this analysis were collected from a random survey of 250 correctional officers. The scale contains nine items consisting of the degree to which the officers reported perceived satisfaction with various dimensions of the job. Each item was measured using a seven-point indicator ranging from 1 (very dissatisfied) to 7 (very satisfied). The actual questionnaire items were structured as follows:

> The following is a list of items relating to various aspects of jobs in the field of corrections. Please put a check mark in the box which best indicates your level of satisfaction with these work related areas.

> The **pay**
> The level of job **security**
> The opportunities for **promotion**
> The fringe **benefits**
> The **hours** of work
> The **challenge** offered by the job
> The extent to which the job is **interesting**

Table 10.1. Data matrix for job satisfaction scale

Pay	**2.081**	.265	.198	.320	.166	.038	.123	.139	.176
Security	.566	**2.187**	.297	.213	.268	.205	.105	.306	.193
Promotion	.510	.784	**3.186**	.248	.278	.342	.368	.403	.429
Benefits	.767	.523	.737	**2.761**	.276	.271	.408	.276	.321
Hours	.444	.735	.921	.851	**3.442**	.320	.276	.297	.309
Tasks	.079	.431	.869	.641	.846	**2.030**	.488	.446	.527
Interest	.298	.373	1.106	1.142	.864	1.171	**2.840**	.509	.674
Skills	.319	.722	1.146	.732	.878	1.012	1.366	**2.541**	.629
Challenge	.432	.487	1.303	.908	.977	1.280	1.934	1.709	**2.902**

$N = 250$

Estimates of item variances are along main diagonal; correlations are above the diagonal and covariances are below.

The variety of **tasks** involved
The opportunities to use your **skills** and training

Next to each question was a box corresponding to one of seven responses.

1 - Very dissatisfied
2 - Dissatisfied
3 - Mildly dissatisfied
4 - Undecided
5 - Mildly satisfied
6 - Satisfied
7 - Very satisfied

Respondents circled what they felt was the most appropriate response.

Split-Half Reliability

Consider an arbitrary six-item scale divided into two parts: items 1–3 and items 4–6. We wish to estimate the reliability of the overall scale by examining the correlation between the first and second halves. The reliability coefficient, r'_{YY}, can be estimated as follows:

$$r'_{YY} = \frac{e}{\sqrt{(a + 2b)(c + 2d)}}$$

where e = sum of the intercorrelations between Y_{1-3} and Y_{4-6}; this should result in nine intercorrelations:

Y_1, Y_4
Y_1, Y_5
Y_1, Y_6
Y_2, Y_4
Y_2, Y_5
Y_2, Y_6
Y_3, Y_4
Y_3, Y_5
Y_3, Y_6

a = number of indicators in the first half (Y_{1-3}), or in this case 3
b = sum of the intercorrelations between Y_{1-3}
c = number of indicators in the second half (Y_{4-6}), or in this case 3
d = sum of the intercorrelations between Y_{4-6}

This coefficient will range between 0 and 1, where 1 represents perfect reliability.

Using the data from Table 10.1, we can estimate the split-half reliability of our job satisfaction scale. Before doing so, however, it is necessary to delete one item from the data matrix, since the split half requires equal numbers of items in each half. For argument's sake, let us delete the item relating to pay and assume that the two halves consist of the following sets: {security, promotion, benefits, hours} and {tasks, interest, skills, challenge}. Reliability, r'_{XX}, is thus estimated as follows:

$$r'_{YY} = \frac{e}{\sqrt{(a + 2b)(c + 2d)}}$$

$$= \frac{4.829}{\sqrt{[4 + 2(1.580)][4 + 2(3.273)]}}$$

$$= .556$$

Overall or total reliability can be estimated from the Spearman–Brown prophecy formula. Generally, overall reliability will be higher than split-half reliability because there are more items in the full scale than in the half-scale. The formula for Spearman–Brown is:

$$r''_{YY} = \frac{2r'_{YY}}{1 + r'_{YY}}$$

where r''_{YY} = reliability coefficient for whole test
$\quad\quad r'_{YY}$ = split-half reliability coefficient

In this instance, the overall reliability is estimated as $2(.556)/1.556 = .715$.

Estimating Reliability for N-Length Scales

If a scale has a given split-half reliability, is it possible to estimate the reliability for a test of a different length? Generalizing from the preceding formula, for a k-tupling we may write:

$$r''_{YY(N)} = \frac{kr'_{YY}}{1 + (k - 1)r'_{YY}}$$

For example, if a five-item split half correlates .22 with another five-item form, how can the reliability of a scale with four times that long be estimated? By substitution:

$$r''_{YY(4)} = \frac{4(.22)}{1 + (4 - 1)(.22)} = \frac{.88}{1.66} = .53$$

Alternately it might be asked: How many times longer would a test have to be to achieve an $r''_{YY(k)}$ of .63? (*Answer:* 6—as an assignment, use the equation above and solve for k.)

Figure 10.1 illustrates the impact of increasing the length of a test up to eight times the length of the original for three selected initial reliabilities. As shown in the figure, initially doubling or tripling the number of items results in substantial increases in reliability, while subsequent increments result in marginal returns to scale. The lower the initial scale reliability, however, the longer substantial gains are made as the number of items is doubled, tripled, quadrupled, and so on. Considering

Figure 10.1. Relationship between reliability and test length.

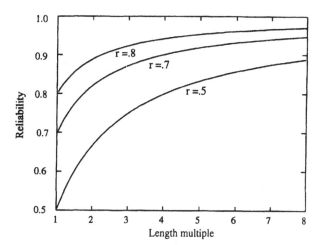

the issue in isolation, one might be led to the conclusion that the problem of achieving a desired reliability estimate is simply a matter of sufficiently increasing test length. Unfortunately, several costs are involved with indiscriminately increasing test length. Clearly one problem is coming up with items equal in reliability to the initial set. As anyone who has tried to construct a scale from scratch soon realizes, this is no mean feat. Other problems relate to the practical issues involved in test administration. The more items there are in a scale, the more likely fatigue will become a problem. Further, time is often an issue, and the more time spent on one set of items, the less time is available for addressing other issues. Finally, a phenomenon known as the *attenuation paradox* has been identified, which shows that after a certain point, not only is there no further increase in overall reliability, but reliability actually *decreases*.

As you might have suspected, a major problem with the Spearman–Brown formula is how one decides to break the scale into two components. For a scale with N items, there are $N!/(N - k)!$ possible combinations of splits. In the current example, where there are $N = 8$ items and they are to be divided into two halves with $k = 4$ items in each half, it is possible to generate 1680 combinations. Consider further that each split can give a different estimate of reliability, and the prospect of relying on the split-half approach gives one pause.

Cronbach's Alpha

Cronbach's (1951) alpha is a very simple and very popular measure of reliability that is often cited in the psychological and sociological literature. It is a generalization of the Kuder–Richardson formulas presented in the 1930s (Kuder and Richardson, 1937). These formulas, generally known as KR20 and KR21, were limited to dichotomous items. Lee Cronbach, however, extended the Kuder–Richardson approach to incorporate continuous variables. This coefficient varies from 0 to 1.0 and represents a lower bound of the reliability estimate. Usually, α increases as the number of items increases in the scale.

Alpha has several advantages over split-half techniques. Computing it is easy; it does not require an even number of parallel items, and one does not have to face the difficulty of deciding how to make splits among the items.

The general formula for alpha is written in terms of the variances of the items; thus,

$$\alpha = \frac{N}{N-1}\left[1 - \frac{\sum_{i=1}^{N} s_{ii}}{\sum_{i=1}^{N} s_{ii} + 2\sum_{i=2}^{N}\sum_{j=i-1}^{N-1} s_{ij}}\right]$$

where N is the number of covariances either above or below the main diagonal of the variance–covariance matrix. Applying alpha to the data in Table 10.1, we can obtain the following estimates: $\Sigma s_{ii} = 2.081 + 2.178 + \cdots + 2.902 = 23.970$; $\Sigma\Sigma s_{ij} = .566 + .510 + \cdots + 1.709 = 29.863$. Since there are nine items in Table 10.1, the value of N is 9. Substituting these values into the equation above, we obtain:

$$\alpha = \frac{9}{8}\left[1 - \frac{23.970}{23.970 + (2 \times 29.863)}\right]$$

$$= .803$$

For summated rating scales with nearly equal variances, some arithmetic can be avoided and alpha can be estimated as follows:

$$\alpha = \frac{N\bar{r}}{1 + (N-1)\bar{r}}$$

where N = number of items in a scale
$\bar{r}$ = average of the item intercorrelations

If this formulation is used, however, it is essential that the item variances be close to equivalent. This is the case in the present example, and the equation above produces an estimate of .808, which is clearly not out of line with our original estimate of .803. Alpha is also useful if all the items have been converted to z scores before use. Novick and Lewis (1967) have shown that unless the test items are parallel, alpha is a lower bound for reliability. As a rule of thumb, α-levels should be .80 or higher to be considered reasonably reliable. According to alpha, then, our example scale barely makes the grade.

It should also be noted that since we are taking the sum of the item covariances, the items should all be scored with the same valence—either positive or negative. Where items are presented with the valence of their wording alternated, the signs of the covariances (and correlations) of mixed-valence items should be made either all positive or all negative to reflect the signs of items similar in valence.

Although alpha is probably the most popular estimate of scale reliability at this time, there are several other common measures based on exploratory factor analytic techniques. Two of the better known of these estimates are theta and omega. The correlation matrix from Table 10.1 was used to conduct a common factor analysis based on the assumption that the items represent a unidimensional scale. Consequently, only one factor was extracted. The pertinent results of this analysis are presented in Table 10.2.

Table 10.2. Results of common factor analysis based on data from Table 10.1

ITEM	FACTOR LOADING	ITEM VARIANCE	$S_{ii} \times h^2$
Pay	.394	2.081	.323
Security	.548	2.187	.657
Promotion	.992	3.186	3.135
Fringe benefits	.799	2.761	1.763
Hours of work	.837	3.442	2.411
Tasks	.898	2.030	1.637
Interest	1.231	2.840	4.304
Skills	1.134	2.541	3.268
Challenge	1.369	2.902	5.439
Sum	22.936		
Largest eigenvalue	8.695		

Theta

Theta (θ) is based on the eigenvalues extracted from a covariance or correlation matrix. Most common factor analysis programs will generate a listing of the eigenvalues. Using the largest eigenvalue, theta may be estimated as:

$$\theta = \frac{N}{N-1}\left(1 - \frac{1}{\lambda_1}\right)$$

where N = number. of items
λ_1 = largest (first) eigenvalue

Given the results of the common factor analysis as presented in Table 10.2, we note that the largest eigenvalue is 8.695. Substituting this into the formula above, we obtain the following estimate:

$$\theta = \frac{9}{8}\left[1 - \frac{1}{8.695}\right]$$
$$= .996$$

At .996, theta provides a higher estimate of reliability than does alpha.

Omega

This statistic also requires that the researcher conduct a factor analysis on the items. From the factor analysis, the communalities, h^2, are estimated. For a common factor analytic solution in which only one factor is extracted, the communalities are easily estimated as the square of the factor loadings.

Omega, then, is defined as follows:

$$\Omega = 1 - \frac{\sum_{i=1}^{N} S_{ii} - \sum_{i=1}^{N} S_{ii} h_i^2}{\sum_{i=2}^{N} \sum_{j=i-1}^{N-1} S_{ij}}$$

Substituting the appropriate values into this equation, we obtain:

$$\Omega = 1 - \frac{23.970 - 22.936}{29.863}$$

$$= .965$$

A somewhat easier formula to use when the item variances are reasonable equivalent is given by

$$\Omega = 1 - \frac{a - \Sigma h_i^2}{a + 2b}$$

where a = number of items

b = sum of the correlations among the indicators or items

h_i^2 = communality for the ith item

While measures of reliability based on common factor analysis have received a great deal of attention in the literature, it should be recognized that they too have several limitations. First, the factor loadings estimated by common factor analysis are indeterminate. This is because the common factor model is based on more parameters than available data points; therefore, any number of models that will reproduce the correlation or covariance matrix can be estimated.

Second, these models do not allow for an explicit examination of the measurement model. That is, are the errors in responses to one item related to another item, or to the errors of another item? A good example of this type of situation occurs when a respondent's answer to one question influences his or her answer to another question.

A third problem with this approach is that it is difficult to decide whether a scale with a low reliability index is inherently nonunidimensional or the items are simply poor items. Extracting more factors under a common factor model does not help this situation very much, for the reasons of indeterminacy outlined under the first limitation.

Correction for Attenuation

Since all measurement involves an error component, clearly the empirical measure between two concepts is likely less than the "true" correlation between those concepts. In the measurement literature, this regression of the true score toward 0 is known as attenuation.

We might raise the following (hypothetical) question: What would the correlation between the scores be *if there were no error*? In other words, can we correct for attenuation? The classical formula for correcting for attenuation is:

$$r_{T_x T_y} = \frac{r_{XY}}{\sqrt{r'_{XX} r'_{YY}}}$$

where $r_{T_x T_y}$ = correlation corrected for attenuation (i.e., the correlation between true scores)

r'_{XX} = reliability of X

r'_{YY} = reliability of Y

A similar approach can be taken to address attenuation in regression parameters. Consider the structural equation: $Y = \beta_0 + \beta_1 X + \varepsilon$. Classical linear regression assumes that the X-values are measured without error. Indeed, this is generally the case in experimental situations where the X-values can be fixed. In much of social research conducted in such fields as sociology, economics, or political science, however, the independent variables are usually random variables measured with varying degrees of precision. As we suggest in Box 10.1, this situation leads to bias, or attenuation, in the estimated parameters. The question we might ask, then, is whether correcting for this bias is possible.

The standard formula for the slope in a simple regression model is:

$$\beta_1 = \frac{\sigma_{XY}}{\sigma_X^2}$$

As we have shown, however, $X = T + e$; therefore we have an attenuated or biased estimate of β_1 that we can term $\hat{\gamma}_1$:

$$\beta_{\text{attenuated}} = \hat{\gamma}_1 = \frac{\sigma_{XY}}{\sigma_X^2 + \sigma_e^2}$$

Dividing $\hat{\gamma}_1$ by the estimated reliability, however, gives us an unattenuated estimate of β. Thus,

$$\hat{\beta}_1 = \hat{\gamma}_1 \hat{\rho}_{XX}^{-1} = \frac{\sigma_{XY}}{\sigma_X^2 + \sigma_e^2} \cdot \frac{\sigma_X^2 + \sigma_e^2}{\sigma_X^2}$$

$$= \frac{\sigma_{XY}}{\sigma_X^2}$$

This procedure can be readily extended to multivariate situations.[3] It is important to remember that these estimates are based on the assumptions that the measurement error in X is independent of both the true scores and the errors (i.e., assumptions 1–4).

Depending upon the issue, it may be necessary for researchers to generate their own reliability estimates. This can often be done in pretests. In other instances, where standard instruments are employed, published reliability estimates may be available. This is particularly the case with many psychometric instruments (see, e.g., Goldman and Saunders, 1974–90; Chun, Cobb, and French, 1975).

EXAMPLE: MEASUREMENT ERROR IN PRACTICE

While a great deal of attention has been directed to the formal aspects of reliability, a salient question is: What impact can measurement error have in practice? One way of getting a taste of the potential impact of the problem is to run a small Monte Carlo study. In this example, an attempt has been made to parallel a real question that arises in social policy contexts: Are gender differences in income *real* or simply statistical

---

3. For a detailed and more rigorous discussion see Fuller (1987). While most computer programs require corrections for attenuation to be done manually, Jöreskog and Sörbom's LISREL program is excellent for such manipulations. See Jöreskog and Sörbom (1993: ch. 5).

artifacts? Since the bulk of the empirical literature holds that these differentials are linked to some form of systemic discrimination, we will play the devil's advocate and construct a data set in which no statistically significant differences by gender exist; rather, all differences depend on differences in productivity and pure error. If productivity seems unpalatable, one can substitute hours worked, widgets produced per unit time, or any other reasonable output measure that can be legitimately used as a reason for differentially distributing rewards.

In the example data set, a total sample of 100 has been generated: 50 fictitious males and 50 fictitious females. These people have been assigned productivity and income levels according to the equation:

$$\text{income} = -49.244 - 15.459 \text{ gender} + 334.29 \text{ productivity}$$

Three new measures of productivity, $P1$, $P2$, and $P3$, were generated by adding a random error component to the existing indicator. Specifically, a random number generator was used to produce a pseudorandom number, z, with a mean of 0 and a variance of 1.0. This standard, normal deviate was then multiplied by a constant to equate its order of size to that of the existing data. Error-prone indicators were thus constructed as follows:

$$P1 = \text{Productivity} + z(5.0)$$

$$P2 = \text{Productivity} + z(10.0)$$

$$P3 = \text{Productivity} + z(15.0)$$

Selected summary statistics are presented in Table 10.3 for all the variables considered. As can be seen, the means for productivity, $P1$, $P2$, and $P3$ are quite similar. The variances increase, however, as the error increases. Since it is assumed that productivity is measured without error, its variance $[s_X^2 = (11.83)^2 = 140.4]$ is an estimate of σ_T^2. The variances associated with $P1$, $P2$, and $P3$ consist of σ_Y^2, which is $\sigma_T^2 + \sigma_e^2$. Thus, the ratio of the variance of productivity to the variances of $P1$, $P2$, and $P3$ are estimates of the reliability of those variables. So, for example, the reliablilty of $P1$ may be estimated as: $\hat{\rho} = (11.83)^2/(12.70)^2 = .87$. The reliability estimates for $P2$ and $P3$ are .61 and .53, respectively.

Regressions were then estimated including income, gender, and the error-prone estimate of productivity for the three new measures. The results are again presented in Table 10.3. What is most notable from these results is that error in the indicator for productivity can have an impact on our perceptions of gender. In Model 0, gender is nonsignificant by any standard judgment (i.e., $t = -.664$ with 1, 97 df). With a reduction in the reliability of productivity to .87 as indicated in Model 1, gender becomes significant at an α-level of .05 ($t = -2.490$ with 1, 97 df). A further reduction in the reliability of productivity to .53, as shown in Model 3, results in gender appearing to be significant at the .01 level (i.e., $t = -3.072$ with 1, 97 df).

In addition, it is evident from our analysis that the substantive parameter values vary widely from one model to the next.

Table 10.3. Results of the reliability simulation

VARIABLE	MEAN	STANDARD DEVIATION	MINIMUM	MAXIMUM
Income	15,910.	3,959.8	10,000.	23,710.
Gender	.5	.503	0.0	1.0
Productivity	47.765	11.834	30.00	71.13
P1	47.567	12.696	20.39	78.87
P2	46.833	15.170	20.26	79.81
P3	48.349	16.208	21.18	79.47

VARIABLE	COEFFICIENT	t-RATIO	p-VALUE
Model 0—reliability = 1.00			
Intercept	−49.244	−.927	.3561
Gender	−15.456	−.664	.5086
Productivity	334.29	337.961	.0000
Model 1—reliability = 0.87			
Intercept	3065.3	4.533	.0000
Gender	−797.88	−2.490	.0145
P1	278.43	21.951	.0000
Model 2—reliability = 0.61			
Intercept	7476.3	8.038	.0000
Gender	−1086.1	−2.101	.0382
P2	191.69	11.196	.0000
Model 3—reliability = 0.53			
Intercept	10,508.	9.748	.0000
Gender	−1,946.8	−3.072	.0028
P3	131.87	6.712	.0000

CONCLUSIONS

All the estimates of reliability discussed in this chapter are derived from what is termed classical test theory. They work reasonably well when the scale is inherently unidimensional, and the underlying assumptions are not violated too severely. Thus, for a quick runthrough, something like Cronbach's alpha is quite useful because it is easy to compute and appears reasonably robust. Unfortunately, real-life data are often complex, poorly behaved, and have a habit of not conforming to the a priori assumptions we set for them. Thus, what is required is a more flexible approach to the situation that will allow for the testing of more complex models. That is, we need models that are multidimensional, and models that do not conform to such restrictive assumptions as requiring that all the error terms be uncorrelated. Fortunately, advances over the last 20 years in structural equation modeling have provided new tools for addressing these issues. It is to this approach that we will direct our attention in the next chapter.

Further Reading

Carmines, E.G., and Zeller, R.A. *Reliability and Validity Assessment*. Beverly Hills, CA: Sage, 1979. A short and very elementary introduction to reliability assessment.

Magnusson, D. *Test Theory*. Reading, MA: Addison-Wesley, 1966. A lucid and comprehensive introduction into scale construction and the determination of reliability and validity within the classical framework.

11

Confirmatory Factor Models

"The time has come," the Walrus said,
"To talk of many things . . ."

—Lewis Carroll

Traditional measures of reliability such as Cronbach's alpha and the split-half reliability coefficient provide only a limited approach to the assessment of scale reliability. In particular, they do not readily allow for an examination of the dimensionality of scales, nor do they allow for an examination of the structure of the error components. Recent advances in linear structural equation modeling, however, allow scales and scale items to be examined in much more detail. The literature in this area is voluminous and growing rapidly. An excellent discussion of the broader aspects of structural equation modeling can be found in Bollen (1989). Initially, we will limit our attention to several basic issues that can be addressed through an approach commonly known as confirmatory factor analysis.

ONE-DIMENSIONAL SCALES

The scale items listed on a questionnaire can be thought of as a series of operational indicators that reflect some underlying factor. Thus, for example, we can view the responses on several questions relating to a person's job as influenced (or *generated*) by the underlying factor that we might understand as *job satisfaction*. In some of the literature, these factors are called *latent variables* and the generated or measured indicators are called *manifest variables*. Each item response can be viewed as a function of the underlying factor plus some error component. A parallel can be drawn with the discussion in Chapter 10 where the observed score, Y, depends on some true score, T, and an error component, e; therefore, $Y = T + e$. Reliability, in this context, is the ratio of the variance of the true score to the variance of the observed score (i.e., $\rho = \sigma_T / \sigma_Y$).

For convenience sake, the notation can be changed, and the true score, T, can be thought of as a latent factor, F. Thus, we may write:

$$Y = F + e$$

Assume for a moment that there is some parameter, λ, and that λ is equal to 1. Without any substantial change in meaning, this formula can be rewritten as follows:

$$Y = \lambda F + e$$

A scale with three items would have three equations, each of which linearly relates the underlying factor, F, to some empirical referent, Y, through an estimable parameter, λ. Thus, we would write:

$$Y_1 = \lambda_1 F + e_1$$
$$Y_2 = \lambda_2 F + e_2$$
$$Y_3 = \lambda_3 F + e_3$$

Graphically, the structural form of this model can be depicted by the path diagram shown in Figure 11.1. Now, whether the λs are or are not truly equal to 1.0 is an empirical question. When the lambdas (λ) are equal and the error variances are equal, the model is consistent with the *parallel* measures model. Relaxing the assumption that the error variances are equal, but retaining the assumption that the lambdas are equal, defines *tau-equivalence*. Eliminating the last constraint and allowing the lambdas to vary results in a *congeneric* measurement model.

Typical summated rating scales in which respondents' scores are summed over all items are implicitly based on a model of parallel measurement. This type of scale assumes that the respective lambdas and error variances are equivalent. While this assumption may be valid under some circumstances, its validity ought ultimately to be an empirical issue rather than one that is decided by fiat.

Congeneric models, where the values of both lambda and the error variances differ, are likely the most common in applied research.

Practically, however, statistical estimation can be a problem in the congeneric model. This is because the congeneric model is mathematically underidentified—a situation that arises because there are more unknowns (parameters) than knowns (observed variables). A solution can be generated, however, by assuming that the underlying factor is a standardized normal deviate (z-score).

The covariance matrix of the observed variables, y, can be broken down as follows:

$$\text{cov}(Y) = \lambda_i \lambda_j + \theta_{ii} = \begin{pmatrix} \lambda_1^2 + \theta_{11} & \lambda_1 \lambda_2 & \lambda_1 \lambda_3 \\ \lambda_2 \lambda_1 & \lambda_2^2 + \theta_{22} & \lambda_2 \lambda_3 \\ \lambda_3 \lambda_1 & \lambda_3 \lambda_2 & \lambda_3^2 + \theta_{33} \end{pmatrix}$$

Figure 11.1. Structural equation model for a scale with a single dimension.

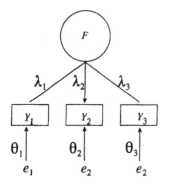

Where cov(Y) is a symmetrical matrix, and in most presentations, the upper diagonal is ignored. The values θ_{ii} represent the variances of the error terms, e_i, where $i = 1, 2, 3$. Again, the *reliability* of any given item is the ratio of the true variance in Y to the total observed variance. Specifically,

$$\rho_{ii} = \frac{\lambda_i^2}{\sigma_{ii}}$$

$$= \frac{\lambda_i^2}{\lambda_i^2 + \theta_{ii}}$$

Already, this view of scaling is an extension beyond the classical approach in that we have allowed for differential weights to relate the observed items to the underlying factor. The model can be further extended by examining the error terms, e_i. For practical reasons, classical measurement theory treats the error terms as being independent of one another. Again, whether this assumption is warranted or not is largely an empirical question. Certain aspects of questionnaire design (such as item sequencing) may lead to significant correlations among the error terms. When this happens we would like to be able to make that determination and include it in our underlying model. A graphic perspective on correlated error terms is presented in Figure 11.2, which shows the possible linkages among the error terms.

Essentially, we may divide our model into two components: the first might be termed a structural model that relates the underlying factor to its empirical referents; the second might be termed the measurement model, which hypothesizes the relationships among the error terms. In classical measurement theory, reliability tends to be addressed as the structural model only; and the measurement model is often ignored.

Classical test theorists did not ignore the measurement model out of theoretical ignorance, however. The problem was far more pragmatic in that software to estimate complex structural equations did not exist until recently. Starting in the late 1960s and throughout the next two decades, Karl Jöreskog solved many of those problems by devising the software package called LISREL. Subsequently, several similar packages

Figure 11.2. Structural equation model for a single dimensional scale with correlated errors.

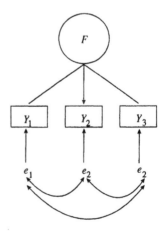

came on the market, including Bentler's EQS, a SAS procedure known as CALIS and SYSTAT's RAMONA. While this software changes rapidly to accommodate both theoretical developments and consumer demand, at the time of this writing, LISREL is the more flexible package, while EQS and RAMONA might be considered more "user friendly."

Essentially, structural equation models attempt to reproduce the observed covariance matrix based on the estimated parameters. The difference between the estimated and the observed covariance matrix is assessed with a likelihood ratio chi-squared test. Where the estimated and observed covariance matrices are very similar, the chi-squared value will be small, hence nonsignificant. Large discrepancies between the two matrices will result in large or statistically significant chi-squared values. In a context such as this, a p-value of approximately .10 is often used as an arbiter of the size of the chi-squared statistic. Thus p-values greater than .10 suggest that the reproduced covariance matrix is satisfactorily *close* to the empirical one.

It is, of course, possible to estimate the overall reliability of the scale. This is done by calculating an R^2 analogue—1 minus the proportion of error or residual variation. In matrix terms, this is defined as 1 minus the ratio of the determinant of the matrix of theta terms to the expected or reproduced covariance matrix. Hence,

$$R^2 = 1 - \frac{|\boldsymbol{\theta}|}{|\hat{\boldsymbol{\Sigma}}|}$$

EXAMPLE: SCALING JOB SATISFACTION

Consider a one-dimensional scale designed to assess level of job satisfaction. The scale is assumed to contain one underlying factor operationalized through four items. The actual data for this analysis were collected from a random survey of 250 correctional officers. The scale contains four items: tasks involved, interesting of job, opportunity to use skills, and the challenge of the job. Each item was measured using a seven-point indicator ranging from 1 (very dissatisfied) to 7 (very satisfied).

The actual questionnaire items were structured as follows:

The following is a list of items relating to various aspects of jobs in the field of corrections. Please put a check mark in the box which best indicates your level of satisfaction with these work related areas.

- The challenge offered by the job
- The extent to which the job is interesting
- The variety of tasks involved
- The opportunities to use your skills and training

Next to each question was a box corresponding to one of seven responses.

1 - Very dissatisfied
2 - Dissatisfied
3 - Mildly dissatisfied

4 - Undecided
5 - Mildly satisfied
6 - Satisfied
7 - Very satisfied

The covariances among the four items were calculated and the results are presented in Table 11.1.[1] From these data, we can test whether the measurement model is parallel, tau-equivalent, or congeneric. Also, we will want to estimate the item reliabilities and the overall model reliability.

The three measurement models were estimated using LISREL Version 8. Table 11.2, which presents the overall goodness-of-fit statistics for the models, shows that the parallel model (i.e., the one that assumes an equivalence between both the true score and error variances) reproduces the observed covariance matrix very poorly. The large χ^2 value and the small p-value suggest that the difference between the two matrices is quite large. Similarly, the tau-equivalent model, which assumes equivalence across true scores but not error variances, provides a very poor fit. Again the χ^2 is large and the p-value extremely small. The congeneric model, however, reproduces the observed covariance matrix quite well, as is suggested by the very small chi-squared value and the large, "nonsignificant" p-value.

Parameter values for both lambdas and thetas in the congeneric model are presented in Table 11.3. This table also shows that the reliability of item 1 is estimated to be:

$$\hat{\rho}_1^2 = \frac{\lambda_1^2}{\lambda_1^2 + \theta_1} = \frac{(.876)^2}{(.876)^2 + 1.263} = .378$$

Table 11.1. Variances–covariances of job satisfaction items

ITEM	TASKS	INTEREST	SKILLS	CHALLENGE
Task	2.030			
Interest	1.171	2.840		
Skills	1.012	1.366	2.541	
Challenge	1.288	1.934	1.709	2.902

Table 11.2. Summary of measurement models for job satisfaction

MODEL	df	χ^2	p-VALUE
Parallel	8	38.44	.000
Tau-equivalent	5	36.38	.000
Congeneric	2	1.79	.408

1. While we use covariance matrices as basic data in this chapter, the analysis could be conducted on correlation matrices without any loss of generality. It should be noted, however, that correlation matrices do produce biased overall chi-squared estimates under certain circumstances.

Table 11.3. Estimates for congeneric model

	PARAMETER	ESTIMATE	SE	$\hat{\rho}$
Lambdas				
Tasks	λ_1	.876	.087	.378
Interesting	λ_2	1.276	.098	.574
Skills	λ_3	1.120	.094	.494
Challenge	λ_4	1.509	.094	.785
Thetas				
Tasks	θ_1	1.263	.126	
Interesting	θ_2	1.211	.144	
Skills	θ_3	1.287	.139	
Challenge	θ_4	.624	.137	

Of the items, task is the least reliable, with a $\hat{\rho}$ value of .378 while challenge is the most reliable, with $\hat{\rho} = .785$.

We might also wish to consider the residuals between the observed covariance matrix (Table 11.1) and the generated covariance matrix. The expected covariance matrix is generated from the parameter estimates. The diagonal elements of this matrix are defined by $\lambda_i^2 + \theta_{ii}$, while the off-diagonals are defined by $\lambda_i \lambda_j$. Thus, we have the original or observed covariance matrix,

$$S = \begin{pmatrix} 2.030 & & & \\ 1.171 & 2.840 & & \\ 1.012 & 1.366 & 2.541 & \\ 1.288 & 1.934 & 1.709 & 2.902 \end{pmatrix}$$

the estimated or generated covariance matrix,

$$\hat{\Sigma} = \begin{pmatrix} 2.030 & & & \\ 1.118 & 2.840 & & \\ .981 & 1.429 & 2.541 & \\ 1.322 & 1.927 & 1.691 & 2.902 \end{pmatrix}$$

and the matrix of residuals,

$$S - \hat{\Sigma} = \begin{pmatrix} 0 & & & \\ .053 & 0 & & \\ .031 & -.063 & 0 & \\ -.034 & .007 & .018 & 0 \end{pmatrix}$$

It is possible to compute standardized residuals by dividing the elements of $S - \hat{\Sigma}$ by their corresponding standard errors. In scalar algebra, the standardized or normed residuals are defined by:

$$\frac{s_{ij} - \hat\sigma_{ij}}{\sqrt{\left(\hat\sigma_{ii}\hat\sigma_{jj} + \hat\sigma_{ij}^2\right)/N}}$$

Performing this operation on each element we get:

$$(\mathbf{S} - \hat{\boldsymbol{\Sigma}})_{\text{standardized}} = \begin{pmatrix} 0 & & & \\ .920 & 0 & & \\ .476 & -1.305 & 0 & \\ -1.305 & .476 & .920 & 0 \end{pmatrix}$$

By any conventional criterion, none of these standardized residuals might be considered statistically significant, thus reasserting the validity of our model.

As shown previously, the R-squared analogue is equal to 1 minus the ratio of the determinant of the theta terms[2] to the determinant of the generated covariance matrix. Given the matrices above, R^2 is estimated to be:

$$R^2 = 1 - \frac{|\boldsymbol{\theta}|}{|\hat{\boldsymbol{\Sigma}}|}$$

$$= 1 - \frac{1.228}{9.000}$$

$$= .868$$

Thus, the *overall* reliability coefficient (as indicated by the coefficient of determination for Y) is .868—a respectable value for this type of scale.

As a final note, since the lambdas and reliabilities vary across the items, it does not make sense to use this scale as a simple summated ratings scale. Instead, if one is contemplating the use of this scale in an aggregate manner, the current evidence suggests that the items should be differentially weighted. Since the scale's underlying metric is somewhat arbitrary, any transformation that retains the relative ratios of the items' true scores would be acceptable. Thus, each item might be weighted by its corresponding λ value or by dividing each lambda by the sum of the lambdas and then weighting the observed scores.

The belief in the underlying measurement structure of this scale should not be based on a single sample, however. For any given sample, even an established parallel test may appear to be tau-equivalent or congeneric. Ideally, we would like to see several replications before coming to a final decision. If future replications produce similar results, then the credibility of the underlying scale structure increases.

Readers who are familiar with the social science literature that has appeared over the last 70 years or so might be wondering what impact mistaking congeneric scales

---

2. In this instance, the matrix $\boldsymbol{\theta}$ is a 4×4 matrix of zeros with the θ_i-values along the main diagonal.

for parallel or tau-equivalent scales has had on our research knowledge. For scales that consist of many items, with similar lambdas across the items, it is unlikely that the results would differ very greatly. Usually, the use of parallel scale assumptions when they are not warranted decreases the power of the study. Thus, it is possible that many "real," but marginal effects have been overlooked in the research literature. On the other hand, where statistically significant effects have been found, the likelihood that these results are "real" is increased.

MULTIDIMENSIONAL SCALES

The basic model for the one-dimensional scale can be extended into multiple dimensions. In fact, most scales commonly employed in social science research have several subcomponents attached to them.

As an extension of the preceding example, we will extend the job satisfaction scale to include another underlying dimension or factor. These factors represent two commonly cited components of job satisfaction—satisfaction with job benefits (extrinsic satisfaction) and satisfaction with "the job itself" (intrinsic satisfaction).

EXAMPLE: JOB SATISFACTION IN TWO DIMENSIONS

The first scale (extrinsic satisfaction) is identified by five items: satisfaction with pay, job security, opportunity for promotion, fringe benefits, and hours of work. The second scale (intrinsic satisfaction) retains the four items cited earlier: tasks, interesting, work, skills, and the challenge of the job. Again, satisfaction with each item was measured through a seven-point indicator ranging from 1 (very dissatisfied) to 7 (very satisfied). Table 11.4 presents a variance–covariance matrix for the nine items.[3]

The hypothesized structural model for this scale is presented in Figure 11.3. Here the relationship between the items and the underlying factors or job satisfaction dimensions is identified. Again, the one-headed arrows flow from the underlying factors to the individual items. Since the two underlying factors are also assumed to be related (although noncausally), they are linked by a curved two-headed arrow. The overall goodness of fit of this model, parameter values, and diagnostic statistics were generated. Since the preceding analysis suggests that the scale associated with the second factor is congeneric, no constraints were placed on either the lambdas or the thetas. Even assuming a congeneric model, the hypothesized scale model does not appear to replicate the observed covariance matrix within acceptable statistical limits. The estimated value of χ^2 for this model is 57.65 with 26 df—indication of an extremely poor fit. Thus, the question might be raised about whether the scale is at all valuable.

---

3. The standard covariance formula was employed:

$$S_{XY} = \frac{\sum (X - \overline{X})(Y - \overline{Y})}{n - 1}$$

Table 11.4. Covariance matrix for job satisfaction dimensions: N=250

ITEM	PAY	SECURITY	PROMOTION	FRINGE	HOURS	TASKS	INTEREST	SKILLS	CHALLENGE
Pay	2.081								
Security	.566	2.187							
Promotion	.510	.784	3.186						
Fringe	.767	.523	.737	2.761					
Hours	.444	.735	.921	.851	3.442				
Tasks	.079	.431	.869	.641	.846	2.030			
Interest	.298	.373	1.106	1.142	.864	1.171	2.840		
Skills	.319	.722	1.146	.732	.878	1.012	1.366	2.541	
Challenge	.432	.487	1.303	.908	.977	1.28	1.934	1.709	2.902

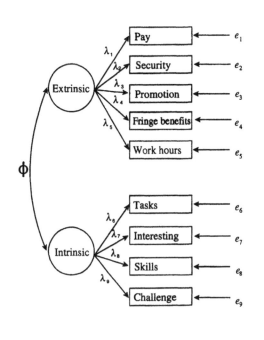

Figure 11.3. Structural model for two-dimensional job satisfaction scale.

Nonsignificant results can arise for many reasons. Perhaps, for example, the items we selected were not generated by the hypothesized factor structure. Or, the model may have been misspecified—that is, we may have selected either the wrong structural model or made the wrong assumptions about the error terms.

Based on prior research and our theoretical convictions, we will assume that the problem is one of misspecification. Furthermore, based on the face validity of the items, we are also reluctant to change the structure of the model. This leaves the suspicion that the lack of fit might be a consequence of incorrect assumptions regarding the error variances. Specifically, it is likely that the assumption that the error terms are *independent* is invalid.

What might produce correlated error terms? Generally, three situations lead to this outcome. First, the model may be slightly misspecified in that some indicators result from the impact of underlying factors not considered in the initial model. That is, a third unconsidered factor may be influencing one or more indicators simultaneously. This phenomenon is similar to the problem we face in ordinary regression problems, where the error term is considered an amalgam of "pure error" and factors not included in the model (Draper and Smith, 1981).

Second, correlated error terms may also be the consequence of the measurement method. Sometimes the sequence of items in a questionnaire can affect the responses to those items. Item A may affect item B if the two are contiguous on a questionnaire. If the items are separated, however, the response to item A will be less likely to influence the response to item B. A good example here is people's attitudes toward abortion and capital punishment. Traditional liberals are often for abortion and against capital punishment. If two items tapping into these factors are placed near each other, respondents might see an inherent contradiction in this stance (i.e., both involve killing) and attempt to resolve the inconsistency in their beliefs.[4] If the items are separated by other indicators, however this contradiction may not be raised in the respondents' minds.

Consider the following patterns of questions as they might appear on a questionnaire:

SEQUENCE	PATTERN 1	PATTERN 2
1	A_1	A_1
2	A_2	B_1
3	A_3	A_2
4	B_1	B_2
5	B_2	A_3
6	B_3	B_3

Questions A_i will be considered to load on one factor; questions B_i on a second. Under pattern 1, it would not be surprising to see larger intercorrelations within the A_is and the B_is than across the A_is and B_is. Under pattern 2 we might expect to see a stronger pattern of correlated errors across the pairings, $A_1 B_1$, $A_2 B_2$, and $A_3 B_3$ than within the A_is and B_is. Depending upon the actual length of either sequence, we might also expect the error variance to depend on the sequence, with the error variance increasing as respondent fatigue and inattentiveness increase with successive questions. Ultimately, whether such error patterns emerge is an empirical question; however, such pattern sequences do provide measurement hypotheses worthy of investigation.

---

4. The opposite tends to be true with regard to conservatives, who often oppose abortion but support capital punishment. Of course there is no apparent contradiction in these stances if one believes that there are intervening or modifying circumstances that need to be considered, such as the role of volition.

A third reason for correlated error terms might, of course, be simple chance. On any one given survey, correlated errors may appear because of the sampling process alone. The relationships may disappear when future samples are obtained, or sometimes, if more subjects are included in the current sample.

Regardless, we will hold onto our belief that the specified structural model is valid and that the problem with goodness of fit in this situation is a result of problems with measurement error.

EXAMPLE: JOB SATISFACTION IN TWO DIMENSIONS (CONTINUED)

An examination of the standardized residuals (Table 11.5) suggests that the error terms are not independent. Several are beyond 2.0 and a number are beyond 2.5. We could use the standardized residuals to decide which parameters we might wish to free in a reestimated model. Another indicator that is very useful in such endeavors, however, is what Jöreskog and Sörbom term *modification indices*. The modification indices are estimates of how much the overall chi-squared value can be expected to change if that parameter is no longer constrained to 0. As with standardized residuals, the modification indices are univariate statistics; thus, only one parameter at a time should be freed, and the results are reexamined after each modification to the model. The largest modification index of 10.375 was associated with indicators 4 and 7 (fringe benefits and skills). Parameters were freed on subsequent iterations to include correlated errors between indicators 4 and 1 (fringe benefits and pay) and 8 and 2 (skills and security).

A revised model diagram for the final model is presented in Figure 11.4. Here correlations between error terms are specifically indicated. Reestimating this model results in a χ^2 value of 31.12 with 23 df. At these values, the chi-squared goodness-of-fit index is no longer significant ($p = .12$); hence, it is unlikely that any difference exists between the observed and reproduced covariance matrix. Parameter estimates for this model are presented in Table 11.6.

Table 11.5. Matrix of standardized residuals: N=250

ITEM	PAY	SECURITY	PROMOTION	FRINGE	HOURS	TASKS	INTEREST	SKILLS	CHALLENGE
Pay	.000								
Security	2.143	.000							
Promotion	0.599	.767	.000						
Fringe	2.885	−0.576	2.401	.000					
Hours	0.423	1.009	−0.926	0.165	.000				
Tasks	−2.660	−0.054	1.379	0.509	1.822	0.000			
Interest	−1.976	−2.536	0.649	2.805	−0.319	0.395	0.000		
Skills	−1.238	1.591	2.080	−0.193	0.621	−0.127	−2.037	0.000	
Challenge	−1.601	−2.724	1.445	−0.696	−0.547	−0.875	1.646	0.903	0.000

Table 11.6. Parameter values for job satisfaction scales

	PARAMETER	ESTIMATE	SE
Phi	ϕ	.740	.056
Lambdas			
Extrinsic factor			
Pay	λ_1	.455	.108
Security	λ_2	.629	.107
Promotion	λ_3	1.125	.127
Fringe benefits	λ_4	.796	.120
Hours of work	λ_5	.948	.133
Intrinsic factor			
Tasks	λ_6	.889	.086
Interesting	λ_7	1.266	.096
Skills	λ_8	1.152	.093
Challenge	λ_9	1.491	.092
Thetas			
Pay	θ_1	1.874	.177
Security	θ_2	1.784	.177
Promotion	θ_3	1.919	.242
Fringe benefits	θ_4	2.140	.219
Hours of work	θ_5	1.542	.269
Tasks	θ_6	1.240	.123
Interesting	θ_7	1.220	.140
Skills	θ_8	1.243	.135
Challenge	θ_9	.678	.125
Pay/fringe	θ_{10}	.420	.140
Fringe/interest	θ_{11}	.388	.119
Security/skills	θ_{12}	.268	.108

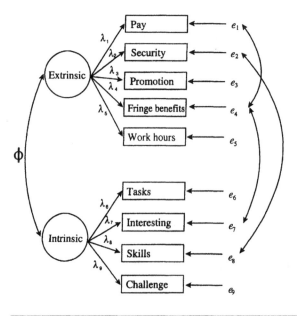

Figure 11.4. Structural model for two-dimensional job satisfaction scale with some correlated errors.

What makes up an adequate measure of goodness of fit is still debated in the statistical literature. Several authors have suggested differing goodness-of-fit indices, many of which can generate quite divergent results. This is a fast developing area of research, and the reader is well advised to keep a close eye on the literature, to refrain from relying too heavily upon any one indicator (especially if it is at odds with several others), and to incorporate a good dose of common sense and theoretical insight into the enterprise. Developing a good scale is as much art as science. Scales that fit "too well" pose both theoretical and statistical problems. An overfitted scale suggests that the information in the data is highly redundant and may lead to multicollinearity. Practically, this means that for a given factor, the operational items may not be tapping into the full domain of the concept.

Miscellaneous

The preceding analysis raises the question of what might be the outcome of changes to the structural model. As proposed, an orthogonal solution was assumed, where the Y indicators are related to one and only one latent factor. However, an oblique solution might also be proposed where one or more of the manifest variables are related to both the latent factors.

This model can be estimated by allowing the Y indicators to load on both factors while assuming independence among the error terms.[5] The model yields a χ^2 value of 36.7 with 19 degrees of freedom. The associated p-value is 0.0088, which would suggest that the model does not reproduce the empirical covariance matrix very well. This finding provides further evidence to lead us to accept the validity of our proposed model.

A further extension would be to incorporate more latent factors. Thus, for example, one might conceive of job satisfaction as having several domains, such as satisfaction with remuneration, the intrinsic tasks, the physical environment, and one's coworkers. Each of these latent factors could then be operationalized through several manifest variables. In this situation, we might wonder whether the latent factors are all part of the same general concept of *job satisfaction*. One way of answering this question is to conduct a higher order factor analysis in which each of the first-order factors is seen as an outcome of some more general second-order factor. Second-order factor analysis is discussed in detail in both Bollen (1989) and Jöreskog and Sörbom (1989). An interesting discussion is also to be found in an article by Beland and Maheux (1989).

VALIDITY

Chapter 6 outlined four basic types of validity: content validity, criterion validity, construct validity, and convergent/discriminant validity. At this stage in the art, content validity is not something that appears open to quantitative assessment. Researchers

---

5. To avoid identification problems, the paths between F_2 and *hours* and F_1 and *challenge* were set to 0.

have tried to quantify the remaining three types of validity in a way similar to how we quantify reliability. Validity, however, is something that seems easy to define but is difficult to operationalize.

Criterion validity

We generally define criterion validity as the correspondence between a measure and a "criterion" variable. The criterion is chosen because of its supposed a priori validity. It is, essentially, a perfect or near perfect measure of the thing that we want to measure. The criterion is the standard against which we gauge all other measures. Typically, the correlation between some measure, Y, and a criterion indicator, C, reflects validity. Through this reasoning, test theory has assessed criterion validity by the size of the correlation, $\rho_{Y,C}$. The implications of this relationship can be explored further by viewing criterion validity within a structural equation framework.

Figure 11.5 presents a path diagram for the conventional definition of criterion validity. By definition, we measure criterion validity through the correlation of an indicator with its latent variable. This correlation, $\rho_{Y,F}$, is represented by the parameter λ_1 in Figure 11.5. F is that which we wish to measure. In this instance, F is operationally signified by its criterion variable, C. If we assume that C is a perfect measure of F, then C is without error and the implied assumptions are that $\theta_2 = 0$ and $\lambda_2 = 1$.

Formally, we can define the correlation between the indicator and the latent variable as

$$\rho_{Y,C} = \frac{\lambda_{11}\lambda_{21}\varphi_{11}}{\sqrt{Var(Y)\,Var(C)}}$$

If we standardize the measures, then the numerator simplifies since $\varphi_{11} = 1$.

Unfortunately, C is rarely a perfect measure of F. Consequently, it is unusual for θ_2 to be zero for either concurrent or predictive instances. Assume, for example, that a criminologist wishes to assess the validity of self-reports of arrest by using police records as the criterion variable. Here, C would only be a perfect measure if all existing police records were available and accurate. Record keepers, however,

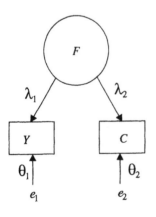

Figure 11.5. Path diagram of construct validity.

have been known to accidentally destroy, lose, or misplace records. Furthermore, the person being surveyed may have been arrested in a different jurisdiction. We usually have no way of knowing whether the error is large or small in these situations.

An instance of predictive validity is using LSATs as a predictor of future success in law school or, even later, in the legal profession. The student's grade point average (GPA) might show success in law school. Nevertheless, this assumes that GPA is a perfect measure of performance. Few instructors are infallible in their grading—even in law school.

Once we acknowledge measurement error in C, it is difficult to decide whether the attenuation in the correlation between Y and C is due to the error in Y or the error in C. Consequently, the theoretical validity of Y, which is defined by the correlation between Y and F, is influenced both by the error in Y and the error in C. Furthermore, substituting different C_is might result in vastly different estimates of $\rho_{Y,C}$. This is obvious if the law school example is revisited. A researcher may wish to validate the LSAT predictively by using career success. The choice of an indicator for "career success," however, is not at all obvious. We could choose any number of indicators from future earnings to number of cases won (for litigators). Undoubtedly, each of these would result in quite different estimates of $\rho_{Y,C}$.

Construct validity

Researchers define construct validity as the correlation between two underlying constructs or factors. For example, they might define IQ as scores on a written test (F_1) or performance on particular tasks (F_2). Construct validity is an attempt to deal with the problem of not having a valid criterion, C, that can be used as a standard against which to compare some measure, Y. A path diagram illustrating construct validity is presented in Figure 11.6.

Conceptually, the correlation between F_1 and F_2 defines construct validity (i.e., $\rho_{F1,F2}$). Operationally, however, we observe the correlation between the indicators Y_1 and Y_2. If we make the assumption that the expected value of the error terms is zero, and that the errors are uncorrelated, then the relationship between the indicator correlation and the factor correlation is given by

$$\rho_{Y_1 Y_2} = \sqrt{(\rho_{Y_1 Y_1} \rho_{Y_2 Y_2})} \rho_{F_1 F_2}$$

$$\therefore \rho_{F_1 F_2} = \frac{\rho_{Y_1 Y_2}}{\sqrt{(\rho_{Y_1 Y_1} \rho_{Y_2 Y_2})}}$$

As with estimating criterion validity, estimating construct validity is fraught with several difficulties. From the definition of ρ_{F_1,F_2} we can see that the reliabilities of the Y-indicators determine the estimation of the construct correlation as well the correlation between the Y-indicators. Looking at this from another point of view, ρ_{Y_1,Y_2} depends on both the construct validity and the reliabilities of the individual indicators. Unreliable indicators will serve to attenuate the validity coefficient. The estimate of validity will also be biased if the error terms, e_1 and e_2, are correlated, or if another latent variable, F_3, influences the indicators. Further difficulties arise when a particular indicator, say Y_1, depends on more than one latent factor.

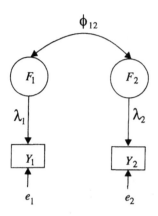

Figure 11.6. Path diagram for construct validity.

Bollen's view

Kenneth Bollen has proposed an alternate view of validity that gets around some limitations of classical definitions of validity. Bollen defines validity as the size of the direct structural relation between an indicator and its corresponding latent factor. At first, this definition appears similar to that for criterion validity. It goes beyond that definition, however, by incorporating the theoretical concept of the latent factor. Classical test theory defines construct validity solely in empirical terms through the correlation $\rho_{Y,C}$. Bollen's definition allows for a more generalized view of the problem. Assume, for a moment, a single latent factor with two indicators. The two indicators can be linked definitionally to the factor through the linear equations[6]

$$Y_1 = \lambda_1 F_1 + e_1$$
$$Y_2 = \lambda_2 F_2 + e_2$$

Within Bollen's definition, the coefficients λ_1 and λ_2 are validity coefficients. The rationale (which does have intuitive appeal) is that λ forms a direct structural link between Y and F. The parameter λ_1, for example, indicates how many units change in Y_1 there will be for every unit change in F_1. We can see the further advantages of this conceptualization in situations where Y_i depends on more than one latent factor. For example, consider the equation

$$Y_1 = \lambda_1 F_1 + \lambda_2 F_2 + e_1$$

with the previous assumptions holding. Classical test theory assumed that y is related to only one factor—a situation that is comparatively rare in the social sciences. By viewing the λs as validity coefficients, we can gauge the impact of each F_i component on a given indicator.

---

6. Assuming, for the moment, that the expected error terms are uncorrelated with the latent factors.

Another advantage of this perspective is that we can choose to use either raw (unstandardized) or standardized estimates of λ. Since the λs are analogous to the b-values found in ordinary regression, the advantages and disadvantages of using standardized and unstandardized b-parameter estimates also hold in this situation. Where units of measurement are arbitrary (as often happens in the social sciences), the use of standardized λs offers the advantage of being able to make *relative* comparisons across Y–F relationships.

Perhaps the most serious limitation of using λ as a validity coefficient parallels the limitation of using b-values as the indicator of the relationship between a dependent and an independent variable. Specifically, neither λs nor b-values show the *strength* of the relationship between the two items they link.

Bollen addresses this issue by suggesting an estimate of the *unique validity variance*, $U_{Y_i F_j}$. That is, the variance in Y that is uniquely attributable to F, $U_{Y_i F_j}$, is

$$U_{Y_i F_j} = R_{Y_i}^2 - R_{Y_i F_j}^2$$

where $R_{Y_i}^2$ is the proportion of variance in Y explained by all factors in the model that have a direct effect on Y_i (excluding the error terms), and $R_{Y_i F_j}^2$ is the proportion of variance in y_i explained by all factors except F_j. In statistics, we often call U the *part* or *semipartial* correlation.

Bollen's reconceptualization of validity does not provide a definitive answer to the estimation of validity. It does serve, however, to open the classical view of validity to a broader appreciation of how we can understand validity.

STRUCTURAL EQUATION MODELS: GENERALIZING THE MODEL

Clearly the latent variable approach helps solve many difficulties surrounding the issue of measurement. Given this advantage, we might question whether generalizing the latent variable approach to the broader class of causal models is possible. The answer is that not only is this generalization possible, it has proven useful in solving many substantive and statistical problems.

Consider the simple model of Figure 11.7 in which some latent factor $F_1^{(Y)}$ is assumed to be the function of two other latent factors, $F_1^{(X)}$ and $F_2^{(X)}$. Each of these latent factors is measured by three indicators. Graphically, we may depict the model as consisting of two components: a *structural model*, which defines how the latent factors are related to one another, and a *measurement model*, which defines how the factors are measured or operationalized. In the structural model, the latent factors, F, are related through a series of parameters, γ_i. The error terms associated with the latent factors are identified as u_i. In the measurement model, the observed Xs and Ys are linked to the latent factors by the lambda parameters as showed earlier. The errors in the observed Xs and Ys are denoted as e_i.

Let us look at the structural model in more detail, since that is the manner in which our substantive hypotheses are generally specified. Formally, we have

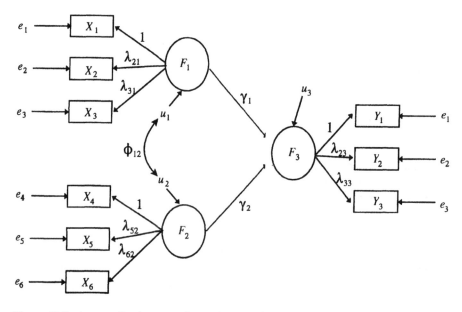

Figure 11.7. A generalized structural equation model.

$$F_1^{(Y)} = \gamma_1 F_1^{(X)} + \gamma_2 F_2^{(X)} + u$$

As in the preceding section, a measurement equation for each of the latent factors may be identified as follows. First, for the dependent factor, $F_1^{(Y)}$:

$$Y_1 = F_1^{(Y)} + e_1^{(Y)}$$
$$Y_2 = \lambda_{21}^{(Y)} F_1^{(Y)} + e_2^{(Y)}$$
$$Y_3 = \lambda_{31}^{(Y)} F_1^{(Y)} + e_3^{(Y)}$$

Second, for the independent factors, $F_1^{(X)}$ and $F_2^{(X)}$:

$$X_1 = F_1^{(X)} + e_1^{(X)}$$
$$X_2 = \lambda_{21}^{(X)} F_1^{(X)} + e_2^{(X)}$$
$$X_3 = \lambda_{31}^{(X)} F_1^{(X)} + e_3^{(X)}$$
$$X_4 = F_2^{(X)} + e_4^{(X)}$$
$$X_5 = \lambda_{52}^{(X)} F_2^{(X)} + e_5^{(X)}$$
$$X_6 = \lambda_{62}^{(X)} F_2^{(X)} + e_6^{(X)}$$

in matrix terms, this may be rewritten as $\mathbf{X} = \lambda \mathbf{F} + \mathbf{e}$, which expands into

$$
\begin{pmatrix} X_1 \\ X_2 \\ X_3 \\ X_4 \\ X_5 \\ X_6 \end{pmatrix} = \begin{pmatrix} 1 & 0 \\ \lambda_{21}^{(X)} & 0 \\ \lambda_{31}^{(X)} & 0 \\ 0 & 1 \\ 0 & \lambda_{52}^{(X)} \\ 0 & \lambda_{62}^{(X)} \end{pmatrix} \begin{pmatrix} F_1^{(X)} \\ F_2^{(X)} \end{pmatrix} + \begin{pmatrix} e_1^{(X)} \\ e_2^{(X)} \\ e_3^{(X)} \\ e_4^{(X)} \\ e_5^{(X)} \\ e_6^{(X)} \end{pmatrix}
$$

Assumptions

As with most multivariate analyses, several assumptions are made to render inferences based on the analysis valid. Specifically, these are:

- The error terms associated with the latent dependent factors and the latent independent factors are assumed to be independent.

- The error terms, $e_i^{(Y)}$, are assumed to be independent of the latent dependent factor(s).

- The error terms, $e_i^{(X)}$, are assumed to be independent of the latent independent factor(s).

- Both the $e_i^{(Y)}$ and the $e_i^{(X)}$ are assumed to be independent of each other.

- No part of the model is underidentified.

- The error terms are multivariate normal in their distribution.

The first four assumptions are consistent with those made when we use classical regression analysis. The fifth assumption—the issue of identification—is the subject of the next section. The sixth assumption, regarding the error terms, is a strong requirement needed if the standard chi-squared test is used to assess the goodness of fit of the overall model. This assumption can be waived if different goodness-of-fit criteria are to be employed, but again, more on that later.

Identification

Most readers will be familiar with the identification problem from classical regression procedures. Classical regression requires more observations than estimable parameters. Without this restriction, no unique solution to the normal equations exists and the $\mathbf{X'X}$ matrix is singular. Another way of viewing this issue is to perceive it as a degrees of freedom problem. Models with more observations than parameters to be estimated have positive degrees of freedom; models with equal numbers of observations and parameters have zero degrees of freedom; and models fewer observations than parameters may be considered to have "negative" degrees of freedom.

Analogously, the identification problem occurs in structural equation models. Instead of relating the number of parameters to be estimated to the number of observations, however, we are concerned about the relationship between the number of estimable parameters and the number of elements in the variance–covariance matrix. Where there is more information in the variance–covariance matrix than is required to estimate the parameters (i.e., we have positive degrees of freedom), the model is considered to be *overidentified*. Models in which there is just enough information in the variance–covariance matrix to estimate the parameters (i.e., zero degrees of freedom) are known as *just-identified* or *saturated* models. Models having too many parameters in relation to the amount of information in the variance–covariance matrix (i.e., "negative" degrees of freedom) are known as *underidentified* models.

The identification problem is one of the thorniest in structural equation modeling, since it may appear in only one part of the model. That is, identification is an issue in the structural components of the model as well the error components of the model. Further, the issue may be relieved in some instances by constraining some parameters to fixed values (typically 0 or 1) or by equating two or more parameters. Because of the complexity of the issue, we will not pursue it in any detail here. Any serious student of structural equation modeling would do well to read the appropriate sections in Bollen (1989: 238–46). Fortunately, the better quality statistical software on the market will identify *most* situations in which identification is a problem. This is not always the case, however, and the researcher should be wary, especially when dealing with complex models.

Goodness of Fit

Once the parameters of a model have been estimated, it is necessary to assess how well the model fits the data. As with determining the adequacy of a scale, this procedure is known as assessing the goodness of fit of the model and usually involves three steps. First, there is the issue of overall fit. That is, how well does the overall model fit the data? This assessment involves two considerations—an assessment of overall statistical significance and an assessment of the size of the fit. The latter component is similar to the practice of looking at the R^2 values in general linear model analyses. Second, there is the issue of evaluating residuals to detect outliers between the empirical and the reproduced or estimated covariance matrices. Third, there is the issue of assessing the significance of individual parameters within the model, especially the parameter estimates of the structural components. It is now worth examining each of these issues in greater detail.

Overall Goodness of Fit

As indicated, the strategy for tests of significance in structural equation modeling differs from that normally employed in statistics. Usually, the objective of the analysis is to reject $H_0 : \mu_1 = \mu_2$ or $\sigma_1 = \sigma_2$; however, the consideration here is to be able to reproduce the observed correlation or covariance matrix with an expected or generated matrix that is as close to the original as possible. Therefore, our interest is in *not* rejecting the null hypothesis.

Essentially, the null hypothesis, H_0, is that $\mathbf{S} = \hat{\mathbf{\Sigma}}(\boldsymbol{\theta})$, where $\mathbf{S}$ is the observed covariance matrix and $\hat{\mathbf{\Sigma}}(\boldsymbol{\theta})$ is the covariance matrix reproduced by the specified model. The closer these two matrices are in terms of some Euclidean distance, the closer the model would appear to fit the data. The most common test for assessing the distance between the two matrices is the likelihood ratio chi-squared test, which is:

$$-2\log\left(\frac{L_1}{L_0}\right) = -2\log L_0 + 2\log L_1$$

Here, L_0 is the log of the likelihood function for the generated matrix, $\hat{\mathbf{\Sigma}}$; L_1 is the log of the likelihood function for an alternate. In this instance, we will use the value for which the log of the likelihood function is at its maximum. Thus, L_0 and L_1 may be defined as follows:

$$\log L_0 = -\frac{N-1}{2}\left[\log|\hat{\mathbf{\Sigma}}| + \text{tr}(\hat{\mathbf{\Sigma}}^{-1}\mathbf{S})\right]$$

$$\log L_1 = -\frac{N-1}{2}\left[\log|\mathbf{S}| + \text{tr}(\mathbf{S}^{-1}\mathbf{S})\right]$$

where tr is the trace of the corresponding matrices. The estimated likelihood ratio chi-squared is then compared with some critical value of χ^2 with $N-1$ degrees of freedom.

Given that we are essentially turning H_0 on its head, the implications for Type I and Type II errors need to be explored. Remember that the power of a test is essentially the likelihood of rejecting H_0 when it is false. Tests with low power have a greater probability of *not* rejecting H_0; thus, one would prefer to avoid low power tests. Again, all things being equal, smaller sample sizes have lower power than large samples and consequently a greater likelihood of not rejecting H_0. That is, by using a small sample size, we have a better chance of getting a good fit to the data. This goes against the basic philosophy of pure research, where one normally attempts to stack the cards against the working hypothesis. Typically, then, we would seek to increase the sample size to reduce the power of the test much in the same manner as we would normally set relatively small alpha levels.

Other Goodness-of-Fit Indices

Several other indices have been developed to assess the relative fit of a hypothesized model to the observed covariance matrix. Two of the more commonly used are known as GFI and AGFI—the *goodness-of-fit index* and the *adjusted goodness-of-fit index*. The actual formula for both is determined by the particular estimation procedure used to generate the model parameters. Since most solutions use maximum likelihood procedures, we will focus on GFI_{ml} and AGFI_{ml} (see Bollen, 1989: 276–81 for a detailed discussion). Both GFI_{ml} and AGFI_{ml} provide an indication of the covariance in $\mathbf{S}$ accounted for by $\mathbf{\Sigma}$. Perfect fit, as suggested by a fitness index of 1, is achieved when $\mathbf{\Sigma} = \mathbf{S}$. The theoretical minimum is 0, but small negative values can be generated under some extreme situations.

Formally, GFI_{ml} is defined as follows:

$$GFI_{ml} = 1 - \frac{tr\left[\left(\hat{\Sigma}^{-1}S - I\right)^2\right]}{tr\left[\left(\hat{\Sigma}^{-1}S\right)^2\right]}$$

where tr signifies the trace of the matrix. Adjusting for the degrees of freedom in the model, we obtain $AGFI_{ml}$:

$$AGFI_{ml} = 1 - \left[\frac{q(q+1)}{2\ df}\right][1 - GFI_{ml}]$$

According to Bollen, however, this adjustment is biased toward simpler models with fewer degrees of freedom, resulting in higher index values for those models.

Residuals

A more informative diagnostic tool in structural equation modeling is a close examination of the residuals. Raw or 'fitted' residuals are obtainable by taking the difference between the observed covariance matrix and the generated or estimated covariance matrix under the hypothesized model. Thus, the residuals are simply $S - \hat{\Sigma}$. As with OLS residuals, large absolute values suggest a poor fit while small absolute values suggest a good fit. Since what defines large and small is often determined by the underlying metric of the measures on which the covariance matrix is based, it is usual practice to estimate standardized residuals.

Again, in nonmatrix notation, the standardized residuals are estimated as follows:

$$\frac{s_{ij} - \hat{\sigma}_{ij}}{\sqrt{(\hat{\sigma}_{ii}\hat{\sigma}_{jj} + \hat{\sigma}_{ij}^2)/N}}$$

Depending upon the sample size, these standardized residuals may be interpreted as t- or z-values. Large standardized residuals (say above 3) would normally suggest that a significant improvement might be obtained by including a parameter associated with that residual. This decision should not be taken automatically, however, since the reasonableness of including extra parameters should be judged in light of the theoretical model underlying the research. Clearly, with enough parameters included in the model, anything can provide a good fit to the observed data. Whether the model makes sense is another issue.

Usually, greater concern is shown for adding structural parameters as opposed to parameters associated with the measurement model. Measurement model failures are often situation specific, and reasonable familiarity with how the data were collected can often suggest why the initially hypothesized measurement model was less than adequate. Inadequacies at the level of the structural model, however, call into question the validity of our substantive theory. "Tinkering" with the structural model should not be taken lightly, since the incorporation of an extra parameter to deal with a large residual can hinder our ability to foresee the consequences for the overall model. Most structural equation models are complex multivariate

■ Box 11.1

A SUMMARY OF STEPS INVOLVED IN
STRUCTURAL EQUATION MODELING

1. Specify the model—this involves two steps. First, specifying the structural model. Second, specifying the measurement model.

2. Examine the raw data for outliers and other abnormalities.

3. Estimate the model parameters.

4. Generate the fitted or expected values.

5. Examine the global measures of goodness of fit.

6. Examine the residuals for outliers and nonnormality.

7. Consider whether minor modifications to the model are required (e.g., inclusion of parameters for correlated error terms). If minor changes to the model seem appropriate, return to step 3.

8. Interpret appropriate results. That is, does the overall model disconfirm the overall null hypothesis? Are the parameters for the structural paths statistically significant? Are individual indicators sufficiently reliable? Do the overall results for both the structural and measurement components of the model make theoretical sense?

9. Confirm results on other samples.

entities, and multivariate consequences are often difficult to grasp until the model is reestimated.

The usual steps followed in constructing a structural equation model are outlined in Box 11.1.

EXAMPLE: IMMUNIZATION PROGRAMS, WOMEN'S EDUCATION, AND SURVIVORSHIP

As an elementary example of how structural equation modeling can be applied, we have chosen to look at the issue of survivorship in Africa. The specific substantive question we want to answer is whether immunization programs have a greater impact on survivorship than the overall level of female education. The data were obtained from the World Bank database for the year 1990. Occasionally, where data were not available for 1990, information from 1989 was substituted. Data on all indicators were available for 42 countries.

The latent dependent variable is identified as survivorship, and the two independent variables are extent of immunization and extent of women's education.

Survivorship

Life expectancy at birth (in years) 1990
Infant mortality (per 1000) 1990
Children under 5 mortality (per 1000) 1990

Immunization

Immunized against tuberculosis (% under age 1 immunized) 1989
Immunized against measles (% under age 1 immunized) 1989
Immunized against polio (% under age 1 immunized) 1989

Women's Education

Adult female illiteracy (% of women aged 15+) 1990
Primary school enrollment ratio (%) 1990
Secondary school enrollment ratio (%) 1990

A variance–covariance matrix for these indicators is presented in Table 11.7, and Figure 11.8 gives the path diagram and estimates of the model parameters.

Estimating the model diagrammed in Figure 11.8, we obtain a χ^2 value of 34.68 with 24 df. As for other goodness-of-fit indices, we obtain a GFI_{ml} of .86 and an $AGFI_{ml}$ of .74. Taken together, these measures suggest a marginal fit to the observed covariance matrix. All the paths between the latent and manifest variables are statistically significant (as indicated by the z-values). Thus, the three scales appear to be sound. It is of major substantive concern, however, that *the path between the female education factor and the survival factor is in the right direction (negative)*

Table 11.7. Covariance matrix for World Bank data

INDICATOR[a]	(1)	(2)	(3)	(4)	(5)	(6)	(7)	(8)	(9)
LIFEEXP	58.19								
IMR	−232.18	1180.68							
UNDER5	−419.19	1957.45	3462.58						
IMTB	67.16	−326.09	−531.67	446.13					
IMPOLIO	125.96	−588.42	−992.77	354.75	592.22				
IMMEASL	73.03	−336.51	−553.65	300.79	415.23	399.28			
ILLFEM	−81.17	337.29	656.72	−134.31	−201.07	−97.86	303.85		
RIMSCH	153.96	−672.31	1157.23	202.86	400.79	215.38	−352.32	733.44	
ECSCH	100.46	−401.38	−697.03	103.39	247.73	139.27	−157.86	314.92	307.96

[a]LIFEXP, life expectancy at birth; IMR, infant mortality rate; UNDER5, mortality rate for children under 5; IMTB, IMPOLIO, IMMEASL, immunization against tuberculosis, polio, and measles; ILLFEM, adult female illiteracy; RIMSCH, ECSCH, ratio of enrollment in primary, secondary school. See text for details.

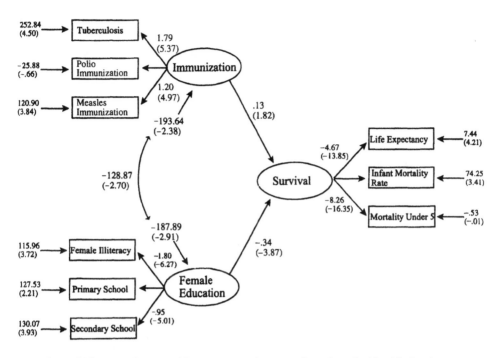

Figure 11.8. Path diagram with parameter estimates and z-values for identified paths (survivorship example).

and statistically significant ($z = -3.87$). This implies that as women's education increases, child mortality decreases. The path between the immunization factor and survival is not statistically significant, however. This suggests that female education is more important than immunization as a determinant of survivorship.

An examination of the standardized residuals and modification indices, however, indicates that some error terms may not be independent. By introducing parameters to allow for correlated errors between the error terms for tuberculosis and polio immunization, and tuberculosis and measles immunization, a χ^2 value of 24.73 with 22 df is obtained. This represents a decrease of about 10 for a loss of only 2 df. This change is reflected in the other goodness of fit indices, where GFI_{ml} becomes .90 and $AGFI_{ml}$ becomes .80.

CONCLUSION

Structural equation modeling is a powerful and flexible technique for addressing both structural and measurement models. In that sense, it is more useful than classical path analysis, which assumes that the independent variables are measured without error (see Box 10.1). Yet despite many advantages over more elementary statistical techniques, structural equation modeling is not without its limitations.

Structural equation models are not easy to construct. As the model becomes more complex and the number of possible links between variables and factors increases, so do the number of estimable parameters. Successful modeling usually requires a firm theory foundation.

This technique is also data intensive. Unfortunately, many existing data sources do not have multiple indicators on key variables. Given the current state of the art, structural equation models are also limited in their ability to specify the functional form between factors. For example, it is exceedingly difficult to define a simple quadratic relationship between two factors. Further, more work needs to be done to extend the framework to include qualitative or polytomous dependent variables.

Further Reading

Cuttance, P., and Ecob, R. *Structural Modeling by Example*. Cambridge: Cambridge University Press, 1987. A collection of articles by several authors dealing with both basic and advance issues relating to structural equation models. More accessible than the Bollen text, this book provides many examples, particularly in the field of education.
Hayduk, L.A. *LISREL Issues, Debates, and Strategies*. Baltimore: Johns Hopkins University Press, 1996. An intermediate level text that addresses special problems with structural equation modeling. Several excellent examples that deal with practical difficulties and solutions. Best for those who have a basic grasp of structural equation modeling.

Appendix: Examples of Program Listings

LISREL, version 8, Program for One-Factor Model

```
One factor example
DA NI=3 NO=250 MA=KM
LA
Firstv Secnd_v 'Third Va'
KM SY
1.0
.63 1.0
.57 .48 1.0
MO NX=3 NK=1
LK
Underly
VA 1.0 LX(1,1)
OU SE TV
```

Note: on the DAta statement, the MA=KM line implies that the data are in the form of a correlation matrix. MA=CM implies that the data are a covariance matrix.

LISREL Program for Two-Factor Model

Confirmatory Factor Analysis: Two-Factor Model

```
DA NI=9 NO=250 MA=CM
LA
Pay Security Promotn Fringe Hours Tasks Interest Skills Challng /
CM SY
data are entered here
MO NX=9 NK=2 LX=FU,FI PH=ST TD=SY,FI
LK
Extrinsic Intrinsic
FR LX 1 1 LX 2 1 LX 3 1 LX 4 1 LX 5 1 LX 6 2 LX 7 2 LX 8 2 LX 9 2
FR TD 1 1 TD 2 2 TD 3 3 TD 4 4 TD 5 5 TD 6 6 TD 7 7 TD 8 8 TD 9 9
OU SE TV MI
```

The LISREL example may be rewritten for SAS PROC CALIS as follows:

```
DATA JOBSAT(TYPE=COV);
TITLE "Two factor model of job satisfaction";
_TYPE_='COV'; INPUT _NAME_$ PAY SECURITY PROMOTN FRINGE
        HOURS TASKS INTEREST
SKILLS CHALLENG;
CARDS;
PAY 2.081 . . . . . . . .
SECURITY .566 2.187 . . . . . . .
PROMOTN .510 .784 3.186 . . . . . .
FRINGE .767 .523 .737 2.761 . . . . .
HOURS .444 .735 .921 .851 3.442 . . . .
TASKS .079 .431 .869 .641 .846 2.030 . . .
INTEREST .298 .373 1.106 1.142 .864 1.171 2.840 . .
SKILLS .319 .722 1.146 .732 .878 1.012 1.366 2.541 .
CHALLENG .432 .487 1.303 .908 .977 1.280 1.934 1.709 2.902
;
PROC CALIS ucov DATA=JOBSAT METHOD=LSML EDF=250 TECH=LM
pestim;
LINEQS
PAY = 1.0 F1 + E1,
SECURITY = LAM2 F1 + E2,
PROMOTN = LAM3 F1 + E3,
FRINGE = LAM4 F1 + E4,
HOURS = LAM5 F1 + E5,
TASKS = 1.0 F2 + E6,
INTEREST = LAM7 F2 + E7,
SKILLS = LAM8 F2 + E8,
```

```
CHALLENG = LAM9 F2 + E9;
STD
e1=err1,e2=err2,e3=err3,e4=err4,e5=err5,e6=err6,e7=err7,e8=err8,e9=err9,
F1=PHI11, F2=PHI22;
COV
F1 F2 = PHI12,
e1 e4 = th10,
e7 e4 = th11,
e2 e8 = th12,
e2 e1 = th13;
run;
```

12

Data Collection Methods
and Measurement Errors

The government are very keen on amassing statistics. They collect them, raise them to the nth power, take the cube root and prepare wonderful diagrams. But you must never forget that every one of these figures comes in the first instance from the village watchman, who just puts down what he damn pleases.

—Sir Josiah Stamp

A primary objective of research design is to minimize measurement error. Unfortunately, less than ideal and poorly implemented designs can exacerbate the measurement problem. Consider, for example, the issue of estimating rates of fertility within a given population. Ideally, one would like to be able to estimate the fertility rate for a cohort of women—say those born 30 years ago. This cannot be done, however, until the cohort has completed childbearing, which will be approximately 15 years from now. For this reason, demographers often estimate fertility trends based on cross-sectional data. The design still has problems, however, since one is left with a series of overlapping samples, each of which is right-censored. Not addressing the issue of censorship leads to biased results. The explicit recognition of this problem, however, has led to a series of statistical solutions that, while again less than ideal, produce reasonable results (Guillaume and Termote, 1978; Lee, 1980).

Examining the issue of estimating fertility in the third world, the Danish demographer Hans O. Hansen has noted that when women participants in a demographic and health survey are asked to list children ever born, the results appear to underestimate short survival times. That is, the number of children who survive for only a few hours or days are fewer than what we would expect, given our knowledge about human fertility patterns. An explanation for this discrepancy is not immediately obvious. Memory lapses may play some role; cognitive suppression of a tragic event may be another cause. Still, it is necessary for the measurement instrument to identify these cases of infant mortality. The recognition of the problem, therefore, can lead to design changes that allow for a much deeper probing into the number of children ever born. Thus, one might focus more attention on the issue of pregnancies and pregnancy outcomes rather than starting with births.[1]

---

1. The same problem is faced by historical demographers who use parish registers to estimate fertility patterns. Historically, unbaptized babies have had an ambiguous status within the Christian church and were generally not included in church registers. Hence, parish records tend to be records of souls rather than people.

The point that is being illustrated, by these examples, is that the error contained in any estimate is very much a function of design and instrumentation. In this chapter, we examine some of the more common methods of collecting survey data with a view to identifying their potential contributions to measurement error.

The focus of our discussion will be errors as they relate to survey designs. Generally, sociologists use one of four primary data collection procedures: interview techniques, mail surveys, diaries, and direct observation. Interview techniques, in turn, fall into two general categories: face-to-face interviews and telephone interviews. Telephone surveys have become the predominant mode of data collection throughout Europe, North America, and most economically developed nations, while face-to-face surveys still dominate in the rest of the world.

STRATEGIES

Telephone Interviews

Because of the high costs of face-to-face interviews and the wide coverage of telephones throughout most North American and European households, telephone interviews have become the predominant form of survey data collection in those regions. The utility of telephone interviewing has also increased with the development of sophisticated computer software that allows for the integration of random digit dialing and the immediate recording and verification of repondents' answers. These CATI (computer aided telephone interviewing) procedures also provide a fast means of producing standardized reports—often overnight. An extensive methodological literature is also appearing as CATI based research expands (Dillman, 1978; Groves et al., 1988).

Overall, telephone interviews offer many advantages over traditional interview techniques. As indicated, telephone interviews are usually less expensive than face-to-face interviews, since travel costs are eliminated. The incorporation of CATI procedures also reduces the need for double-coding (once on the interview schedule and once to convert the answers to electronic form), thus reducing labor costs and lowering the likelihood of coding error. Typically, telephone interviewing is highly centralized, with several interviewers working in a common location under the scrutiny of a supervisor. Thus, the supervisor is readily available to answer any questions that may arise during the interview (a refinement seldom found in field settings). Quality control is enhanced, as well, since supervisors can determine whether interviewers are asking all questions and recording the responses actually given by the interviewees. Through monitoring, supervisors can also determine that consistency is maintained across interviewers.

While most survey units do use the centralized model, the technique potentially offers a great deal of flexibility, and it is also possible that a cottage industry model could develop around interviews conducted from interviewers' homes, with the results uploaded to a central database at the end of each session.

Interviewees often prefer telephone interviews because they afford an increased level of anonymity with respect to both the interviewer and other household members. This feature may be important when particularly sensitive issues are being addressed.

A further advantage of telephone interviews is that the physical characteristics of the interviewer are unlikely to affect the interviewee's responses. Thus, some traditional concerns raised in face-to-face interviews concerning the effects of age, race, or general physical appearance on the rate and quality of response become moot.

On the other hand, some disadvantages are associated with this procedure. For example, visual aids cannot be used with telephone interviewees unless the materials are distributed in advance.[2] This can be a drawback, particularly when complex issues are being addressed or the interviewer wishes to give the respondent a large number of predetermined responses. In some types of market research, for example, it is desired to elicit the respondents' opinions of different products or types of packaging. Further, whereas face-to-face interviews allow interviewers to make assessments of an interviewee's behavior and physical surroundings, telephone interviews do not allow for this type of verification.

Another drawback of telephone interviews lies in the likelihood that any interviewer effects that might exist will be magnified, since interviewer productivity is often greater in telephone interviews than in face-to-face interviews (Groves and Magilavy, 1980; Groves, Magilavy, and Mathiowetz, 1981).

In recent years, the biggest threat to telephone surveys has been declining response rates. Part of this trend is due to the increasing number of surveys being conducted and a feeling of inundation and fatigue by many respondents. Another part is due to the unethical practices of some commercial interests, who falsely claim to be conducting disinterested survey research as a vehicle for targeting potential customers for their products. Furthermore, with growing numbers of crank and obscene phone calls, ever more subscribers are reverting to unlisted numbers. While this does not pose a problem for true random digit dialing, it does increase the costs associated with calling, since more noneligibles are reached.

Face-to-Face Interviews

Traditionally, the face-to-face interview has been the workhorse of survey research, and despite the steady encroachment of telephone interviewing, the face-to-face interview is still dominant in most parts of the world. Trewin and Lee note that as late as 1987, only 11 countries had telephone coverage rates over 90%; thus, relying totally upon telephone interviewing in most countries would likely result in substantial bias due to undercoverage (Trewin and Lee , 1988). While universally popular, face-to-face interviews are expensive to administer in economically developed nations and are fraught with many potential sources of measurement error. Still, some situations might justify the additional costs associated with face-to-face interviews. On-site interviewers can monitor respondents' body language and, by their presence, may encourage respondents to provide more, and more thorough responses. Some researchers believe that it is easier to build trust in a face-to-face situation, and thereby

---

2. Visual aids are sometimes distributed in advance, particularly by mail. This approach thus has the advantages and disadvantages associated with being able to set up an interview with the respondent beforehand. See Bradburn (1983).

obtain better quality responses, particularly to delicate issues, although this claim has not been proven empirically.

Clearly, the greatest benefit of face-to-face interviews is the far greater ease with which visual aids can be employed, when called for. As indicated in the discussion of telephone interviewing, on-site interviewers can verify such visually evident issues as lifestyle, approximate apparent value of the person's home, and the general social environment in which the interviewee resides.

The high costs associated with face-to-face interviews become evident when we compare them with telephone surveys. Not only is there the extra cost associated with transportation, but face-to-face interview schemes generally require more supervision, both for managing the interviewing and in providing oversight. While supervisors can easily monitor telephone interviews by listening in on an auxiliary headset, oversight in face-to-face interviewing generally involves a supervisor accompanying an interviewer or the use of some type of reinterview procedure. Furthermore, since interviewer productivity is generally lower in face-to-face interviews, more interviewers are usually hired, thus incurring higher interviewer training costs.

As Lyberg and Kasprzyk (1991: 241) note, however, whether dealing with telephone interviews or face-to-face interviews, "the most disturbing component of measurement error in both methods is the interviewer variance component." While the literature does suggest that interviewer bias is often overstressed, particularly among professional interviewers, apparently the personal style of the interviewer (body cues, recording techniques, etc.) and the general visual impression given by the interviewer can be problematic (DeLeeuw and Van der Zouwen, 1988). Although many interviewer characteristics have been explored in the literature, the overall conclusion is that most impacts are idiosyncratic as opposed to systematic (Kish, 1962; Bailey, Moore, and Bailar, 1978; Groves and Magilavy, 1986; U.S. Bureau of the Census, 1979). Furthermore, these problems usually can be overcome through proper training and supervision (Fowler and Mangione, 1990; Fowler, 1991); still, the visual anonymity of the telephone interview provides a more secure guarantee that such problems will be minimized.

Mail Surveys

The least expensive survey mode for addressing a wide target group is still the self-administered mail survey. Whether mail surveys will retain this relative cost advantage is questionable, however, as postal rates rise. Particularly with short questionnaires, the costs associated with printing questionnaires, packaging them in envelopes, mail-out and return postage, postage for follow-up reminders, and the transcribing of completed questionnaires quickly approach the costs associated with efficient telephone interviews. This convergence becomes a particular issue when response rates are considered.

Beyond cost, mail surveys offer other advantages as a vehicle for data collection. They allow for the distribution of visual aids. They also allow respondents the time and opportunity to consider the issues involved and to collect pertinent data. It is difficult for telephone and face-to-face survey takers to wait while respondents check their pantries for various products or poll other family members on daily expenses. Similarly, finding out how many indigenous clients a professional served in the last month might be an unacceptably time-consuming task for interviewer and interviewee alike. Furthermore, in mail surveys the issue of interviewer bias is mooted (Dillman, 1978).

Some evidence suggests that question ordering can have an impact on interviewees' responses under certain circumstances (Abramson, Silver, and Anderson, 1987). Even when the possibility for bias exists, however, response and question order effects are minimal for mail surveys in most cases; yet situations do arise in which the ordering of questions is very important (Ayidiya and McClendon, 1990).

Clearly, though, mail surveys have some flagrant limitations. They are far less flexible than telephone or face-to-face surveys, and it is very difficult to monitor respondents' understandings and interpretation of questions until the survey is virtually completed. Thus researchers must have a well-pretested schedule with the questions matched to the literacy skills and knowledge base of the target sample. It is likely for these reasons that mail surveys are often most successful with small, clearly defined samples (such as professionals), where the issues and jargon are salient. While interviewer bias may be eliminated, the interviewer's proxy—the cover letter—can have a significant impact on responses.

Generally, mail surveys have lower response rates than do interviews, although this does vary with the target sample. Broad-scale, nonspecific market surveys sent to "occupant" are often lucky to achieve response rates in the 5–15% range. On the other hand, tightly focused questionnaires sent to specific groups for whom the issues are particularly relevant can yield response rates over 80%. Lyberg and Kasprzyk, for example, note a report by DeLeeuw that in some instances mail surveys do marginally better with respect to measurement error than telephone and face-to-face interviews. The basic point is, however, that the lower the response rate (despite modality), the greater the opportunity for all types of nonreponse bias to affect the estimates, and mail surveys generally yield lower response rates than most other modes of data collection.

Diary Surveys

Diaries are a specialized form of record keeping that have become very popular in certain areas. Essentially, diaries are self-administered records in which one or more members of a household keep track of ongoing events, such as household expenditures (Neter, 1970; Pearl, 1979; Tucker and Bennett, 1988), television viewing, time use (Plewis, Creeser, and Mooney, 1990), or sexual behavior. Diaries are used to avoid problems associated with recall error when events take place regularly.

In some respects, diaries combine the attributes of interviews and mail surveys. Since they often deal with complex issues (such as timekeeping or expenditure breakdowns), it is generally necessary for interviewers to provide detailed instructions on the use of the survey instrument. Examples of completed diary entries are often left with the respondent, and the phone number of a contact person is provided, should further assistance be required. Because of the work required to maintain the diary, interviewers also must be sure that the respondents understand the merits of the project.

In reality, diary surveys are fraught with many problems, and a great deal of planning and advanced preparation is necessary to ensure any degree of success. A particularly good analysis of issues surrounding diaries is to be found in the review article by Silberstein and Scott (1991). Difficulties often start upon delivery. As Silberstein and Scott note, in one study where record keeping was supposed to start the day following the distribution of the diaries, 5% of the respondents started recording on the date of delivery. A few other respondents were several days late, and as time progressed, many respondents forgot to maintain their diaries regularly. Some events are omitted, and forgetting becomes a problem as respondents allow entries to pile up over a one- or two-day period. Patterns of reporting can also change both for the better (as respondents become more adept at using the instrument) and for the worse (as they become less diligent). Thus, entry reliability can be an issue, particularly over extended periods. Furthermore, the fact that the data are being recorded "in real time" can influence the respondents' behavior. For example, smokers may come to realize how much they spend on cigarettes; parents may be surprised to learn how much time their children spend watching televised cartoon shows and consequently, change their heretofore normal behavior. Problems may also arise when respondents truly do not understand how the diary should be maintained yet fail to report their difficulties to an interviewer or supervisor.

A further difficulty with some diary studies arises because of the intended or unintended use of proxy reporting. Proxy reporting refers to the reporting of a respondent's behavior by another person, usually a family member. This may be intentional, as in U.S. consumer expenditure surveys, where one person in a household is nominated as the record keeper, or unintentional, as in U.K. expenditure surveys, which use separate diaries for different family members, a practice almost inviting errors of inadvertency. All the problems associated with individuals keeping their own diaries are magnified in proxy reporting, where one person is expected to monitor the behavior of another.

The major drawback of diary use is the requirement for active, ongoing participation by the respondent. Because respondents often lose interest in a project, diary reporting periods are typically short: from 1 to 14 days. Kemsley et al. (1980) note that a 14 day period is generally optimal for most diary-based research. Still, the problem of attentiveness is pervasive. Commenting on the 1987 U.S. Consumer Expenditure Survey, Silberstein and Scott (1991: 325) write:

> Declines in reporting after the first diary day and in the second diary week are found to be sizable. Estimates derived from diaries completed solely by respondents show that the first day of the week exhibits means 35% greater than means for the combined two weeks.

They further go on to note that "These effects have been noted in other expenditure diary surveys . . ."

A final difficulty associated with diaries involves the problem of *allocation*. In expenditure surveys, for example, it may be necessary to decide to which of a group of categories an item belongs. Communal products (e.g., soap) may also require allocation among users. Problems of allocation should not be seen as unique to expenditure surveys, however, since they can arise regarding any behavior or attribute a diary is designed to record. These allocation judgments by the respondents may lead to bias depending upon how the allocation is conducted.

Direct Observation

Direct observation is the least common form of data collection, largely because it is inordinately expensive. In the traditional, and most costly form, direct observation involves waiting for events to happen rather than relying upon other people's accounts. Perhaps the last significant vestiges of direct observers are to be found in the anthropological community, where researchers still engage in significant amounts of participant observation, or "qualitative" research. Some social psychologists also use unobtrusive direct observation (such as one-way mirrors) to study certain types of behavior—such as children playing in a day care center. The primary advantage of direct observation lies in the supposed reduction of bias. Instead of having the dual perceptual filter of a researcher interpreting a respondent's interpretation of an event, we simply have the single filter of the researcher's interpretation of the event.

To avoid the cost issue, some researchers look to technological solutions. Thus, for example, many market researchers have resorted to electronic monitors or "black boxes" to provide continuous records of television use, instead of relying upon diaries. Most readers are probably familiar with roadside monitoring devices used to count vehicles in traffic flow and, increasingly, electronic scanners are used to keep track of everything from supermarket purchases to commuter patterns. Photoreconnaissance cameras can be used in stores, not only to record acts of theft, but also to monitor the movements of patrons. On the street, similar video devices are used to record traffic accidents, monitor compliance with seat belt laws, and identify speeders.

At a macro level, satellite surveillance can be used to identify changes in settlement patterns and pollution problems, or to monitor natural resource use and agricultural output. With recent developments in pattern recognition software, it is likely that such technologies will gain greater favor as it becomes possible to code and analyze immense volumes of information automatically. Suffice it to say that automated data collection is still in its infancy.

While these technologies initially have a high level of intuitive appeal, they have unique drawbacks. Donmyer, Piotrowski, and Wolter (1991), for example, provide a very interesting analysis of some problems surrounding the use of scanners to monitor grocery sales.

At its best, direct observation through on-site recording results in the accurate, unobtrusive, and continuous collection of data. At its worse, we are left with a single surveyor who simply records selected personal perceptions ad nauseam. And, of course, the more paranoid among us see such developments as yet another step toward the privacy-invading, Big Brother world of George Orwell.

Multimode Procedures

Increasingly, for large-scale surveys, researchers are resorting to multimode or mixed-mode surveys. These procedures involve the combining of two or more single-mode procedures in an attempt to reduce costs, minimize error, and increase response rates. Ideally, multimode procedures allow us to take advantage of the best parts of different modes while sidestepping or mitigating their weaknesses.

It makes sense, for example, to combine a prescreening telephone interview with in-depth, in-person interviews and then to leave a diary or send out a mail survey as a follow-up. By matching the technique to the particular data requirements, we ought to be able to combat memory effects and interviewer biases.

Unfortunately, while multimode approaches sound reasonable at first, they do have their limitations. They are obviously more costly to conduct than single-mode studies. Duplicate instruments need to be created, different sampling frames may need to be constructed, and it may be necessary either to hire additional staff or to retrain existing staff in different data collection procedures. Clearly the cost of administration is increased, and many survey organizations find themselves choosing between developing new expertise and subcontracting to other agencies.

Multimode approaches may also create analysis problems. The use of more than one mode may introduce mode-specific errors that may be difficult to estimate. Matching problems may arise if different modes are used to collect the same information from different respondents. The same problems we face with reinterviews arise here also. For example, if differences arise in parameter estimates according to mode, how do we decide which is the most accurate?

As with all approaches, multimode procedures will solve some problems and create others.

Conclusions

One obvious question we might raise is whether any one form of data collection is *inherently* superior to the others. As Lyberg and Kasprzyk (1991: 239) note in their review of data collection modalities, little evidence exists to date to suggest that one mode is a priori superior to another:

> In general, the literature on mode comparisons has not shown large differences in estimates between modes. This may just mean, however, that the sum of measurement errors associated with one mode is similar to that of the other mode. The common situation is that the choice of mode depends on a number of factors . . . where measurement error is just one. Given a mode with its specific set of design parameters, we may identify factors affecting measurement errors and in some cases estimate these errors. The issue of mode and measurement errors then is more concerned with errors associated with each mode and how they can be corrected or eliminated rather than with a choice between alternative modes.

Thus, the decision about which mode of data collection is most appropriate for a given project is usually exogenous to the issue of measurement error. The driving factors behind the selection process are the costs involved, the issue of timeliness, and concerns with response rates. Once the decision regarding collection modality has been made, however, it is imperative to maximize the quality of the data collected within the chosen framework.

REDUCING INTERVIEW ERRORS: INTERVIEWERS

Reducing Interviewer Errors

In most survey research, the interview is critical; it is here, as the common saying goes, that the rubber meets the road. Assuming the availability of a well-developed and pretested instrument, the primary concern for most researchers is that the interviewers do their jobs to the best of their abilities. Depending upon the study design, interviewers are in a uniquely powerful position to influence the quality of the data collected. Often, they are the ones who are responsible for contacting and enlisting the cooperation of respondents. They present the questions, record the answers, and largely control the interview environment. As the representatives of the project, they are the people who convey to respondents the objectives of the study and the meanings of the questions. Competent, well-trained interviewers can motivate interviewees to provide complete and accurate responses; incompetent and demoralized interviewers, on the other hand, not only may lead to the generation of vacuous data, but can poison the atmosphere to such a degree that interviewees will actively campaign against the research by writing letters of complaint to newspapers and regulatory agencies. A single bad experience can leave people with an extremely negative view of social research and spoil their value as participants for future research.[3]

Reinterview Procedures

Several procedures have been developed in an attempt both to reduce the impact of interviewer error and to obtain a better estimate of the components of error variance in interview settings. A more commonly used procedure, especially for ongoing, large-scale surveys, is the *reinterview*. According to Gösta and Schreinger (1991), the basic reinterview method was developed in the United States and India in the 1940s. At present, reinterview procedures are commonly used by U.S. Bureau of the Census and by Statistics Canada for their large-scale recurring surveys and population censuses. The technique is also employed by many private research organizations.

As indicated, the major purposes for the reinterview are to evaluate fieldwork and to estimate the size of the error components in a survey. Regarding fieldwork, reinterviews are beneficial in identifying any interviewers who are falsifying their data, as well as any who misunderstand data collection procedures and require remedial training. When respondents are reinterviewed and a second measure is obtained, both sample response variance and response bias can be estimated.

---

3. On the other side of the coin, being involved in survey research soon makes one appreciate the wondrous diversity found within the human psyche. It is not uncommon for interviewers to report that some respondents use the experience as a therapy session to purge psychic demons or to assuage feelings of loneliness. Some individuals will rail at the very fact that they have been contacted and will write inflammatory letters to newspapers or make harassing and nuisance calls to the research office. Some of the more paranoid (or more perceptive?) will see your research as yet another instance of the great government/communist/fascist/whatever conspiracy to monitor and control their lives. As with all enterprises that deal with the general public, one must be prepared for any eventuality.

Once the decision to reinterview has been made, the researcher faces several important decisions. Should the same mode of data collection be used (e.g., another face-to-face interview), or should another mode be employed (e.g., follow up a face-to-face interview with a telephone call)? The use of cross-modalities has some advantages, including reduced cost (when switching from face-to-face interview interviews to telephone) and the ability to evaluate modalities. Unfortunately, when discrepant results occur under such circumstances, it is not always clear whether the mismatch is due to measurement error or modality effects.

Another decision that needs to be faced is the assignment of a reinterviewer. Should the initial interviewer, who has already established rapport with the respondent, do the second interview, or should it be someone else—another interviewer or a supervisor? Just as in the case of using cross-modalities in reinterviews, we must ask how we ought to attribute any estimated variance: Is it due to simple respondent variance, or variance within or across interviewers?

Finally, we have already alluded to the issue of handling discrepancies: Should the initial response be left as it is? Should it be replaced by the follow-up response? Or should some imputed value (such as the mean of the two responses) be used? Clearly, reconciliation is the biggest problem facing the researcher. It is not always clear which of varying or conflicting responses is correct. Yet, as Gösta and Schreinger (1991: 288) point out, even consistent responses do not always get the researcher out of the woods:

> The most obvious limitation of a reinterview program using reconciliations to measure validity is that a respondent may knowingly report false information. If he or she is consistent in the reporting of that information then there is no way in which the reinterview will yield "true" information. In a study of the quality of the CPS [Current Population Survey] reinterview data, [two researchers] concluded that up to 50 percent of the errors in the original interview are not detected in the reconciled interview.

The consistent reporting of false or misleading information clearly decreases with the time elapsed between the initial interview and the reinterview. With short intervals, a respondent's follow-up response is more likely to be conditioned on the initial interview. On the other hand, the longer the time between interviews, the more likely it is that the threats to internal validity outlined by Campbell (history, maturation, etc.) will come into play.

After reviewing the available literature, Gösta and Schreinger noted some major findings of reinterview research, namely, where interviewer problems occur, personnel with shorter service records are more likely to falsify data, and experienced interviewers often have "more sophisticated falsification patterns" than newer interviewers.

Interviewer Selection

Since the inception of survey research, researchers have wondered how interviewer characteristics affect responses, particularly in face-to-face situations. The primary concern has been with visual characteristics of the interviewer such as gender and race or ethnicity. Several older studies purport to find differences by gender (Hyman et al., 1954), race (Pettigrew, 1964; Williams, 1964), religion (D. Robinson and Rhode, 1946), or combinations of these factors. More recent studies, however, find almost no impact (Groves and Magilavy, 1986). A particular exception is reported by Schuman and Converse (1971), who noted that the interviewer's race affected interviewees' responses to racial questions.

Some of these findings may be tied to specific sociohistorical circumstances, to times and places in which issues of ethnicity, religion, or gender are salient. In summary, Fowler (1991: 273) concludes: "Most of the positive findings of interviewer demographic characteristics affecting answers tend to be consistent with the generalization that respondents tend to avoid answers that they believe will make the relationship to the interviewer uncomfortable." Since most questions do not fall into this category, the problem is likely not significant. Complicating this issue is the existence in many jurisdictions of antidiscrimination laws that forbid the selection of employees based on stigmatic characteristics. Thus, the systematic selection of interviewers to match interviewees might be problematic.

Overall, though, current research does give some solace insofar as it indicates that ascribed characteristics of interviewers are not very important. Most of the literature suggests that clear, objective questions are the least likely to be influenced by the interviewer's personal characteristics. Furthermore, well-trained, well-supervised, professional interviewers can elicit accurate responses, even in difficult circumstances (Weiss, 1968, 1970). Finally, as Fowler suggests, where interviewer characteristics might be a problem, attempting to estimate the error associated with interviewer demographics is probably better than trying to control it. Selecting the wrong control strategy may introduce bias where none existed in the first instance, or even make a bad situation worse.

Clearly the key to reducing interviewer effects is adequate training and supervision. Fowler and Mangione (1990) show that data quality depends on how well interviewers are trained. More training leads to higher levels of standardization in the asking and coding of questions, and fewer incomplete or nonresponses are incurred. With an appropriate mix of lectures, demonstrations, and supervised practice, all skills, and in particular probing skills, show significant improvement. How much training is optimal for interviewers has not been investigated in great detail; however, some research by Fowler and Mangione suggests that well-structured 2- to 5-day training sessions may be optimal. In one study they introduced an inordinately long (10-day) training session, and few marked skill improvements were noted.

Good training does not stop when the interviewer has completed the initiation procedure, however. Although much supervision is oriented to monitoring costs and productivity, ongoing feedback is an essential component in maintaining optimal interviewer performance. Monitoring interviewers in telephone surveys is relatively easy, since supervisors can listen in through auxiliary headsets. With face-to-face interviews, adequate supervision may require supervisors to accompany interviewers on occasion. Specific guidelines for monitoring and supervising interviewers are presented in the more specialized literature (Cannell and Okensberg, 1988; Fowler and Mangione, 1990).

Overall, Fowler (1991: 263) identifies five general strategies that research directors can use for reducing interviewer-related error. These are:

1. Give interviewers procedures to follow that will minimize the extent to which they will distinctively influence the answers that are given.
2. Attempt to control interviewer behavior through training and supervision.
3. Select interviewers least likely to affect answers.
4. Design questions that can be administered consistently.
5. Reduce the size of the interviewer assignment, which will reduce the impact of whatever error is generated by interviewers on the total error of the survey estimates.

Fowler further identifies what we might call the golden rules, which are given to almost all interviewers with the intent of teaching them how to be consistent.

1. Read the questions exactly as written.
2. In the event that a respondent fails to answer a question adequately in response to the initial reading, follow-up probes and questions should be nondirective.
3. Answers should be recorded without interviewer interpretation or editing.
4. Interviewers should maintain a professional, neutral relationship with the respondent, which minimizes any sense of evaluation of the content of the answers produced.

Perhaps surprisingly, given the importance of the matter, little systematic research exists on the impact of interviewer characteristics on response outcomes. Some empirical studies are available, but the results are often contradictory. What goes for expertise in the area is often as not based on intuition and conventional wisdom rather than systematic knowledge.

Estimating Interviewer Effects

How can we estimate interviewer effects? If interviews are assigned systematically (e.g., more experience interviewers are assigned to "more difficult" cases), the issue becomes extremely difficult to explore. Any differences we discover under these circumstances may be a consequence of the assignment procedure rather than interviewer bias. On the other hand, if interviews are assigned randomly, as happens with random digit dialing, the problem offers certain clear approaches. For any given item, it is possible to conduct a one-way ANOVA in which the different interviewers form the categorical variable and the item response is the outcome measure. This approach can be expanded to include many items; however, consideration must be given to two issues. First, if a series of one-way ANOVAs is conducted, the researcher should be aware that the nominal α-level will not be the actual α-level unless some correction is made. One might, for example, use the Bonferroni approach. Otherwise, for an α-level of .05 say, we could expect 1 out of every 20 items to produce significant results by chance alone.

Another tack one might try is to conduct a two-way ANOVA, with the interviewers as the column effects and the items as the row effects. A second issue arises here, however, since the row effects are not mutually independent. That is, the same respondents are represented in all the rows. This difficulty might be addressed by treating the problem analogously to other test–retest or nonindependence problems (Winer, 1971).

The use of ANOVA also assumes that the responses to the items are continuous. Analogous approaches can be used with categorical data by resorting to any number of contingency table or log-linear modeling techniques (Agresti, 1990).

When the item outcomes are continuous, the calculation of a correlation coefficient is often informative. The most commonly used, however, is the rho ($\hat{\rho}_{int}$) statistic attributable to Kish (1962; also see Groves, 1989). Formally, this statistic is defined as follows:

$$\hat{\rho}_{int} = \frac{\dfrac{V_a - V_b}{m}}{\dfrac{V_a - V_b}{m} + V_b}$$

where V_a is the between-groups mean square in a one-way ANOVA with interviewer as the column factor, V_b is the within-group mean square, and m is the total number of interviews conducted by interviewer. The values of $\hat{\rho}_{int}$ range from 0 to 1, with 0 meaning that answers to a particular question are unrelated to the interviewer. Values of $\hat{\rho}_{int}$ are unique to each item, hence are calculated for each item. The standard F-ratios alluded to above can be used to test for significance; however, the aforementioned caveats concerning the α-levels must be observed.

REDUCING INTERVIEWER ERROR: THE INSTRUMENT

Question Wording

As Fowler (1991: 14) says, the "key defining criterion for good measurement in surveys is 'standardization,' " and this is achieved through the selection, training, and supervision of interviewers.

Clearly, interviewers who are socially inept are a problem as are those who cheat in their data collection. On the other hand, problems may arise even with good interviewers. For example, several studies have shown that many interviewers do not read the questions exactly as they are written, even in telephone surveys (Cannell and Okensberg, 1988; Groves, 1989; Fowler and Mangione, 1990). Fowler and Mangione report that sometimes over 50% of the questions asked are reworded to some extent. The significance of these rewordings is an empirical question. In a series of experiments, Schuman and Presser (1981) show that occasionally, small changes in the wording of questions can have a profound impact on the responses obtained.

In reality, the researcher faces a conundrum over the issue of question rewording. On the one hand, the rewording of well-developed and well-tested questions can clearly introduce bias of the form discussed by Schuman and Presser. On the other hand, the fact that interviewers feel the need to reword questions might be an indication that the material is poorly formulated or poorly matched to the target sample. Some authors question whether having the same item wording for all respondents is best (Mishler, 1986; Suchman and Jordan, 1990). Their argument is that each situation is unique, and each respondent; therefore, some flexibility is called for. Ultimately, this argument is that the connotation of the items is more important that the specific denotation. While this position has some initial appeal, it still begs the issue of the degree to which there is commonality within the connotations. Perhaps the best solution is to identify the questions on which changes are made and discuss each such issue with the interviewers. If word changes are the result of interviewees consistently not understanding the question, a rewording of the question may be in order. If interviewers are rewording questions out of boredom or fancy, further training in the importance of consistency is likely to be required.

Clearly, total consistency will never be achieved, and interviewers will always have to use some discretion about how much rewording and supplemental information to give to a respondent to obtain a clear and accurate answer. To cover these eventualities, Converse (1987) recommends providing interviewers with a series of well-developed scripts.

Memory Effects

Groves (1989: 407–408) suggests that interviewees go through five stages of information processing that influence their responses to questions.

1. Encoding of information: that is, the process of observation or obtaining information
2. Comprehension: understanding the issue or phenomenon and making sense of it.
3. Retrieval or recall.
4. Judgment of appropriate answer: that is, matching information in memory to response requirement.
5. Communication: the judgment of the context in which answer given; an assessment about whether the answer socially desirable, and so on.

Unfortunately, as Bradburn and Sudman (1991: 34) note: "It is well known that respondents usually do not make strenuous efforts to search their memories completely. Rather, they do just enough memory search to arrive at some kind of estimate." This lack of motivation, combined with normal memory decay (legitimate forgetting), undoubtedly contributes to much of the error variance in survey results. Further systematic bias can be contributed through the phenomenon known as telescoping, where respondents underestimate how much time elapsed between the occurrence of an event and the present.

One major difficulty with assessing memory effects is the lack of "objective" data with which one can compare respondents' answers. Most of the laboratory research in cognitive psychology focuses on the ability of undergraduates to recall prepared material over a short time. Survey research on the matter is generally based on test–retest assessments. There are, however, some examples within the literature of survey responses that have been compared with external criteria. Poulain, Riandey, and Firdion (1991) compared the responses of participants in a Belgian life history survey to data in the national population registers. The study involved 445 middle-aged couples who were asked a series of questions relating to several family matters, including when they were born, when they were married, the birth dates of their children, when the children left home, and household movements (migrations). The spouses were first interviewed separately and then as a couple. In the joint interview, the couples were allowed to refer to any documentation they had that could resolve such discrepancies as might have appeared between their responses.

The results obtained by Poulain and his associates, summarized in Table 12.1, show a clear pattern. Dates relating to marriages and to births of children are quite accurate, whereas dates relating to children leaving home and household migration are far less accurate. It is also the case that in this instance the women were more accurate in their recollections than are the men, and that together, the couples were more accurate than are the spouses singly.

Other attempts to verify survey results have been reported in the literature. Clarke and Tift (1966), for example, cross-validated self-reported delinquent behavior with polygraph responses, and Erickson and Empey (1963) correlated self-reported delinquency with court records.

Several techniques can be employed to help reduce memory effects. Longer questions, for example, often provide cues that elicit higher response rates. Further, unlike open-ended questions, which place the entire burden of recall on the respondent, closed-end questions provide response categories that serve as cues.

In a review of interviewee response propensities, Groves notes that there is substantial social psychological evidence that recall is also related to the circumstances surrounding the initial observation or experience: "the quality of recall is a function of whether the schema evoked at the time of recall is the same as that used at the encoding phase" (1989: 411). Thus, some aspects of recall are situation specific. We have noted that cues can enhance recall, just as imagining oneself in the same environment can. Saliency and the social desirability of the behavior may also affect recall, with some respondents actively suppressing personally painful or socially undesirable events.

On the other hand, *crossover* effects can muddy a respondent's recall of events. That is, respondents may fill in details from experiences to make their recall more coherent (Bower and Gillian, 1979). Old soldiers, for example, often amplify accounts of specific battles with experiences from other events.

Nonattitudes

A particularly interesting group of respondents, initially studied in detail by Converse (1970), consists of those who hold what are termed *nonattitudes*. Initially, Converse observed a group of respondents who presented inconsistent views on a range of political issues. Some gave "no response" while others provided detailed but inconsistent ones. Thus it appeared that these individuals were simply responding for responding's sake, generating answers off the top of their heads.

Table 12.1. Belgian life history survey concordance with population register

	MARRIAGE			BIRTH OF CHILDREN			LEAVING HOME			HOUSEHOLD MIGRATION		
	MEN	WOMEN	COUPLE	MEN	WOMEN	COUPLE	MEN	WOMEN	COUPLE	MEN	WOMEN	COUPLE
Total events	445	445	445	1078	1078	1078	310	310	310	1388	1388	1388
Number of dated events	440	445	445	1076	1077	1078	222	228	222	1169	1196	1237
Exact date (±1 month)	94.1%	98.9%	99.6%	90.8%	97.8%	98.2%	39.0%	50.4%	53.6%	55.7%	60.5%	67.3%
Antedated												
≤1 year	1.8%	0.2%	0.0%	4.4%	0.5%	0.7%	20.0%	17.1%	17.1%	23.0%	22.8%	20.8%
>1 year	0.4%	0.0%	0.0%	0.7%	0.3%	0.3%	18.9%	15.8%	15.3%	8.6%	6.9%	4.3%
Postdated												
≤1 year	2.9%	0.6%	0.2%	3.2%	1.0%	0.7%	10.8%	9.2%	7.7%	8.8%	6.9%	5.1%
>1 year	0.7%	0.2%	0.2%	0.9%	0.4%	0.1%	11.3%	7.5%	6.3%	3.9%	2.9%	2.5%

Source: Compiled from Poulain, Riandey, and Firdion (1991).

Further analysis suggested that most of those people had very little interest in the political events that were the objective of the survey. Most also had lower levels of education.

A wonderful example of responses to nonattitude issues is given by Schuman and Presser (1981), who note that one group of people gave what appeared to be considered responses to a nonissue. In this study, researchers asked people what they thought of a nonexistent agricultural reform act. Bishop, Tuchfarber, and Oldendick (1986) have also examined this problem in some detail. They asked respondents to a telephone survey to answer questions about three fictitious public affairs issues. The results seem to suggest that part of the problem is created by a combination of the pressure to answer the survey by the interviewer and the manner in which interviewers handle "do not know" responses. This study also suggests that there is no relationship between a respondent's willingness to admit ignorance on an issue and his or her inclination to answer fictitious questions.

Smith (1984), who evaluated the literature on nonattitudes, suggests two remedies to the problem. The first is to use screening questions to identify respondents who had given some reasonable thought to the issue at hand. These questions should be framed to encourage nonattitudinal respondents to give an honest "don't know" if they truly do not. Second, follow-up questions can be used to delve into the intensity of the respondents' opinions.

Techniques for Sensitive Questions

Many researchers believe that respondents often underreport sensitive or "socially undesirable" behaviors. That is, many respondents either will not respond or will falsify responses to questions relating to such issues as criminality, sexual behavior, or social attitudes toward racial or religious minorities. To avoid this problem, several techniques have been suggested that allow the researcher to deduce the occurrence of the behavior or attitude without eliciting a direct response from a respondent.

The earliest suggested procedure is the randomized response technique outlined by Warner in the mid-1960s and subsequently elaborated upon by several others (Warner, 1965; Fox and Tracy, 1986). Here respondents are presented with a pair of questions: one is innocuous, the others socially problematic. In its most basic form, this procedure leaves the choice of question to a randomization device. For example, the interviewer might bring along a box containing black and white balls. When the box is shaken, a ball randomly appears in a window on the side of the box, but the situation is managed so that only the respondent can see the ball. The respondent is told that if a black ball appears, he or she is to answer the question: "Were you born in July?" If a white ball appears, the respondent is to answer the sensitive question: "Have you ever stolen from your employer?" A "yes" or a "no" answer is expected in either case.

A priori, the researcher knows both the distribution of balls in the box and the distribution of people born in July. Based on this information, it is possible to estimate the proportion of respondents who have stolen from their employers as:

$$p_s = \frac{\lambda - p_J(1 - \pi)}{\pi}$$

where p_s = the estimated proportion who have stolen from their employers
p_J = the proportion who were born in July
λ = the proportion of "yes" answers
π = proportion of balls of one color

While intuitively elegant, this procedure has posed many problems in practice. From the researcher's point of view, there is the encumbrance of the randomization device. Furthermore, while bias is reduced, it is not eliminated. The standard errors of the estimates obtained from studies of these types are also higher than those estimated from direct questions. Some respondents also appear to have difficulty understanding the instructions, and the complexity of the task makes others suspicious (Greenberg et al., 1969; Wiseman, Moriarty, and Schafer, 1975-76; Shimizu and Bonham, 1978; J. Miller, 1981). On the other hand, Bradburn and Sudman (1979) reported few difficulties in applying the technique.

Another procedure that has most of the benefits of the randomized response procedure but is somewhat easier to carry out is the item count technique (Droitcour et al., 1991). In this procedure one group of respondents is presented with a series of items and asked to say how many items are applicable to them. A second group is given the same series of items plus a disapproved item and asked how many are applicable. The difference in the mean number of items reported for each form provides an estimate of the prevalence of the disapproved item.

As with the randomized response model, the item count procedure produces significantly larger standard errors than more direct approaches. In an extensive analysis of a pretest involving both item counts and direct questions, Droitcour et al. (1991) also noted that 70% of their respondents considered the direct question approach to be the better of the two procedures. Furthermore, when these researchers analyzed the responses to questions relating to intravenous drug use and receptive anal intercourse (both related to prevalence of HIV infection), no statistically significant differences appeared between the estimates produced by the two procedures. In defense of the item count procedure, however, it should be noted that in the study by Droitcour et al., the nonresponse rates for the direct questions relating to receptive anal intercourse (especially among the men) were significantly higher than for the item count technique. According to the authors, this was "primarily due to men apparently not understanding that they were to answer this question."

In conclusion, it would appear that indirect estimation procedures work better in theory than in practice. The procedures are often cumbersome to administer and, while they may result in a small reduction in bias, the price one pays is a higher estimate of the standard error. Furthermore, except for generating prevalence estimates, it is difficult to subject the results to the types of sophisticated statistical analysis that can be applied to direct answers, since specific respondents cannot be linked to the behavior in question. Ultimately, it may be surmised that respondents who are not convinced that anonymity will be preserved with direct answer approaches probably are not convinced that indirect approaches afford them any further protection. Perhaps the most compelling reason for randomized response techniques lies in the legal protection it affords both the researcher and the respondent. In principle, data collected by social researchers are not privileged in the way client communications are privileged in the legal and medical professions. Thus, it is possible that sensitive information collected by social researchers could become subject to judicial oversight.

CONCLUSION

There are three primary sources of error in surveys: the respondent, the measurement instrument (including the mode), and the recording process. Depending upon the instrument used, the latter category may include interviewers and coding clerks. The researcher has only minimal control over respondent error. However, the researcher can assist respondents by honing the measurement instrument, providing an aide-mémoire, and convincing respondents of the importance of the study. Most researchers would be delighted if respondent error were the only source of error in their data.

The researcher has much more control over errors due to the measurement instrument and the mode of collection. In many situations, poor survey data result from a lack of attention to detail, a lack of pretesting, and a tendency to rush the instrument into the field before it has been adequately prepared. Ultimately, all instruments have their limitations; however, it is through the instrument that the researcher has the greatest opportunity to ensure that the data collected are reliable and valid. As indicated earlier, no amount of statistical manipulation after the fact can make up for a poorly conceived design or a sloppy instrument.

Errors due to recording can be minimized through proper training, and supervision, and the appropriate use of technology. Interviewers and coding clerks make fewer errors and are more likely to identify instrument problems early if they are well trained and well versed in the objectives of the study. Too often researchers treat interviewers as mechanical "black boxes," whose only role is to ape questions, check boxes, and key responses into a database. By the same token, many researchers abnegate their responsibility for the measurement instrument by assuming that interviewers can work around poorly conceived and awkwardly worded questions.

Table 12.2 summarizes some of the advantages, disadvantages, and solutions to problems with the different modes of data collection discussed in this chapter. A priori, no one mode is superior to the others; the key to successful data collection is to match the procedure to the problem at hand and to the available resources. Once that decision has been made, it is the researcher's task to maximize the quality of data collection.

While it is common for texts to identify arcane sources of error in data collection, the fact remains that most error stems from a lack of attention to basics. For researchers constrained by a fixed budget, greater returns are generally realized by increasing the resources put into planning, pretesting, and training than into increasing the size of the sample.

Further Reading

Groves, R.M. *Survey Errors and Survey Costs*. New York: Wiley, 1989. A comprehensive review of issues relating to measurement error in surveys. This is a good starting point, with an exhaustive review of literature up to the date of publication.

Table 12.2. A comparison of survey modes

MODE	ADVANTAGES	DISADVANTAGES	SOURCES OF ERROR	SOLUTIONS
Telephone	Inexpensive Ease of quality control (esp. with CATI software) Timeliness Respondent anonymity Ability to explain questions to respondents Ability to control sequencing of questions	Inability to view respondent in context Difficult to conduct with lengthy and complex material More difficult to build rapport than in face-to-face interviews Increased reluctance of respondents to participate Cost savings attributable to fewer interviewers may be offset by increased interviewer bias	Respondent Instrument (questionnaire) Interviewer	Increase interviewer training Enhance supervision Offset response rate problem by using different modes of data collection (e.g., mail)
In-person	Ability to collect contextual information Ability to develop rapport with respondent Works well with long interviews Ability to use visual and other aides-mémoires Greater ability to determine whether respondents actually understand questions by observing visual cues Interviewer has control over how questions are presented	Generally very expensive Little control or supervision over field staff Potential for interviewer bias	Respondent Instrument (questionnaire) Interviewer	Enhance training Increase supervision Conduct ongoing interrater reliabilities Use of reinterview techniques

Method	Advantages	Disadvantages	Unit	Strategies
Mail	Relatively inexpensive No interviewer bias No time pressure on respondent, thus allowing for more opportunity to track and verify information Ability to distribute large quantities of material, such as aides-mémoires and samples	Instrument is self-coded, thereby raising problems of coding inconsistency Often lower response rates than other modes Inability to sequence questions; one or two "offensive" questions can lead to abandonment of instrument Limited ability to explain question or prompt respondent for answers No control over who actually fills out the instrument	Respondent Instrument (questionnaire)	Supply telephone number (toll-free if long distance) of contact person to answer respondent questions Construct questionnaire so that sequencing is not an issue Focus on crafting of instructions to accompany questionnaire Use a variant of Dillman's "total design" approach
Diaries	Allow for ongoing recording of information No interviewer bias Ability to collect very detailed information	Instrument is self-coded, thereby raising problems of coding inconsistency Limited ability to explain question or prompt respondent for answers Coding may become increasingly unreliable over time as fatigue sets in No control over who actually records the information	Respondent Instrument (questionnaire)	Supply telephone number (toll-free if long distance) of contact person to answer respondent questions Focus on crafting of instructions to accompany questionnaire Provide training to respondents outlining coding procedures and purpose of survey

Continued

Table 12.2. Continued

MODE	ADVANTAGES	DISADVANTAGES	SOURCES OF ERROR	SOLUTIONS
Direct observation	Problem of self-report bias nullified Ability to extensively record contextual information "Technology-assisted" direct observation (e.g., use of VCRs) allows for data to be collected in continuous time, 24 hours a day Recorded observations minimize interviewer bias; allow for multiple judges and estimation of interrater reliability	Costly and time-consuming Potential for observer bias Heavy reliance on integrity of observer to actually collect and record data Inefficient for recording rare events Potential lack of flexibility where mechanical devices are used	Observer Recording protocol	Increase observer training Construct and use standard protocols for coding while in field Use multiple observers/judges to estimate coding reliability
Multimodal	Can increase response rate by capturing respondents who will not respond to certain modes Potential to estimate mode bias Ability to better control costs by matching mode to type of data to be collected Ability to incorporate advantages of different modes while avoiding major disadvantages of each	Comparability may be a problem where different respondents are measured on items using different modes Less viable for small surveys, where duplicate efforts are needed to construct instruments, find sampling frames, and train personnel in different modes Cost, particularly relating to administration, can be high	Respondent Instrument (questionnaire) Interviewer Mode	Techniques used for single-mode studies apply to subcomponents of multimode surveys Restrict applicability to large surveys where resources are available

13

Missing Data

One cannot make totally objective probability statements about how nonrespondents would respond without some response data from them; however, one can formalize subjective notions about the similarity of respondents and nonrespondents and thus formalize notions about what effect their responses would have had on results.

—Donald Rubin

INTRODUCTION

Seldom is one fortunate enough to have data on all the cases drawn from the sampling frame, and seldom are complete observations on all the cases surveyed available. In planned experiments, some subjects refuse to participate, some drop out before the study is completed, and yet others are available at different points in the study. In survey research, we face similar problems of selective nonparticipation and also the unwillingness or inability of some respondents to provide answers to all our questions. To complicate matters, the reason for the missing observations might be fortuitous, thus resulting in what we call data missing at random (MAR) or, the data might also be missing for systematic reasons that have a direct bearing on the results of the study. Often, however, missing data pose problems for both the internal and the external validity of our research.

Note that we say "often," since in some cases missing data have little or no impact on the final analysis. The difficulty is that we often do not, and sometimes cannot, determine whether the missing data produce biases or inefficiencies in our parameter estimates. Of course, not all questions we pose require efficient estimates. Griliches (1986) distinguishes between what he terms *ignorable* and *nonignorable* situations. If the missing data are unrelated to the outcome or criterion variable, then we may be satisfied with generating point estimates that might be inefficient. This is Griliches's *ignorable case*, and we may choose not to deal with the problem. More commonly, the data are not missing at random but are the result of some form of systematic selection bias.

As will be shown later in this chapter, our decision to address or not address the issue of missing data explicitly implies certain assumptions. Ignoring the issue allows those assumptions to stand unquestioned; addressing them makes the assumptions explicit, and allows the researcher to make an informed if not necessarily correct decision regarding further analysis. As is obvious from the inclusion of the topic in this chapter, it is our belief that addressing the problem head-on is preferable to remaining ignorant of the possible consequences of our (in)action.

It should be kept in mind that post hoc attempts to deal with the problem are less desirable than strategies developed to avoid the situation in the first instance. In social research, there is no truer adage than "An ounce of prevention is worth a pound of cure." This is particularly so regarding the problem of missing observations. Certainly, some aspects of the research process, especially in large-scale survey research, are not totally within the researcher's control. Respondents cannot be forced to respond, for example. On the other hand, issues such as putting together a complete sample frame, drawing a correct sample from the frame, controlling the quality of data coding and entry, and making sure that questionnaires and data entries are not lost or garbled are dimensions over which the researcher does have control. When breakdowns in management and quality control take place, those factors should be documented, for often they provide insight into whether the missing cases are systematic or random.

Even respondent participation can be influenced by the researcher. Good instrument design, including adequate pretesting, a clear and appealing explanation of the value of the research, and follow-up reminders, can all influence the quality of the data.

DIRECT ANALYSIS WITH MISSING DATA

It is probably fair to say that unless they are working with secondary data generated by an organization such as the census bureau, most researchers do not attempt to deal with the issue of missing data by "filling in the blanks." Most statistical packages are programmed to identify missing values (e.g., those coded −999, SYSMIS, or simply ".") and to deal with those observations by either deleting the case, skipping the observation (for univariate analysis), or conducting a "pairwise" analysis that includes only pairs of observations for which data exist on both dimensions.

The conundrum can lead to considerable mental anguish—"Should I casewise delete, or pairwise delete?" In many situations, the conscience is assuaged by compromising. Delete those cases for which a considerable amount of data is missing (say more than 50%) and then perform pairwise analysis on the remainder. For most of us, pairwise deletion has greater intuitive appeal than casewise deletion, since more of the information in the available data is retained. But as with many things scientific, intuition can be misleading, so it is worthwhile to question whether pairwise deletion is a superior approach to a given problem.

The simple answer to this question is that while the pairwise approach is easy to conduct with modern statistical software and is intuitively appealing, it proves not to be a universal solution and often performs more poorly than casewise deletion. In a typical regression analysis, for example, Haitovsky (1967) shows that casewise deletion under OLS estimation is consistently superior to pairwise deletion with respect to both efficiency and bias. A succinct but clear analysis of the relative impact of straightforward casewise and pairwise deletion can be found in Little and Rubin (1989–90).

Overall, using the standard default options available in most statistics packages is less than ideal. A far better approach is to address the problem of missing data directly. Before entering that discussion, however, it is worthwhile considering a series of dimensions along which the discussion can be organized.

CHARACTERISTICS OF MISSING DATA

The available tactics for handling missing data are influenced by three primary dimensions. We must first determine whether we have a *unit nonresponse* or an *item nonresponse*. "Unit nonresponse" implies that the case itself is missing, while "item nonresponse" implies that although some data are available for the case, selected information is missing.

The second dimension, which has already been discussed, is whether the nonresponse is ignorable or nonignorable. This distinction is based on whether the missing piece is information on the criterion or dependent variable or information on one or more of the covariate or independent variables. Where data are missing on the dependent variable, it is highly likely that sample selection bias exists. Most of the statistical techniques required to address this issue are beyond what is assumed here (see Berk, 1983; Winship and Mare, 1992, for discussions). Furthermore, while this distinction is highly relevant for analysis, its usefulness is determined largely by whether the survey has one or multiple purposes. Limiting the optimization of multipurpose surveys are the possibilities that the criterion variable will not be clearly identified or that there are several diverse indicators that ultimately would serve this purpose.

The third dimension to consider is whether the data are missing systematically or at random. Furthermore, if the data are missing at random, we often distinguish between data referred to as MCAR (missing completely at random) and simply MAR (missing at random). The distinction is subtle but important: unlike the case of MCAR data, the randomness of MAR data is conditional upon some covariate. For example, the probability of an observation's not being included in a survey may be dependent upon region, but within each region, the data are missing randomly. MCAR data, however, are assumed not to be related to any identified covariate.

The random/nonrandom and ignorable/nonignorable dimensions affect many of the techniques we use to handle missing data. The unit/item nonresponse distinction forms the basis for a primary categorization of approaches to handling missing data. The problem of unit nonresponse will be addressed first; however, the primary focus of this chapter is on approaches to addressing item nonresponse.

UNIT NONRESPONSE

Cases may be missing for several reasons. They may not have been included in the initial frame; the respondent may have been impossible to locate; the respondent may have refused to participate in the survey; the researcher may have decided to limit the number of callbacks; or the data may have been lost through sloppy data administration. Regardless of the cause, the result is that data for selected cases are not available. To retain the overall sampling fraction, researchers typically decide either to augment the sample by selecting another case from the frame or to reweight the existing cases. If the data are missing completely at random (MCAR), selecting another case or weighting the existing cases by n/m (where n is the original sample size and m is the number of respondents excluding the missing cases) will suffice.

Statistics prone to bias even under MCAR conditions, such as totals and standard errors, will be corrected by either approach.

Unfortunately, data are rarely MCAR. More often, the data either are MAR conditional on some covariate or stratifying variable, or they are selectively available depending upon the values of the dependent or criterion measures, thereby raising the specter of sample selection bias. Data MAR but dependent upon a covariate are often corrected through some form of weight adjustment.

Population Weight Adjustment

Population weight adjustments reweight or adjust the sample to reflect the known distribution of the population. Typically, we are aware of age, sex, or income distributions of the population through census data or ancillary surveys. Weights are thus attached to the sample cases to reflect the proportion of the population known to be within certain strata. In this respect, population weight adjusting is similar to poststratification. The crucial difference, however, is that in poststratification, the weights sum to the total number of cases in the sample. In population weight adjusting, the sum of the weights is greater than the number of cases in the sample.

For the simple case of data divided into H strata, stratum weights are given as follows:

$$w_h = \frac{N_h}{N} \times \frac{n}{m_h}$$

where N_h and N are the known stratum and population totals; m_h is the obtained, within-stratum total, and n is the original sample size (including respondents and missing cases).

The advantage of population weight adjusting is that biases in both point estimates and variances can be corrected. For this approach to be successful, however, accurate external data must exist, and those data must reflect the distribution of the weighting covariate that is related to the missing data mechanism. It is further assumed that within these strata, the data are missing at random. Stratifying and weighting the sample according to some covariate that is *not* related to the reason for the missing data will not correct the problem and, in some circumstances, can introduce even more bias.

If one's statistical software cannot accept fractional weights, the sample can be effectively reweighted through case duplication. Case duplication involves randomly selecting cases within each stratum and duplicating them until the appropriate number of stratum-specific cases has been achieved. Because of the potential for clumping (duplicating the same case several times), case duplication techniques tend to work best with larger data sets.

Weighting to adjust for a known population distribution is relatively simple when the adjustment is made over one or two variables. In the multivariate instance, involving several covariates or stratifying factors, a procedure known as *raking* is invoked. Raking utilizes the iterative proportional fitting algorithms often used in log-linear modeling to smooth the data (Bishop, Fienberg, and Holland, 1975; Kalton and Kasprzyk, 1986).

Sample Weighting Adjustments

Unlike population weight adjusting, sample weight adjusting uses only data within the sample to make the adjustments. Again, sample weight adjusting assumes that the sample can be stratified according to a covariate that is meaningfully related to the missing data process. Within each stratum, the available data are weighted according to the inverse of the response rate. That is, if the response rate is m_h/n_h, the appropriate weight factor is given by

$$w_h = n_h/m_h$$

with m_h being the obtained, within-stratum total, and n_h the original within-stratum sample size (including respondents and missing cases).

Many sampling plans attempt to increase the precision of the dependent variable through stratification. The variables that are related to the dependent variable, however, may not be related to the missing data mechanism. Consequently, the bias problem may not be addressed and may even be exacerbated. Under ideal circumstances, sample weight adjusting can reduce the amount of point estimate bias. Unfortunately, it often leads to increases the variance of the estimate.

Statistically, sample weight adjusting is relatively easy to do, but it generally poses many practical problems. Potential covariates or stratifying variables are usually limited in availability, and those that are linked to the missing data mechanism are often not incorporated into the survey at the design phase. Furthermore, determining which variables are related to the missing data mechanism is often a more daunting task than solving the objective of the substantive research addressed by the survey. When the sample size is small, or a large number of strata result in small n_h values, there may also be a substantial loss in precision as stratum variances are inflated.

Potentially, the impact of unit nonresponse on survey data can be quite complex. More detailed discussions of the nature of the biases produced and the impact of weighting to correct for nonresponse can be found in Cochran (1977: ch. 13), Kalton and Kasprzyk (1986), and Kish (1965: sec. 13.4–13.6).

ITEM NONRESPONSE

Unlike unit nonresponse, item nonresponse results when some case information is available. Typically, respondents who cooperate for much of a survey may refuse to answer particular questions, or may be unable to answer because they do not have the information at hand. Questions relating to income, for example, are generally a problem from both these perspectives. Many respondents who will provide information on issues that might typically be described as sensitive (e.g., issues relating to criminal acts or sexual behavior) will balk at providing an estimate of their income. Further, it is common for many household members to be unable to provide estimates of the household's total income.

Two primary strategies are used to handle item nonresponse. One is to attempt to analyze the data directly; the second is to impute the missing value. While this analytical distinction is often made on a practical basis, the substantive distinction is moot because most techniques used to analyze the data directly actually perform an implicit imputation of the missing value. For example, some statistical techniques serve to "smooth" the items in a covariance matrix that have differing numbers of observations. This smoothing process often produces results that are equivalent to those obtained from some explicit regression imputation techniques.

Since the differences in results between implicit and explicit imputation are usually indistinguishable, and explicit imputation is generally preferred for practical reasons. We will focus on that approach for the remainder of this chapter.

The issue of imputing (or "guesstimating") missing values has received a great deal of attention in the statistical literature. It is a very popular way of dealing with missing data, since it presents the researcher with a data set that is more easily handled by standard statistical packages, which often accept only rectangular and complete data matrices. Despite its many nice properties, however, imputation can lead to significant difficulties. Poor attempts to impute can generate greater biases in the estimated parameters than would have resulted from a simple casewise or pairwise deletion of the data.

Little and Rubin (1989–90) also note that a major pitfall of imputation is the possibility the imputed data will be considered "real" by some, thereby leading to an overestimation of the precision. In one example provided by these authors, an assumed 5% significance level had a true level of close to 50%. This overestimation is not a necessary condition, but extreme care is required to avoid comparable situations.

The point being made here is not that imputation should be avoided. On the contrary, ignoring missing values carries a set of assumptions that might be more or less warranted than those underlying the chosen imputation procedure. Rather, we must consider what actions are most appropriate given the data, the intended analysis, and the consequences of the estimated results. Ultimately, the only solution to a severely inadequate data set may be to abandon it, learn what lessons we can from the experience, and start anew.

Dimensions of Imputation

The literature is replete with imputation techniques, and a review of the publications available often leaves one with the feeling that there is more chaos than order to the enterprise. It is possible, however, to categorize imputation techniques along a series of dimensions. Briefly, these are as follows.

- **Autogenerative vs. predictive**: missing values imputed from information contained in the responses from the same variable may be termed autogenerative, while those based on some other indicator may be termed predictive. Substituting the mean of the observed values would be an instance of autogenerative imputation; regressing the observed Y-values on some indicator X and then replacing the missing values with an estimated Y-hat value ($\hat{Y}$) is an example of a predictive approach.

- **Deterministic vs. stochastic**: replacing the missing values with the mean of the observed values or a predicted value from the equation $\hat{Y}_{(NR)_i} = b_0 + b_1 X_i$

is an instance of a deterministic approach. Stochastic approaches add a random component, e_i, drawn from a stochastic distribution. Thus, an example of stochastic imputation might be $\hat{Y}_{(NR)_i} = \overline{Y} + e_i$, where $e \approx N(0, \sigma^2)$.

- **Single vs. multiple missing items**: here the distinction is between cases that have missing information on only one item or variable as opposed several items.

- **Single vs. multiple imputation**: traditional approaches to imputation have tended to generate a single estimate of $\hat{Y}_{(NR)}$. More recently, the benefits of generating a range of $\hat{Y}_{(NR)_i}$-values have been raised.

Autogeneration vs. Prediction

Autogeneration: Mean Substitution

One common method of imputing data is *mean substitution*. Essentially, this approach involves the substitution of the mean of the known observations for the missing values. The primary advantage of this approach is its simplicity. The drawbacks are that it does not take advantage of other information that might be available within the data, and invariably leads to an underestimation of the variance. This, in turn, results in an underestimation of the standard error and an increase in the likelihood of a Type I error. The overall mean, however, remains constant.

Because of its fundamental importance, examining the impact of mean substitution in more detail is worthwhile. First, it can be shown that when the newly completed data are analyzed, the overall mean remains constant. To see this, let m represent the number of observations with complete data, and n the total cases sampled. For the known data, the expected value (or mean) is the familiar:

$$E(Y) = \overline{Y} = \frac{\sum_{i=1}^{m} Y_i}{m}$$

For the missing $n - m$ observations, we substitute the constant, $\overline{Y}$. The mean of a constant is equal to that constant; therefore, the expected value of the imputed cases is equal to the mean of the observed cases.

Occasionally, as when the data are MCAR, this results in an overall unbiased estimate of the population mean, . If the data are not MCAR, however, it is likely that the estimated $\overline{Y}$ will be biased. A typical example occurs when the variable of interest is income. Generally, response rates are lower from high income respondents than others. This implies that the true mean for the missing values is somewhat higher than that for the observed values; hence, the true value of μ is underestimated by the quantity $\mu - \overline{Y}$.

The use of mean substitution for missing values has a far greater impact on the estimate of the variance, however. Specifically, it can be shown that even when the data are MCAR, mean substitution leads to a bias in the estimate of s^2 in the order of m/n. For the known observations, s^2 is estimated by:

$$s^2 = \frac{\sum_{i=1}^{m} (Y_i - \overline{Y})^2}{m}$$

The variance of the missing values, however, is:

$$s^2 = \frac{\sum_{i=m}^{n} (\bar{Y} - \bar{Y})^2}{n - m}$$

$$= \frac{0}{n - m}$$

$$= 0$$

Pooling these variances through mean substitution, however, leads to:

$$s^2 = \frac{\sum_{i=1}^{m} (Y_i - \bar{Y})^2 + \sum_{i=m}^{n} (\bar{Y} - \bar{Y})^2}{m + (n - m)}$$

$$= \frac{\sum_{i=1}^{m} (Y_i - \bar{Y})^2 + 0}{n}$$

Thus, while the numerator remains the same, the denominator has increased from m to n. The overall sample variance can be retained, however, by multiplying the variance of the computed data by n/m. This is a simple procedure for univariate statistics but can be somewhat cumbersome for multivariate modeling.

More elaborate autogenerative procedures are sometimes used to impute missing values, particularly when there is substantial autocorrelation in the data. This auto-correlation in time series data, for example, can often be exploited to generate a more accurate estimate than simple mean substitution. While there are many approaches to the analysis of autocorrelative data, the techniques discussed in Chapter 14, on interpolation and smoothing, can serve as a starting point.

Doing Nothing Is Doing Something

It is often tempting to avoid the issue of missing values by simply "doing nothing" and analyzing the existing data. Unfortunately, with missing data, doing nothing is tantamount to doing mean substitution. By not addressing the problem directly, one is assuming that the data are MCAR and that the expected value of the missing observations is equal to the expected value of the observed cases. If the data are MCAR, this might not be a bad assumption to make. On the other hand, data are often missing for a reason.

Thus, ignoring the problem by doing nothing is fraught with the same potential pitfalls of biased estimates of μ and σ as are inherent with mean substitution. The difference between the approaches is that by ignoring the problem, researchers are deluding themselves into believing the problem does not exist when, in fact, it does.

Prediction: Regression Approaches to Imputation

A major improvement over mean substitution is to impute the missing values by means of a standard regression procedure. This approach uses the available observations in the data matrix and considers that $\hat{Y}_{(NR)}$ might also be conditional upon the distribution of the other X variables.

Let us consider the simple bivariate case, with two variables, Y and X, where Y contains missing elements and X is complete. The sample correlation between these two variables may be estimated using the standard formula:

$$r = \frac{s_{XY}}{s_X s_Y}$$

Clearly, however, the variances and other statistics will be based on different sample sizes. For Y, the sample estimate of s (and the inclusive $\overline{Y}$) will be based on m cases; for X, the estimates will be based on n cases. If this model is reparameterized as a predictive equation, we get $\hat{Y}_{(NR)} = a + bX$, where $b = s_{XY}/s_X^2$, and $a = \overline{Y} - b\overline{X}$. This model is easily extended to the multivariate case where, in matrix terms, $\hat{Y}_{(NR)} = \mathbf{X}\boldsymbol{\beta}$.

Predictive approaches can result in less bias if the predictive model is correctly specified. As with any substantive research, misspecified models can result in bad predictions and in the case of missing data, usually aggravate the problem of bias. This is not a trivial issue. Further, as with any attempt at prediction, the researcher needs to address the standard modeling issues relating to what variables ought to be included in the model, the adequacy of the functional form (including whether to include interaction terms), whether to use OLS, maxim likelihood, or some other estimation procedure, and the other such concerns.

Deterministic vs. Stochastic Approaches

Another approach for univariate imputation that retains both the expected value and the variance of the observed data is to generate a random variate with a mean of zero and a distribution similar to that of the observed data. Thus, if the observed data are normally distributed with a variance of s^2, a random normal deviate, z_i, with mean 0 and variance s^2 should be generated. The imputed value, $\hat{Y}_{(NR)_i}$, would consist of the value $\overline{Y} + z_i$. This procedure is adequate for maintaining the univariate integrity of the data but should be used cautiously when multivariate analyses are proposed, since it decreases the efficiency of the parameter estimates.

As with mean imputation, this model, even in the multivariate formulation, is not fully efficient. However, considerable improvement can be made by again adding a random component z, so that the prediction equation becomes $\hat{Y}_{(NR)_i} = a + bX + z_i$. Assuming the regression is properly specified, z would be drawn from a distribution of normal deviates, $N(0, s_e^2)$, where s_e^2 is based on an estimate of the mean squared error of the estimated regression equation. For the multivariate situation, we would substitute $\hat{Y}_{(NR)} = \mathbf{X}\boldsymbol{\beta} + \mathbf{z}$.

Since the true error variance, σ_e^2, is estimated by s_e^2, it remains the case that the imputation will be inefficient, although less so than where z is not included. Empirically, the limitations of the regression approach are small compared with the benefits involved. Certainly, ease of computing is a major strength of this approach. Recent advances in computing, however, have allowed for the greater availability of an estimation technique that overcomes the residual limitations of ordinary regression–maximum likelihood.

Where the independent variables are categorical, this type of prediction model is analogous to a standard analysis of variance (ANOVA). It is also parallel to the practice of substituting subclass means when the sample is stratified along some dimensions known (or more often assumed) to be related to the missing data mechanism.

In the examples above, heavy reliance has been placed on the assumption that the random component, z, is a standard normal deviate. While this may be the case for some well-specified uni- and multivariate models, it remains a fairly strong and limiting assumption. As suggested, where this assumption is not warranted, the researcher can substitute a selection from the empirical distribution of residuals estimated from the respondents' data.

Another approach is to use a "hot-deck" (see below) variant, in which a residual is selected from a respondent who is a close match to the nonrespondent. If the two cases are the same on the matching variables, the value of the respondent can be given to the nonrespondent. One of the major attractions of the hot-deck approach is that it generally avoids problems of homosckedasticity. It also gets around the larger problem of identifying the correct specification for the regression equation. Needless to say, a misspecified model will result in misspecified residuals, thus aggravating an already less than ideal situation.

Hot-Deck Procedures

An imputation technique that is very popular among the world's census and statistical bureaus is that known as the *hot-deck* approach. The term "hot deck" is somewhat confusing, since it actually relates to a series of procedures that involve some element of computer matching and the mechanical substitution of known for missing data. As originally conceived, the responses (profile) of the last similar case to that with the missing item(s) are kept in an *active* file. When a case with missing data arises, the known value from the most similar case in the active file is donated to the missing item. This is known as a hot-deck procedure because the substitute responses in the active file are continually updated.

Variations on the hot-deck approach involve *random within-class imputation, sequential hot-deck imputation*, and *hierarchical hot-deck imputation*, as well as distinctions on whether the original data or just the residual from the donor case ought to be substituted.

These techniques are conceptually very simple and work well with categorical data, but they are intensive in terms of computing resources, especially for large data sets. On the other hand, hot-deck procedures work best with large data sets (as in the census). Small data sets often result in multiple use of the same donor, which can lead to a loss of precision. Detailed comparisons of the effectiveness of hot-deck procedures can be found in Bailar and Bailar (1983) and Sande (1983). Fundamentally, hot-deck imputation is similar to regression imputation, where the independent or matching variables are categorical or categorized.

Single vs. Multiple Missing Items

Another important issue arises when a case has more than one missing item. Essentially the issue is one of whether we should impute the missing values independently of one another or allow the imputed values of one variable to influence the values of a missing value on a second variable. Several suggestions have been made to address the multiply missing items problem. Most focus on the covariance matrix generated from the items included in the analysis, and most involve a maximum likelihood (ML) approach.

Usually, maximum likelihood approaches provide better estimates than those based on more direct procedures such as simple regression. Generally, ML requires us to assume that the data matrix was drawn from a multivariate normal distribution [i.e., $N(\mu, \Sigma)$, where μ is a vector of means for each of the y_i variables of interest, and Σ is a variance–covariance matrix for those variables. If that assumption seems valid, then it is possible to proceed by specifying a partitioned likelihood equation for the data as follows:

$$L(y_{i,m} \mid \theta_j) = L_1(y_{i,m} \mid y_{i,n-m}, \theta_j) L_2(y_{i,n-m} \mid \theta_j)$$

where $y_{i,m}$ are the complete data; $y_{i,n-m}$ are the incomplete data, and θ_j are the parameters to be estimated. Details of how the estimates for the missing data and for the parameters θ_j are generated are provided in several sources, including Anderson (1957), Orchard and Woodbury (1972), and Little and Rubin (1987, ch. 6).[1] Suffice it to say that the estimated parameters, $\hat{\Theta}$, and estimates of the missing values, $\hat{y}$, are produced by combining the ML estimates of the parameters for the complete cases with those for the incomplete cases. If the underlying model is valid, the estimates achieve both consistency and efficiency—two factors whose absence bedevils many other approaches.

One disadvantage of maximum likelihood is that its theoretical foundation is based on the assumptions surrounding large sample estimates. Thus, with small data sets, ML may not produce reliable estimates.[2] Also, one might question the basic distributional assumptions underlying the model. Clearly, this is a major item of contention. The assumptions are not too problematic, however, if we consider that the overall approach is extremely flexible and allows for tremendous variation in model specification. In particular, one can incorporate explicit information regarding how the data were corrupted, as well as the specific functional form that best predicts the missing elements.

Increasingly, standard statistical packages are incorporating ML procedures that can be adapted to impute missing values. The most common ML implementation takes advantage of the EM or expectation maximization algorithm.

Single vs. Multiple Imputation

A more recent extension of the maximum likelihood approach is multiple imputation. Single imputation, or the generation of one replacement value, usually results in an attenuation of the standard error and an increase in the likelihood of a Type I error.

---

1. A popular approach to the problem seems to be the application of Dempster's (EM) expectation-maximization algorithm. For details, see Dempster, Laird, and Rubin (1977).
2. Little and Rubin (1987, sec. 6.3.2) indicate that one way of dealing with this problem is to use a Bayesian approach, which allows the incorporation of prior knowledge into the procedure.

Multiple imputation retains consistency in the estimation of means and variances, a prime advantage of the ML procedure, but extends it to other parameters of interest. Multiple imputation also generates more accurate estimates of the standard errors (in the long run) and consequently maintains the integrity of the chosen α-level.

Instead of providing just one estimate of a missing value, multiple imputation (MI) generates a variety of estimates. This approach makes sense because the singly imputed value is an estimate around which there is a sampling distribution. In some ways the procedure is analogous to the previously mentioned approach of using mean substitution with a random component to retain the overall variance. If instead of using $\overline{Y}$, we generate another "best estimate" through a maximum likelihood approach, that estimate can be represented by $\hat{Y}_{(NR)}$. Adding a random component, we get $\hat{Y}_{(NR)_i} + z_i$, where z is drawn from a distribution of normal deviates. Since z is based on a distribution [here, $N(0, s^2)$], our results may vary depending upon the specific value of z.

Perhaps the biggest advantage of MI is that it forces us to avoid taking too precise a view of our $\hat{Y}_{(NR)}$ imputed values. Generating several estimates serves to reinforce the uncertainty about our estimate.

Unfortunately, MI is costly in that it increases the amount of future analysis on the substantive model of interest. However, that cost does carry some advantages. We can, for example, estimate the sensitivity of the model to different assumptions, such as comparing MAR with non-MAR imputation strategies. While one can theoretically generate many imputed matrices, research into practical MI procedures suggests that often imputations of two or three variations on the data set can give valid estimates, even when substantial amounts of data are missing (Little and Rubin, 1987).

EXAMPLE: IMPUTING VALUES ON FERTILITY AND THE STATUS OF WOMEN

We examine a data set used to address the issue of fertility and the status of women in economically developing countries (Balakrishnan and Hou, 1993). The data were obtained on total fertility rates (TFRs) and various indicators of the status of women for 1990 from a series of World Bank development reports, the United Nations Yearbooks, and several publications of the Population Reference Bureau. The sample consisted of 109 countries outside Europe and North America. The basic data are presented in Table 13.1.

As with any analysis, it is prudent to start with a close visual examination of the available data. The amount of missing data differs across the chosen variables. Data were available for all 109 cases on total fertility rate, while only 78 cases were available for average age of marriage for males. Figure 13.1 presents box plots for each variable in the data set. Most of the distributions look reasonably good; however, clearly something is amiss with GNP. Given what we know about income distribution and the results of the box plot, it was decided to take a log transformation of the data before doing anything else.

Although the data could be analyzed with several packages, the present imputations were conducted using the AM procedure in BMDP (Dixon et al., 1988). This is an

Table 13.1. Data for analysis of fertility and status of women in economically developing countries[a]

COUNTRY	(1)	(2)	(3)	(4)	(5)	(6)	(7)	(8)	(9)	(10)	(11)	(12)
Afghanistan	6.8	24	102.4	9	*	18	61.0	9	42.0	53.3	17.8	25.3
Algeria	5.1	56	103.3	5	2060	52	13.9	35	64.1	23.6	21.0	25.3
Angola	6.4	46	107.2	64	610	28	73.8	23	46.1	*	*	*
Argentina	2.9	99	110.0	27	2370	86	13.0	94	74.0	10.1	22.9	25.3
Bangladesh	5.3	43	98.8	7	200	16	56.5	19	50.4	65.4	16.7	23.9
Barbados	1.8	100	106.9	89	6540	45	7.6	99	77.0	0.6	*	*
Benin	7.1	45	107.2	31	360	38	70.2	12	48.1	45.5	18.2	24.9
Bhutan	5.5	42	97.2	48	190	5	92.5	19	47.1	*	*	*
Bahrain	3.9	81	106.3	11	6420	83	3.0	63	72.9	14.5	*	*
Bolivia	5.9	80	108.9	49	620	51	46.5	65	55.4	15.6	22.1	24.5
Botswana	6.7	74	110.6	55	2040	28	43.2	60	61.5	7.0	26.4	30.8
Brazil	3.3	96	108.6	39	2680	75	25.2	77	67.6	14.6	22.6	25.9
Burkina Faso	6.5	27	107.0	87	330	9	86.6	6	48.9	53.4	17.4	27.0
Burundi	6.8	60	107.1	90	210	6	92.8	32	50.7	19.2	20.8	24.4
Cameroon	6.9	58	105.7	42	940	41	74.0	36	53.0	44.3	18.8	26.2
Central African Republic	6.2	43	110.6	86	390	47	83.7	19	47.1	45.5	*	*
Chad	5.8	37	107.1	21	190	30	83.2	13	47.1	*	*	*
Chile	2.7	99	110.3	29	1940	86	18.3	92	75.1	10.4	23.6	25.7
China	2.4	69	104.6	76	370	33	73.7	55	70.9	4.3	22.4	25.1
Colombia	3.0	98	108.8	52	1240	70	*	84	67.2	16.5	20.4	24.0
Cambodia	4.6	40	106.0	64	*	12	74.4	17	49.9	*	*	*
Comoro Islands	7.0	71	101.8	69	480	28	83.0	40	53.8	26.0	19.5	25.8
Congo	6.3	58	110.2	64	1010	40	62.4	38	50.2	15.7	21.9	27.0
Costa Rica	3.1	100	106.4	27	1910	47	25.9	92	77.0	15.4	22.2	25.1
Cuba	1.9	97	104.9	46	*	75	23.8	91	75.8	26.9	19.9	23.5
Djibouti	6.5	72	107.1	0	*	81	*	13	48.7	*	*	*
Dominican Republic	3.5	95	106.6	17	820	60	45.7	79	68.1	*	20.5	26.1
Ecuador	4.1	94	106.6	26	960	56	38.5	81	67.6	17.8	21.1	24.3
Egypt	4.3	49	104.1	16	600	47	38.2	30	62.0	21.1	21.3	26.9
El Salvador	4.7	90	111.0	33	1100	44	43.2	65	66.5	20.5	19.4	24.7
Equatorial Guinea	5.9	53	107.0	69	330	29	66.0	31	48.1	*	*	*
Ethiopia	6.8	*	107.4	61	120	13	79.8	*	42.6	53.2	17.7	25.5
Fiji	3.0	89	106.9	23	1770	39	46.0	75	72.7	12.8	21.6	24.5
Gabon	5.2	62	106.5	61	3220	46	75.5	43	53.2	*	*	*
Gambia	6.3	35	107.6	69	730	23	84.0	11	44.6	*	*	*
Guatemala	5.6	73	107.9	19	900	39	49.8	44	64.4	26.4	20.5	23.5
Ghana	6.3	67	106.7	67	390	33	59.3	42	55.8	31.8	19.3	26.9
Guinea	7.0	33	102.3	43	480	26	78.1	8	43.8	*	*	*
Guyana	2.6	97	109.2	27	370	35	27.0	94	72.3	11.6	20.7	26.0
Haiti	4.9	77	106.2	51	370	28	50.4	42	56.4	8.0	23.8	27.3
Honduras	5.2	92	106.7	22	590	44	60.4	65	66.1	29.2	20.0	24.4
Hong Kong	1.4	85	107.2	59	11540	94	1.1	81	79.1	2.0	25.3	28.7
India	4.2	50	100.6	34	350	27	62.6	29	57.9	43.5	18.7	23.4
Indonesia	3.3	79	105.9	52	560	31	54.4	64	57.4	17.3	20.0	24.1
Iran	5.0	61	101.3	21	2450	57	36.4	36	65.5	33.9	19.7	24.2
Iraq	6.2	64	103.3	6	*	71	12.5	41	64.8	31.5	20.8	25.2
Ivory Coast	7.4	55	106.6	52	730	40	65.2	34	54.2	52.5	18.9	27.1
Jamaica	2.5	100	106.2	45	1510	52	25.3	98	76.7	9.1	25.2	30.5

Continued

Table 13.1. Continued

COUNTRY	(1)	(2)	(3)	(4)	(5)	(6)	(7)	(8)	(9)	(10)	(11)	(12)
Jordan	5.8	72	105.6	11	1240	68	10.2	62	67.8	20.1	22.6	26.8
Kenya	6.9	69	106.9	67	370	24	81.0	53	60.5	28.8	20.4	25.8
Korea, North	2.5	*	109.5	85	*	60	42.8	*	72.7	*	*	*
Korea, South	1.7	93	109.2	51	5400	72	19.0	91	72.5	0.9	24.1	27.3
Kuwait	3.7	84	106.0	16	16150	96	30.9	63	75.0	14.3	22.9	26.3
Laos	6.7	*	106.2	81	200	19	75.7	*	50.0	*	*	*
Lebanon	3.6	80	106.1	37	*	84	14.3	69	69.0	*	*	*
Lesotho	5.8	135	117.1	78	470	20	23.3	84	60.5	25.9	20.5	26.3
Liberia	6.7	50	104.7	44	450	46	74.2	21	56.0	42.3	19.4	26.6
Libya	6.8	57	105.7	10	5320	70	18.1	40	62.5	*	*	*
Madagascar	6.5	80	105.7	66	230	24	80.9	68	55.4	34.3	20.3	23.5
Malaysia	3.8	78	106.1	45	2340	43	41.6	65	71.6	8.2	23.5	26.6
Maldive Islands	7.0	100	*	*	450	30	*	93	49.5	43.1	*	*
Mali	7.1	50	107.4	20	270	19	85.5	15	45.6	48.9	18.1	28.2
Malawi	7.6	60	102.9	72	200	12	81.8	31	47.7	47.0	17.8	22.9
Mauritania	6.5	40	107.2	28	500	47	69.4	16	47.6	36.9	19.2	*
Mauritius	1.9	87	107.6	35	2250	40	19.0	77	71.7	10.9	21.7	24.7
Mexico	3.3	94	110.0	30	2490	73	22.9	82	72.3	20.1	20.6	23.6
Mongolia	4.9	*	104.2	83	*	52	39.9	*	65.6	*	*	*
Morocco	4.5	54	105.7	26	950	48	45.6	30	62.5	16.9	22.3	27.2
Mozambique	6.3	42	107.1	92	80	27	84.5	16	48.1	47.7	17.6	22.7
Myanmar	3.9	78	105.9	60	*	25	63.9	69	61.8	16.0	22.4	24.6
Nepal	6.7	32	97.9	51	170	10	93.0	11	50.3	50.1	17.9	21.5
Nicaragua	5.3	101	104.4	27	810	60	46.5	78	64.6	22.7	20.2	24.6
Niger	7.1	35	107.3	89	310	19	85.0	11	46.1	*	*	*
Nigeria	6.7	57	106.9	25	370	35	44.6	31	52.2	*	18.7	*
Oman	7.1	26	105.6	9	5220	11	50.0	12	56.8	*	*	*
Pakistan	6.2	41	100.0	7	380	32	41.3	18	56.5	29.1	19.8	24.9
Panama	3.0	100	105.8	37	1830	53	26.1	86	74.1	20.1	21.2	25.0
Papua–New Guinea	5.0	53	102.7	64	860	16	76.3	32	54.8	16.7	*	*
Paraguay	4.5	94	106.6	62	1110	47	48.6	86	69.1	14.1	21.8	26.0
Peru	3.8	83	106.3	49	1160	70	35.1	75	63.4	14.2	22.7	25.7
Philippines	4.1	99	106.1	46	730	43	43.4	87	65.4	14.0	22.4	25.3
Qatar	5.5	94	107.2	8	15860	89	3.0	73	71.8	16.1	*	*
Rwanda	8.1	54	107.0	92	310	8	92.8	32	50.2	15.0	21.2	24.5
Saudi Arabia	7.1	61	105.6	8	7050	77	48.5	43	65.2	*	*	*
Senegal	6.3	43	104.2	20	710	38	80.6	19	47.4	33.3	18.3	28.3
Sierra Leone	6.5	30	107.8	49	240	32	69.6	6	42.6	*	*	*
Singapore	1.8	85	107.8	61	12310	100	0.4	76	75.7	2.3	26.2	28.4
Somalia	6.6	33	107.2	64	150	36	75.6	9	46.6	*	20.1	26.5
South Africa	4.3	*	110.1	32	2520	59	13.6	*	63.5	5.1	25.7	27.8
Sri Lanka	2.6	88	106.1	33	470	21	42.6	81	72.5	9.7	24.4	27.9
Sudan	6.4	25	104.8	27	*	22	64.9	10	51.0	*	21.3	*
Surinam	2.8	99	107.4	41	3050	47	20.0	92	72.1	*	*	*
Swaziland	6.5	94	106.6	67	820	33	74.0	66	57.3	*	*	*
Syria	6.5	59	106.1	7	990	50	24.9	44	66.9	24.6	21.5	25.7
Tahiti	3.7	70	102.6	15	1420	54	21.6	47	66.1	6.5	24.3	28.1
Tanzania	7.1	*	106.5	93	120	33	85.6	*	54.7	35.7	19.1	24.9
Thailand	2.4	92	106.4	82	1420	23	72.4	87	67.1	15.6	22.7	24.7
Togo	6.6	49	106.8	58	410	26	64.3	25	54.8	40.6	18.5	26.5
Trinidad	2.8	98	107.3	38	3470	69	11.9	94	72.8	24.8	22.3	27.9

Continued

Table 13.1. Continued

COUNTRY	(1)	(2)	(3)	(4)	(5)	(6)	(7)	(8)	(9)	(10)	(11)	(12)
Turkey	3.5	73	105.5	32	1630	61	45.3	64	65.8	20.8	20.6	23.6
Uganda	7.3	51	106.6	71	220	10	85.9	29	52.7	*	*	*
Uruguay	2.4	99	109.4	45	2560	85	15.3	95	74.4	12.2	22.4	25.4
United Arab Emirates	4.6	*	106.3	7	19860	78	4.5	*	72.9	55.0	18.0	25.9
Venezuela	3.6	104	109.2	27	2560	90	12.5	88	72.8	18.4	21.2	24.8
Vietnam	3.9	89	107.3	88	*	22	67.5	80	63.6	*	*	*
Yemen	7.5	44	101.3	15	*	29	62.5	20	52.4	*	17.8	22.2
Zaire	6.1	67	106.6	56	230	39	71.5	53	54.2	*	20.1	25.4
Zambia	7.2	77	103.9	40	420	50	37.9	59	54.5	29.4	19.4	25.1
Zimbabwe	5.6	79	106.2	54	640	28	64.7	55	60.1	24.5	20.4	25.4

[a]Asterisk indicates missing data.
(1), total fertility rate; (2), female-to-male literacy ratio; (3), female-to-male life expectancy ratio; (4), female-to-male LFP rate; (5), gross national product; (6), percent population urban; (7), percent labor force in agriculture; (8), percent female literacy; (9), female life expectancy; (10), percent females married, ages 15–19; (11), mean age at marriage, females; (12), mean age at marriage, males.

excellent package for both prescreening and imputation because it generates several useful diagnostic statistics and allows for a range of imputation procedures.

For those using other statistical packages, the generation of the following indicators is a good starting point:

- numbers and percentage of missing cases for each variable
- means, minimum, and maximum values, standard deviations
- the number of missing cases in common on a pairwise basis
- correlations of the dichotomized variables, where each variable is coded on a present/missing basis
- a casewise distribution of the missing data
- a graphical presentation of the available data for each variable

In fact, the researcher has the obligation to approach the issue of missing data as a substudy in its own right. Not only can this ease further analysis and avoid some crucial pitfalls, it might also produce some substantive insight into the underlying mechanisms that generated the data in the first instance.

If it is decided to impute missing values, it is also worthwhile to screen the data to look for overall patterns again and to investigate any oddities because of the imputation process.[3] One very useful approach is to generate a series of casement plots or a scatter plot matrix (Cleveland, 1985). Again, this can be accomplished with any number of commercial statistics and graphics packages. This *verification* of the imputation process provides an excellent starting point for the actual substantive analysis of the data.

3. As an example, if one were to leave GNP in its original state, negative imputed values could be generated for a number of countries.

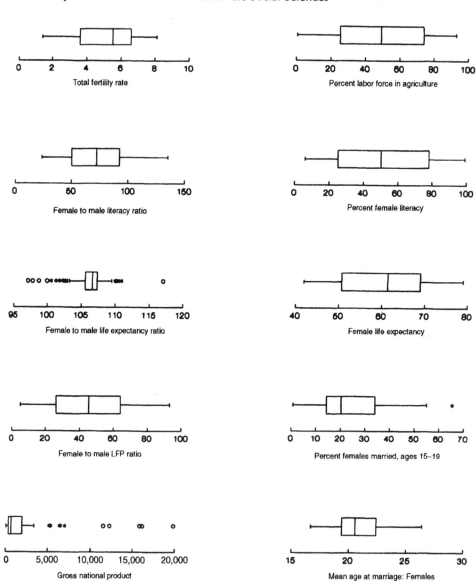

Figure 13.1. Box plots of data in Table 13.1.

Table 13.2. Summary statistics for mean substitution and maximum likelihood imputations

VARIABLE	AVAILABLE DATA			MEAN SUBSTITUTION		MAXIMUM LIKELIHOOD	
	N	MEAN	SD	MEAN	SD	MEAN	SD
TFR	109	5.1	1.7	5.1	1.7	5.1	1.7
F:M Literacy	102	69.6	23.9	69.6	23.2	69.8	23.6
F:M Life Exp.	108	106.3	2.8	106.3	2.8	106.3	2.8
Labor force participation	107	44.8	25.0	44.8	24.7	44.6	24.8
GNP	97	2.9	0.5	2.9	0.5	3.0	0.5
Urbanization	109	43.7	23.4	43.7	23.4	43.7	23.4
Agriculture	106	50.3	26.6	50.3	26.2	50.4	26.3
Literacy rate	102	51.1	28.9	51.1	28.0	51.4	28.6
Life Expectancy	109	60.4	10.2	60.4	10.2	60.4	10.2
Married	81	24.5	15.3	24.5	13.2	25.9	14.1
Age married							
Female	81	20.9	2.3	20.9	1.9	20.8	2.0
Male	78	25.6	1.7	25.6	1.4	25.7	1.5

Table 13.2 presents three sets of estimates for the means and standard deviations of the 12 variables: the first are based on the available data; the second on mean substitution, and the third on ML imputed values. These results illustrate three main points. First, for this data set, there is little discrepancy among any of the results; however, the greatest discrepancies generally occur where the proportion of missing data are greatest. Thus, for example, the estimates for GNP are more consistent than for mean age at marriage for either males or females.

Second, the estimated means for the maximum likelihood estimates are virtually identical with those for the available data, even where the proportion of missing cases is large. Third, while there are not great differences in the estimates of the standard deviations, both the mean substitution approach (as we found earlier) and the maximum likelihood approach tend to underestimate the standard deviation based on the available data.

Multiple Imputation: Combining Estimates

The process of multiple imputation is straightforward: the researcher simply applies the imputation process M times on the same data set. Once those M sets have been generated, however, we must ask how the results are to be combined or summarized to form an appropriate estimate.

Let us assume that the required imputations have been generated. The objective is to estimate some overall parameter, θ, from each of the $\hat{\theta}_i$ estimates given by each replicate. This combined estimate of θ, across the M now complete data sets, is

$$\bar{\theta}_M = \sum_{i=1}^{M} \frac{\hat{\theta}_i}{M}$$

To obtain an estimate of the variance of $\overline{\theta}_M$, it is necessary to combine the average of the within-group variances of the imputed data sets with the between-group variance of the imputed data sets. The average within-imputation variance is estimated by

$$\overline{s}_w^2 = \frac{\sum_{i=1}^M s_w^2}{M}$$

and the between-imputation variance is estimated by

$$s_b^2 = \frac{\sum_{i=1}^M \left(\hat{\theta}_i - \overline{\theta}_M\right)^2}{M-1}$$

The total estimated variance of $\overline{\theta}_M$ is now determined as

$$s_M^2 = \overline{s}_w^2 + \frac{M+1}{M}s_b^2$$

The component $(M+1)/M$ is the finite correction factor. Once an estimate of the total variability has been obtained, a confidence interval about $\overline{\theta}_M$ is given by

$$\overline{\theta}_M \pm t_{v,\alpha/2}\sqrt{s_M^2}$$

where the v degrees of freedom are approximated as

$$v = (M-1)\left[1 + \frac{1}{m+1}\frac{\overline{s}_w^2}{s_b^2}\right]^2$$

EXAMPLE: MULTIPLY IMPUTING AVERAGE AGE AT MARRIAGE FOR FEMALES

The data for this example are again drawn from Table 13.1. Two variables are of interest: mean age at marriage for females and female life expectancy. In 28 of the 109 cases, however, information on mean age at marriage is missing for women. Consequently, this variable is a prime candidate for imputation.

Research suggests that mean age at marriage is strongly related to life expectancy. With this information, using female life expectancy to predict the missing values seems reasonable. Taking the 81 cases with available data, age at marriage is regressed on life expectancy and the estimated equation is determined to be $\hat{Y}_R = 11.7796 + .1476X$ (where X is life expectancy). This equation is significant at $p < .001$; the coefficient of determination, R^2, is .42; and, the standard error of the estimate is 1.6684.

Five data sets are created in which the missing ages at marriage values are imputed with $\hat{Y}_R + z_i$, where z is drawn from the normal distribution with a mean of 0 and a standard deviation equal to the standard error of the estimate. The estimated means for age at marriage in those five complete data sets are 20.76, 20.70, 20.68, 20.63, and 20.63 years resulting in an overall mean, $\overline{Y}_M$, of 20.68 years. The between group variance is .003. The corresponding within-group variances are 4.52, 5.19, 4.65, 5.04, and 5.28. The mean within group variance, $\bar{s}^2_w$, based on these five estimates is 4.94. Thus, the total variance of the estimate is

$$s^2_M = s^2_W + \left(\frac{5+1}{5}\right) s^2_b = 4.94 + 1.2(.003) = 4.94$$

Because the ratio $\bar{s}^2_w / S^2_B$ is large, the degrees of freedom associated with the t-distribution also becomes very large. Consequently, a 95% confidence interval is estimated by $\overline{Y}_M \pm z \sqrt{\overline{Y}^2_M} = 20.68 \pm 1.96\sqrt{4.94}$, or the interval 16.3, 25.0.

Different models of imputation would produce different (and perhaps better) estimates for the missing values. The same procedure to aggregate the results from the M imputed data sets that is used here would be applied in those instances. It should also be noted that the method is not limited to those situations in which the statistic of interest is the mean. Further examples with applications to more complex samples can be found in Rubin (1987), and Little and Rubin (1987: ch. 12) although these references may be difficult for those with a minimal statistical background.

Multiple imputation is a procedure that works well with complex data sets, where the impact of single value imputation may not be obvious. When used across several imputation procedures, it also acts as a type of sensitivity analysis, informing us about the possible relative impact the of different procedures on the results. Overall, the application of multiple imputation solutions need not be too onerous, particularly with the availability of powerful and inexpensive desktop computers. Most "professional" statistical software can be readily adapted to generate several replicates with imputed values. Further, Rubin (1987) has shown that even when M is limited to three or four replicates, results with respectable sampling characteristics can be obtained.

ASSESSING IMPUTATION PROCEDURES

The impact of imputation on the bias and precision of estimates can be determined analytically for some simple imputation procedures such as mean substitution. In many more instances, however, the impact of the imputation cannot be determined analytically. Furthermore, since many procedures are stochastically based, the behavior of any given procedure may be known only asymptotically or "in the long run." Under these circumstances, the best way to investigate the behavior of a particular procedure, or even a particular variable in a particular data set, is to conduct a simulation analysis.

Most attempts to assess imputation procedures involve some form of jackknife or Monte Carlo procedure (see Chapter 15). To obtain a flavor for the variety of approaches to examining the behavior of imputation techniques, two examples are provided. The first is a review of a study by Landerman, Land, and Pieper (1997) that examines the behavior of a mean substitution method for imputing missing income values. The second involves a suggestion by Rubin (1977) for a Bayesian approach to assessing the impact of missing values.

EXAMPLE: LANDERMAN, LAND, AND PIEPER'S ASSESSMENT OF MEAN MATCHING

Landerman, Land, and Pieper (1997) conducted a Monte Carlo–style study of the impact of what they term the "predictive mean matching method for imputing missing values" in an epidemiological survey of the elderly. The investigation surveyed 4162 respondents, and complete data were available in 3213 cases. The variable that accounted for most of the missing data was income. The dependent variable in the study was the number of depressive symptoms the respondents had recounted during the past week.

The researchers generated a regression model in which the logarithm of the number of depressive symptoms was regressed on eight independent variables (including income) for the 3213 cases with known data. Subsequently, the researchers randomly set income to missing on some of the known cases, used the same variables to impute the deleted income values, and then assessed the impact of the imputation procedure by reestimating the original regression.

The imputation procedure employed the "mean matching method, where a missing value is assigned the value of a donor whose regression-predicted score . . . is closest to that of the nonrespondent" (Landerman, Land, and Pieper, 1997: 8). This is a variant on the hot-deck approach, and it has the advantage that not all the imputed values within a subclass defined by the regressors have the same score. The effect is that of imputing a regression mean and adding a random component, e_i, that reflects that of the sample data.

The researchers generated 600 test samples, 200 each with 5, 10 and 20% of the cases with income set to missing. They also examined the impact of multiple imputation on the results. In this instance, five imputed values were generated for the analysis. By recalculating the original regression equation on each sample, the researchers obtained a distribution of parameter values for each of the independent variables that could be compared with those obtained from the sample of 3213 complete cases. Overall, Landerman, Land, and Pieper (1997: 26) concluded:

- The imputed data results "became increasingly biased as the predictive power of the imputation model declined and the percentage set to missing increased." The coefficients were slightly more biased than the standard errors, with the coefficients for income being underestimated and the coefficient bias for the other predictors varying with the sign of the relationship with the dependent variable.
- In comparison to multiple imputation, "additional bias to standard errors resulted from the use of single-value imputation methods that underestimated standard errors and inflated t values." Unlike the bias mentioned in the preceding point (which ranged from 1% to 24%), this additional bias was relatively minor at 2% and under.
- "The predictive power of the imputation model had a substantially greater impact on precision than did the use of multiple-imputation methods." This result is consistent with other studies of this type and suggests that finding substantive variables that correlate highly with the variable with missing data is generally more important than the specific procedure used to impute the missing values.

The latter conclusion is of particular importance because it suggests that if missing data are a problem, it would be worthwhile exploring and attempting to construct adequate models of the missing data mechanism. Since some variables (such as income) appear in a wide range of substantive investigations, determining the best correlates of those items would pay large dividends.

A Bayesian Approach to Assessing the Impact of Missing Values

Rubin (1977) has outlined another technique for assessing the sensitivity of parameter estimates to censored data. The technique is particularly appealing because it allows for the incorporation of the researcher's subjective or prior knowledge of the problem, along with estimates of differences in the profiles of respondents and nonrespondents based on the collected data. The approach can be used to estimate the sensitivity of many different parameter estimates to situations in which some outcome measures are missing but some data are available on the censored cases. Here, the focus will be on regression modeling, since this is perhaps the most common form of statistical analysis applied to survey data.

Assume that a model is constructed in which Y is regressed on a series of independent variables defined by the matrix $\mathbf{X}$. The regression model conforms to all the standard assumptions, including the assumption that the errors (residuals) are identically and independently distributed.

Let $\overline{Y}_R$ be the mean for the respondents and $\overline{Y}_{NR}$ be the unknown mean for the nonrespondents. The proportion of respondents in the sample is signified by p and the proportion of nonrespondents is $1 - p$. $\mathbf{S}_{XX}$ is the sums of squares and cross-product of the matrix of independent variables, $\mathbf{X}$, and s_e^2 is the residual mean squared error.

A confidence interval can be constructed around $\overline{Y}$ by

$$\overline{Y}_R \left[1 + h_0 \pm z \left(\theta_1^2 h_1^2 + \theta_2^2 h_2^2 + h_3^2 \right)^{1/2} \right]$$

where z is a value corresponding to a given confidence interval (e.g., 1.96 for a 95% interval) and

$$h_0 = \frac{p \left(\overline{X}_{NR} - \overline{X}_R \right) b_R}{\overline{y}_R}$$

$$h_1^2 = h_0^2 + \left(\frac{p^2 s_e^2}{\overline{Y}_R^2} \right) \left(\overline{X}_{NR} - \overline{X}_R \right) S_{XX}^{-1} \left(\overline{X}_{NR} - \overline{X}_R \right)'$$

$$h_2^2 = p^2 \left[\frac{1 + s_e^2}{\overline{Y}_R^2 n (1 - p)} \right]$$

$$h_3^2 = p^2 \left(s_e^2 / \overline{Y}_R^2 \right) \left[\frac{1}{np - np^2} + \left(\overline{X}_{NR} - \overline{X}_R \right) S_{XX}^{-1} \left(\overline{X}_{NR} - \overline{X}_R \right)' \right]$$

The h_0 term above represents the relative bias resulting from different means on the independent variables (X) for respondents and nonrespondents. A large value for

h_0 suggests that the respondents and nonrespondents differ widely on the predictor variables; small values for h_0 suggest that their expected values on the predictors are similar.

The $\theta_1^2 h_1^2$ component reflects the relative variance due to uncertainty about the regression slopes for the two groups. A small value for θ_1 indicates that we believe that a substantial difference in the regression parameters across the two groups is unlikely.[4] A small value for h_2 suggests that there is little in the sample data to suggest any substantial variation exists across the regression slopes for the two groups.

The term $\theta_2^2 h_2^2$ is the relative variance related to the uncertainty about the equality of the expected Y-values based on the means of the respondents ($\overline{\mathbf{X}}_R$): that is, the expected values of Y if the predictor variable means were the same for nonrepondents and for respondents. Again, the value of θ_2 represents our subjective contribution to this uncertainty, while the data contribution to this component is reflected in the size of h_2.

The final term, h_3^2, is the uncertainty that exists even when our subjective belief is that the regression slopes are unlikely to be substantially different across the two samples. In other words, this is the uncertainty that remains even when $\theta_1 = \theta_2 = 0$; or, as Little and Rubin (1987: 233) point out, where the nonresponse mechanism is ignorable. The uncertainty captured in h_3 is essentially due to sampling variability.

If the h-values are near zero, the sample data suggest that the respondents and nonrespondents are unlikely to differ substantially on their average outcome value. Thus, we probably would not be too concerned about response bias *unless* we have strong a belief that there is something awry with the sample. This subjective concern would be based on factors such as our external knowledge of how those who choose either to respond or not to respond vary on the outcome measure. For example, a survey that attempts to investigate the social correlates of paranoia would raise substantial concerns over response bias even if the data hold little to suggest the responding and nonresponding groups differ. Substantive knowledge of how the data were collected could also influence this judgment. Again, these subjective concerns are reflected in the values we select for θ_1 and θ_2.

The θ-values may seem mystical to those not used to thinking in Bayesian terms. With some reflection, however, most researchers can soon generate reasonable estimates, given their "feel" for the problem. The thetas are subjective estimates of the coefficients of determination (the standard deviation divided by the mean) for their respective variance components. As Rubin (1977) points out, coefficients of determination work well because their magnitudes are intuitively appealing. That is, a value of .01 or .05 is usually judged to be small and a value of 1.00 is judged to be large. If we believe, for example, that given similar mean values on the predictor variables, the mean values of Y differ substantially between the respondents and the nonrespondents, then we might assess θ_2 to be .6 or .75. If we have little reason to

---

4. Another way of thinking about this is to draw a parallel with analysis of covariance. The respondent–nonrespondent dichotomy forms the grouping variable, with X being a covariate. Setting $\theta_1 = 0$ supports the standard ANCOVA assumption that the Y-on-X regression slopes are similar for both groups. The larger we set θ_1, however, the less we believe in the validity of that assumption.

believe that there ought to be much difference, then a relatively small value of θ_2 might be chosen—say, .1 or .2.

EXAMPLE: FEMALE LABOR FORCE PARTICIPATION IN DEVELOPING COUNTRIES

Once again using the data in Table 13.1, we estimate the impact of national variations in female life expectancy and female labor force participation rates on mean age of marriage for women. As shown earlier, mean age of marriage is missing for 25% of the nations included in the study (27 out of 108). For the known cases, the overall mean age at marriage, $\bar{Y}_R$, is 20.8975 years. We use the known data to construct an OLS regression model, and the two independent variables end up explaining about 46% of the variance in average age of marriage. This is significant beyond a p-value of .001. The estimated b-values for female labor force participation and female life expectancy are .0178 and .1579 respectively, and the mean squared error (s_e^2) is 2.6557. Based on the available data and our subjective knowledge of the problem, we wish to construct a 95% confidence interval about the expected value of $\bar{Y}$ based on $\bar{X}_R$.

Substituting the appropriate quantities into the equations for the estimates of h, it is found that

$$h_0 = .00717$$

$$h_1 = .00005$$

$$h_2 = .56263$$

$$h_3 = .00017$$

The estimate of the bias, h_0, is quite small: based on differences between the mean values for $\mathbf{X}_R$ and $\mathbf{X}_{NR}$, the bias-adjusted estimate of the mean becomes $\bar{Y}_R(1 + h_0) = 20.8975(1.0072) = 21.0479$. To conduct a sensitivity analysis, we select what we believe to be a series of reasonable values for θ_1 and θ_2. In this instance, values for θ_1 are chosen to be .1 and .3, while .1, .2, and .3 are selected as the corresponding values for θ_2. Based on the h-values estimated from the data and these subjective values, the following corresponding 95% intervals about the adjusted mean are estimated:

θ_1	θ_2	ESTIMATED INTERVAL
.1	.1	18.74, 23.35
.1	.2	16.44, 25.66
.1	.3	14.13, 27.96
.3	.1	18.74, 23.35
.3	.2	16.44, 25.66
.3	.3	14.13, 27.96

Normally, the values for θ_1 and θ_2 are selected independently from the data. In practice, this implies that we should select the θ-values before conducting the data analysis.

An examination of the results shows that the estimated intervals are relatively insensitive to variations in θ_1 but vary considerably with the value of θ_2. This is because the estimate of h_1 is very close to zero, while the estimate for h_2 is about .56. This pattern is consistent with a model of nonresponse in which the regression parameters are stable across both respondents and nonrespondents, but the expected values of $\overline{Y}$ differ across the two groups when the mean values of the predictor variables are held to be those of the respondents (i.e., $\overline{X}_{NR}$ is set at $\overline{X}_R$).

Despite the obvious insights it generates for the researcher, Rubin's approach has seen few applications in the social science literature. Land and McCall (1993), however, examine the impact of missing cases on the estimate of community standards for obscenity. They reported on a sample of residents who were asked to participate in a viewing of a sexually explicit film and then comment on whether the film was offensive according to community standards. The study method involved drawing a sample of residents, administering a prefilm questionnaire, showing the film, and administering a postfilm questionnaire. Some people refused to participate "up front," and others completed the background questionnaire but refused to view the film when they were told that it contained X-rated material. Land and McCall wanted to find how the results might have differed if the nonrespondents had participated in the study.

The researchers use θ-values of .1, .2, and .4 to assess the sensitivity of the results to the self-censorship problem. These values were selected, in large part, to illustrate the applicability of the procedure to the problem at hand. Subjectively, it seems clear that the refusal to participate in the study is highly related to the respondent's judgment of the material. Thus, a more realistic scenario for this application would probably involve setting θ_2 at a reasonably high value, say .65 or .75.

SPECIAL ISSUES

Categorical Variables and Complex Data Structures

In the preceding example, we assumed that all the variables were continuous. In many situations, however, the data set may contain categorical variables or variables that can take only integer values. The previous logic still applies, however, with the accommodation that different procedures such as probit or logit analysis must be used.

A far more difficult situation arises when there are complex relationships within the data structure. Some combinations of outcomes are logically impossible. Thus, for example, care must be taken not to impute hysterectomies to men or incomes to dead persons. Such impossibilities often occur in actual survey data—as a result of coding errors, random responses, or fabrications by respondents. Good screening procedures will capture these anomalies in collected data; good researchers avoid generating such structures in imputed data.

Rotating Samples

Occasionally, observations are deliberately excluded from the database. One example is the Canadian Labour Force Survey, which attempts to estimate rates of unemployment. In total, approximately 60,000 households are contacted monthly. Each month, one-sixth of the respondents interviewed in the preceding month are dropped and are replaced by a random subsample of a similar size. The initial sample is randomly divided into sixths, and the sample is rotated so that after the first 5 months, each sixth will have been observed over half a year. Since both the initial allocations into the six groupings and the selection of the replacement subsample are under the control of the researcher, it is possible to assure that the cases are selected in and out randomly.

This type of sampling procedure is generally used when the cost to individuals responding to the survey is relatively high (regarding time investment) and natural attrition over time would be high. Of course, attrition does take place; however, the restricted duration of the follow-up period serves to minimize its impact. This type of design results in two types of problem for the researcher: that posed by natural attrition, which may or may not result in cases MAR, and that posed by the deliberate rotation known to be MAR.

The algebra involved in analyzing rotating panels is somewhat messy, and the details of this approach are beyond the scope of the statistical background we have assumed. For those interested in pursuing this topic, a clear and succinct discussion of how to deal with estimates for rotating panels can be found in Hsiao (1986: 193–97).

The point to be made, however, is twofold. First, there are situations in which the assumptions of MAR are known to hold with a fair degree of certainty. Second, unbiased, efficient, and consistent techniques developed for handling missing data problems solve a wider range of problems than might be imagined at first glance.

Truncation

Another form of sampling bias that has an impact on our research results from truncation. In many studies, the researcher chooses to focus on a limited range of the data. For example, income maintenance programs might limit their scope to individuals within some multiple of a predefined poverty level. In the preceding example, the original study limited the focus to countries defined as *developing*. Thus, the wealthier countries of Europe, North America, and Australasia were excluded from the analysis.

For a moment, let us assume that in the fertility example above there is a strong negative linear relationship between gross national product (GNP) and a country's total fertility rate (TFR). The relationship might be exemplified by Figure 13.2. Note that the line *T* represents an arbitrary cutoff point above which data are not included in the analysis. If all the data were available, the *true* regression line would be the solid line. Because the observations in the upper left-hand portion of the graph are omitted, the regression the researcher would end up estimating is represented by the hashed line. In this instance, the estimated slope is somewhat less than the true slope, thereby underestimating the actual relationship between the two factors.

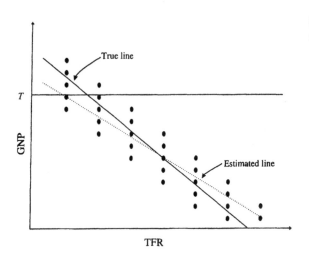

Figure 13.2. Regression bias resulting from truncation.

Selection bias can be the result of sampling truncation introduced by the researcher; or, it can be the result of self-selection by certain classes of subjects. Many income studies, for example, do not capture the truly rich or the truly poor.

The problem of correcting for sample selection bias has received considerable attention, particularly in the econometric literature. Again, the ideal solution is to augment the existing, truncated data set with auxiliary data. Where this is not possible, statistical approaches are used to address the problems. Two of the more popular statistical corrections now are the use of Tobit analysis and Heckman's procedure (Berk, 1983; Maddala, 1983; Winship and Mare, 1992). While these and other procedures address the problem with varying degrees of success, none is ideal across a broad range of problems.

Other Approaches

Imputation approaches to dealing with the problem of missing data involve two steps: imputation of the missing values, followed by proceeding with the statistical analysis originally intended. Several procedures have been developed that allow for addressing the problem of missing data without explicitly going through the imputation step. Most of these approaches involve "adjusting" the covariance matrix before analysis. Allison (1987), for example, outlines a maximum likelihood method that can be implemented within a structural modeling framework using such readily available statistical programs as LISREL. This procedure allows for the combination of data from two or more samples where there might even be slight differences in the actual indicators used. Within this framework, one can conduct most standard statistical procedures, such as ordinary regression and path modeling, as well as more general structural equation modeling.

Table 13.3. Summary of some commonly used techniques for imputing values

APPROACH	ADVANTAGES	DISADVANTAGES
Casewise deletion	Simplifies analysis (default option in most statistical packages) May produce unbiased results if cases are missing at random Produces unbiased variances for known cases	Implicitly assumes missing cases are indistinguishable from available cases; may result in significant bias if cases not missing at random Assumes "mean substitution" May disregard ancillary information on missing cases
Pairwise deletion	Easy to use (standard option within many statistical packages) Takes advantage of partial case data where available Effective increase in sample size on variables where data are available May produce unbiased results if data are missing at random Produces unbiased variances for known cases	Implicitly assumes missing cases are indistinguishable from available cases; may result in significant bias if cases not missing at random Assumes "mean substitution" Can introduce more bias in results than casewise deletion in some circumstances
"Doing nothing"	Implicitly assumes either casewise or pairwise deletion, depending upon default option in software	See discussions of casewise and pairwise deletion
Autogenerative (generally "mean") substitution	Easy to use; mean substitution is available as option in most statistical software Retains mean for known cases as estimate of the overall mean	Results in underestimate of overall variance unless correction factor is used in final estimates Assumes that Y is the same for both known and missing cases Implies that there is no variance among the missing cases
Predictive imputation based on covariates (e.g., using regression estimates)	Relatively easy to use; increasingly available in many software packages Makes use of case information available in observed values Often results in less underestimation of variance than univariate substitution procedures, since imputed values vary with covariates	Results usually underestimate overall variance unless correction factor is used in final estimates Assumes that Y is the same for both known and missing cases within the strata defined by the covariates Implies that there is no variance among the missing cases within the strata defined by the covariates "Quality" of results depends upon estimation procedure; maximum likelihood and iterative procedures generally produce better estimates than single-stage estimates
Addition of random (stochastic) component	Can improve on both mean substitution and substitution with covariates if	Most applications assume that the random component is normal with a mean of zero and a variance

Continued

Table13.3. Continued

APPROACH	ADVANTAGES	DISADVANTAGES
	appropriate distribution is chosen for selecting random element May lead to more valid estimate of population mean and variance, particularly where data are not missing at random and researcher has some prior notion of the distribution of the missing data Relatively easy to use if data are assumed to be missing at random	equal to that for the known cases Where $z_i \approx N(0, \sigma^2)$ is assumed: a) the estimate of the individual variances is improved but often results in a slight overestimate, and b) $\overline{Y}$ is assumed to be the same for both known and missing cases Improper selection of distribution for random component may introduce substantial bias
Single imputation	Can reduce bias in point estimates and standard errors if used correctly, especially if data are not missing at random Explicitly addresses problems inherent casewise and pairwise deletion Simplifies analysis May take advantage of ancillary data available to original researcher that are not part of final data set	If done improperly, may introduce more bias in results than either casewise or pairwise deletion Leaves researcher with impression that imputed values are as valid as known observations Implies that imputed values are "real" as opposed to "estimates"; that is, the uncertainty about $\hat{Y}$ is not incorporated into the distributed data
Multiple imputation	Clearly identifies missing cases/values Can reduce bias in point estimates and standard errors if used correctly, especially if data are not missing at random Explicitly addresses problems inherent casewise and pairwise deletion Retains essence of missing values as estimates as opposed to observed values Readily amenable to sensitivity analysis	Involves extra computing resources in terms of time and storage space May require distribution of multiple data sets May still contribute a false sense of awareness if done poorly
"Hot-deck" procedures	Makes use of case information available in observed values Often results in less underestimation of variance than univariate substitution procedures, since imputed values vary with covariates With large data sets, may be a more efficient procedure than developing an explicit model for imputing missing values	Disadvantages similar to substitution based on covariates Most "hot-deck" approaches require specialized software and are memory intensive

CONCLUSION

Some of the advantages and disadvantages of various approaches to handling missing data are outlined in Table 13.3. Clearly, there is no one best approach for dealing with the problem of missing data, and while it is equally clear that we ought to enhance our data collection procedures as a primary line of defense, obviously we cannot avoid the issue entirely. The two best approaches to the problem may be the use of ML techniques and, when possible, multiple imputation.

While this sage advice is passed on to the analyst, we have not addressed the choice of means by which to place data sets in the public domain. Should one distribute a data set with missing values noted, or is it better to distribute a "sanitized" version in which all missing values are either purged or imputed? In general, preprocessing data sets by including imputed values is not a good strategy. It is far better to retain the integrity of the data as they were collected, which allows future researchers to decide how they might wish to deal with the problem.

On the other hand, some organizations (such as census bureaus) make a practice of distributing only preprocessed data sets. How can this approach be justified? Beyond the self-evident observation that preimputed values save considerable effort for the individual researcher, Little and Rubin (1989–90) point out several valid justifications. These include the following.

- The data are readily amenable to complete case analysis, thus averting the need for researchers to use specialized software or procedures.

- The original data collector might be privy to confidential information that cannot be publicly distributed but might prove useful in providing more efficient and less biased estimators than could be obtained with the public data alone. This is especially the case with government agencies such as census bureaus.

- The problem is addressed only once, thus providing a consistency in any further analyses that might be conducted. If idiosyncratic imputations were allowed, it might be difficult, if not impossible for other researchers to verify or replicate published results.

- The data collector may often have special insight into how the data were collected, and thus can make more informed judgments about how the imputation ought to be done. Often, that insight is not passed along when data are publicly distributed.

The issue of missing data is a difficult one. As we have argued, however, it is one that does not go away if ignored.

Further Reading

Madow, W.G., Nisselson, H., and Olkin, I. *Incomplete Data in Sample Surveys*, Vol. 1: *Report and Case Studies*. New York: Wiley, 1983.

Madow, W.G., Olkin, I. and Rubin, D.B. *Incomplete Data in Sample Surveys*, Vol. 2: *Theory and Bibliographies*. New York: Wiley, 1983.

Madow, W.G., and Olkin, I. *Incomplete Data in Sample Surveys*, Vol. 3: *Proceedings of the Symposium*. New York: Wiley, 1983.

These three volumes represent an assessment of the state of the art in the analysis of missing data. Individual articles vary in their level of difficulty, however, with some requiring an extensive background in statistics. Overall, this is a good starting point when one is faced with a particularly difficult situation.

Rubin, D.R. *Multiple Imputation for Nonresponse in Surveys*. New York: Wiley, 1987. This text examines the application of multiple imputation to a wide range of data situations. Later chapters deal with difficult problems such as panel studies.

14

Interpolating and Smoothing

I never could make out what those damned dots meant.
—Lord Randoph Churchill

Frequently summarized data are too "rough" for our purposes. This roughness may arise for many reasons, such as the categorization of summary data into groupings that have inappropriate boundaries. Alternatively, the upper and lower bounds may not be consistent with other available data, or they may not coincide with theoretically relevant boundaries. Ordinary sampling variability may also produce distributions that do not coincide with known distributions at the population level. Furthermore, when relatively rare events are of interest, we may find that several cells have empirical zero values. In these and other situations, it is often worthwhile adjusting the data to be more consistent with known empirical or theoretical patterns.

Two procedures that are used extensively in this adjustment process are interpolation and smoothing. Although the statistical literature often deals with these as separate issues, the two are simply variations on the same theme.

INTERPOLATION

Often, published data are categorized into groups. For example, it is common to see age distributions reported in 5- or 10-year groups or to see income reported in groups of $10,000. On certain occasions, however, those groupings are inconvenient. The category limits of one income distribution may differ from those of another, thus making comparisons difficult. In other situations, we may be interested in knowing the likely distribution of values between the published limits. In these and many other situations, interpolating values between the reported limits is useful. The practice of interpolation is discussed extensively in demographic techniques, but it has a wide range of applications in many substantive areas.

Fitting curves to incomplete empirical distributions has many uses beyond being simply able to "fill the gaps" in published data. We may, for example, wish to construct microsimulation models based on samples or populations for which detailed data are not available. In these circumstances, an empirical function fitted to known data fragments can define a quasi-population distribution from which Monte Carlo or simulation data can be generated.

We will explore a couple of flexible procedures that have a wide range of applicability.[1]

---

1. For a more detailed exposition of interpolation, see discussions in Shryock and Siegel (1973: 681–712) and Keyfitz (1974: 223–45). Many standard computer packages can be used to

As with all statistical techniques, the use of interpolation procedures should be preceded by consideration of the process that generated the data in the first instance. Figure 14.1 shows three data points and four out of many possible ways of connecting these points. At the extremes, we have a stepwise function and shortest distance straight lines connecting the points. Between, two curves exist that assume very different ways of joining the points. Which of these lines is the more appropriate for interpolating values between the points? This is an important issue. Occasionally, the issue can be resolved theoretically; at other times especially if more data points are available, an empirical estimate can be reached.

Polynomial Fitting

Any curve or function with n data points can be fit perfectly by a polynomial of degree $n - 1$. This insight has been used by many authors to propose several solutions to the interpolation problem. In its crudest form, the approach is quite simple. Let us assume that an instructor had a class of 450 students, who were graded on a five-point scale, incorporating the whole numbers 1 through 5 inclusive. Some time later, it is desirable to determine how many students scored between 2.5 and 3.0. Unfortunately, the instructor went insane and burned the gradebook, thereby making it difficult to recover the original scores. A record of the grade distribution is maintained in the office of the chair, however, and it is reproduced in Table 14.1

In fact, custom dictates that the recorded grades represent the upper limits of the grade intervals. Thus, a student with a grade of 1 could likely have received anything from 0 to 1, just as a student with a 5 could have a grade between 4 and 5. The student's

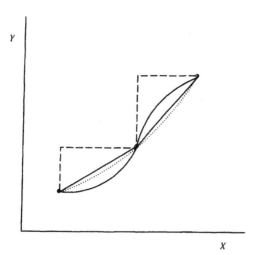

Figure 14.1. Some possible interpolations between points.

Y

X

perform interpolation. Those with programming experience can find useful algorithms in Press et al. (1992).

Table 14.1. Hypothetical grade distribution

GRADE	n	CUMULATIVE (n)	p
1	50	50	0.1111
2	100	150	0.3333
3	150	300	0.6667
4	100	400	0.8889
5	50	450	1

most likely grade, then, is the midpoint of the intervals, or the corresponding values .5, 1.5, 2.5, 3.5, and 4.5. The grade distribution and the cumulative grade distributions are graphed in Figures 14.2 and 14.3. Usually, it is easier to work with the cumulative distribution to maintain the limits of 0 and 1.0 in the cumulative distribution function (cdf), although this is not a necessarily true in all situations.

Since there are five data points, the cdf can be fit by a fourth-degree polynomial. That is,

$$\hat{p} = a_0 + \sum_{i=1}^{4} a_i X^i$$
$$= a_0 + a_1 X^1 + a_2 X^2 + a_3 X^3 + a_4 X^4$$

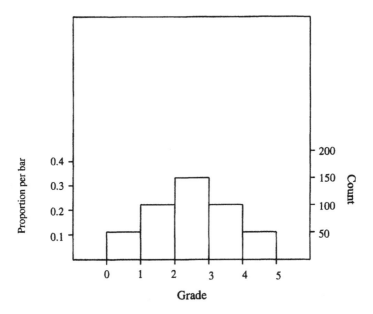

Figure 14.2. Histogram of grade distribution.

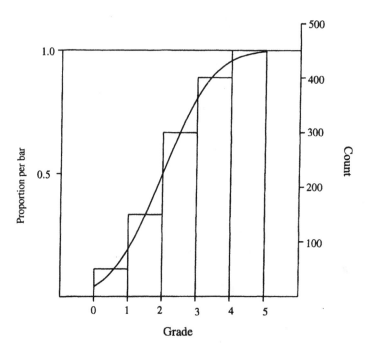

Figure 14.3. Cumulative histogram of grade distribution with fourth-order polynomial fit.

Allowing x to be the grade point scores, we have:

$$X = \begin{bmatrix} X & X^2 & X^3 & X^4 \\ 1 & 1 & 1 & 1 & 1 \\ 1 & 2 & 4 & 8 & 16 \\ 1 & 3 & 9 & 27 & 81 \\ 1 & 4 & 16 & 64 & 256 \\ 1 & 5 & 25 & 125 & 625 \end{bmatrix} \qquad P = \begin{bmatrix} 50/450 \\ 150/450 \\ 300/450 \\ 400/450 \\ 450/450 \end{bmatrix}$$

Solving the system of linear equations, $(X'X)^{-1}X'P$, it is possible to obtain the coefficients[2]:

$$a_0 = .44444$$

$$a_1 = -.81481$$

---

2. Systems of linear equations can be solved using almost any general statistical software. Some general regression package OLS routines will balk at trying to estimate a perfect fit. However, almost any matrix package (e.g., GAUSS, MATHCAD) or statistical package with an embedded matrix language (e.g., SYSTAT, SAS) can be used for generalized curve fitting.

$$a_2 = .60185$$

$$a_3 = -.12963$$

$$a_4 = .00926$$

In the original question, we wished to know the likely number of individuals with scores between 2.5 and 3.0. From Table 14.1 we know that 300 students had scores of 3.0 or less. The proportion of students with scores of 2.5 or less may now be calculated as:

$$\hat{p}_{(2.5)} = .44444 - .81481(2.5) + .60185(2.5)^2 - .12963(2.5)^3 - .00926(2.5)^4$$

$$= .50521$$

Multiplying .50521 by 450 gives 227.3. Thus, approximately $300 - 227 = 73$ students could be expected to have grades between 2.5 and 3.0. The cumulative distribution based on the fourth-order polynomial is given by the curved line in Figure 14.3.

The approach outlined above works reasonably well in a wide range of circumstances. However, difficulties can arise when one is estimating in the tails. Specifically, predicted values below 0 and above 1.0 may be generated. In this situation, using the logistic transformation is beneficial. The logistic equation is:

$$\ln\left(\frac{p}{1-p}\right) = a_0 + \sum_{i=1}^{n-1} a_i X^i$$

Once the logits have been estimated—that is, the expected $\ln[p/(1-p)]$ values—it is possible to recover the estimated cumulative probabilities as follows:

$$\hat{p} = \frac{\exp\left(a_0 + \sum_{i=1}^{n-1} a_i X^i\right)}{1 + \exp\left(a_0 + \sum_{i=1}^{n-1} a_i X^i\right)}$$

Fortunately, many statistical packages will generate the $\hat{p}$-values as an option, saving us considerable arithmetic. If this option is not available, the formula for generating the $\hat{p}$-values can be programmed easily into a spreadsheet or matrix language of a general statistical package such as SAS or SYSTAT.

The preceding example allows us to estimate the parameters under the logistic model. One minor adjustment is made to the data, however, and that is to replace the cumulative probability of 1.0 with .9999. This is done to avoid the problem of log $[1/1 - 1)]$. From a practical point of view, one must keep in mind the precision of the estimation software to avoid internal rounding back to 1.0.

Again solving the normal equations, we estimate the coefficients for the logistic model:

$$a_0 = 6.8709$$

$$a_1 = -20.148$$

$$a_2 = 15.074$$

$$a_3 = -4.3069$$

$$a_4 = .43069$$

For those who are less familiar with working with logistic models, some intermediate values are presented in Table 14.2. Here we have substituted the original X-values into the equation. The column of Y-values consists of the estimates $a_0 + \sum a_i x^i$; $\exp(Y)$ is a column of the Y-values exponentiated, and p consists of $\exp(y)/[1 + \exp(Y)]$. As is to be expected, the cumulative probabilities reproduce themselves faithfully.

As mentioned previously, fitting to the cdf is not necessary; however, fitting to proportions instead of to the raw numbers does have some advantages. The expected values at the limits can be constricted to 0 and 1. Furthermore, by making the distribution independent of the magnitudes in the distribution, the generic distribution can be easily applied to samples of any size. This is very useful if an empirical distribution is to be used for simulation modeling (e.g., Monte Carlo studies) or if one wishes to impose a distribution of a particular shape on another sample. We might, for example, want to estimate how large the Mexican middle class might be if Mexico had the same income distribution as the United States.

Special Issues with Polynomials

Occasionally, functions will occur that are not amenable to the procedure outlined above. In those situations, more creative approaches will be necessary.[3] Most good statistical packages include "nonlinear" routines that can be used to great advantage in these situations. Many problems, however, require an initial estimate of the parameter values. Often values obtained from an OLS estimation are adequate for the job.

Care must also be taken not to generate values that exceed the precision of either the software or hardware chosen to conduct the numerical analysis. Even small numbers raised to the nth power soon achieve large magnitudes. Sometimes this practical problem can be solved by shifting the X-values so that they center on 0. Conducting a simple linear transformation on these quantities (e.g., subtracting 50 or 55 from a set of values 50, 51, . . . , 75) does not undermine the generality of the results, but 10 or 20 raised to the nth power is less likely to create problems than 60 or 70 raised to

Table 14.2. Logistic model fit to hypothesized grade distribution

X	Y	$\exp(Y)$	$\hat{p}$
1	−2.0794	0.125	0.1111
2	−0.69315	0.5	0.3333
3	0.69315	2	0.6667
4	2.0794	8	0.8889
5	6.107	98,688	0.9999

3. For those faced with intransigent problems, Acton (1990) and Cuyt and Wuytack (1987) might prove to be useful.

the nth power. As a rule, generating the polynomials internally is better than reading them in as raw data. Many statistical packages treat input data as single precision while internal calculations are conducted in double precision.

Other difficulties can arise when using ordinary least squares procedures are used to fit distributions. Usually we encounter few problems when fitting curves to simple counts. However, if the function to be fitted is based on the logarithm of those counts, then it is necessary to do weighted regression using Y^2 (where Y is the original count) as a weighting factor if the results are to be exponentiated back into counts.[4] Again, most decent statistical packages will do weighted least squares regression.

Splines

Another general way of interpolating data is to use spline functions. Originally, splines were flexible strips of metal that draftsmen used to generate smooth lines among a series of plotted points. The fit was produced by fixing the spline to the points by means of weights. The spline was bent into shape and the draftsman drew the desired line by hand. With the coming of digital computers, spline functions gradually came to replace the mechanical contrivance. Mechanical splines are now as rare as slide rules, and the term "spline" has essentially become synonymous with the mathematical notion of spline function.

Mathematical splines are functions consisting of sets of polynomials, known as segmented or piecewise polynomials, jointed at the data points.[5] Because the lines are joined at the data points, the data points themselves are often called knots in reference to the mechanical heritage.

Spline functions are simple to define and have several properties that make them more desirable in many circumstances than nth-order polynomials. Usually, splines give a smoother fit to the data than do polynomials, and splines often provide a better solution to the boundary problem (i.e., what to do with the intervals $-\infty, X_0$ and $X_n, +\infty$) than do polynomials. As with nth-order polynomials, splines can be estimated as a series of linear equations. The computation effort required to estimate splines is comparable to that involved in estimating nth-order polynomials. For technical reasons that we will appreciate in a moment, only splines of odd orders need be considered (cubic, quintic, etc.).

Assume that we have a series of outcome observations, Y, defined along an X-axis. The earlier example concerning the grade distribution would be typical. The X-values

---

4. The appropriate weight is actually $1/Y^2$; however, most statistical packages require Y^2 to be input, with the reciprocation conducted internally. See Greene (1990: ch. 14) for a general discussion of weighted least squares. Chapter 11 also provides a good introduction to nonlinear regression estimation.

5. The literature on splines is extensive. For treatments of the theory underlying splines, see Greville (1969) and De Boor (1978). Computational aspects are addressed in Hopkins and Phillips (1988) and Thisted (1988). Those wishing to gain an appreciation of what life was like before the advent of microcomputers would do well to track down a copy of Sard and Weintraub (1971).

must be ordered monotonically, usually from lowest to highest. The spline function is then defined as follows:

$$s(X) = \sum_{j=0}^{m} a_j X^j + \sum_{i=1}^{n} b_i (X - X_i)_+^m$$

where $(X - X_i)_+$ implies that the difference $(X - X_i)$ is greater than or equal to 0 (or, as the subscript implies, a positive value), and the a_j and b_i are estimable coefficients. Because of the constraint $(X - X_i) > 0$, spline functions are often called systems of *truncated polynomials*.

To set up the linear equations, it is necessary to separate the lower and upper boundaries from the data set. Thus, for example, we would segment the five-point grade distribution as follows:

$0 = X_0$ lower boundary
$1 = X_1$
$2 = X_2$ n inner data points
$3 = X_3$
$4 = X_n$
$5 = X_{n+1}$ upper boundary

Each of the inner data points is defined by a single linear equation that would be termed the first derivative in elementary calculus (see Box 14.1). Depending upon the

---

■ **Box 14.1.**

DERIVATIVES

Derivatives of elementary algebraic functions are quite easy to calculate.
    Assume we have some function $y = f(x)$.

1. If that function is a constant (e.g., $y = 10$), then the derivative is 0. The derivative of any constant is 0.

2. If that function is specified by $y = x^n$, then subsequent derivatives are based on decremental values of n, hence:

    First derivative x^n
    Second derivative nx^{n-1}
    Third derivative $(n - 1)x^{n-2}$

        .
        .
        .

This assumes that n is a real number greater than 0. For any given function, the derivatives may not exist or may be undefined.

order of the spline function (cubic, quintic, etc.), the boundaries are defined by two or more equations. For a spline of order m, the boundaries are defined by $k = (m+1)/2$ equations. These represent the various derivatives of the boundary equations; thus, the boundaries of a cubic spline would require the first and second derivative to be specified [since $k = (3+1)/2 = 2$]. A quintic spline would require the specification of the first, second, and third derivatives. While the ordering of equations in a matrix is totally arbitrary, the equations for the inner data points are usually specified first, followed by the derivatives for the lower and upper boundaries. It is also because of the relationship between k and m that only splines of odd orders are used, since an even value of m will result in a fractional value for k.

For each knot, or data point, we can write out the $a_j X^j$ and $b_i (X - X_i)_+^m$ and present the results in matrix form. Assuming for a moment a quintic spline, ($m = 3$; hence, $k = 2$), the $n + m + 1$ normal equations can be gathered to form the matrix **D**. The corresponding matrix of coefficients consists of the matrix **A**.

$$D = \begin{bmatrix}
X_1^0 & X_1^1 & X_1^2 & X_1^3 & 0 & 0 & \cdots & 0 & 0 \\
X_2^0 & X_2^1 & X_2^2 & X_2^3 & (X_2 - X_1)^3 & 0 & \cdots & 0 & 0 \\
& & & & & & \vdots & & \\
X_n^0 & X_n^1 & X_n^2 & X_n^3 & (X_n - X_1)^3 & (X_n - X_2)^3 & \cdots & (X_n - X_{n-1})^3 & 0 \\
X_0^0 & X_0^1 & X_0^2 & X_0^3 & 0 & 0 & \cdots & 0 & 0 \\
0 & X_0^0 & 2X_0^1 & 3X_0^2 & 0 & 0 & \cdots & 0 & 0 \\
X_{n+1}^0 & X_{n+1}^1 & X_{n+1}^2 & X_{n+1}^3 & (X_{n+1} - X_1)^3 & (X_{n+1} - X_2)^3 & \cdots & (X_{n+1} - X_{n-1})^3 & (X_{n+1} - X_n)^3 \\
0 & X_{n+1}^0 & 2X_{n+1}^1 & 3X_{n+1}^2 & 3(X_{n+1} - X_1)^2 & 3(X_{n+1} - X_2)^2 & \cdots & 3(X_{n+1} - X_{n-1})^2 & 3(X_{n+1} - X_n)^2
\end{bmatrix}$$

$$A = \begin{bmatrix}
a_0 \\
a_1 \\
a_2 \\
\vdots \\
a_m \\
b_1 \\
b_2 \\
\vdots \\
b_n
\end{bmatrix}$$

As can be seen in **D**, the first n rows consist of the first derivatives for the inner data points, 1 to n inclusive. The last four rows in **D** consist of the first and second derivatives for the lower boundary (X_0) and the first and second derivatives for the upper boundary (X_{n+1}) respectively.

As a set of linear equations, where **D** consists of the $(n + m + 1) \times (n + m + 1)$ matrix defined above (based on the X-axis values); **Y** is an $(n + m + 1) \times 1$ matrix of outcome observations, and **A** is an $(n + m + 1) \times 1$ matrix of coefficients to be estimated, we have:

$$DA = Y$$

Since **D** is a square matrix, **A** is obtained simply by premultiplying both sides of the equation by $\mathbf{D}^{-1}$. Hence,

$$A = D^{-1}Y$$

EXAMPLE: SPLINES AND THE GRADE DISTRIBUTION

Returning to the grade distribution example (Table 14.1), we may fit a cubic spline by substituting the X-values into the matrix **D**, giving us:

$$\mathbf{D} = \begin{bmatrix} 1 & 1 & 1 & 1 & 0 & 0 & 0 & 0 \\ 1 & 2 & 4 & 8 & 1 & 0 & 0 & 0 \\ 1 & 3 & 9 & 27 & 8 & 1 & 0 & 0 \\ 1 & 4 & 16 & 64 & 27 & 8 & 1 & 0 \\ 1 & 0 & 0 & 0 & 0 & 0 & 0 & 0 \\ 0 & 1 & 0 & 0 & 0 & 0 & 0 & 0 \\ 1 & 5 & 25 & 125 & 64 & 27 & 8 & 1 \\ 0 & 1 & 10 & 75 & 48 & 27 & 12 & 3 \end{bmatrix} \quad \mathbf{Y} = \begin{bmatrix} 50/450 \\ 150/450 \\ 300/450 \\ 400/450 \\ 0 \\ 0 \\ 450/450 \\ 0 \end{bmatrix}$$

Here, the first four rows of **D** are the first-order derivatives for the four inner data points. Row 5 is the first derivative for the lower boundary ($X_0 = 0$); row 6 is the second derivative for the lower boundary; row 7 is the first derivative for the upper boundary ($X_{n+1} = 5$); and finally, row 8 is the second derivative for the upper boundary.

The corresponding entries in the **Y** matrix reflect the coordinates for the **D** matrix. The first four rows are the outcomes for the inner categories, X_1 to X_4. The last four entries represent the outcome values corresponding to the lower and upper boundaries. In this instance, the first derivatives for the lower and upper boundaries are set to 0 and 1.0 (i.e., 450/450) respectively, while both the Y-values for the second derivatives are set to zero. Inverting **D** and postmultiplying it by **Y** gives the matrix of coefficients, **A**.

$$\mathbf{A} = \begin{bmatrix} .0 \\ .0 \\ .15789 \\ -.04678 \\ .07602 \\ -.09942 \\ .09942 \\ -.07602 \end{bmatrix}$$

Checking our arithmetic, we can substitute some X-values (say 2 and our desired value of 2.5) into our predictive equation to obtain:

$$\hat{p}_2 = \sum_{j=0}^{m} a_j X^j + \sum_{i=1}^{n} b_i (2.0 - X_i)_+^m$$

$$= 0(2)^0 + 0(2)^1 + .15789(2)^2 - .04678(2)^3 + .07602(2 - 1)^3$$

$$- .09953(0) + .09942(0) - .07602(0)$$

$$= 0(1) + 0(2) + .15789(4) - .04676(8) + .07602(1) - .09942(0)$$

$$+ .09942(0) - .07602(0)$$

$$= .3333$$

$$\hat{p}_{2.5} = \sum_{j=0}^{m} a_j X^j + \sum_{i=1}^{n} b_i (2.5 - X_i)_+^m$$

$$= 0(2.5)^0 + 0(2.5)^1 + .15789(2.5)^2 - .04678(2.5)^3 + .07602(2.5 - 1)^3$$

$$- .09953(2.5 - 2)^3 + .09942(0) - .07602(0)$$

$$= 0(1) + 0(2) + .15789(4) - .04676(8) + .07602(1) - .09942(0)$$

$$+ .09942(0) - .07602(0)$$

$$= .5000$$

As with polynomial regression, substantial care is required with the numerical analysis. The **D** matrix is often ill conditioned, particularly for high m and large ns, thus making it often difficult to invert.

Special Issues with Splines

As with any form of curve fitting, the effective use of splines calls for as much art as theory. While cubic splines are essentially the workhorses in most applications, resorting to higher order splines, such as quintic or septic splines, may be necessary. The final choice should be based on a visual check of the interpolations against the known values. In some circumstances, particularly in the tails, splines may produce illogical fits (e.g., negative values for population counts) that require higher order splines or a different estimation of the higher order derivatives. In some situations the problem is best solved by doing separate fits on different segments of the function.

Many comments concerning numerical estimation as applied to polynomial regression also apply to splines. While the presentation above has theoretical merit, it often creates difficulties in practice—especially as n and m increase. The two major difficulties revolve around the large absolute values that can be obtained though exponentiation, and the problem of inverting an ill conditioned **A**-matrix. Solutions to these problems do exist, and anyone investigating splines seriously should become familiar with these approaches. Among the best-known practical implementations that do not involve simple matrix inversion are the *B*-splines. Discussions on these and other spline functions are found in the references cited earlier.

EXAMPLE: DIVORCES IN DENMARK

The Danish vital statistics include numbers of divorces that have taken place during a given year by the age of the partners.[6] The figures are provided in 5-year age groupings 15–19, 20–24, . . . , 74+ in the original tables. The number of divorces recorded for 1990 by husband's age are presented in Table 14.3.

Both a cubic spline and a twelfth-order polynomial were fit to the data. The interpolated results are presented in Figure 14.4. Although not specifically shown on the graph, the points on the graph for each age multiple of 5 years are the values represented in the empirical distribution.

While both interpolation procedures provide similar results for the midrange of the interpolated values, some divergence is to be seen in the tails. Figure 14.5 provides a greater detail of the left-hand tail for the Danish divorce data. Here, the spline is best behaved, providing a much smoother fit to the data, especially between the ages of 15 and 20. Unfortunately, the spline function does interpolate small negative values (an impossibility with a cdf) for ages 16–18 inclusive. These values are small enough to be imperceptible in the graph. The twelfth-degree polynomial, on the other hand, does not suffer from this difficulty at the low end of the distribution (although it does interpolate values above 1.0 in the 70+ range), but it behaves much more erratically. As can be seen from the graph, the polynomial bulges upward in the 15–20 year age interval—again, producing impossible results for a cdf. Similar poor behavior is seen at the upper end of the distribution. Here, the polynomial produces expected values

Table 14.3. Danish divorce by duration of marriage: 1990

		CUMULATIVE VALUES	
HUSBAND'S AGE (YEARS)	*n*	*n*	*p*
<15	0	0	0.0000
20	44	44	0.0031
25	955	999	0.0693
30	2369	3,368	0.2336
35	2766	6,134	0.4254
40	2735	8,869	0.6150
45	2537	11,406	0.7910
50	1524	12,930	0.8967
55	769	13,699	0.9500
60	378	14,077	0.9762
65	194	14,271	0.9897
70	98	14,369	0.9965
≥75	51	14,420	1.0000

---

6. Danmarks Statistik (1992) *Befolkningens bevægelser 1990*, Copenhagen, Table 51 p. 78.

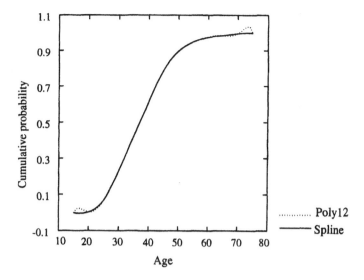

Figure 14.4. Interpolated Danish divorce data by age of husband: 1990.

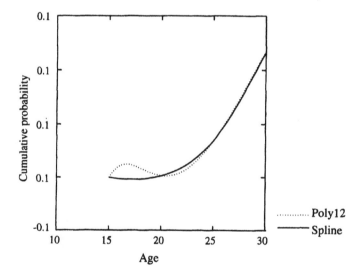

Figure 14.5. Detail of interpolated values in left tail of Figure 14.4.

beyond the theoretical limit of 1.0. This behavior is typical of polynomial functions and can often be solved either by fitting a lower order polynomial or by doing a logarithmic or logistic transformation on the data. The spline function, however, is quite well behaved at the upper end of the distribution.

GRADATION AND SMOOTHING

The same basic approaches that can be used to interpolate data between known points can also be used to smooth distributions assumed to be jagged because of measurement error. For example, fitting an eleventh-order polynomial to the Danish divorce data is cumbersome and, where the data are relatively smooth, largely redundant, since the distribution can often be fit by a polynomial of a lower order. Furthermore, selecting a lower order polynomial can be useful in smoothing out errors and perturbations in the data. For illustrative purposes, polynomials of orders 2, 3, and 4 have been fit to the data. The results of these exercises are given in Table 14.4.

The second-degree polynomial provides a reasonable fit to the data, although a substantial increase in fit is achieved by adding another additional term. As the last row in the table shows, the sum of squared error decreases from .0032 to .0006, going from a second- to a third-order polynomial. The addition of another term, however, provides only a marginal increment in fit as the sum of squared error decreases from .0006 to .0005.[7]

The greatest "lack of fit" appears in the distribution of marriages less than 2 years in duration. This feature could result from many sources, including simple data error. Some marriages recorded as less than 1 year in duration could, in fact, have lasted 1 to 2 years. This is not highly likely, since recording errors or memory decay problems tend to occur less often over such a short period. More than likely, true behavioral differences are at play. Substantively, the observed pattern would suggest that the risk factors associated with divorce are quite different for extremely short duration marriages and for those of a longer duration. Marriages that result in divorce within the first year are more likely to be marriages of convenience or marriages of impulse

Table 14.4. Estimated cumulative probabilities based on second-, third-, and fourth-order polynomials, $\hat{p}^{(2)}$, $\hat{p}^{(3)}$, and $\hat{p}^{(4)}$

DURATION (YEARS)	CUM. (p)	$\hat{p}^{(2)}$	$\hat{p}^{(3)}$	$\hat{p}^{(4)}$
<1	0.0247	0.0386	0.0151	0.0125
1	0.0757	0.1003	0.0909	0.0908
2	0.1553	0.1597	0.1609	0.1622
3	0.2291	0.2168	0.2255	0.2273
4	0.3458	0.2715	0.2850	0.2867
5	0.3397	0.3240	0.3397	0.3408
6–7	0.4366	0.4218	0.4362	0.4353
8–9	0.5131	0.5104	0.5174	0.5148
10–14	0.6646	0.6911	0.6707	0.6685
15–19	0.7914	0.8137	0.7848	0.7884
20–24	0.8980	0.8782	0.8999	0.8987
≥25	1.0000			
$\sum e^2$		0.0032	0.0006	0.0005

---

7. Although, as we shall soon see, small changes in proportions can have a major impact when distributed over large numbers.

than those that last longer. This lack of fit in the tails is not uncommon. Interpolating life tables creates similar problems, since rates of mortality are extremely high in the first year of life (infant mortality) and among the most elderly.

For convenience sake, let us assume that the lack of fit between the empirical distribution and that estimated by the third-order polynomial is simply due to error. On this basis, and assuming that the model $\hat{p} = a_0 + a_1 X + a_2 X^2 + a_3 X^3$ adequately models the cumulative divorce distribution, we will generate the expected numbers of divorces by discrete year (see Table 14.5). For comparison's sake, the cumulative probabilities and the expected numbers of persons in each duration are presented for the tenth-order polynomial. As a comparison of the numbers under $\hat{n}^{(3)}$ and $\hat{n}^{(10)}$ indicates, the discrepancy in the extrapolated values can be quite large, depending upon how close the fitted function is to the empirical function. Here, of course, we must ask, Which set of estimates is most appropriate?

Age Heaping

Even "good" data can have substantial error in the observed distribution. One well-known example is that of age heaping, or spiking—the result of a tendency by survey respondents to "round out" their age to numbers ending in 5 or 0. Thus, most empirical age distributions report too many people aged, say, 30 or 35 and too few aged 31, 32, 33, and 34. This phenomenon is common and has been the subject of substantial investigation and commentary.

Smoothing is a precarious endeavor at the best of times, since it calls for several judgments involving a choice of a smoothing technique and some estimate of the mechanism underlying the spiking. The choice of technique is a statistical judgment.

Table 14.5. Estimated values based on third- and tenth-order polynomials, $\hat{p}^{(3)}$, $\hat{n}^{(3)}$ and $\hat{p}^{(10)}$, $\hat{n}^{(10)}$

DURATION (YEARS)	$\hat{p}^{(3)}$	$\hat{n}^{(3)}$	$\hat{p}^{(10)}$	$\hat{n}^{(10)}$
<1	0.0151	217	0.0247	355
2	0.0909	1091	0.0757	734
3	0.1609	1008	0.1553	1146
4	0.2255	930	0.2291	1062
5	0.2850	857	0.2919	904
6	0.3397	787	0.3458	776
7	0.3900	724	0.3934	685
8	0.4362	665	0.4367	623
9	0.4786	610	0.4765	573
10	0.5174	559	0.5131	527
11	0.5531	514	0.5453	464
12	0.5860	474	0.5727	394
13	0.6163	436	0.5969	348
14	0.6444	405	0.6241	392
15	0.6707	379	0.6646	583

Note: Expected numbers, $\hat{n}$, are obtained by multiplying the difference between contiguous year's proportions by 14,396.

Two possible procedures were outlined in the preceding section—polynomial regression and splines. Many other options are available, including moving average techniques, kerneling, and various forms of "filtering." Of more concern than the technical properties of the statistical procedure used for the smoothing is some notion of *why* the spiking or heaping takes place.

The most common assumption underlying spiking is the "symmetrical error" model. This model assumes that there is rounding on both sides of numbers that are multiples of 5 toward that multiple. There are, however, other plausible models for explaining the phenomenon. In societies that attribute status to great age, it is likely that there is much more rounding up toward the multiple than rounding down. This would mean, for example, that persons who are 42, 43, or 44 years of age are likely to report their age as 45, but those who are 46 or 47 are unlikely to round downward. This is an "asymmetrical error" model. The complementary asymmetrical error model arises where a premium is placed on youth. Thus, people will tend to round down but not up.

EXAMPLE: THE KENYAN DHS SURVEY

The DHS survey conducted for Kenya in 1991 presents a good example of age heaping (see Figure 14.6).

Figure 14.7 illustrates the results of applying quintic spline smoothing to DHS data. In all three instances, the spline knots were identified by taking the midpoint of the data collapsed into 5-year intervals. Smoothed values were then generated by interpolating the points between the knots or the intervals of the midpoints.

The line in Figure 14.7 identified as Model 1 assumes that the respondents underestimated their ages to the nearest digit ending in a 5 or a zero. Thus, the data are smoothed upward, or shifted slightly to the right. Model 2 assumes a rounding

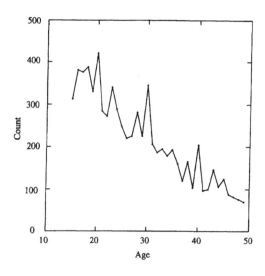

Figure 14.6. Age distribution of Kenyan women interviewed in DHS II survey, 1990.

Figure 14.7.
Smoothing models
for DHS II Kenya
survey.

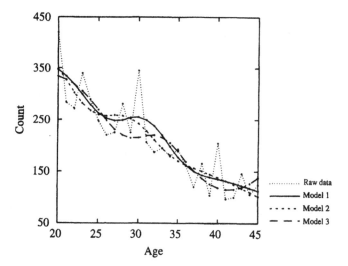

up to the highest digit ending in a 5 or a zero. These data are smoothed downward or
shifted proportionately to the left. Model 3, however, assumes that ages ending in a 5
or a zero are the midpoints of the categories and smooths proportionately onto both
sides of the digit.

The results of this analysis make two significant points. First, it is clear that
smoothing has a substantial impact on the data, leveling out the peaks and the troughs.
Second, there are considerable variations in the smoothed results depending upon
which set of assumptions we wish to make about the mechanism that produced the
spiking. Of course, the relative correctness of the assumptions could be determined
either by questioning a knowledgeable informant or by conducting a small amount of
fieldwork. Researchers are aware that other numbers besides those that are multiples
of 5 can have special cultural significance. Thus, in some societies, it is common to
find secondary spiking on numbers ending in 7 or 9.

Running Medians

Running means, another popular form of smoothing, are sometimes easier to apply
than either polynomial regression or splines. Running means smooth the data by
substituting an average of a series of contiguous values for each data point. For
example, a running mean of span 3 (i.e., that takes three consecutive data points)
involves replacing X_t with $(X_{t-1}, X_t, X_{t+1})/3$. A running mean with a span of 5
would average over five consecutive numbers. As in all algorithms involving means,
however, the results are highly susceptible to outliers. A far more robust approach to
smoothing that is structurally similar to running means involves the use of *running
medians*. Instead of substituting an actual data point with the mean of a run, the data
point is replaced with the median. The use of medians is attributable to Tukey (1977);

the elaboration and popularization of the technique is attributable to Velleman and Hoaglin (1981).

As we found with running means, the length of the span influences the amount of smoothing that appears, with longer spans producing smoother patterns than shorter ones. A difficulty with medians that does not appear with means is the difference between using even and odd numbers of observations in a run. When odd numbers of observations are used, the middle value of the observations constitutes the substitution point. With even numbers of observations, the median is determined by taking the arithmetic mean of the two middle values. For example, if a run of five number consists of the values {5, 7, 6, 1, 4}, the median value is 5. For the run {5, 6, 3, 4}, the median is the mean of the two middle values or $(4 + 5)/2 = 4.5$.

Typically, running medians are calculated on five or seven sequential data points. Medians based on a span of 3 are rarely used because this span is too short to correct for two outliers in a row. Spans beyond 7 tend to produce a result that is too "flat" and not sufficiently responsive to the fluctuations in the data. As Velleman and Hoaglin indicate, an initial smoothing based on a run of 4 is often optimal, since it eliminates the largest and smallest values in the run and settles on the mean of the two middle values.

Even-numbered smoothers do pose a minor problem, however. Technically, the values on the horizontal axis (X-values) should also be adjusted to coincide with the adjustment of the outcome measure on the vertical axis (Y-values). Even-numbered smoothers generate an expected value at the midpoint of the run instead of at an observed point on the horizontal axis. A solution to this problem is to recenter the values by applying a second smoothing with a running median of 2. This "realigns" the data to fall on an observed X-value.

Applying a second smoothing to an already smoothed sequence is known as *resmoothing*. The repeated application of a running median on a sequence results in a much smoother pattern with fewer kinks. Resmoothing also addresses some oddities in the data. For example, data with the pattern $+1, -1, +1, -1, +1, \ldots$ are left unchanged by the application of a running median of 5, and are inverted with a running median of 3. Velleman and Hoaglin suggest that in most instances good results can be obtained by means of an initial smoothing with a span of 4, with a recentering by span 2, followed by resmoothings of spans 5 and 3. That is, the resulting trend line is reasonably insensitive to outliers but sensitive enough to reflect variation in the data.

A succinct notation has been adopted in the literature to reflect the level of smoothing to which a sequence is subjected. A 4-span followed by 2-span, 3-span, and 5-span smooths is referred to as a **4253** smooth. The repeated application of a 5-span smooth until the data converge (i.e., there are no further changes in the smoothed values) is denoted as **5R**. Since spans beyond nine sequential points are almost never used, the application of a **35** resmooth cannot be confused with smooth on a span of 35 data points.

A further element that is used in the smoothing process is known as *hanning*. Hanning involves the calculation of a weighed average on a span of data. Typically, a value Y_t would be replaced by w_t, where

$$\hat{Y}_t = w_1 Y_{t-1} + w_2 Y_t + w_3 Y_{t+1}$$

Any number of elements can be used in a span as long as the weights sum to 1. Typically, $\hat{y}$ is calculated as follows:

$$w_t = 1/4 Y_{t-1} + 1/2 Y_t + 1/4 Y_{t+1}$$

This particular example is commonly used because it generates a gentler pattern than, say, a **53** smooth alone. For exploratory work, it is not uncommon to apply a **4253H** smooth, where the **H** refers to a hanning application after the final 3-span smooth.

EXAMPLE: RECORDED LYNCHINGS IN THE UNITED STATES: 1882–1930

Table 14.6 presents the number of recorded lynchings in the United States between the years 1882 and 1930 (U.S. Bureau of the Census, 1975: 422, series H 1168). This series is graphed in Figure 14.8. While it is obvious that there is a strong downward trend over time, there is also considerable variability from year to year. Figure 14.9 shows the results of applying a **4253H** smoother to the data.

Table 14.6. Recorded lynchings in the United States: 1882–1930

YEAR	PERSONS LYNCHED	YEAR	PERSONS LYNCHED	YEAR	PERSONS LYNCHED
1882	113	1899	106	1916	54
1883	130	1900	115	1917	38
1884	211	1901	130	1918	64
1885	184	1902	92	1919	83
1886	138	1903	99	1920	61
1887	120	1904	83	1921	64
1888	137	1905	62	1922	57
1889	170	1906	65	1923	33
1890	96	1907	60	1924	16
1891	184	1908	97	1925	17
1892	230	1909	82	1926	30
1893	152	1910	76	1927	16
1894	192	1911	67	1928	11
1895	179	1912	63	1929	10
1896	123	1913	52	1930	21
1897	158	1914	55		
1898	120	1915	69		

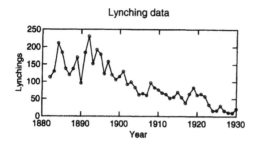

Figure 14.8. Lynching data.

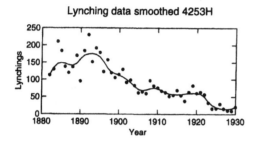

Figure 14.9. Lynching data smoothed 4254H.

Pseudo–Bayes Cell Estimators

Often when we address a contingency table, some of the cells have empirical zero values. These zero frequencies result from the fact that some cells are empirically rare; thus, for any given sample, it is likely that we will not capture any representative elements. This is particularly the case when the sampling scheme is a simple random sample, as opposed to a stratified or a more complex sampling strategy. Samples of 500 or 1000 individuals are unlikely to capture events that have a 1/500 or 1/1000 chance of occurring. Even events with probabilities of 1/100 may not appear. Furthermore, as Bishop, Fienberg, and Holland (1975: 401) note, it may be misleading to report cells with expected frequencies of 0/5 and 0/500 as both being equal to zero.

In many analyses, particularly in log-linear or logistic analysis of contingency tables, it is common practice to "correct" zero cells by adding a constant such as .5 to each cell. In many circumstances, we can do better. If a population distribution is known (from say census data), it is possible to adjust the sample data to reflect the known distribution. This process is akin to the poststratification approach discussed earlier. Adjusting for a known or a theoretically relevant distribution is also used in some disciplines to generate a "standardized" distribution. For example, an age-specific mortality distribution in a city with an inordinately high rate of elderly people may be adjusted to reflect the pattern of mortality for a more normal or typical age distribution. In this way, we can generate an age-standardized rate. Such standarized rates allow for the comparison of mortality experiences across a range of cities with widely varying age distributions.

Another approach is to adjust the cell frequencies through smoothing. A particularly useful approach is to generate a pseudo-Bayes estimate based on some known or assumed prior distribution. While there are several approaches outlined in the literature, that presented by Bishop, Fienberg, and Holland (1975) is particularly appealing because of its simplicity and flexibility. Given an observed array of data, where $N = \sum X_{ij}$, there are three steps to follow.

1. Identify a prior array of probabilities, λ_{ij}, based on either the data or some theoretically relevant distribution.

2. Compute a weighting factor

$$\hat{K} = \frac{N^2 - \sum_{i,j} X_{ij}}{\sum_{i,j}(X_{ij} - N\lambda_{ij})^2}$$

3. Determine the expected cell frequencies:

$$\hat{f}_{i,j} + \frac{N}{N + \hat{K}}\left(X_{ij} + \hat{K}\lambda_{ij}\right)$$

The latter two steps are easy to implement either by means of a spreadsheet or by employing the matrix language of one of the more common statistical packages.

One of the obvious advantages of the formula outlined in step 3 is that cells with structural zeros are identified with X_{ij} and λ_{ij} both being set to zero. Consequently, for structurally identified empty cells, the expected frequencies, f_{ij}, will remain as zero.

EXAMPLE: CONSISTENCY OF PRESIDENTAL VOTES BY PARTY IDENTIFICATION: 1956–60

The data presented in Table 14.7 represent a subset of respondents taken from a larger sample of Americans who were interviewed in 1956 and in 1960 and asked about both their political party affiliation and their voting patterns. These data were analyzed extensively by Hout and Knoke (1976) and by Duncan (1981). The original multiway table consisted of 786 repondents broken down by religious affiliation; however, for illustrative purposes, only the 584 non-Catholic respondents will be examined.

Although there are many different ways of determining the λ-values, our first approach will be to base the lambdas partially on the empirical distribution of the table itself. Dashed lines in the table subset the data on the basis of party identification, highlighting the concentration of cell values along the diagonals. The observed frequencies along the party identification blocks (i.e., Democrat, 1956/ Democrat, 1960; Independent, 1956/Independent, 1960; Republican, 1956/ Republican, 1960) are higher than those in the off-diagonal blocks. Further, within each block, the cells along the main diagonals tend to have higher frequencies than the off-diagonal cells.

This suggests that there is a strong pattern of consistency to both party affiliation and voting across the two elections. We might hypothesize that 85% of voters are

Table 14.7. Presidential votes by party identic ation and year: 1956–60

PARTY/VOTE: 1956	1960					
	Dem/Dem	Dem/Rep	Ind/Dem	Ind/Rep	Rep/Dem	Rep/Rep
Dem/Dem	127	29	17	2	0	0
Dem/Rep	15	24	4	4	0	3
Ind/Dem	11	3	9	5	0	1
Ind/Rep	1	6	21	52	1	33
Rep/Dem	1	0	3	0	1	1
Rep/Rep	2	0	2	16	9	181

Note: In Tables 14.7–14.9, Rep, Republican; Ind, Independent; Dem, Democrat.

consistent in their pattern over time, while only 15% are inconsistent. Since there are 18 consistent and 18 inconsistent cells, we might choose to start with λ-values of .85/18 = .0472 for the diagonal elements and .15/18 = .0083 for the off-diagonal elements. This results in the pattern outlined in Table 14.8.

With the λ-values in Table 14.8, K becomes 6.794. The pseudo-Bayes estimates of the cell frequencies are shown in Table 14.9, with the completion of step 3 in the calculations. The values do not change very much from Table 14.7 to Table 14.9. All the zero cells have been replaced, with the zeros along the diagonals in each block being replaced by slightly higher values than those on the off-diagonals.

Table 14.8. Lambda values for initial smoothing

PARTY/VOTE: 1956	1960					
	Dem/Dem	Dem/Rep	Ind/Dem	Ind/Rep	Rep/Dem	Rep/Rep
Dem/Dem	0.0472	0.0083	0.0472	0.0083	0.0472	0.0083
Dem/Rep	0.0083	0.0472	0.0083	0.0472	0.0083	0.0472
Ind/Dem	0.0472	0.0083	0.0472	0.0083	0.0472	0.0083
Ind/Rep	0.0083	0.0472	0.0083	0.0472	0.0083	0.0472
Rep/Dem	0.0472	0.0083	0.0472	0.0083	0.0472	0.0083
Rep/Rep	0.0083	0.0472	0.0083	0.0472	0.0083	0.0472

Table 14.9. Expected frequencies for presidential votes by party identic ation and year: 1956–60

PARTY/VOTE: 1956	1960					
	Dem/Dem	Dem/Rep	Ind/Dem	Ind/Rep	Rep/Dem	Rep/Rep
Dem/Dem	125.86	28.72	17.12	2.03	0.32	0.06
Dem/Rep	14.88	24.04	4.01	4.27	0.06	3.28
Ind/Dem	11.19	3.02	9.21	5	0.32	1.04
Ind/Rep	1.04	6.25	20.81	51.72	1.04	32.94
Rep/Dem	1.31	0.06	3.28	0.06	1.31	1.04
Rep/Rep	2.03	0.32	2.03	16.13	8.95	179.24

Lambda-values were also generated by means of a more complex consistency model in which the blocks on the main diagonal were initially weighted by .85 and the off-diagonal blocks by .15. Thus, each block on the main diagonal received a weight of $.85/3 = .283$ and each off-diagonal block received a weight of $.15/6 = .025$. Within each main diagonal block, the cells on the diagonal were then weighted by .85 and the off-diagonals by .15. Thus, for example, in the Democrat/Democrat block, the cell lambdas were calculated as $.283 \times .85/2 = .1204$ for the on-diagonal cells and $.283 \times .15/2 = .021$ for the off-diagonal cells. Hence, the diagonal blocks consisted of the lambda patterns

$$\begin{vmatrix} .120 & .021 \\ .021 & .120 \end{vmatrix}$$

For the off-diagonal blocks, the lambda patterns were

$$\begin{vmatrix} .011 & .002 \\ .002 & .001 \end{vmatrix}$$

With these lambdas, K becomes 10.117. The expected frequencies, however, are closer to the original values and the smoothed zeros are much closer to zero than those obtained in Table 14.9.

CONCLUSIONS

The procedures discussed in this chapter have a wide range of application and, depending upon the circumstances, can be used to interpolate missing values, provide exploratory insights to the data, or transform a discrete distribution into a continuous one. While data interpolating and smoothing have many uses, normally it makes little sense to smooth the data before they have been used for further analysis. For example, if one is conducting a multivariate analysis of international crime data, smoothing the data beforehand will likely reduce the error within the data and result in an optimistic fit to those data. As with all forms of data manipulation, the theoretical implications of the manipulation should not be forgotten while one is caught up in the mechanisms of the calculations.

Further Reading

Chambers, J.M., Cleveland, W.S., Kleiner, B., and Tukey, P. *Graphical Methods for Data Analysis*. Belmont, CA: Wadsworth, 1983. A fascinating book that outlines the state of the art in graphics-oriented descriptive statistics. Very accessible.

Simonoff, J.S. *Smoothing Methods in Statistics*. New York: Springer-Verlag, 1996. A general introduction to smoothing and graphics. Heavy focus on kerneling procedures.

15

Computer-Intensive Hypothesis Testing

> Good *simple ideas, of which the jackknife is a prime example, are*
> *our most precious intellectual commodity . . . .*
>
> —Bradley Efron

This chapter introduces a number of procedures that are typically referred to as "computationally intensive" techniques for solving a wide range of statistical and methodological problems. The commonality among these procedures is that they require a substantial amount of computing power to generate repeated and often random samples from one or more sets of data. The three procedures we will focus on—randomization tests, jackknifing, and bootstrapping—are part of what we term simulation or *resampling* techniques.

Although hypothesis testing procedures generally fall in the domain of statistics as opposed to methods, the approaches discussed here take advantage of the insights developed in the discussion of sampling in Chapters 5 and 6. Furthermore, variations on resampling themes can be used to estimate standard errors and assess bias in complex sampling plans.

Essentially, these techniques start with a given set of data from which we then proceed to draw repeated samples. The techniques differ, however, according to the type of sampling plan used to generate replicated subsamples from the collected data. *Randomization tests* and *jackknife* procedures are based on permutations—an enumeration of all possible combinations of subsets that can be constructed from the observed data. Variations in the procedures are based on the number of observations included in the subsets, and on whether all permutations are calculated.

Bootstrap procedures, on the other hand, involve sampling with replacement. Thus, for any given replicate, some observations may not be included while others may be included several times. Typically, for small samples, the replicates are based on the same n as the original sample. For large samples, the replicates are often based on a smaller n than was found in the original sample. This latter approach to subsampling the sample parallels that commonly known at the *Monte Carlo* procedure.

Monte Carlo studies are also based on repeatedly drawing subsamples (or replicates) from a large parent population. Monte Carlo procedures, however, are usually based on sampling *without* replacement.[1] As indicated, the researcher generally either

---

1. Needless to say, enumerating all possible permutations can also be seen as a form of sampling without replacement.

starts with a very large sample drawn from an empirical population or generates a data set that conforms to some known distribution using a random number generator.[2] Once the original sample has been identified, repeated subsamples are drawn to study their distributional characteristics. As with standard sampling procedures, a crucial question in Monte Carlo studies is how large the replicates or subsamples ought to be (see Chapters 5 and 6).

The theory behind most resampling techniques has long been known. It is only recently, however, that these methods have started to come into their own as a valuable component of the quantitative analyst's toolbox. Although this chapter focuses on three major techniques, the underlying approach they represent is infinitely flexible and will undoubtedly become a major component of much future research. Until recently, most introductory and intermediate statistics and methods texts have given little consideration to resampling approaches.[3] Undoubtedly, this was due to the lack of preprogrammed statistical software. The inclusion of standardized routines to conduct resampling analysis in mainstream packages such as STATA and SYSTAT, and some specialty packages such as LISREL, will likely rectify that situation.

Another reason for the limited use of resampling techniques is the tendency of researchers, like other human beings, to stick with what is familiar. To quote Noreen (1989: 7), "Out of necessity, researchers have fallen into the habit of selecting a test statistic from the large (but nevertheless limited) set of test statistics for which the sampling distributions are known." Unfortunately, as Noreen continues, "sometimes this has been like fitting a square peg in a round hole."

RANDOMIZATION TESTS

Many times in classical statistics it is difficult or impossible to use a reasonable test statistic because we do not know what its sampling distribution looks like. Thus, for example, we rarely examine the difference in the median value between two samples, or test to see whether a statistically significant difference exists between the interquartile ranges of two batches of numbers. For some applications, such test statistics might be more consistent with the substance of the null hypothesis than traditional measures of central tendency and variation such as the mean and variance.

Fortunately, in many applications the data are amenable to what we term a randomization test. Randomization tests are based on our ability to estimate the sampling distribution empirically rather than relying upon its analytical derivation.

With randomization tests, the fundamental hypothesis may be stated thus: Is the observed allocation of results similar or dissimilar to what we could expect if the data were distributed (allocated) at random? If the data were allocated at random, we would expect no difference between the statistic of interest across the groups. In this

---

2. Most statistics and numerical analysis software packages can be used to generate samples from any number of distributions, including the uniform, normal, negative exponential, gamma, and beta.

3. One notable exception at the more elementary level is Hamilton (1992).

sense, the test is no different from, say, testing the null hypothesis that $\overline{Y}_2 = \overline{Y}_1$. This null hypothesis might also be stated as $\theta = \overline{Y}_2 - \overline{Y}_1 = 0$.

Since θ will have a sampling distribution, the objective is to define the form of that distribution empirically. Once that distribution has been defined, we can compare the observed value of θ with the distribution to estimate the likelihood of the observed value given the distribution.

Randomization tests appear in one of two variants. We may use an *exact* randomization test, where all possible allocations are enumerated. This is the basis of Fisher's exact test. While theoretically sound, exact randomization does have practical limitations. In particular, N elements allocated to two conditions with n and m elements in each results in $N!/(n!m!)$ combinations or sets. Partitioning 10 elements into two equal sets of five results in $10!/5!5!$ or 252 possible combinations. Doubling that number to 20 elements results in 184,756 possible combinations of sets with 10 elements in each. Even with modern computers, enumerating several hundred thousand combinations and calculating a test statistic for each combination can involve a substantial amount of computational time.

One way of getting around this data glut is to use an *approximate* randomization test. In many circumstances enumerating *all* possible permutations is not necessary. A sufficiently large sample of permutations can suffice. Specifically, instead of enumerating all combinations, we repeatedly allocate the sample to conditions randomly. Even when the exact number of combinations goes into the hundreds of thousands (or, more typically, several billion), a random sample of 1000–5000 will generally suffice. Some situations may require samplings of up to 10,000 to obtain enough estimates in the far tails of the distribution. Still, this amount of computation falls short of the number of combinations often demanded by an exact approach.

Overall, permutation tests have several advantages over their classical counterparts. Typically, they allow for a much wider range of test statistics; they are far simpler for most analysts to understand and interpret; and, as Efron and Tibshirani (1993: 210) state, "the greatest virtue of permutation testing is its accuracy." It is likely that permutation tests will dominate much of our statistical analysis in the future as computers become increasingly powerful and more software incorporates the routines and algorithms necessary to take advantage of this approach.

EXAMPLE: A PERMUTATION TEST OF DEPENDENCY AND URBANIZATION IN AFRICA

The data for this example were collected by the World Bank from 45 countries in Africa for 1990. The outcome variable is the dependency ratio—the number of dependents per 100 persons of working age. The independent variable is a dichotomous indicator "urban" or "rural," based on whether more than 40% of the population resides in urban areas. Examining the data (given in Table 15.1), it is noted that 18 countries might be classified as "urban" and 27 as "rural." The working hypothesis is that the dependency ratio should be higher in rural as opposed to urban areas. The rationale for this prediction is based on the supposition that rural families tend to be

Table 15.1. Dependency ratios and percent urban dwellers for 45 countries in Africa

COUNTRY	DEPENDENCY RATIO	PERCENT URBAN
Angola	92	28.3
Burundi	98	7.3
Benin	101	42.0
Botswana	103	23.6
Central African Republic	82	46.6
Côte d'Ivoire	105	46.6
Cameroon	104	49.4
Comoro Islands	103	27.6
Congo	96	42.2
Cape Verde	97	28.0
Djibouti	88	80.7
Algeria	90	44.7
Egypt	77	48.8
Ethiopia	99	12.9
Gabon	78	45.7
Ghana	99	33.0
Guinea	95	25.6
Gambia	87	22.5
Guinea-Bissau	87	30.8
Equatorial Guinea	78	64.5
Burkina Faso	95	9.0
Kenya	113	23.6
Liberia	92	44.0
Libya	94	70.2
Lesoto	89	20.3
Morocco	80	48.5
Madagascar	99	25.0
Mali	99	19.2
Mozambique	89	26.8
Mauritania	92	42.1
Mauritius	53	42.3
Malawi	97	14.8
Namibia	96	57.0
Niger	99	19.5
Nigeria	100	35.2
Rwanda	102	7.7
Sudan	92	22.0
Senegal	98	38.4
Sierra Leone	87	27.2
Somalia	96	38.1
São Tomé and Principe Island	85	42.3
Swaziland	103	33.1
Seychelles	73	59.3
Chad	84	33.3
Tanzania	99	32.8

more extended and complete than urban families. The alternate, or null hypothesis, is that no relationship exists between dependency and residential status.

The data do not form a random sample, so it could be argued that applying a standard t-test is inappropriate. A better approach might be to consider the problem in the context of randomization.

If the null hypothesis were true, then from the perspective of dependency, the appearance of a country in one residential category rather than the other could be considered a random event. It makes sense, therefore, to consider all the possible assignments of countries to the two conditions. We could enumerate all possible subsets of assignments where 18 countries are allocated to the urban condition and 27 are allocated to the rural one. For each subset, the difference between the two means can be calculated.

Mathematically, it can be shown that if we wish to allocate N elements into two groups of size n and m, respectively, there are $g = \binom{N}{n}$ combinations. Substituting the values for the current example, we obtain

$$\binom{N}{n} = \frac{N!}{n!\,m!} = \frac{45!}{18!\,27!}$$

or approximately 1.7×10^{12} possible sets, of which the observed allocation is but one. The question then becomes, What is the proportion of differences of means among these sets that are less likely to occur than the observed one?

For the urban sample of 18 countries, we observe a mean dependency ratio of 86.889, with a standard deviation of 12.769. For the sample of 27 rural countries, the corresponding values are 96.333 and 6.409, respectively. Our test statistic, θ (the difference between the means), is $96.333 - 86.889 = 9.444$. Traditionally, we would use a difference of means t-test to decide whether that difference was statistically significant.

Since the variances of the two groups are different ($F = 163.05/41.08 = 3.97$ with 17, 26 df), normal practice would be to use Welch's or the pooled variance formulation. Doing the appropriate computations results in a t-value of 2.85 with 43 df, for a one-tailed p-value of .001. Hence, we would typically reject H_0 and assume that the difference between the mean dependency ratios is "real."

The randomization approach, however, involves allocating the 45 countries to the two groups at random. Doing this 4999 times, we obtain the distribution appearing in Figure 15.1, which represents the sampling distribution of the difference of means under randomization (i.e., under the situation in which H_0 is true). As can be seen from Figure 15.1, the distribution is approximately normal and roughly centered around the expected value of 0.

Assessing whether the observed mean difference is consistent with the null hypothesis of a mean difference of zero is fairly straightforward. We simply select a percentile above or below which we consider an observed value of θ to be unlikely, given H_0. Thus, one might typically choose the upper 95th percentile for a directional test, or the middle 95% of values (the 2.5th percentile to the 97.5th percentile) for a nondirectional test. In conventional analysis, these decisions would correspond to the rejection of H_0 at the 5% level for one- and two-tailed tests, respectively.

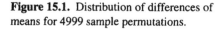

Figure 15.1. Distribution of differences of means for 4999 sample permutations.

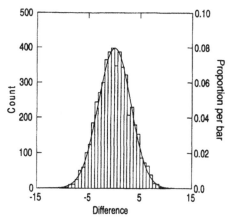

Rank-ordering the 4999 generated values and including the observed difference in the distribution results in the value of 9.444 ranking fifth out of the 5000 differences of means. Thus, the *p*-value for 9.444 can be estimated as 5/5000 or .001. Perhaps not unsurprisingly, this result corresponds with that of the two-sample *t*-test conducted earlier.

For difference of means, the randomization test appears to offer little more than what we get by using the classical approach. In fact, Welch's *t*-test involves much less computation and can generally be calculated in far less time.[4] This approach comes into its own, however, when the test statistic is less amenable to the classical parametric approach. A test statistic based on a difference of medians would be one example; differences in interquartile ranges would be another. In fact, one might be tempted to "invent" any number of descriptive statistics that better reflect the substantive hypothesis than the traditional measures of means or variances. The sampling distributions of those invented statistics can be generated empirically using this approach.

The basic procedure for conducting a simple randomization test is outlined in Figure 15.2. In summary, the following steps are carried out:

1. An appropriate test statistic, θ, is calculated for the whole sample (e.g., a difference of means).

2. The same test statistic is calculated for *n* pairs of subsamples drawn at random and with replacement from the original sample.

---

4. This similarity of results should not be unexpected. Early in this century Fisher introduced the concept of permutation tests to validate the use of Student's *t*-test for nonnormal samples (Efron and Tibshirani, 1993: 208).

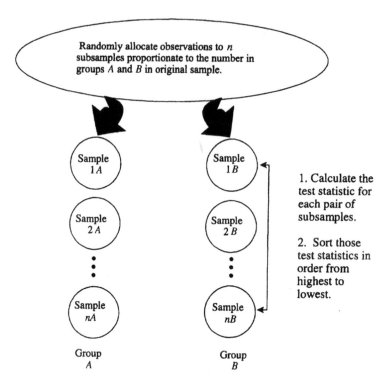

Figure 15.2. Method underlying simple permutation test.

3. The *n* test statistics calculated from the random subsamples are sorted in order of magnitude.

4. Boundaries or cut points are identified according to the level of accuracy required by the researcher. For example, a 95% confidence interval required the identification of the cases of the 2.5th and 97.5th percentile. The values associated with those cases are noted.

5. A determination is made as to whether θ falls within the confidence limit boundaries, as is the case in standard confidence interval analysis.

Statistical Power

The issue of statistical power was discussed at some length in Chapter 4. Essentially, power is the ability of a test to reject the null hypothesis when it is, in fact, false. Statisticians study statistical tests to determine which test is the most powerful under any given set of circumstances. Ideally, one wishes to employ the uniformly most powerful test available.

Randomization tests are generally not *directly* comparable to most conventional tests (e.g., *t*-tests for differences of means) since they usually test slightly different null hypotheses. Some situations can be created, however, in which the null hypotheses closely parallel one another. In those circumstances, it does appear that randomization tests are at least as powerful as traditional parametric tests, even when all the assumptions underlying the parametric test are met. When one or more assumptions underlying the parametric test are violated, randomization tests seem to perform better (Hoeffding, 1952).

Some interesting examples of how Monte Carlo procedures can be used to assess the power of permutation tests are outlined by Noreen (1989: 33–41).

Limitations

As with any statistical procedure, randomization tests are no panacea. The primary limitation of the randomization test is that the null hypothesis is based on the assumption of randomization. In some circumstances, simply knowing that the observed test statistic is not likely to belong to a randomized process will not tell us very much. More complex hypotheses may be difficult, if not impossible to formulate in a manner that incorporates a meaningful null based on some assumption of randomization.

Another problem associated with randomization tests is that while they offer a greater variety of test statistics for us to ponder, not all test statistics are of equal utility. With increased choice comes the necessity for the researcher to ensure that the test statistic (say, the comparison of interquartile ranges) is meaningful within the context of the substantive hypothesis. Selecting a "bad" test statistic carries a price. As Efron and Tibshirani (1993: 211) note, "The penalty for choosing a poor test statistic $\hat{\theta}$ is low power—we don't get as much probability of rejecting H_0 when it is false."

Still, just as the classical hypothesis testing approach based on distributional assumptions has almost infinite variability in the hands of a creative and experienced researcher, so too does the randomization approach. Furthermore, as the literature on empirical simulations of sampling distributions increases, it is likely that more varied elaborations will be developed. Undoubtedly, those elaborations will have as their core some variant on the method just outlined.

THE JACKKNIFE AND THE BOOTSTRAP

Consider a situation common in the social sciences. A researcher is studying a parent population with some unknown distribution but wishes to estimate a characteristic of that population, Θ. The researcher first randomly selects a series of observations Y_1, $Y_2, \ldots, Y_n$ from the population, then calculates the statistic of interest, θ, from the sample, hoping that θ will be a good estimate of Θ. Since θ will vary somewhat from sample to sample, boundaries are constructed about the estimate to define the range within which Θ is likely to appear given a certain level of confidence. Typically this attempt to measure the accuracy of θ involves the estimation of its standard error.

Under classical statistics, we can estimate the standard error and a confidence interval if (a) we know the distribution of the parent population or (b) the sample size, n, is sufficiently large. This latter condition applies because under the central limit theorem, the sampling distribution of many point estimates (such as $\overline{Y}$) approaches normality as n increases. Specifically in the case of $\overline{Y}$, we know that $SE(\overline{Y}) = \sqrt{(\sigma_{\overline{Y}}^2/n)}$. When the variance of the sampling distribution is not known, it can be estimated by S^2; hence, $SE(\overline{Y}) \doteq \sqrt{(S_{\overline{Y}}^2/n)}$.

Unfortunately, problems arise with small samples and with "complicated" statistics such as the median, the interquartile range, Pearson's r, or more esoteric features such as the largest eigenvalue of a covariance matrix. The appropriate formulas for the standard errors for these statistics are either unknown or subject to crude approximations. It is for circumstances of these types that two computationally intensive techniques—the jackknife and the bootstrap—were devised.

THE JACKKNIFE

The development of the jackknife approach is generally credited to John Tukey (1958), although it is recognized that the impetus for the idea came from Quenouille's (1949) work on the nonparametric estimation of bias. Tukey supposedly gave the technique its name because of its apparent flexibility in dealing with a wide range of statistical problems.

In many respects the jackknife procedure is similar to exact permutation tests. For a set of observations, $Y_1, Y_2, \ldots, Y_n$, one creates n subsets, leaving out one observation

---

■ **Box 15.1**

SOME LIMITATIONS OF CONVENTIONAL STATISTICAL ESTIMATES

Several problems are often encountered with traditional estimates of the standard errors of test statistics. Among the more common are the following:

- Traditional estimates, since they are often asymptotic approximations, may require very large sample sizes. In many situations, it is neither feasible nor possible to increase the amount of data collected.

- The traditional estimate is often based on a model incorporating fairly restrictive assumptions. Minor violations of those assumptions (e.g., non-normal errors in regression models) may undermine the accuracy of the estimate.

- The theoretical formula (or even a close approximation) may not be known for any given application.

- The proper solution or derived formula may not be available to the researcher. This is particularly the case when one is working in the field and access to a good library is limited. Resampling statistics are generally practical and easy to implement. Exact solutions may be beyond the technical expertise of the researcher or may not be implemented in the available software. Some recent implementations of resampling software are exceedingly flexible.

at a time. For each subset, some statistic of interest (θ) is calculated and the variability among those n thetas is used to determine the standard error of the estimate.

Let us define $\bar{\theta}^*$ as the mean of the n estimated thetas (where θ_i^* represents the ith estimate of θ). Formally, this is defined as

$$\bar{\theta}^* = \frac{\sum_{i=1}^n \theta_i^*}{n}$$

Quenouille discovered that it was possible to determine the bias of θ (the sample estimate of Θ, the population parameter) as follows:

$$\widehat{\text{bias}} = (n-1)(\bar{\theta}^* - \theta)$$

Using this information, it is possible to estimate a bias-corrected or jackknife estimate of θ by means of

$$\tilde{\theta} = \theta - \widehat{\text{bias}}$$

While we shall not pursue this line in any detail, it is interesting to note that the estimated bias for the mean, $\bar{Y}$, is 0, and the bias inherent in using s^2 (the sample variance) as an estimate of σ^2 (the population variance) can be corrected by using $n - 1$ in the denominator of s^2 instead of n. These results are so basic that they are assumed to be known to all who have studied elementary statistics. Thus, the jackknife procedure adds little to our understanding of the estimates of the population mean and variance. On the other hand, there are many other statistics for which the bias is either unknown or extremely difficult to estimate by means of a closed form equation. Quenouille's use of the jackknife provides a procedure for estimating that bias no matter how complex or esoteric the statistic of interest might be.

Tukey's extension of the jackknife procedure went beyond the simple but important ability to estimate bias, to provide a possible general approach for calculating standard errors. Parametric estimates of the standard errors of many common statistics (such as $\bar{Y}$) have been long known. There is a large class of statistics, however, for which the standard error is either unknown or, again, difficult to estimate.

Tukey suggested that through the jackknife, the standard error of any sample statistic, θ, may be calculated as

$$\widehat{SE}(\theta)_{\text{jack}} = \sqrt{\frac{n-1}{n} \sum_{i=1}^n (\theta_i^* - \bar{\theta}^*)^2}$$

This formula applies regardless of what θ might be. Thus, θ may be a sample mean, the median, a correlation coefficient, or the eigenvalue mentioned above. The general procedure for drawing jackknife samples is outlined in Figure 15.3.

While the jackknife approach is simple to execute, powerful, and applicable to a wide range of problems, it is not without its drawbacks. As Efron points out, Quenouille's estimate of bias is not always dependable, and the jackknife estimate of the standard error is often moderately inflated (Efron, 1982). Thus, care should be exercised in situations for which accuracy is paramount. On the other hand, much can be learned from the application of the jackknife, especially when one examines

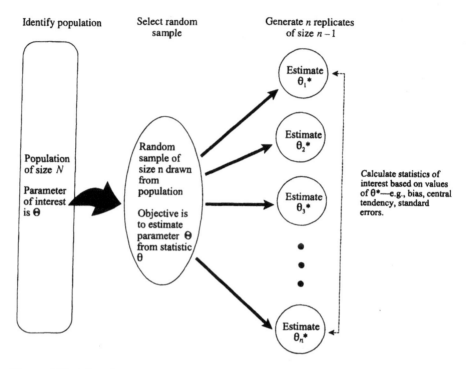

Identify population

Select random sample

Generate n replicates of size $n-1$

Population of size N

Parameter of interest is Θ

Random sample of size n drawn from population

Objective is to estimate parameter Θ from statistic θ

Estimate $\theta_1{}^*$

Estimate $\theta_2{}^*$

Estimate $\theta_3{}^*$

Estimate $\theta_n{}^*$

Calculate statistics of interest based on values of θ^*—e.g., bias, central tendency, standard errors.

Figure 15.3. Allocation method underlying jackknife.

the distribution of results graphically. Perhaps as with its mechanical namesake, the jackknife is better for whittling away at a problem than for sculpting the final solution.

We will take a quick look at the jackknife in application and then turn our attention to another, and in some ways more general procedure, the bootstrap. The data for the following examples is drawn from the World Bank's Social Development Indicators for 1992. Data are available for 192 countries (out of 207) on a nation's total fertility rate (TFR) and its corresponding child mortality rate, or CMR (number of deaths under age 5 per 1000 live births). From that population, a simple random sample of 16 nations was drawn for analysis. The values for those nations are presented in Table 15.2.

EXAMPLE: THE MEAN

The data in Table 15.2 permit us to estimate the mean and the standard error for both the TFR and the CMR. The traditional formulas for the means and standard deviations result in estimates of $\overline{Y}_{(TFR)} = 3.522$ and $\overline{Y}_{(CMR)} = 58.094$, and $S_{(TFR)} = 1.685$ and $S_{(CMR)} = 55.707$. Thus, the standard errors of the respective means $(S/\sqrt{n})$ are .421 and 13.927. In the original population of 192 nations, the mean values were determined to be $\mu_{(TFR)} = 3.803$ and $\mu_{(CMR)} = 69.484$. Constructing 95% confidence intervals for the TFR (2.670, 4.347) and the CMR (30.797, 85.391) suggests that we ought not

Table 15.2. Total fertility rate (TFR) and child mortality rate (CMR) for a random sample of 16 nations

COUNTRY	TFR	CMR
Albania	2.850	39.6
Bahamas	2.132	30.6
Czech Republic	1.900	12.3
Ecuador	3.500	57.6
France	1.780	9.3
Guyana	2.643	62.0
Kenya	5.350	102.4
Liberia	6.200	212.0
Libya	6.390	83.4
Luxembourg	1.650	10.7
Namibia	5.400	85.8
New Zealand	2.120	9.3
Pakistan	5.600	135.5
Sri Lanka	2.480	21.6
Trinidad and Tobago	2.750	18.2
Venezuela	3.600	39.2

to reject the null hypothesis that $\overline{Y} = \mu$ in either instance, since the population means are encompassed by both intervals.

We may now ask how well the jackknife performs. Generating the 16 jackknife subsamples based on $n-1$ observations results in estimates of {3.516, 3.573, 3.591, 3.383, 3.615, 3.396, 3.646, 3.330, 3.343, 3.400, 3.580, 3.638, 3.523, 3.630, 3.614, 3.566} for the mean TFR and estimates of {59.353, 60.753, 60.527, 52.933, 61.347, 56.247, 61.253, 56.407, 47.833, 55.140, 57.833, 61.347, 58.127, 61.147, 59.927, 59.327} for the mean CMR. Allowing each subsample or replicate mean to be represented by θ_i^*, we estimate the mean of the sample means as $\overline{\theta}^* = \Sigma\theta_i^*/n$. Thus, for the TFR, $\overline{\theta}_{\text{TFR}}^* = 3.5216$ and for the CMR, $\overline{\theta}_{\text{CMR}}^* = 58.0938$. Both these values are equivalent to those obtained from the original sample. This is empirically consistenct with the assertion that the sample mean is an unbiased estimator of the population mean.

Recall that the jackknife standard errors for these means can be determined from the subsamples as

$$\widehat{SE}(\theta)_{\text{jack}} = \sqrt{\frac{n-1}{n}\sum_{i=1}^{n}\left(\theta_i^* - \overline{\theta}^*\right)^2}$$

For the TFR, we may determine the jackknife standard error as

$$\widehat{SE}(\theta_{\text{TFR}})_{\text{jack}} = \sqrt{\frac{n-1}{n}\sum_{i=1}^{n}\left(\theta_i^* - \overline{\theta}^*\right)^2}$$

$$= \sqrt{\frac{15}{16} \times 1892}$$

$$= .421$$

The corresponding estimate of the standard error for the CMR is $[(15/16) \times 206.882]^{1/2} = 13.927$. In this instance, the jackknife estimates of the standard error and the estimates based on the normal approximation are the same.

This coincidence of values is not typical. Results from theoretical research show that estimates of the variance (hence the standard errors) obtained from the jackknife are usually biased upward. Thus, the jackknife generally provides a more conservative estimate of the variance and the standard error of the estimate. As Efron (1982: 26) notes, however, for any given set of data this is not always true, since the jackknife variance is based on subsamples of size $n - 1$ instead of size n.

EXAMPLE: THE COEFFICIENT r

In the foregoing example of 16 nations, we had continuous measures for both the TFR and the CMR. For the original population of 192 nations, the correlation (Pearsonian r) between these two variables is $\Theta = \rho = .8477$. The corresponding estimate for the 16 nations is $\theta = r = .8593$. Using the jackknife, we might wish to estimate the bias and the standard error of this estimate.

Again, the first step in using the jackknife is to generate 16 replicates of size $n - 1 = 15$. The correlation coefficient is then calculated for each subsample. The distribution of those correlations is presented in Figure 15.4. As a final step, we can calculate the mean of those 16 sample correlations. This turns out to be .8620.

The estimate of the bias is suggested as $(n - 1)(\bar{\theta}^* - \theta)$, or in this case, where θ represents the sample correlation coefficient, r, bias $= (15)(.8620 - .8593) = .0405$. Notice, however, that bias is defined as the difference between the mean of the jackknifed replicate correlations and the correlation coefficient based on the entire sample of 16 (i.e., θ). It is a common error to assume that the difference is between the mean of the jackknifed replicates and the population parameter—in this case, Θ.

Figure 15.4. Jackknife distribution of Pearson r values for 16-nation data.

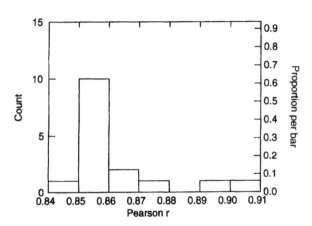

For the jackknife estimate of the standard error, we calculate

$$\widehat{SE}(\theta)_{jack} = \sqrt{\frac{n-1}{n} \sum_{i=1}^{n} \left(\theta_i^* - \bar{\theta}^*\right)^2}$$

$$= \sqrt{\frac{15}{16} \times .0044}$$

$$= .0642$$

The traditional formula for the standard error of r^2 gives

$$SE(r^2) = \frac{1 - r^2}{\sqrt{n-3}}$$

Thus, the typical estimate of $SE(r^2)$ would be $[1 - (-.8593)^2]/\sqrt{13} = .0726$.

In this instance, the estimated standard error of .0642 under the jackknife is smaller than the .0726 that we would normally estimate. Again, however, this is an anomalous case (Efron, 1982: ch. 4). Typically, the jackknife estimate of the standard error tends to be greater than the true estimate although, again, not by much.

Limitations

The traditional jackknife has several limitations, not the least of which is the necessity to calculate n subsamples. For statistics that Efron and Tibshirani refer to as nonlinear or having a "lack of smoothness," the jackknife can also be *inconsistent*. That is, the estimated standard error may fail to converge to the true standard error as $n \to \infty$. Some of those nonsmooth estimates include statistics for which the jackknife approach would appear to be most useful, such as the median (Efron and Tibshirani, 1993: 147–48).

Suggestions have been made to address this problem of inconsistency for nonsmooth statistics. The most successful has been the delete-d jackknife. In this case, we leave out d as opposed to one observation at a time. Here, d is some value greater than $\sqrt{n}$ but less than n; hence, $\sqrt{n} < d < n$. By following this procedure, $\binom{n}{d}$ samples are drawn instead of n, thus requiring considerably more computation. This correction, however, moves the jackknife more closely into the realm of another, and more general procedure, known as the bootstrap.

THE BOOTSTRAP

The jackknife can be seen to be a special application of the more encompassing bootstrap approach elaborated by Bradley Efron. In the bootstrap, repeated random samples (with replacement) of size n are drawn from the original sample. Since the number of replicates is not determined by the sample size (as it is with the simple jackknife), a slight change in notation is in order. It is up to the researcher to decide how many replicates, designated as b, should be generated. Where bootstrap statistics are consistent, it is clear that large values for b have the advantage of increasing the accuracy of the estimate. On the other hand, depending upon the size of the sample and the algorithm of the statistic of interest, substantial computing time can be consumed. The consensus in the literature appears to be that for estimating standard errors, 50 to 200 replicates is generally adequate. For estimating bootstrap confidence intervals, however, b necessarily increases to values of 1000 and more. As with the permutation test, the further out into the tails one wishes to go, the larger b needs to become. Replicates in the vicinity of 5000 or even 10,000 are not out of order in such instances.

Again, some sample statistic, θ, is calculated. The standard deviation of the replicates, θ_i^*, is thus used to estimate the standard error of θ.

As with the jackknife, the measure of centrality for the bootstrap is defined by

$$\bar{\theta}^* = \frac{\sum_{i=1}^{b} \theta_i^*}{b}$$

where θ is once again the parameter of interest and b is the number of subsamples or replicates.

The estimate of the bootstrap standard error is different from that of the jackknife, however. For the bootstrap, the estimate of the standard error of θ is defined as the standard deviation among the θ_i^*s. For b replicates, therefore, the standard error is estimated as

$$\widehat{SE}(\theta)_{\text{boot}} = \sqrt{\frac{1}{b-1} \sum_{i=1}^{b} \left(\theta_i^* - \bar{\theta}^*\right)^2}$$

It is also possible to use the bootstrap to estimate bias. As in the case of the jackknife, bias is estimated as the expected difference between the mean of the θ_i^* bootstrap subsamples and θ as estimated from the entire sample. Formally, this may be defined as

$$\widehat{\text{bias}} = \frac{\sum_{i=1}^{b} \theta_i^*}{b} - \theta$$

$$= \bar{\theta}^* - \theta$$

The obvious question here is, Why go to the bother of estimating this bias? The answer is that we hope that the estimate of the bias $\bar{\theta}^* - \theta$ parallels that of $\theta - \Theta$. Whether that parallel exists in any given situation is an empirical question. However, it is unlikely that this parallel will exist if the sampling plan by which the original sample was drawn from the population is not followed in the selection of the elements used to determine the θ_i^*s. If the original sample was drawn srs, then the replicate ought to be so drawn, as well. If the original sample was drawn as a stratified cluster sample, then so must be the replicates. Clearly, this requirement complicates the analysis, but it is the only way of maintaining the integrity of the analysis.

The general procedure for drawing bootstrap samples is outlined in Figure 15.5. These concepts are illustrated in the following examples.

Identify population	Select random sample	Generate b replicates or subsamples

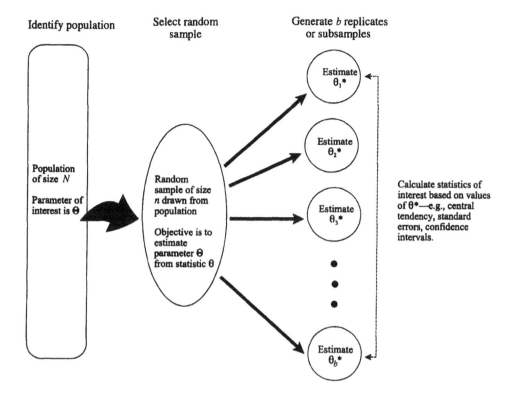

Figure 15.5. Allocation method underlying bootstrap.

EXAMPLE: THE MEDIAN

In the 16-nation sample, the median values for the TFR and the CMR are 2.8 and 39.4, respectively. Both values are lower than the corresponding means, which are approximately 3.5 and 58.1. This fairly large discrepancy between these two measures of central tendency is one of the reasons the median is often the preferred descriptive statistic. Overall, the median is less sensitive to "outliers" or extreme values; hence it is often considered the more robust estimate.

As with the mean, however, we may wish to calculate a measure of the standard error and to construct a confidence interval. In the current example, b replicates of size 16 were drawn with replacement from the original set of data. For illustrative purposes, four bootstraps were run with b set at 50, 200, 1000, and 5000. The results for both variables are presented in Table 15.3.

For the entire group of 192 nations, the median values (Θ) for TFR and CMR are 3.450 and 39.400, respectively. For the random sample of 16 nations, the corresponding medians (θ) for TFR and CMR are 2.800 and 39.400. Clearly, the sample estimate for CMR poses no difficulty as a point estimate. It is identical to the population

Table 15.3. Bootstrap results where θ is the median for various sizes of b

	TFR	CMR
$b = 50$		
θ^*	2.905	43.400
$SE\left(\overline{\theta}^*\right)$	0.538	14.765
$b = 200$		
θ^*	3.061	43.292
$SE\left(\overline{\theta}^*\right)$	0.705	16.256
$b = 1000$		
θ^*	3.050	42.697
$SE\left(\overline{\theta}^*\right)$	0.649	15.622
$b = 5000$		
θ^*	3.052	42.800
$SE\left(\overline{\theta}^*\right)$	0.661	15.662
θ (median) for 16 nations	2.800	39.400
Θ (median) for 192 nations	3.450	39.400

parameter. There is, however, a reasonable discrepancy between the population and sample estimates for the TFR. We might thus wish to test the null hypothesis as to whether $\Theta = \theta$—that is, whether the population and sample medians are equal.

As Efron suggests, for estimates of the standard error, 200 replicates appears to give reasonable results. To construct a 95% confidence interval, however, it was decided to go with 5000 replicates. Once these values had been sorted, the 125th case (the lower 2.5th percentile) for the TFR was determined to have a value of 2.272, and the 4875th case (the upper 97.5th percentile) was noted as 5.350.

Since the population median ($\Theta = 3.450$) clearly falls within the bootstrap limits of 2.272 and 5.350, we would likely decide not to reject H_0 and conclude that there is no statistically significant difference between the sample statistic and the population parameter.

The asymmetrical distribution of the θ_i^* about $\overline{\theta}^*$ for a statistic such as the median is evident here. The distance between the estimate of the median (2.800) and the upper limit (a difference of .525) is much greater than that between the median and the lower limit (a difference of 2.255). This is in stark contrast to statistics such as the mean, which have symmetrical probability distributions for their standard errors.

Bias-Corrected Bootstrap

Researchers use the bootstrap primarily because for a given situation, no theoretically defined solution exists to calculate the standard error of the estimate. In certain special cases, however, statistical theory provides an exact solution. In those circumstances, it is possible to observe how well the bootstrap performs in comparison to the "correct" solution. In these situations, it is also possible to compare one formulation of the bootstrap with another.

Generally, in those limited applications that permit the estimation of an exact solution, both the bootstrap calculation of standard errors and the percentile approach to estimating confidence intervals are less than perfect. The situation is well summarized by Efron and Tibshirani (1993: 178), who tell us, "The bootstrap-t intervals have good theoretical coverage probabilities, but tend to be erratic in actual practice. The percentile intervals are less eratic, but have less satisfactory coverage properties."

Several modified versions of the bootstrap have been developed that address those concerns. The references provide a broad discussion of many of those approaches. One of the simpler modifications is a version of the percentile method called the bias-corrected (BC) method. This variation is worth examining because it provides some general insight into how improvements can be made to the standard approaches. The BC approach takes slightly more computation but comes closer to the behavior of the known theoretical solutions.

One of the issues surrounding bootstrapping that has been discussed but not directly incorporated into our estimations is that of bias. Because no correction for bias was included in our estimates of various confidence intervals, it is likely that the estimated confidence bands are shifted too far to the left or the right of where they ought to be. Furthermore, where the distribution is asymmetrical around its midpoint, not correcting for the centrality of the confidence interval likely results in the bounds not being the proper width.

The BC approach discussed here starts with the percentile approach and corrects for the "median" bias. In other words, where the median of the distribution is not equal to θ, the confidence interval is shifted over by an amount equal to the estimated bias resulting from that inequality. Since we are dealing with an adjustment to the percentage bootstrap approach, it is assumed that the value of b is quite large, likely over 1000.

Essentially, this method starts by estimating the bias and calculating its corresponding zs or standard score. This may be written as follows:

$$z_0 = \Phi^{-1}\left(\frac{\#\left[\theta_i^* < \theta\right]}{b}\right)$$

The numerator term in the parentheses, $\#\left[\theta_i^* < \theta\right]$, represents the number of cases in which the θ_i^* are less than θ. This is turned into a proportion by dividing by the number of replicates, b. For example, if 600 of 1000 θ_i^* replicates were less than the value of θ, that proportion would be .60. The Φ^{-1} component of the equation simply means that we should calculate the corresponding z-score for the value within the parentheses.[5] For example, $\Phi^{-1}(.975) = 1.96$. In this instance, $\Phi^{-1}(.60) = .253$. Once z_0 has been determined, the upper and lower boundary percentiles can be calculated. The percentiles for a BC interval with a coverage of $1 - \alpha$ are given by

$$p_{LO} = \Phi\left[2z_0 - z_{(1-\alpha/2)}\right]$$
$$p_{UP} = \Phi\left[2z_0 + z_{(1-\alpha/2)}\right]$$

For an $\alpha = .05$ or a 95% confidence interval, $z_{(1-\alpha/2)}$ would be .975. The uppercase phi (Φ) indicates that we ought to find the standard normal cdf value that corresponds to the quantities within the square brackets (i.e., $\Phi[1.96] = .975$).

Once p_{LO} and p_{UP} have been determined, those values are multiplied by b to identify which cases correspond to the upper and lower intervals. Having identified those cases, we determine their values, to locate the actual boundary points of the confidence interval (θ_{LO}^* and θ_{UP}^*).

EXAMPLE: THE CORRELATION

We may repeat the example presented in the jackknife section to generate bootstrap estimates of the standard error and confidence intervals for the correlation between the TFR and the CMR for the 16-nation sample. One of the first things we might wish to investigate is the impact of different sizes of b. Estimates of $\overline{\theta}^*$, and θ_i^* where θ is the Pearson product moment correlation coefficient, are presented in Table 15.4 for the values $b = 50, 100, 200,$ and 5000.

In the section on the jackknife, the population correlation coefficient is reported as .848 and that for the 16 randomly selected nations is .859. The traditional formula for the standard error of r provides a value of .070; thus, a 95% confidence interval about the sample correlation easily encompasses the population value. In contrast to the traditional approach, the jackknife procedure generated an estimate of the standard error for this sample of .064.

As shown in Table 15.4, the bootstrap estimates of the standard error of θ^* are all substantially lower than either of these values. Depending upon the number of replicates, b, the bootstrap estimate ranges from .044 to .048. If we use SE(θ^*)$_{boot}$, based on $b = 5000$, the 95% confidence interval ranges from .765 to .953 (i.e., $\theta^* \pm 1.96 \times .048$), which clearly includes the population correlation of .848. An alternate approach is to calculate the bootstrap confidence limits based on the upper and lower percentiles of the distribution of the θ_i^* estimates.

To ensure that there are enough observations in the tails to generate a reliable estimate, it was decided to use $b = 5000$ for estimating the 95% bootstrap confidence limits. A frequency histogram for the 5000 replicates is illustrated in Figure 15.6. One of the obvious characteristics of this distribution is its asymmetry. This would

---

5. More precisely, it is telling us to take the inverse of the standard normal cumulative distribution function.

Table 15.4. Bootstrap results where θ is the correlation coefficient for various sizes of b

	ESTIMATE
$b = 50$	
θ^*	.882
$SE(\overline{\theta}^*)$	.048
$b = 100$	
θ^*	.877
$SE(\overline{\theta}^*)$	.044
$b = 200$	
θ^*	.876
$SE(\overline{\theta}^*)$	.044
$b = 5000$	
θ^*	.881
$SE(\overline{\theta}^*)$	.048
θ (sample r) for 16 nations	.859
Θ (population ρ) for 192 nations	.848

suggest that the traditional approach to estimating the confidence interval based on $\theta^* \pm z_{\alpha/2} \, SE(\theta^*)$ might be inappropriate. Using the bootstrap approach to estimating the limits, however, we note that the value of the 125th case is .781 and that of the 4875th case is .962. This latter range is slightly narrower than that estimated using the $\theta^* \pm z_{\alpha/2} \, SE(\theta^*)$ procedure and is shifted a little to the right.[6]

It is also possible estimate the bias of θ. Recall that bias is defined as the difference between the mean of the $b\,\theta_i^*$ values and θ. For the jackknife, this bias turns out to be $.862 - .859 = .041$. Turning to Table 15.4, we note that the mean of the θ_i^* values for $b = 5000$ is .881 Thus, the bootstrap bias is estimated as $.881 - .859 = .022$ This value is about half that obtained under the jackknife. Part of the difference between the bias estimated under the jackknife and that estimated under the bootstrap is due to the

6. It is because the sampling distribution of r is asymmetrical once one moves away from r being centered on 0 that most sources recommend using the normalizing transformation $z = .5\ln(1 + r^2)/(1 - r^2)$. The standard deviation of this distribution is approximated by $1/(n-3)^{1/2}$. Confidence intervals are estimated in the normalized form and then transformed back to the original metric. For the sake of simplicity, we have not persued this step. However, it is an interesting assignment to conduct this exercise and compare the result with those presented here.

basing of the jackknife estimates of θ on $n - 1$ observations instead of n. Obviously, the estimates of bias under the bootstrap will vary somewhat according to the value of b and the particular combination of subsamples that happen to be drawn on any given run. However, it should be noted that calculating the bias for the three other conditions in Table 15.4 ($b = 50$, 100, and 200) results in little variability. Those estimates turn out to be .023, .028, and .017 respectively.

Another point of comparison between the jackknife and the bootstrap is the difference in the distributions of the replicates (shown in Figures 15.4 and 15.6). The major difference between Figures 15.4 and 15.6 is the relative smoothness of the latter. With the greater number of replicates, the bootstrap simply has more data points for defining the sampling distribution than does the jackknife approach.

Having calculated the bias in the bootstrap, we can estimate a bias-corrected confidence interval. Looking at the last run, where $b = 5000$, it was discovered that in 1567 out of 5000 replicates, the estimated value of θ_i^* was less than that of θ. Thus, z_0 becomes the inverse normal probability of 1567/5000 or $\Phi^{-1}(.313) = -.486$. For convenience, let $\alpha = .05$; consequently, $z_{1-\alpha/2} = 1.96$. Based on these values, it is possible to obtain the percentiles for the cases that define the lower and upper bounds as follows:

$$p_{LO} = \Phi\left[2z_0 - z_{1-\alpha/2}\right]$$
$$= \Phi\left[2(-.486) - 1.96\right]$$
$$= .002$$

and

$$p_{UP} = \Phi\left[2z_0 + z_{1-\alpha/2}\right]$$
$$= \Phi\left[2(-.486) + 1.96\right]$$
$$= .838$$

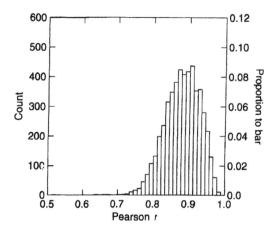

Figure 15.6. Distribution of $b = 5000$ correlation coefficients for the 16-nation data.

Table 15.5. Comparison of confidence intervals for three different estimation procedures for a 95% confidence interval around r ($b = 5000$)

METHOD	95% CONFIDENCE INTERVAL	
Normal	.764	.955
Percentile	.779	.962
Bias-corrected	.708	.932
θ (correlation)	.859	
Estimated bias	.022	
Standard error	.048	

Multiplying these values by 5000 identifies the 9th and the 4190th cases, which define the boundaries of the inner 95% of cases as .708 and .932.

Table 15.5 compares the resulting confidence intervals for the normal, percentile, and bias-corrected methods. In this particular instance, while the BC method does encompass both the sample correlation coefficient ($\theta = .859$) and the population correlation coefficient ($\Theta = .848$), it shifts the intervals to the left of the distribution because of the direction of the bias estimate between $\overline{\theta}^*$ and θ.

EXAMPLE: THE RATIO MEAN

In Chapter 5 we discussed the problem of estimating the standard error of the ratio mean within cluster samples. It is worthwhile revisiting that problem to see how it might be addressed using the bootstrap. The data for this problem are taken from Table 5.2 in Chapter 5. The data consist of 42 random road sites where investigators stopped a number of vehicles and determined which drivers were over the legal blood alcohol limit. For the sites used in the example, the total number of drivers over the legal limit was 90 and the total number of vehicles stopped was 1693. The ratio mean is therefore $90/1693 = .05316$ or .053. The standard error was estimated to be $.69 \times 10^{-4}$; thus, a 95% confidence interval would be approximately $.036 \leq r \leq .069$.

Upon setting up the bootstrap, 5000 replicates of 42 clusters were generated. The total number of vehicles and the total number of drivers over the limit was calculated for each replicate and those numbers were used to generate an estimate of the ratio mean for each replicate. The distribution of replicates is given in Figure 15.7.

The mean of those ratio means also turned out to be .053. At five decimal places, the difference between the two estimates of the ratio means (essentially $\overline{\theta}^* - \theta$) is $.05329 - .05316 = .0013$, indicating a minimal bias. This is not unexpected, since, as indicated in Chapter 5, the bias in cluster samples is in the order of $1/X$.

Although Figure 15.7 suggests that the bootstrap distribution is close to normal, there are slight deviations, partly because the lower limit for r is truncated at 0. The skewness of the means turns out to be .2567 (as opposed to an expected value of

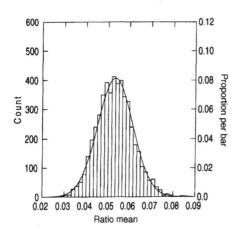

Figure 15.7. The 5000 bootstrap replicates of the ratio mean for the proportion of drivers over the legal blood alcohol limit.

0), suggesting that the distribution is skewed somewhat to the right. The kurtosis value is 3.1517 (as opposed to an expected value of 3), indicating a slight amount of leptokurtosis. Thus, the tails of the distribution are somewhat thinner than expected. Together, the skewness/kurtosis test for normality indicates a statistically significant deviation from the normal curve ($\chi^2 = 57.73$; $p < .001$) (D'Agostino, Balanger, and D'Agostino, 1990). While the deviation is of little substantive importance in this application, it does suggest that we might wish to estimate a confidence interval using the bootstrap percentile approach.

In this case, the inner 95% of cases (cases 125–4875) are defined by the limiting values of .038 and .071. The standard parametric estimate gave the range .036 $\leq$ $r \leq$ .069; thus, the bootstrap percentile narrows the range slightly and shifts the confidence boundaries slightly to the right.

Clearly, the advantage of the bootstrap here (aside from dealing with the non-normality problem) is the relative simplicity of calculating the standard error. The standard approximation is relatively complex, and would be even more so if the cluster sample involved stratification or some form of multistage sampling. Those wishing to pursue the applicability of the bootstrap to sampling problems might start with the discussion in Shao and Tu (1995).

Limitations

Some of the limitations inherent in jackknifing also apply to the bootstrap. The naïve bootstrap in particular can be unreliable and is generally not very good for long-tailed distributions or for time series and stochastic data. However, work on the bootstrap continues, and solutions to some of the difficulties inherent in the naïve bootstrap have been devised (see LePage and Billard, 1992).

Despite its limitations, resampling has much to offer the researcher. Resampling procedures such as the jackknife and the bootstrap provide the opportunity to use test statistics that make more sense given the substantive hypothesis. Thus, one is not limited to the relatively narrow range of classical statistics for which direct formulas (or large sample approximations) for their standard errors have been established. Our confidence in the application of resampling statistics can be enhanced by using a few basic precautions. First, be sure to employ more than one approach as a means to cross-verify the results. If parametric approximations are suggested in the literature, compare the results given by those procedures with what you obtain. Second, do not simply accept the summary outcomes; examine the data and the result firsthand by means of various graphical presentations. Most successful researchers spend more of their time examining descriptive statistics and graphical presentations than calculating and testing model parameters. Third, search the literature (relating to both theory and applications) for work similar to your own application. Resampling procedures are currently among the most actively researched areas in methods, and between the publication of this book and your reading it, several hundred articles have likely appeared across any number of disciplines.

VARIATIONS

This chapter has outlined but a few of the core ideas underlying the jackknife and bootstrap. There are numerous variations on these themes that can work either better or worse than those outlined here, depending upon the circumstances. One common modification that is seen in the literature is the bootstrap-t. The bootstrap-t creates its own normal and t-percentiles from the data rather than taking them from a standard table. Briefly, the bootstrap-t produces a distribution of standardized differences about the center of the distribution. That is, instead of creating a confidence interval based on the percentile distribution of the raw values of θ_i^*, it is created on the basis of

$$z_i = \frac{\theta_i^* - \theta}{\widehat{SE}(\theta)}$$

The major difficulties surrounding the bootstrap-t involve a substantial increase in the amount of calculation required (estimation involves performing a "double bootstrap") and the potential for erratic performance in small-sample, nonparametric applications.

The bias correction method can be modified to include changes to the shape of the distribution as well as the amount of estimated bias. This modification, known as the accelerated bias correction (BCa) approach, takes into account the possibility that the standard error of θ will not be constant with respect to Θ.

Instead of estimating, for example, the upper interval as $p_{UP} = \Phi[2z_0 + z_{(1-\alpha/2)}]$, we use

$$p_{UP} = \Phi \left[z_0 + \frac{z_0 + z_{1-\alpha/2}}{1 - a\left(z_0 + z_{1-\alpha/2}\right)} \right]$$

If a (in the denominator) is zero, then the BCa formula reduces to the simpler BC one. As with the bootstrap-t, BCa involves more computation than the simple BC approach. Although a can be estimated through a variety of means (including a preapplication of the jackknife), Efron has developed a modification commonly known as the ABC algorithm.

Again, how well BCa or ABC works in practice is largely an empirical issue, depending upon the statistic to be bootstrapped, the sample size, and the vicissitudes of sampling variability. These and other modifications are dealt with in some detail in the readings listed at the end of the chapter.

CONCLUSIONS

Research into resampling techniques is ongoing, and new results appear on a regular basis. Traditional parametric approaches are superior to resampling techniques in some situations, and there are clearly some instances in which resampling techniques are the appropriate response. Resampling techniques seem to require two conditions in order to work: (a) there needs to be reasonable continuity in the distribution of the θ_i^* values, and (b) the estimates must be consistent such that $\theta \to \Theta$ as $n \to \infty$. Summarizing the literature to date, the following recommendations are offered.

Resampling techniques, especially the bootstrap, do *not* work well when the sampling distribution is not a continuous function. They will not work, for example, on estimates such as the minimum and the maximum, or for statistics such as the median when the θ_i^*s take on only two or three discrete values. Often, the jackknife will be inconsistent for statistics that are not very smooth. This can sometimes be addressed, however, by means of modifications such as the delete-d jackknife.

Generally, resampling techniques require that the data be distributed i.i.d., that is, identically and independently. Certainly "naïve" bootstrap procedures cannot handle dynamic data with the kind of strong dependencies found in many time series and spatially correlated examples. In some instances, modification (such as the "wild bootstrap" of Shao and Tu, 1995) can be used for non-i.i.d. situations. When resampling approaches do work with dependent samples, the generating process is usually stationary as opposed to dynamic.

It also makes little sense to use bootstrap procedures when a traditional parametric approach is simpler and is known to work well. Few, for example, would go to the trouble of bootstrapping to find the standard error of a simple binomial when it is possible to calculate it as $(pq/n)^{1/2}$ in a matter of seconds.

Jackknife statistics do, however, appear to be particularly useful for estimating standard errors in complex sampling plans, such as multistage and stratified cluster samples (Shao and Tu, 1995).

Bootstrap statistics appear to work well with quantiles and with most statistics amenable to t-type distributions (e.g., regression weights). Bootstraps are also valuable when minor violations of assumptions, such as residuals in a regression application that are not centered on 0, can cause havoc with traditional approaches. Some research suggests that the bootstrap works well with most linear model applications, including many "robust" techniques. However, significant difficulties arise when the number of variables included in the analysis becomes large.

Resampling approaches such as the bootstrap also are beneficial at times even when classical normal approximations work. In many instances, bootstraps will work better in that they produce additional accuracy.

Further Reading

The literature on resampling techniques is voluminous and ranges from the very accessible to the arcane. Generally, the notions underlying resampling techniques are elementary, so much of the literature is accessible to those with an intermediate level background in statistics.

Efron, B., and Tibshirani, R.J. *An Introduction to the Bootstrap*. London: Chapman & Hall, 1993. An excellent intermediate level introduction to the subject. The text is fairly comprehensive and attempts to provide a reasonably sophisticated understanding of the procedures without resorting to extensive formal proofs.

Mammen, E. *When Does Bootstrap Work?* New York: Springer-Verlag, 1992. The title pretty well says it all. The discussion is quite advanced, however, with emphasis on formal proofs. Best for those with a strong formal background in statistics.

Manly, B.F.J. *Randomization, Bootstrap and Monte Carlo Methods in Biology*, 2nd ed. London: Chapman & Hall, 1997. While oriented toward biological applications, this book is eminently readable. Most of the applications have parallels in the social sciences.

Mooney, C.Z., and Duval, R.D. *Bootstrapping: A Nonparametric Approach to Statistical Inference*. Newbury Park, CA: Sage, 1993. This is a good introduction to resampling from the social science perspective. Very accessible, with a minimum of mathematical or statistical background assumed.

Noreen, E.W. *Computer Intensive Methods for Testing Hypotheses*. New York: Wiley, 1989. Another basic introduction with several good examples that are easy to replicate. Invaluable source of computer code for do-it-yourselfers.

Shao, J., and Tu, D. *The Jackknife and Bootstrap*. New York: Springer-Verlag, 1995. A more formal introduction to the topic. Requires upper intermediate/advanced level understanding of statistics. Excellent chapter on the applicability of jackknifing to sampling problems.

References

Abramson, P.R., Silver, B.D., and Anderson, B.A. "The effects of question order in attitude surveys: The case of the SRC/CPS citizen duty items." *American Journal of Political Science*, 31: 900–908, 1987.

Acton, F.S. *Numerical Methods That Work* (corrected edition). Washington, DC: Mathematical Association of America, 1990.

Adair, J.G., Sharpe, D., and Huynh, C.L. "Placebo, Hawthorne and other artifact controls: Researchers' opinions and practices." *Journal of Experimental Education*, 57: 341–55, 1989.

Agresti, A. *Categorical Data Analysis*. New York: Wiley, 1990.

Aiken, L.S., and West, S.G. *Multiple Regression: Testing and Interpreting Interactions*. Newbury Park, CA: Sage, 1990.

Alliger, G.M., and Williams, K.J. "Relating the internal consistency of scales to rater response tendencies." *Educational and Psychological Measurement*, 52: 337–43, 1992.

Allison, P.D. "Estimation of linear models with incomplete data." *Sociological Methodology*, 17: 71–103, 1987.

Anderson, A.B., Balilevsky, A., and Hum, D.P.J. "Missing data." In Rossi, P.H., Wright, J.D., and Anderson, A.B., eds. *Handbook of Survey Research*. New York: Academic Press, 1983.

Anderson, A.B., et al. "Measurement: Theory and techniques." In Rossi, P.H., Wright, J.D. and Anderson, A.B., eds., *Handbook of Survey Research*. New York: Academic Press, 1983.

Anderson, T.W. "Maximum likelihood estimates for a multivariate normal distribution when some observation are missing." *Journal of the American Statistical Association*, 52: 200–203, 1957.

Andrich, D. "An elaboration of Guttman scaling with Rasche models for measurement." In Tuma, N. ed., *Sociological Methodology 1985*. San Francisco: Jossey-Bass, 1985.

Athearn, D. *Scientific Nihilism*. Albany, NY: State University of New York Press, 1994.

Ayer, A.J. ed. *Logical Positivism*. New York: Free Press, 1959.

Ayidiya, S.A., and McClendon, M.J. "Response effects in mail surveys." *Public Opinion Quarterly*, 54: 229–88, 1990.

Bailar, B.A. "Information needs, surveys and measurement errors." In Kasprzyk, D., Duncan, G., Kalton, G., and Singh, M.P. eds., *Panel Surveys*. New York: Wiley, 1989.

Bailar, B.A., and Bailar, J.C. "Comparison of the biases of the hot-deck imputation procedure with an 'equal weights' imputation procedure." In Madow, W.G., Olkin, I., and Rubin, D.B., eds., *Incomplete Data in Sample Surveys*, Vol. 2: *Theory and Bibliographies*. New York: Wiley, 1983.

Bailey, L., Moore, T.F., and Bailar, B.A. "An interviewer variance study for the eight impact cities of the national crime survey cities sample." *Journal of the American Statistical Association*, 73: 16–23, 1978.

Balakrishnan, T.R., and Hou, F. "Status of women, economic development and fertility." IUSSP XXIInd General Conference, Montreal, Canada, August 24–September 1, 1993.

Bebbington, A.C. "A simple method of drawing a sample without replacement." *Applied Statistics*, 24: 136, 1975.

Bechtoldt, P. "Construct validity: A critique." *American Psychologist*, 14: 619–29, 1959.

Beland, F., and Maheux, B. "Construct validity and second-order factorial model: The second-order factor model." *Quality and Quantity*, 23: 143–159, 1989.

Bendig, A.W. "Reliability and the number of rating scale categories." *Journal of Applied Psychology*, 38: 38–40, 1954a.

Bendig, A.W. "Reliability of short rating scales and the heterogeneity of the rated stimuli." *Journal of Applied Psychology*, 38: 167–70, 1954b.

Benson, J., and Hocevar, D. "The impact of item phrasing on the validity of attitude scales for elementary school children." *Journal of Educational Measurement*, 22: 231–40, 1985.

Berk, R.A. "An introduction to sample selection bias in sociological data." *American Sociological Review*, 48: 386–98, 1983.

Bierstedt, R. "Nominal and real definitions in sociological theory." In Gross, L., ed., *Symposium on Sociological Theory*. Evanston, IL: Row, Peterson and Co., 1959.

Bishop, G.F, Tuchfarber, A.J., and Oldendick, R.W. "Opinions on fictitious issues: The pressure to answer survey questions." *Public Opinion Quarterly*, 50: 240–50, 1986.

Bishop, Y.M.M., Fienberg, S.E., and Holland, P.W. *Discrete Multivariate Analysis: Theory and Practice*. Cambridge, MA: MIT Press, 1975.

Blalock, H. *Causal Inferences in Nonexperimental Research*. Chapel Hill: University of North Carolina Press, 1964.

Blanchard, O.J., and Fischer, S. *Lectures on Macroeconomics*. Cambridge, MA: MIT Press, 1989.

Bloor, M., Leyland, A., Barnard, M., and McKeganey, N. "Estimating hidden populations: A new method of calculating the prevalence of drug-injecting and non-injecting female street prostitutes." *British Journal of the Addictions*, 86: 1477–83, 1991.

Blossfeld, H.-P. *Event History Analysis*. Hillsdale, NJ: Erlbaum, 1989.

Bock, D.R. *Multivariate Statistical Methods in Behavioral Research*. New York: McGraw-Hill, 1975.

Bollen, K.A. *Structural Equations with Latent Variables*. New York: Wiley, 1989.

Bonjean, C.M. *Sociological Measurement: An Inventory of Scales and Indices*. San Francisco: Chandler, 1967.

Boote, A.S. "Reliability testing of psychographic scales: Five-point or seven-point? Anchored or labeled?" *Journal of Advertising Research*, 21: 53–60, 1981.

Booth, A., and Johnson, D.R. "Tracing respondents in a telephone interview panel selected by random digit dialing." *Sociological Methods and Research*, 14: 53–64, 1985.

Borgatta, E.F., and G.W. Bohrnstedt. "Level of measurement—once over again." *Sociological Methods and Research*, 9: 147–60, 1980.

Boruch, R.F., McSweeny, A.J., and Soderstrom, E.J. "Randomized field experiments for program planning, development and evaluation." *Evaluation Quarterly*, 2: 655–95, 1978.

Bower, G.H. and Gillian, S.G. "Remembering information relating to one's self." *Journal of Research in Personality*, 13: 420–32, 1979.

Bradburn, N.M. "Response effects." In Rossi P.H, Wright, J.D., and Anderson, A.B., eds., *Handbook of Survey Research*. New York: Academic Press, 1983.

Bradburn, N.M., Sudman, S., and Associates. *Improving Interview Method and Questionnaire Design*. San Francisco: Jossey-Bass, 1979.

Bradburn, N.M., and Sudman, S. "The current status of questionnaire research." In Biemer, P., Groves, R.M., Lyberg, L.E., Mathiowetz, N.A., and Sudman, S., eds., *Measurement Errors in Surveys*. New York: Wiley, 1991.

Breakey, W.R., and Fischer, J. "Homelessness: The extent of the problem." *Journal of Social Issues*, 46: 31–47, 1990.

Brecht, M.-L., and Wickins, T.D. "Application of multiple-capture methods for estimating drug use prevalence." *Journal of Drug Issues*, 23: 229–50, 1993.

Bridgman, P.W. *The Logic of Modern Physics*. New York: Macmillan, 1928.

Broad, N. and Wade, N. *Betrayers of Truth*. New York: Simon & Schuster, 1982.

Brodsky, S.L., and Smitherman, H.O. *Handbook of Scales for Research in Crime and Delinquency*. New York: Plenum Press, 1983.

Brown, G., Widing, R.E., and Coulter, R.L. "Customer evaluation of retail salespeople utilizing the SOCO scale: A replication, extension, and application." *Journal of the Academy of Marketing Science*, 9: 347–51, 1991.

Browne, M.W., and Cudeck, R. "Single sample cross validation indices for covariance structures." *Multivariate Behavioural Research*, 24: 445–55, 1989.

Bunde, H., and Havlin, S. *Fractals and Disordered Systems*. New York: Springer-Verlag, 1991.

Bunge, M. *Causality: The Place of the Causal Principle in Modern Science*. Cambridge, MA: Harvard University Press, 1959.

Bunge, M. *Causality and Modern Science*, 3rd ed. New York: Dover, 1979.

Burgess, R.D. "Major issues and implications of tracing survey respondents." In Kasprzyk, D., Duncan, G., Kalton, G., and Singh, M.P., eds., *Panel Surveys*. New York: Wiley, 1989.

Campbell, D.T. " Factors relevant to the validity of experiments in social settings." *Psychological Bulletin*, 54: 297–311, 1957.

Campbell, D.T. "Reforms as experiments." *American Psychologist*, 24: 409–29, 1969.

Campbell, D.T., and Boruch, R.F. "Making the case for randomized assignment to treatments by considering the alternatives: Six ways in which quasi-experimental evaluations in compensatory education tend to underestimate effects." In Bennett, C.A., and Lumsdaine, A.A., eds., *Evaluation and Experiment: Some Critical Issues in Assessing Social Programs*. New York: Academic Press, 1975.

Campbell, D.T., and Fiske, D.W. "Convergent and discriminant validation by the multitrait–multimethod matrix." *Psychological Bulletin,* 52: 281–302, 1959.

Campbell, D.T., and Stanley, J. "Experimental and quasi-experimental designs for research on teaching." In Gage, N.L., ed., *Handbook of Research on Teaching*. Chicago: Rand-McNally, 1963.

Campbell, D.T., and Stanley, J. *Experimental and Quasi-experimental Designs for Research*. Chicago: Rand-McNally, 1966.

Cannell, C.F., and Okensberg, L. "Observation of behaviour in telephone interviews." In Groves, R., Biemer, P., Lyberg, L., Massey, J., Nicholls, W., and Waksberg, J., eds., *Telephone Survey Methodology*. New York: Wiley, 1988.

Capra, F. *The Tao of Physics*. London: Fontana, 1979.

Carnap, R. (1931/2) "Überwindung der Metaphysik durch logische Analyse der Sprache," *Erkenntnis*, 2. Translated version reprinted as "The elimination of metaphysics through logical analysis of language." In Ayer, A.J., ed., *Logical Positivism*. New York: Free Press, 1959, pp. 60–81.

Carnap, R. *The Logical Structure of the World and Pseudoproblems in Philosophy*. Berkeley: University of California Press, 1969.

Cartwright, N. *Nature's Capacities and Their Measurement*. Oxford: Clarendon Press, 1989.

Champney, H., and Marshall, H. "Optimal refinement of the rating scale." *Journal of Applied Psychology*, 23: 323–31, 1939.

Chang, L. "A psychometric evaluation of 4-point and 6-point Likert-type scales in relation to reliability and validity." *Applied Psychological Measurement*, 18: 205–15, 1994.

Chao, A. "Estimating the population size for capture–recapture data with unequal catch probabilities." *Biometrics*, 43: 783–91, 1987.

Choldin, H.M. *Looking for the Last Percent: The Controversy over Census Undercounts*. New Brunswick, NJ: Rutgers University Press, 1994.

Chun, K., Cobb, S., and French, J.R.P. *Measures for Psychological Assessment*. Ann Arbor, MI: Survey Research Centre, 1975.

Cicchetti, D.V., Showalter, D., and Tyrer, P.J. "The effect of number of rating scale categories on levels of interrater reliability." *Applied Psychological Measurement*, 7: 249–53, 1985.

Clark, J.P., and Tifft, L.L. Polygraph and interview validation of self-reported deviant behavior." *American Sociological Review*, 31: 516–523, 1966.

Cleveland, W.S. *The Elements of Graphing Data*. Monterey, CA.: Wadsworth, 1985.

Cochran, W.G. *Sampling Techniques*. New York: Wiley, 1977.

Coeffic, N. "Le recensement de 1990: L'Enquete de mesure d'exhaustivité." *Journal de la Societé de Statistique de Paris*, 134: 3–20, 1993.

Cohen, J. "The statistical power of abnormal-social psychological research: A review." *Journal of Abnormal and Social Psychology*, 65: 145–53, 1962.

Cohen, J. *Statistical Power Analysis for the Behavioral Sciences*. New York: Academic Press, 1969.

Cohen, J. *Statistical Power Analysis*, 2nd ed. Hillsdale, NJ: Erlbaum, 1988.

Collins, R., and Waller, D. "Did social science break down in the 1970s?" In Hage, J., ed., *Formal Theory in Sociology*. Albany: State University of New York Press, 1994.

Converse, P. "Attitudes and nonattitudes: Continuation of a dialogue." In Tufte, E.R., ed., *The Quantitative Analysis of Social Problems*. Reading, MA: Addison-Wesley, 1970.

Converse, J.M. *Survey Research in the United States*. Berkeley: University of California Press, 1987.

Cook, T.D., and Campbell, D.T. *Quasi-Experimental Designs*. Chicago: Rand-McNally, 1974.

Cook, T.D., and Campbell, D.T. *Quasi-Experimentation: Design and Analysis Issues for Field Settings*. Chicago: Rand-McNally, 1979.

Coombs, C.H. *A Theory of Data*. New York: Wiley, 1964.

Copi, I.M. *Symbolic Logic*. New York: Macmillan, 1967.

Cormack, R.M. "The statistics of capture–recapture methods." *Annual Review of Oceanography and Marine Biology*, 6, 455–506, 1968.

Costner, H.L., and Leik, R.K. "Deductions from 'axiomatic theory.'" *American Sociological Review*, 29: 819–35, 1964.

Courgeau, D. *Event History Analysis in Demography*. Oxford: Oxford University Press, 1992.

Crider, D.M, Willits, F.K., and Bealer, R.C. "Tracing respondents in longitudinal surveys." *Public Opinion Quarterly*, 35: 613–20, 1971.

Crilly, A.J., Earnshaw, R.A., and Jones, H. *Application of Fractals and Chaos*. New York: Springer-Verlag, 1993.

Cronbach, L.J. "Coefficient alpha and the internal structure of tests." *Psychometrika*, 16: 297–334, 1951.

Cronbach, L.J., and Meehl, P.E. "Construct validity in psychological tests." *Psychological Bulletin*, 52: 281–302, 1955.

Cudeck, R., and Browne, M.W. "Cross-validation of covariance structures." *Multivariate Behavioural Research*, 18: 147–57, 1983.

Cuyt, A., and Wuytack, L. *Nonlinear Methods in Numerical Analysis*. Amsterdam: North-Holland, 1987.

D'Agostino, R.B., Balanger, A., and D'Agostino, R.R. "A suggestion for using powerful and informative tests of normality." *American Statistician*, 44; 316–21, 1990.

D'Andrade, R. "Three scientific world views and the covering law model." In Fiske, D.W., and

Shweder, R.A, eds., *Metatheory in Social Science.* Chicago: University of Chicago Press, 1986, pp. 26–27.

Dallago, B. *The Irregular Economy.* Aldershot, U.K.: Dartmouth, 1990.

Danmarks Statistik. *Befolkningens bevægelser 1990.* Copenhagen, 1992.

Darroch, J.N., Fienberg, S.E., Glonek, G.F.V., and Junker, B.W. "A three sample multiple-recapture approach to census population estimation with heterogeneous catchability." *Journal of the American Statistical Association,* 88: 1137–48, 1993.

De Boor, C. *A Practical Guide to Splines.* New York: Springer-Verlag, 1978.

DeLeeuw, E.D., and Van der Zouwen, J. "Data quality in face to face surveys: A comparative meta analysis." In Groves, R., Biemer, P., Lyberg, L., Massey, J., Nicholls, W., and Waksberg, J., eds., *Telephone Survey Methodology.* New York: Wiley, 1988.

Dempster, A.P., Laird, N.M., and Rubin, D.B. "Maximum likelihood from incomplete data via the EM algorithm." *Journal of the Royal Statistical Society (B),* 34: 1–38, 1977.

Dillman, D.A. *Mail and Telephone Surveys: The Total Design Method.* New York: Wiley, 1978.

Dillman, D.A. "The design and administration of mail surveys." *Annual Review of Sociology,* 17: 225–249, 1991.

Dixon, W.J., Brown, M.B., Engelman, L., Hill, M.A., and Jennich, R.I. *BMDP Statistical Software Manual,* Vol. 2. Berkeley: University of California Press, 1988.

Doby, J.T. "Logic and levels of scientific explanation." In Borgotta, E.F., ed., *Sociological Methodology.* San Francisco: Jossey-Bass, 1961.

Donmyer, J.E., Piotrowski, F.W., and Wolter, K.M. "Measurement error in continuing surveys of the grocery retail trade using electronic data collection methods." In Biemer, P., Groves, R.M., Lyberg, L.E., Mathiowetz, N.A., and Sudman, S., eds., *Measurement Errors in Surveys.* New York: Wiley, 1991.

Draper, N.R., and Smith, H. *Applied Regression Analysis,* 2nd ed. New York: Wiley, 1981.

Droitcour, J., Caspar, R.A., Hubbard, M.L,. Parsley, T.L,. Visscher, W., and Ezzati, T.M. "The item count technique as a method of indirect questioning: A review of its development and a case study application." In Biemer, P., Groves, R.M., Lyberg, L.E., Mathiowetz, N.A., and Sudman, S., eds., *Measurement Errors in Surveys.* New York: Wiley, 1991.

Dumont, R.G., and Wilson, W.J. "Aspects of Concept Formation, Explication, and Theory Construction in Sociology." *American Sociological Review,* 32: 985–95, 1967.

Dunbar, R. *The Trouble with Science.* London: Faber, 1994.

Duncan, O.D. "Path analysis: Sociological examples." *American Journal of Sociology,* 72: 1–16, 1966.

Duncan, O.D. "Two faces of panel analysis: Parallels with comparative cross-sectional analysis and time-lagged association." *Sociological Methodology 1981.* San Francisco: Jossey-Bass, 1981.

Edmonston, B., and Schultze, C. *Modernizing the U.S. Census.* Washington, DC: National Academy Press, 1995.

Efron, B. "The jackknife, the bootstrap and other resampling plans." *CBMS-NSF Regional Conference Series on Applied Mathematics,* Vol. 38. Philadelphia: Society for Industrial and Applied Mathematics, 1982.

Efron, B., and Tibshirani, R.J. *An Introduction to the Bootstrap.* London: Chapman & Hall, 1993.

Erickson, M.L., and Empey, L. "Court records, undetected delinquency and decision-making." *Journal of Criminal Law, Criminology and Police Science,* 54: 456–69, 1963.

Fairley, W.B., and Glenn, J.E. "A question of theft." In DeGroot, M.H., Fienberg, S.E., and Kadane, J.B., eds., *Statistics and the Law.* New York: Wiley, 1986.

Feyerabend, P.K. *Against Method: Outline of an Anarchistic Theory of Knowledge.* London:

Humanities Press, 1975. The third edition appeared in 1993, published by Verso, New York.

Finn, R.H. "Effect of some variations in rating scale characteristics on the means and reliabilities of ratings." *Educational and Psychological Measurement*, 34: 885–92, 1972.

Fisher, R.A. *Statistical Methods for Research Workers*, 12th ed. Edinburgh: Oliver & Boyd, 1954.

Fisher, N., Turner, S.W., Pugh, R., and Taylor, C., "Estimating numbers of homeless and homeless mentally ill people in Northeast Westminster by using capture–recapture analysis." *British Medical Journal*, 308: 27–30, 1994.

Fowler, F.J. "Reducing interviewer-related error through interviewer training, supervision, and other means." In Biemer, P., Groves, R.M., Lyberg, L.E., Mathiowetz, N.A., and Sudman, S., eds., *Measurement Errors in Surveys*. New York: Wiley, 1991.

Fowler, F.J., and Mangione, T.W. *Standardized Survey Interviewing*. Newbury Park, CA: Sage, 1990.

Fox, J.A., and Tracy, P.E. *Randomized Response: A Method for Sensitive Surveys*. Sage Series in Quantitative Applications in the Social Sciences. Beverly Hills, CA: Sage, 1986.

Frank, D.J., Meyer, J.W., and Miyahara, D. "The individualist polity and the prevalence of professionalized psychology: A cross-national study." *American Sociological Review*, 60: 360–77, 1995.

Frankel, B. "Two extremes in the social science commitment continuum." In Fiske, D.W., and Shweder, R.A., eds., *Metatheory in Social Science*. Chicago: University of Chicago Press, 1986, pp. 353–61.

Fuller, W.A. *Measurement Error Models*. New York: Wiley, 1987.

Ghiselli, E.E., and Brown, C.W. *Personnel and Industrial Psychology*. New York: McGraw-Hill, 1948.

Ghiselli, E.E., Campbell, J.P., and Zedeck, S. *Measurement Theory for the Behavioral Sciences*. San Francisco: Freeman, 1981.

Gibbs, J. *Social Theory Construction*. Hinsdale, IL: Dryden Press, 1972.

Gibbs, J.P. "Resistance in sociology to formal theory construction." In Hage, J., ed., *Formal Theory in Sociology*. Albany: State University of New York Press, 1994.

Giere, R. *Understanding Scientific Reasoning*. New York: Holt, Rinehart & Winston, 1984.

Giere, R. *Explaining Science*. Chicago: University of Chicago Press, 1988.

Glenn, N.D. "Cohort analysts' futile quest: Statistical attempts to separate age, period and cohort effects." *American Sociological Review*, 41: 900–904, 1976.

Goldberg, L.R. "Unconfounding situational attributions from uncertain, neutral, and ambiguous ones: A psychometric analysis of descriptions of oneself and various types of others." *Journal of Personality and Social Psychology*, 41: 517–52, 1981.

Goldman, B.A., and Saunders, J.L. *Directory of Unpublished Experimental Mental Measures*. New York: Human Sciences Press, 1974–1990.

Good, I.J. *Good Thinking: The Foundations of Probability and Its Applications*. Minneapolis: University of Minnesota Press, 1983.

Gösta, F., and Schreinger, I. "The design and analysis of reinterview: An overview." In Biemer, P., Groves, R.M., Lyberg, L.E., Mathiowetz, N.A., and Sudman, S., eds., *Measurement Errors in Surveys*. New York: Wiley, 1991.

Gottfredson, M.R., and Hirschi, T. *A General Theory of Crime*. Stanford, CA: Stanford University Press, 1990.

Government of Ontario, Interministerial Committee on Drinking-Driving. *The 1986 Ontario Survey of Nighttime Drivers*. Toronto: Ministry of Transportation, 1988.

Goyder, J. *The Silent Minority*. Cambridge: Blackwell, 1987.

Granger, C.W.J. "Investigating causal relations by econometric models and cross-spectral methods." *Econometrica*, 37: 424–38, 1969.

Granger, C.W.J., and Newbold, P. *Forecasting Economic Time Series*. New York: Academic Press, 1977.

Green, P.E., and Rao, V.R. *Applied Multidimensional Scaling*. New York: Holt, Rinehart & Winston, 1972.

Greenberg, B., Abul-Ela, A., Simmons, W., and Horvitz, D. "The unrelated questions randomized response model theoretical framework." *Journal of the American Statistical Association*, 64: 520–39, 1969.

Greene, W.H. *Econometric Analysis*. New York: Macmillan, 1990.

Greer, S. *The Logic of Social Inquiry*. New Brunswick, NJ: Transaction, 1989.

Gregg, J.R. *Language of Taxonomy*. New York: Columbia University Press, 1954.

Greville, T.N.E. *Theory and Applications to Spline Functions*. New York: Academic Press, 1969.

Griliches, Z. "Economic data issues." In Griliches, Z., and Intrilligator, M., eds., *Handbook of Econometrics*, Vol. 3. Amsterdam: North-Holland, 1986.

Groves, R.M. *Survey Errors and Survey Costs*. New York: Wiley, 1989.

Groves, R.M. Biemer, P., Lyberg, L.E., Massey, J.T., Nicholls, W.L., and Waksberg, J., eds. *Telephone Survey Methodology*. New York: Wiley, 1988.

Groves, R.M., and Lyberg, L.E. "An overview of nonresponse issues in telephone surveys." In Groves, R.M., Biemer, P., Lyberg, L.E., Massey, J.T., Nicholls, W.L., and Waksberg, J., eds., *Telephone Survey Methodology*. New York: Wiley, 1988.

Groves, R.M., and Magilavy, L.J. "Estimates of interviewer variance in telephone surveys." *Proceedings of the Section on Survey Research Methods, American Statistical Association*, 1980, pp. 622–27.

Groves, R.M., and Magilavy, L.J. "Measuring and explaining interviewer effects." *Public Opinion Quarterly*, 50: 251–56, 1986.

Groves, R.M., Magilavy, L.J., and Mathiowetz, N.N. "The process of interviewer variability evidence from telephone surveys." *Proceedings of the Section on Survey Research Methods, American Statistical Association*, 1981, pp. 438–43.

Guba, E.G., and Lincoln, Y.S. "Naturalistic and rationalistic enquiry." In Keeves, J.P. *Educational Research, Methodology, and Measurement: An International Handbook*. Oxford: Pergamon, 1988.

Guilford, J.P. *Psychometric Methods*. New York: McGraw-Hill, 1954.

Guillaume, J.W., and Termote, M.G. *Introduction to Demographic Analysis*. New York: Plenum, 1978.

Gulliksen, H. *Theory of Mental Tests*. New York: Wiley, 1950.

Habermas, J. *Knowledge and Human Interests*. Beacon Press: Boston, 1971.

Hacking, I. *Logic of Statistical Inference*. Cambridge: Cambridge University Press, 1965.

Hagenaars, J.A., and Cobben, N.P. "Age, cohort and period: A general model for the analysis of social change." *Netherlands Journal of Sociology*, 14: 587–98, 1978.

Haitovsky, Y. "Missing data in regression analysis." *Journal of the Royal Statistical Society (B)*, 30: 67–82, 1967.

Hamilton, L.C. *Regression with Graphics*. Pacific Grove, CA: Brooks/Cole, 1992.

Hansen, M.H., Hurwitz, W.N., and Madow, W.G. *Sampling Survey Methods and Theory*, Vols. I and II. New York: Wiley, 1953.

Harré, R. *Varieties of Realism: A Rationale for the Natural Sciences*. New York: B. Blackwell, 1986.

Harrop, J.W., and Velicer, W.F. "Computer programs for interrupted time series analysis: II. A quantitative evaluation." *Multivariate Behavioral Research*, 25: 233–248, 1990.

Harvey, A. *The Econometric Analysis of Time Series*, 2nd ed. Cambridge, MA: MIT Press, 1990.

Hauser, P.M. "The US Census undercount." *Asian and Pacific Census Forum*, 8: 1–16, 1981.

Hays, W.L. *Statistics*, 4th ed. Orlando, FL: Harcourt, Brace, Jovanovich, 1988.

Heckman, J. "Sample selection bias as a specification error." *Econometrica*, 45: 153–61, 1979.

Hempel, C. *Fundamentals of Concept Formation in Empirical Science*. Chicago: University of Chicago Press, 1952.

Hempel, C. *Aspects of Scientific Explanation*. New York: Free Press, 1965.

Hempel, C. *Philosophy of Natural Science*. Englewood Cliffs, NJ: Prentice-Hall, 1966.

Henshel, R.A. *Reacting to Social Problems*. Don Mills, Ont.: Longman, 1976.

Henshel, R.A. "The boundary of the self-fulfilling prophecy and the dilemma of social prediction." *British Journal of Sociology*, 33: 511–28, 1982.

Henshel, R.A. "Do self-fulfilling prophecies improve or degrade predictive accuracy?" *Journal of Socio-Economics*, 22: 85–104, 1993.

Henshel, R.A., and Johnston, W.A. "The emergence of bandwagon effects: A theory." *Sociological Quarterly*, 28: 493–511, 1987.

Hirsch, E.D. *Validity in Interpretation*. New Haven, CT: Yale University Press, 1967.

Hobcraft, J., Menken, J., and Preston, S. "Age, period and cohort effects in demography: A review." *Population Index*, 48: 4–43, 1982.

Hoeffding, W. "The large sample power of tests based on permutations of observations." *Annals of Mathematical Statistics*, 23, 169–92, 1952.

Hogan, H. "The forward trace study: Its purpose and design." *Proceedings of the Section on Survey Research Methods*, American Statistical Association, 1983, pp. 168–72.

Holland, P.W. "Statistics and causal inference." *Journal of the American Statistical Association*, 81: 945–60, 1986.

Holland, P.W. "Causal inference path analysis and recursive structural equation models." In Clogg, C.C., ed. *Sociological Methodology*. San Francisco: Jossey-Bass, 1988.

Hoover, K.D. "The logic of causal inference. Economics and the conditional analysis of causation." *Economics and Philosophy*, 6: 207–34, 1990.

Hopkins, T., and Phillips, C. *Numerical Methods in Practice: Using the NAG Library*. Wokingham, U.K.: Addison-Wesley, 1988.

Hout, M., and Knoke, K. "Change in voting turnout, 1952–1972." *Public Opinion Quarterly*, 39, 52–68, 1975.

Howson, C., and Urbach, P. *Scientific Reasoning: The Bayesian Approach*. La Salle, IL: Open Court, 1989.

Hox, J.J., and DeLeeuw, E.D. "A comparison of nonresponse in mail, telephone, and face-to-face surveys." *Quality and Quantity*, 28: 329–44, 1994.

Hoyningen-Heune, P. "Context of discovery and context of justification." *Studies in the History and Philosophy of Science*. 18: 501–16, 1987.

Hsiao, C. *The Analysis of Panel Data*. Cambridge: Cambridge University Press, 1986.

Hyman, H., Cobb, W.J., Feldman, J., Hart, C.W., and Stember, C. *Interviewing in Social Research*. Chicago: University of Chicago Press, 1954.

Jaspers, K. "Is science evil?" *Commentary*. 9: 229–33, 1950.

Jenkins, G.D., and Taber, T.D. "A Monte Carlo study of factors affecting three indices of composite scale reliability." *Journal of Applied Psychology*, 62: 392–98, 1977.

Jennis, A.L. "The census undercount: Issues of adjustment." *Columbia Journal of Law and Social Problems*, 18: 381–417, 1984.

Johnstone, D.J., and Lindley, D.V. "Bayesian inference given data 'significant at alpha': Tests of point hypotheses." *Theory and Decision*, 38: 51–60, 1995.

Jones, S.R.G. "Worker interdependence and output: The Hawthorne studies reevaluated." *American Sociological Review*, 55:176–90, 1990.

Jones, S.R.G. "Was there a Hawthorne effect?" *American Journal of Sociology*, 98: 451–68, 1992.

Jöreskog, K.G., "Statistical analysis of sets of congeneric test." *Psychometrika*. 36: 109–34, 1971.

Jöreskog, K.G., and D. Sörbom. *LISREL 7 User's Reference Guide*. Mooresville, IN: Scientific Software, Inc., 1989.

Jöreskog, K.G., and D. Sörbom. *LISREL 8 User's Reference Guide*. Chicago: Scientific Software International, 1993.

Judge, G.G., Hill, R.C., Griffiths, W.E., Lutkepohl, H., and Lee, T.-C. *Introduction to the Theory and Practice of Econometrics*. New York: Wiley, 1988.

Jurow, G.L. "New data on the effect of 'death qualified' jury on the guilty determination process." *Harvard Law Review*, 5: 53, 1971.

Kalton, G., and Kasprzyk, D. "The treatment of missing survey data." *Survey Methodology*, 12: 1–16, 1986.

Kalton, G., Kasprzyk, D., and McMillen, D.B. Nonsampling errors in panel surveys." In Kasprzyk, D., Duncan, G., Kalton, G., and Singh, M.P., eds., *Panel Surveys*, New York: Wiley, 1989.

Kaplan, A. "Definition and the specification of meaning." In Lazarsfeld, P.F., and Rosenberg, M., eds., *The Language of Social Research*. New York: Free Press, 1955, p. 527.

Keene, C., Maxim, P., and Teevan, J. "Drinking and driving, self-control, and gender: Testing a general theory of crime." *Journal of Research in Crime and Delinquency*, 30: 30–46, 1993.

Keeves, J.P. *Educational Research, Methodology, and Measurement: An International Handbook*. Oxford: Pergamon Press, 1988.

Kemsley, W.F.F., Redpath, R.U., and Holmes, M. *Family Expenditure Survey Handbook*. London: Office of Population and Surveys, HMSO, 1980.

Keppel, G. *Design and Analysis: A Researcher's Handbook*. New York: Prentice-Hall, 1991.

Kerlinger, F.N. *Foundations of Behavioral Research*, 3rd ed. New York: Holt, Rinehart & Winston, 1986.

Keyfitz, N. *Introduction to the Mathematics of Population*. Menlo Park, CA: Addison-Wesley, 1974.

Kim, J., and Rabjohn, J. "Binary variables and index construction." In Schuessler, K.F., ed., *Sociological Methodology 1980*. San Francisco: Jossey-Bass, 1979.

King, G. *A Solution to the Ecological Inference Problem*. Princeton, NJ: Princeton University Press, 1997.

Kish, L.T. "Studies of interviewer variance for attitudinal variables." *Journal of the American Statistical Association*, 57: 92–115, 1962.

Kish, L.T. *Survey Sampling*. New York: Wiley, 1965.

Kish, L.T. *Statistical Design for Research*. New York: Wiley, 1987.

Kohn, A. *False Prophets, Fraud and Error in Science and Medicine*. Oxford: Basil Blackwell, 1986.

Kraemer, H.C., and Thiemann, S. *How Many Subjects? Statistical Power Analysis in Research*. Newbury Park, CA: Sage, 1987.

Krishnaiah, P.R., and Rao, C.R. *Handbook of Statistics*, Vol. 6: *Sampling*. New York: North-Holland, 1988.

Kuder, G.F., and Richardson, M.W. "The theory of the estimation of test reliability." *Psychometrika*, 2: 135–38, 1937.

Kuhn, T.S. "Logic of discovery or psychology of research?" In Lakatos, I., and Musgrave, A., eds., *Criticism and the Growth of Knowledge*. Cambridge: Cambridge University Press, 1970, pp. 8–10.

Lakatos, I. "Falsification and the methodology of scientific research programs." In Lakatos, I., and Musgrave, A., eds., *Criticism and the Growth of Knowledge*. Cambridge: University of Cambridge Press, 1970.

Lakatos, I. *Philosophical Papers*, 2 vols. Cambridge: Cambridge University Press, 1978.

Land, K.C. "Mathematical formalization of Durkheim's theory of division of labour." In Borgatta, E.F., and Bohrnstedt, G.W., eds., *Sociological Methodology*. San Francisco: Jossey-Bass, 1970.

Land, K.C., and McCall, P.L. "Estimating the effect of nonignorable nonresponse in sample surveys." *Sociological Methods and Research*, 21, 291–316, 1993.

Landerman, L.R., Land, K.C., and Pieper, C.F. "An empirical evaluation of the predictive mean matching method for imputing missing values." *Sociological Methods and Research*, 26: 3–33, 1997.

Larson, A., Stevens, A., and Wardlaw, G. "Indirect estimates of 'hidden' populations: Capture–recapture methods to estimate the numbers of heroin users in the Australian Capital Territory." *Social Science and Medicine*, 39: 823–31, 1992.

Lee, E.T. *Statistical Methods for Survival Data Analysis*. New York: Lifelong Learning Press, 1980.

LePage, R., and Billard, L. *Exploring the Limits of Bootstrap*. New York: Wiley, 1992.

Leplin, J., ed. *Scientific Realism*. Berkeley: University of California Press, 1984.

Levin, B. "Comment." In DeGroot, M.H., Fienberg, S.E., and Kadane, J.B., eds., *Statistics and the Law*. New York: Wiley, 1986.

Lieberson, S. *Making It Count*. Berkeley: University of California Press, 1985.

Likert, R. "A technique for the measurement of attitudes." *Archives of Psychology*, 140: 5–55, 1932.

Lippmann, W. *Public Opinion*. New York: Macmillan, 1932.

Lissitz, R.W., and Green, S.G. "Effects of the number scale points on reliability: A Monte Carlo approach." *Journal of Applied Psychology*, 60: 10–13, 1975.

Little, R.J.A., and Rubin, D.B. *Statistical Analysis with Missing Data*. New York: Wiley, 1987.

Little, R.J.A., and Rubin, D.B. "The analysis of social science data with missing values." *Sociological Methods and Research*, 18: 292–326, 1989–90.

Lord, F. "On the statistical treatment of football numbers." *American Psychologist*, 8: 750–51, 1953.

Luce, R.D., Krantz, D.H., Suppes, P., and Tversky, A. *Foundations of Measurement*, Vol. 3. New York: Academic Press, 1990.

Lyberg, L., and Kasprzyk, D. "Data collection methods and measurement error: An overview." In Biemer, P., Groves, R.M., Lyberg, L.E., Mathiowetz, N.A., and Sudman, S., eds., *Measurement Error in Surveys*. New York: Wiley, 1991.

Mackie, J.L. *The Cement of the Universe: A Study in Causation*. Oxford: Clarendon Press, 1980.

Maddala, G. S. *Limited-Dependent and Qualitative Variables in Econometrics*. Cambridge: Cambridge University Press, 1983.

Madge, J.H. *The Tools of Social Science*. New York: Doubleday, 1965.

Madow, W.G., and Olkin, I. *Incomplete Data in Sample Surveys*, Vol. 3: *Proceedings of the Symposium*. New York: Wiley, 1983.

Madow, W.G., Olkin, I., and Rubin, D.B. *Incomplete Data in Sample Surveys*, Vol. 2: *Theory and Bibliographies*. New York: Wiley, 1983.

Madow, W.G., Nisselson, H., and Olkin, I. *Incomplete Data in Sample Surveys*, Vol. 1: *Report and Case Studies*. New York: Wiley, 1983.

Magnusson, D. *Test Theory*. Reading, MA: Addison-Wesley, 1966.

Makridakis, S.G., Wheelwright, S.C., and McGee, V.E. *Forecasting, Methods and Applications* 2nd ed. New York: Wiley, 1983.

Mammen, E. *When Does Bootstrap Work?* New York: Springer-Verlag, 1992.

Manly, B.F. J. *Randomization, Bootstrap and Monte Carlo Methods in Biology*, 2nd ed. London: Chapman & Hall, 1997.

Marcantonio, R.J. and Cook, T.D. "Convincing quasi-experiments: The interrupted time series and regression-discontinuity designs." In Wholey, J.S., Hatry, H.P., and Newcomer, K.E. (eds.) *Handbook of Practical Program Evaluation*, San Francisco: Jossey-Bass, 1994.

Martin, E. "Assessment of S-Night street enumeration in the 1990 census." *Evaluation Review*, 16, 418–38, 1992.

Masters, G.N. "A comparison of latent trait and latent class analysis of Likert-type data." *Psychometrika*, 50: 69–82, 1985.

Mastro, T.D., et al. "Estimating the number of HIV-infected injection drug users in Bangkok: A capture–recapture method." *American Journal of Public Health*, 84: 1094–99, 1994.

Matell, M.S., and Jacoby, J. "Is there an optimal number of alternatives for Likert Scale items? Study I: Reliability and validity." *Educational and Psychological Measurement*, 31: 657–74, 1971.

Maxim, P.S. "Cohort size and juvenile delinquency: A test of the Easterlin hypothesis." *Social Forces*, 63: 661–81, 1985.

Maxim, P.S. "The impact of design effects on standard errors in roadside traffic surveys." *Evaluation Review*, 13: 157–73, 1989.

Meehl, P.E. "What social scientists don't understand." In Fiske, W.D., and Shweder, R.A., eds., *Metatheory in Social Science*. Chicago: University of Chicago Press, 1986, p. 323.

Miller, J. "Complexities of the randomized response solution." *American Sociological Review*, 46: 928–30, 1981.

Miller, R.W. *Fact and Method*. Princeton, NJ: Princeton University Press, 1987.

Miller, P.V., and Groves, R.M. "Matching survey responses to official records: An exploration of validity in victimization reporting." *Public Opinion Quarterly*, 49: 366–80, 1985.

Miller, T.R., and Cleary, T.A. "Direction of wording effects in balanced scales." *Educational and Psychological Measurement*, 53: 51–60, 1993.

Mincer, J. *School Experience and Earnings*. New York: National Bureau of Economic Research, 1974.

Mishler, E. *Research Interviewing*. Cambridge, MA: Harvard University Press, 1986.

Mooney, C.Z., and Duval, R.D. *Bootstrapping: A Nonparametric Approach to Statistical Inference*. Newbury Park, CA: Sage, 1993.

Mosteller, F., and Tukey, J.W. *Data Analysis and Regression: A Second Course in Statistics*. Reading, MA: Addison-Wesley, 1977.

Murphy, M., and Sullivan, O. "Housing, tenure and family formation in contemporary Britain." *European Sociological Review*, 1: 230–43, 1985.

Nagel, E. "On the statement 'The whole is more than the sum of its parts.' " In Lazersfeld, P.F., and Rosen, M., eds., *The Language of Social Research*. New York: Free Press, 1955.

Nagel, E. *The Structure of Science*. New York: Harcourt, Brace & World, 1961.

Nelson, C.R. *Applied Time Series Analysis for Managerial Forecasting*, San Francisco, Holden-Day, 1973.

Neter, J. "Measurement errors in reports of consumer expenditures." *Journal of Marketing Research*, 7: 11–25, 1970.

Nettler, G. *Explanations*. New York: McGraw-Hill, 1970.

Nettler, G. *Explaining Crime*. New York: McGraw-Hill, 1984.

Neurath, O. "Soziologie im Physikalismus," *Erkenntnis*, 2, 1931/32. Translated version reprinted as "Sociology and physicalism," In Ayer, A.J., ed., *Logical Positivism*. New York: Free Press, 1959, pp. 282–317.

Nickles, T. *Scientific Discovery, Logic and Rationality*. Dordrecht: Reidel, 1980.

Noreen, E.W. *Computer Intensive Methods for Testing Hypotheses*. New York: Wiley, 1989.

Novick, M., and Lewis, C. "Coefficient alpha and the reliability of composite measurements." *Psychometrika*, 32: 1–13, 1967.

Nunnally, J.C. *Psychometric Theory*. New York: McGraw-Hill, 1970.

Orchard, T.A., and Woodbury, M.A. "A missing information principle: Theory and applications." *6th Berkeley Symposium of Mathematics and Probability*, 1: 697–715, 1972.

Otto, R. *The Idea of the Holy*, 2nd ed. London: Oxford, 1957.

Pampel, F.C. "Relative cohort size and fertility: The socio-political context of the Easterlin effect." *American Sociological Review*, 58: 496–514, 1993.

Pawson, R. *A Measure for Measures*. London: Routledge, 1989.

Pearl, R.B. "Reevaluation of the 1972–73 U.S. Consumer Expenditure Survey." *U.S. Bureau of the Census Technical Papers, No. 46*. Washington, DC: Government Printing Office, 1979.

Pettigrew, T.F. *A Profile of Negro America*. New York: Van Nostrand, 1964.

Pfanzagl, J. *Theory of Measurement*. New York: Wiley, 1968.

Phillips, D.C. *Philosophy, Science and Social Inquiry*. New York: Pergamon Press, 1987.

Phillips, D.C. *The Social Scientist's Bestiary*. New York: Pergamon Press, 1992.

Plewis, I., Creeser, R., and Mooney, A. "Reliability and validity of time budget data: Children's activities outside school." *Journal of Official Statistics*, 6: 411–20, 1990.

Polachek, S.W., and Siebert, W.S. *The Economics of Earnings*. Cambridge: Cambridge University Press, 1993.

Popper, K.R. *The Logic of Scientific Discovery*. London: Hutchinson, 1959.

Popper, K.R. *Poverty of Historicism*, 2nd ed. New York: Basic Books, 1960.

Portes, A., and Sensenbrenner, J. "Embeddedness and immigration: Notes on the social determinants of economic action." *American Journal of Sociology*, 98: 1320–50, 1993.

Poulain, M., Riandey, B., and Firdion, J.-M. "Enquête biographique et registre Belge de population: Une confrontation des données." *Population*, 46: 65–88, 1991.

Poundstone, W. *Labyrinths of Reason: Paradoxes, Puzzles and the Frailty of Knowledge*. New York: Anchor/Doubleday, 1988.

Press, W.H., Teukolsky, S.A., Vetterling W.T., and Flannery, B.P. *Numerical Recipes*. Cambridge, Cambridge University Press, 1992.

Psacharopoulos, G. "Returns to education: An updated international comparison." *Comparative Education*, 17: 321–41, 1974.

Quenouille, M. "Approximate tests of correlation in time series." *Journal of the Royal Statistical Society, Series B*, 11: 18–44, 1949.

Quine, W.V.O. "Two dogmas of empiricism." In Quine, W.V.O., ed., *From a Logical Point of View*. Cambridge, MA: Harvard University Press, 1953, pp. 20–46.

Ramsay, J.O. "The effect of number of categories in rating scales on precision of estimation of scale values." *Psychometrika*, 38: 513–33, 1973.

Rasch, G. "An individualistic approach to item analysis." In Lazarsfeld, P.F., and Henry, N.W., eds., *Readings in Mathematical Social Science*. Chicago: Science Research Associates, 1966.

Reynolds, P.D. *A Primer in Theory Construction*. Indianapolis: Bobbs-Merrill, 1971.

Robinson, D., and Rhode, S. "Two experiments with an anti-Semitic poll." *Journal of Abnormal Psychology*, 41: 136–44, 1946.

Robinson, J.P. Athanasiou, R., and Head, K. *Measures of Occupational Attitudes and Occupational Characteristics*. Ann Arbor, MI: Institute for Social Research, 1969.

Robinson, J.P. Rusk, J.G., and Head, K.B. *Measures of Political Attitudes*. Ann Arbor, MI: Institute for Social Research, 1968.

Robinson, J.P., and Shaver, P.R. *Measures of Social Psychological Attitudes*. Ann Arbor, MI: Institute for Social Research, 1973.

Robinson, W.S. "Ecological correlation and the behavior of individuals." *American Sociological Review*, 15: 351–57, 1950.

Roethlisberger, F.J., and Dickson, W.J. *Management and the Worker: An Account of a Research Program Conducted by the Western Electric Company, Hawthorne Works, Chicago.* Cambridge, MA.: Harvard University Press, 1939.

Rogers, W.L. "Estimable functions of age, period and cohort effects." *American Sociological Review*, 47: 843–61, 1982.

Ross, H.L. "Law, science and accidents: The British Road Safety Act of 1967." *Journal of Legal Studies*, 2: 1–75, 1973.

Ross, H.L., Campbell, D.T., and Glass, G.V. "Determining the social effects of a legal reform: The British 'Breathalyser' crackdown of 1967." *American Behavioral Scientist*, 13: 493–509, 1970.

Rubin, D.R. "Formalizing subjective notions about the effect of nonrespondents in sample surveys." *Journal of the American Statistical Association*, 72: 538–43, 1977.

Rubin, D.R. *Multiple Imputation for Nonresponse in Surveys*. New York: Wiley, 1987.

Russell, B. *Mysticism and Logic*. London: Allen & Unwin, 1929.

Rutherford, R.D., and Choe, M.K. *Statistical Models for Causal Analysis*. New York: Wiley, 1993.

Salmon, W. "Statistical explanation." In Salmon, W., ed., *Statistical Explanation and Statistical Relevance*. Pittsburgh: University of Pittsburgh Press, 1971.

Samuelson, P. "Problems of methodology—discussion." *American Economic Review, Papers and Proceedings*, 53: 232–36, 1963.

Samuelson, P. "Theory and realism: A reply." *American Economic Review*, 54: 736–40, 1964.

Samuelson, P. "Professor Samuelson on theory and realism: A reply." *American Economic Review*, 55: 1162–72, 1965.

Sande, I.G. "Hot-deck imputation procedures." In Madow, W.G., Olkin, I., and Rubin, D.B., eds., *Incomplete Data in Sample Surveys*, Vol. 2: *Theory and Bibliographies*. New York: Wiley, 1983.

Sard, A., and Weintraub, S. *A Book of Splines*, New York: Wiley, 1971.

Saunders, P.T. *An Introduction to Catastrophe Theory*. New York: Cambridge University Press, 1980.

Scandura, J.M., and Wells, J.N. "Advanced organizers in learning abstract mathematics." *American Educational Research Journal*, 4: 295–301, 1967.

Schaeffer, N.C. "Hardly ever or constantly? Group comparisons using vague quantifiers." *Public Opinion Quarterly*, 55: 395, 1991.

Schmitt, N., and Stults, D.M. "Factors defined by negatively phrased items: The result of careless respondents?" *Applied Psychological Measurement*, 9: 367–73, 1985.

Schuman, H., and Converse, J.M. "The effects of black and white interviewers on black responses in 1968." *Public Opinion Quarterly*, 35: 44–68, 1971.

Schuman, L., and Jordan, B. "Interactional troubles in face-to-face survey interviews." *Journal of the American Statistical Association*, 85: 232–41, 1990.

Schuman, L., and Presser, S. *Questions and Answers in Attitude Surveys: Experiments on Question Form, Wording and Context*. New York: Academic Press, 1981.

Schutz, A. *The Phenomenology of the Social World*. Evanston. IL: Northwestern University Press, 1967 (originally published in 1932).

Schwartz, N. "Assessing frequency reports of mundane behaviors: Contributions of cognitive psychology to questionnaire construction." In Hendrick, C., and Clark, M.S., eds., *Review of Personality and Social Psychology*. Beverly Hills, CA: Sage, 1990.

Scriven, M. *The Legacy of Logical Positivism,* Achinstein, P., and Barker, F., eds., Baltimore: John Hopkins Press, 1969.

Scriven, M. "The logic of cause." *Theory and Decision,* 2: 49–66, 1971.

Seber, G.A.F. *Estimation of Animal Abundance,* 2nd ed. London: Griffin, 1982.

Sedlmeier, P., and Gigerenzer, G. "Do studies of statistical power have an effect on the power of studies?" *Psychological Bulletin,* 105: 309–16, 1989.

Selltiz, C., Jahoda, M., Deutsch, M., and Cook, S.W. *Research Methods in Social Relations,* rev. ed. New York: Holt, Rinehart & Winston, 1959.

Shao, J., and Tu, D. *The Jackknife and Bootstrap.* New York: Springer-Verlag, 1995.

Shannon, L.W. *Criminal Career in Continuity: Its Social Context.* New York: Human Sciences Press, 1988.

Shaw, M., and Wright, J. *Scales for the Measurement of Attitudes.* New York: McGraw-Hill, 1967.

Shearing, C.D. "How to make theories untestable: A guide to theorists." *American Sociologist,* 8: 33–37, 1973.

Sheatsley, P.B. "Questionnaire construction and item writing." In Rossi, P.H., Wright J.D., and Anderson, A.B., eds., *Handbook of Survey Research.* New York: Academic Press, 1984.

Shimizu, I., and Bonham, G. "Randomized response in a national survey." *Journal of the American Statistical Association,* 73: 35–39, 1978.

Shryock, H.S., and Siegel, J.S. *The Methods and Materials of Demography,* Vol. 2. Washington, DC: U.S. Bureau of the Census, 1973.

Silberstein, A.R., and Scott, S. "Expenditure diary surveys and their associated errors." In Biemer, P., Groves, R.M., Lyberg, L.E., Mathiowetz, N.A., and Sudman, S., eds., *Measurement Errors in Surveys.* New York: Wiley, 1991.

Simpson, S.N. "Coverage of the Great Britain census of population and housing." *Journal of the Royal Statistical Society, Series A,* 157: 313–16, 1994.

Singer, B. "Self-selection and performance-based ratings: A case study in program evaluation." In Wainer, H., ed., *Drawing Inference from Self-Selected Samples.* New York: Springer-Verlag, 1986.

Skinner, B.F. "Are theories of learning necessary?" *Psychological Review,* 57: 193–216, 1950.

Smart, J.C.C. *Between Science and Philosophy.* New York: Random House, 1968.

Smith, T.W. "Nonattitudes: A review and evaluation." In Turner, C.F., and Martin, E., eds., *Surveying Subjective Phenomena.* New York: Russell Sage Foundation, 1984.

Snijders, T.A.B. "Estimation on the basis of snowball samples: How to weight?" *Bulletin de Méthodologie Sociologique,* 36: 59–70, 1992.

Spearman, C. "Correlation calculated from faulty data." *British Journal of Psychology,* 3: 271–95, 1910.

Spreen, M. "Rare populations, hidden populations, and link-tracing designs: What and why?" *Bulletin de Méthodologie Sociologique,* 36: 34–58, 1992.

Steiner, M. "The application of mathematics to natural sciences." *Journal of Philosophy,* 86: 449–80, 1989.

Stevens, S.S. "On the theory of scales and measurement." *Science,* 103: 667–80, 1946.

Stevens, S.S. "Mathematics, measurement, and psychophysics." In Stevens, S.S., ed., *Handbook of Experimental Psychology.* New York: Wiley, 1951.

Stinchcombe, A.L. *Constructing Social Theories.* New York: Harcourt, Brace and World, 1968.

Stoll, R.R. *Sets, Logic, and Axiomatic Theories.* San Francisco: Freeman, 1961.

Stolzenberg, R.M., and Relles, D.A. "Theory testing in a world of constrained design research." *Sociological Methods and Research,* 18: 395–415, 1990.

Straubhaar, T. "The impact of international labor migration for Turkey." In Zimmerman, K.F., ed., *Migration and Economic Development*. Berlin: Springer-Verlag, 1992.

Stroh, C.M. *Alcohol and Highway Safety; Roadside Surveys of Drinking Driving Behavior: A Review of the Literature and a Recommended Methodology*. Ottawa: Transport Canada, Road and Motor Vehicle Traffic Safety Branch, 1974.

Suchman, L., and Jordan, B. "Interactional troubles in face-to-face survey interviews," *Journal of the American Statistical Association*, 85: 232–41, 1990.

Sudman, S. *Applied Sampling*. New York: Academic Press, 1976.

Sudman, S. and Bradburn, N.M. *Response Effects in Surveys—A Review and Synthesis*. Chicago: Aldine, 1974.

Symonds, P.M. "On the loss of reliability in ratings due to coarseness of the scale." *Journal of Experimental Psychology*, 7: 456–61, 1924.

Synthese, Volumes 67 and 68. Dordrecht, Holland, 1986.

Talbot, M. *Mysticians and the New Physics*. London: Routledge & Kegan Paul, 1981.

Thisted, R.A. *Elements of Statistical Computing*. New York: Chapman & Hall., 1988.

Thompson, S.K. *Sampling*. New York: Wiley, 1992.

Thurstone, L.L. "Attitudes can be measured." *American Journal of Sociology*, 33: 529–54, 1928.

Tiryakian, E.A."Typological classification." *International Encyclopedia of the Social Sciences*, New York: Macmillan, 1968.

Torgerson, W.S. *Theory and Methods of Scaling*. New York: Wiley, 1958.

Tracy, P.E., Wolfgang, M.E., and Figlio, R.E. *Delinquent Careers in Two Birth Cohorts*. New York: Plenum Press, 1990.

Trewin, D., and G. Lee. "International comparisons of telephone coverage." In Groves, R.M., Biemer, P.P., Lyberg, L.E., Massey, J.T., Nicholls, W.L., and Waksberg, J., eds., *Telephone Survey Methodology*. New York: Wiley, 1988.

Trochim, W.M.K. *Research Design for Program Evaluation: The Regression-Discontinuity Approach*. Newbury Park, CA: Sage, 1984.

Trott, D.M., and Jackson, D.N. "An experimental analysis of acquiescence." *Journal of Experimental Research in Personality*, 2: 278–88, 1967.

Trussell, J., Hankinson, R., and Tilton, J., eds. *Demographic Applications of Event History Analysis*. Oxford: Clarendon Press, 1992.

Tucker, C., and Bennett, C. "Procedural effects in the collection of consumer expenditure information." *Proceedings of the Section on Survey Research, American Statistical Association*, 1988, p. 256–61.

Tukey, J.W. "Bias and confidence in not quite large samples." *Annals of Mathematical Statistics*, 29: 614, 1958.

Tukey, J.W. *Exploratory Data Analysis*. Reading, MA: Addison-Wesley, 1977.

U.S. Bureau of the Census. *Historical Statistics of the United States, Colonial Times to 1970, Bicentennial Edition*, Part 2. Washington, DC: Government Printing Office 1975.

U.S. Bureau of the Census. "Enumerator variance in the 1970 Census." *Evaluation and Research Program,* Series PHC(E)-13. Washington, DC: Government Printing Office 1979.

Velleman, P.F., and Hoaglin, D.C. *Applications, Basics and Computing of Exploratory Data Analysis*. Belmont, CA: Duxbury Press, 1981.

Velleman, P.F., and Wilkinson, L. "Nominal, ordinal, interval and ratio typologies are misleading." *American Statistician*, 47: 65–72, 1993.

Wainer, H. "The SAT as a social indicator: A pretty bad idea." In Wainer, H., ed., *Drawing Inference from Self-Selected Samples*. New York: Springer-Verlag, 1986.

Warner, S.L. "Randomized response: A survey technique for eliminating evasive answer bias." *Journal of the American Statistical Association*, 60: 63–69, 1965.

Weiss, C.H. "Validity of welfare mothers' interview response." *Public Opinion Quarterly*, 32: 622–33, 1968.

Weiss, C.H. "Interaction in the research interview: The effects of rapport on response." *Proceedings of the Social Science Section, American Statistical Association*, 1970, pp. 17–20.

Wilkinson, L. *SYGRAPH: The System for Graphics*. Evanston, IL: SYSTAT, Inc., 1990.

Williams, J.A. "Interviewer–respondent interaction: A study of bias in the information interview." *Sociometry*, 27: 338–52, 1964.

Winer, B.J. *Statistical Principles in Experimental Design*. New York: McGraw-Hill, 1971.

Wiseman, F.M. Moriarty, M., and Schafer, M. "Estimating public opinion with the randomized response model." *Public Opinion Quarterly*, 73: 35–39, 1975–76.

Winship, C., and Mare, R.D. "Models for sample selection bias." *Annual Review of Sociology*, 18: 327–50, 1992.

Winship, C., and Radbill, L., Sampling weights and regression analysis." *Sociological Methods and Research*, 23: 230–57, 1994.

Wonnacott, R.J., and Wonnacott, T.J *Econometrics*. New York: Wiley, 1970.

Wright, S. "Correlation and causation." *Journal of Agricultural Research*, 20: 557–85, 1921.

Wright, S. "The method of path coefficients." *Annals of Mathematical Statistics*, 5: 161–215, 1934.

Yule, G.U., and Kendall, M.G. *An Introduction to the Theory of Statistics*. London: Griffin, 1950.

Zeller, R.A., and Carmines, E.G. *Measurement in the Social Sciences*. Cambridge: Cambridge University Press, 1980.

Zetterberg, H.L. *On Theory and Verification in Sociology*. Totowa, NJ: Bedminster Press, 1965.

Author Index

Subject Index

CPSIA information can be obtained
at www.ICGtesting.com
Printed in the USA
BVHW04*0916080718
520595BV00012B/57/P

9 780195 114652